"*The Game Changer* is a source o [barcode] and young executives. Alistair deliver [barcode] ts of strategic management supporte[barcode] and sport. I have taken benefit from [barcode] e the University's strategy."

Professor Sir Jim . ncellor,
athclyde

"It is one thing to write about strategy and how it should be done. It is a completely different thing to write about strategy and to have actually done it. Alistair Gray provides the latter in his book. It is a tremendous read packed with insight into how to deliver meaningful strategic change."

Harry Sminea, Professor of Strategic Management,
Strathclyde Business School,
University of Strathclyde

"Top business frequently turns to sport for strategies to improve performance. Alistair Gray benefits from his unique combination of a successful voluntary leader in sport and respected consultant to leading businesses and sports around the world. The articles and case studies in the book deliver real insight into how to succeed."

Martin Gilbert, CEO Standard Life Aberdeen PLC

"Altogether, a really useful book whose articles and case studies will be invaluable for anyone facing the prospect of competing in the challenging global markets of the 21st century."

Sir Tom Farmer KBE, Founder of Kwik Fit

The Game Changer is a demonstration and evolution of the importance of out-of-the-box thinking in providing winning performance. It emphasises the benefits of embracing change in mindset and strategic perspective.

Sir Bill Gammell FRSE, Founder and former Chair
and CEO of Cairn Energy PLC; Chair of
Winning Scotland Foundation

"This is a very enlightening and well-researched read from a wise sage who knows – from first-hand experience – more than a bit about what provides the zeitgeist in business."

Andy Nash, Portfolio Chair and former Director of
Taunton Cider PLC

"For many years I have appreciated Alistair's unique insight across business, elite sport and other sectors. *The Game Changer* captures that and will be stimulating for executives in business and sport at any stage in their career – from MBA classes to the Board Room."

Charles Berry, Chairman of The Weir Group PLC

"The creation of Scotland Food & Drink was the ultimate game changer for the food and drink industry in Scotland. Alistair led us through the journey that initially created an industry strategy group. He further guided us through a process that included industry leadership, the Scottish Government, Scottish Enterprise and Highland & Islands Enterprise to create Scotland Food & Drink. We began the journey with the complexity of the cluster strategy and concluded with a pragmatic approach to deliver the platform for Scotland Food & Drink. In doing so, we created a collaborative model, with strong strategic direction that has now transformed the value and reputation of Scotland's food and drink industry."

David Kilshaw, Former Chair of Scotland Food & Drink

"In helping make the best strategic choices, Alistair always considers whether they can be successfully implemented, taking into account leadership qualities and optimal use of resources. This invaluable book is full of pragmatic insights on how to decide and then deliver."

David Gray, Non-Executive Director

"Alistair Gray has a lifetime of experience in business and sport and this book provides an insight into the strategic management, innovation and drivers needed to change the game."

Baroness Sue Campbell CBE, Director of Women's Football at The FA. Chair of UK Sport (2003–2013) and Youth Sport Trust (2005–2017)

"*The Game Changer* is easy to read and follow and challenges the reader to think differently, with clarity. Full of examples and strategic models, it provides an excellent framework to develop winning strategies and improve performance in business and sport."

Sir Ian McGeechan OBE, Head Coach, British and Irish Lions (four tours) and Director of Rugby for Scotland, Northampton and Wasps

"A supportive infrastructure is key to ensuring coaches and other performance specialists in sport can exercise their skills effectively. Alistair applies his unique skills set to creating such infrastructure by tackling culture shift head on. Putting it another way, he facilitates performance excellence."

Professor Frank Dick OBE, Coach and Motivational Speaker

"Nowadays sport operates more like business and must employ best business practice in its operations, within systems of good governance for its athletes, officials, volunteers and supporters. Alistair Gray presents his own considerable experience achieving these goals which those in sport and business will find most valuable."

"Alistair Gray draws upon behind-the-scenes insights into the change process to provide a much needed and revealing insider account of sports management in the real world. It relegates data and evidence, promotes people and relationships to answer some important contemporary sporting questions – How can small nations win at sport? How can sport build integrity? How do you manage sustainable change?"

"This book will be a great resource for all management professionals and those building their career. The content and case studies reflect the open-minded, ambitious and check and challenge approach of Alistair in his many roles and experiences across organisations in business and sport."

"In my experience in sport, especially in Ireland, Alistair Gray and Brian MacNeice are the first names mentioned for strategy development. Genesis were instrumental in supporting us to achieve our ambition to secure Test status in Cricket. Their approach is inclusive and uncomplicated and focuses on clear targets and accountability. Their honesty and integrity set them apart and they are a pleasure to work with."

"The Genesis report on the 2002 FIFA World Cup and subsequent projects provided the FAI with the practical impetus to make many significant changes within the Association and improve our performances on and off the field. The reforms made along the way have helped Ireland's position in European football administration and the Association is proud to occupy a place among UEFA members as a modern progressive governing body."

"Alistair is someone who challenges you to think the unthinkable and has undoubtedly influenced my professional development. Winning in business and sport is a golden thread through his philosophy and his contribution to Scottish Cycling and Scottish sport has definitely been a Game

Changer. This really useful book provides the opportunity to learn from one of the best."

"Alistair's insights into what makes elite athletes perform and his knowledge of how sports organisations can improve their performance through the execution of a carefully-crafted strategy were of enormous value to the Scottish FA during my time as CEO."

The Game Changer

The Game Changer powerfully demonstrates how some organisations in business and sport have done more than raise their performance; they have also changed the rules of the game or the game itself within their industry. It gives examples of the strategies and governance programmes that have emerged to accomplish this, and the challenges of executing them.

This book brings to life strategic management in business, sport and not-for-profit organisations. It explores many of the theories taught on MBA and other professional programmes through case studies from the worlds of sport and business, written by authors who have actively played a part in the change. Alistair Gray has spent much of his career in senior roles in these sectors and brings a unique insight to the field, as well as providing the reader with tools and techniques for improvement in governance and performance.

The Game Changer is essential reading for both professionals looking for methods to improve their own performance and to embed strong principles of governance, and business students looking for real-life lessons from practice.

Alistair Gray is the founder and Managing Director of Renaissance & Co, UK, and one of Europe's leading strategic management consultants. He is also a lecturer on strategic management on the MBA programme at Strathclyde Business School, UK. A director of a number of companies, he has held a range of board positions in business and sport.

The Game Changer

How Leading Organisations in
Business and Sport Changed
the Rules of the Game

Alistair Gray

LONDON AND NEW YORK

First published 2019
by Routledge
2 Park Square, Milton Park, Abingdon, Oxon OX14 4RN

and by Routledge
711 Third Avenue, New York, NY 10017

Routledge is an imprint of the Taylor & Francis Group, an informa business

British Library Cataloguing-in-Publication Data
A catalogue record for this book is available from the British Library

Library of Congress Cataloging-in-Publication Data
Names: Gray, Alistair (Management consultant), author.
Title: The game changer : how leading organizations in sport and
    business changed the rules of the game / Alistair Gray.
Description: Abingdon, Oxon ; New York, NY : Routledge, 2019. |
    Includes bibliographical references and index.
Identifiers: LCCN 2018027490| ISBN 9781138362703 (hbk) | ISBN
    9781138362727 (pbk)
Subjects: LCSH: Strategic planning. | Management. | Organizational
    change. | Sports—Management.
Classification: LCC HD30.28 .G727 2019 | DDC 658.4/012—dc23
LC record available at https://lccn.loc.gov/2018027490

ISBN: 978-1-138-36270-3 (hbk)
ISBN: 978-1-138-36272-7 (pbk)
ISBN: 978-0-429-43189-0 (ebk)

Typeset in Baskerville
by Swales & Willis Ltd, Exeter, Devon, UK

Contents

Figures and images

Foreword

By Sir Tom Farmer, KBE

I am delighted to have the opportunity to write this foreword to *The Game Changer*, a book full of real-life case studies and associated articles on how businesses, sports and other organisations not only improved performance, they also changed the rules of the game in their industry.

I started my first tyre discount business in 1964, taking advantage of changes in the Retail Price Maintenance Act. In 1968 we merged with Albany Tyre Services, which was eventually bought by an American company in 1970. I then founded Kwik-Fit in 1971 when I saw an opportunity to create a new business model in the automotive repair industry. I saw real scope to improve the level of service and the customer experience. The success of our first business was because we realised very quickly the importance of looking after our own people. We were obsessed with the level of service we provided our customers and the high standards we set ourselves. We took the chance to change the game.

Most businesses, business schools and students of business focus on the importance of customers and shareholder value. In Kwik-Fit we saw our own people as our key asset. They were the ambassadors of our brand, our business and our values. 'You can't get better than a Kwik-Fit fitter; we're the boys to trust!' was no idle boast. Our people were well trained for their role and regarded as equals in our democratic company – we had respect for each other. Second, we built genuine partnerships with our suppliers to ensure the quality and range of our products. The stocks we held supported our business and our service charter. With these in place we would attract and retain our customers and finally investors would be keen to provide funds for our development and expansion. This model and its priorities turned the traditional business model on its head and gave us a real advantage over others.

In *The Game Changer* I was particularly drawn to the business case studies on NCR and The Famous Grouse. In both instances the businesses and their local management took on and defeated the might of IBM and Diageo respectively to achieve global leadership in their segment of the market. They achieved this by challenging and changing the accepted paradigm for their industries. Their great people and leaders delivered a performance that was difficult to imitate. Their passion and commitment to improve kept them ahead of the chasing pack.

The '*Braveheart*' article in Chapter 8 reveals lessons from the inspiring leadership of Robert the Bruce and William Wallace, from as far back as the 13th and 14th centuries, in winning strategically important battles against the superior numbers of their opponents. The key to their successful victories lay in the passion and loyalty of their front-line troops, fighting for a cause in the face of superior numbers. These and other lessons contained in each chapter – not from theories or academic research studies but real-life case studies – are particular features of what is a readable, informative and useful book for any MBA student or young professional in business, sport, the arts and any area of the public sector or professions.

Alistair also brings his extensive experience working and consulting in sport as well as business to provide invaluable insight into where sport, especially at the performance end, provides additional pointers for breaking traditional models to leaders and executives in other sectors. Examples from the New Zealand All Blacks, Irish Golf, Cricket, Rugby and Football and the author's work with Scottish Football and The FA demonstrate that 'instant success takes time' when changing performance in sport and show how these lessons can be applied elsewhere.

My life, my family and my time in business have taught me that success is down to two things – engaging and developing great people with a passion for success, be it personal or corporate in business, as well as their families and the chance to fulfil their potential. This passion goes alongside an obsession, nothing less, for building an enterprise to be the best it can be.

Altogether, a really useful book whose articles and case studies will be invaluable for anyone facing the prospect of competing in the challenging global markets of the 21st century.

Sir Tom Farmer
Edinburgh

Acknowledgements

The idea for a book came as I reflected on the consulting work carried out by Genesis, my firm, working with great clients over a period of nearly 20 years. The case studies contained within *The Game Changer* build on a number of assignments carried out with clients who responded to the challenges we provided and the supportive style we adopted.

To those clients who feature in the book I give special thanks for working with us to secure their future success. Second, I would like to thank and acknowledge the contribution made to our clients' success by those we employed and deployed. First to James, Brian and Fiona, my fellow directors, who along with John contributed chapters to the book; to Brian Porteous, Kevin Parker, Brian Mooney and Caroline Vance who shared the leadership of the company, and to David Simpson, Bob Pettigrew, John Marti, Mike Fitzpatrick and David Coates who provided good counsel and advice as non-executive directors over the years.

Our aim was to enable our consultants and staff to fulfill their potential and I hope for those we employed the time spent with Genesis equipped them for a successful future. In addition, a number of associates brought special skills, experience and personality to the work with our clients. First among these are Margaret (MAD) Dewhurst, Mike Fitzpatrick, Lynn McHattie, Sally Horrox and Ann Astell who delivered excellent service over many years and appreciated being part of the family that was Genesis.

From my beginning as a consultant in 1982 I have been supported by a number of dedicated support staff and my thanks and appreciation go to Shelly-Anne, Louise, Elaine, Sian, Ann and Allan in the UK and Grace and Ciara in Ireland for their service and loyalty.

In my career prior to entering consulting I was especially influenced by my time with Unilever NV and the John Wood Group PLC and the empowerment I was given at an early age by the likes of Norman Sawdon in Unilever and Sir Ian Wood in the Wood Group. At Arthur Young my leader and mentor in strategic management was Mike Davidson, who gave me so many basics on which to build my consulting style and approach, and John Barbour at PA for encouraging my entrepreneurial desires. My thanks also go to all those in Scottish Hockey who allowed me to lead the sport through merger in 1989. This gave me the launch pad for much of my work in sport as well as colleagues at the European and International Hockey Federations. My thanks also to Graeme Simmers and Alan Alstead at **sports**-cotland for entrusting me with the leadership of the Scottish Institute of Sport, and to Baroness Sue Campbell and Dame Liz Nicoll at UK Sport for their encouragement to make change happen in sport in the UK.

The publication of this book would not have been possible without the encouragement of Kenny Kemp, the former Business Editor at *The Herald* and a fellow board member of the Winning Scotland Foundation, who encouraged me to start this project, and to Rebecca Marsh and Judith Lorton at Routledge (Taylor and Francis) who made publication a reality. I would also like to thank Sir Tom Farmer for contributing the foreword to this book – an honour from one of the ultimate great game changers in business.

Lastly, and first without equal, is my family. All this would not have been possible without the encouragement and support of Sheila, my wife, and Kathryn and Nicola my daughters. Sheila gave me the push to set up Genesis in 1991, to take the risk it represented at the time. She joined Genesis in 1999 from a career in teaching that culminated in her appointment as head teacher of Park School in Glasgow. It was a special pleasure to see her develop a new career in consulting and to be appointed, in her own right, a World Class Adviser to UK Sport and **sport**england, where her work led to the improvement in performance of a number of sports in the UK and Ireland. She has also carried out the hard yards of proofing this text. I am so proud of what my family has achieved and the love and support they have given me over my career and as husband and father. I hope *The Game Changer* reflects this and that they are also proud.

Our authors

Alistair Gray

- Academic qualifications: MA (Maths and Economics), University of Edinburgh.
- Professional qualifications and membership: ACMA (Cost and Management Accountants), Fellow – Institute of Directors, Fellow – Institute of Consultants, Professional Pension Fund Trustee, Entrepreneurship Scotland (Founder Member).
- MIT Sloan Management School: Alumnus of Executive Management Programme.
- University of Strathclyde: current Faculty Member – Strategy and Organisation (2016 UK Business School of the Year).
- Loughborough University: Faculty Member – Sports Management MBA (2013–2015).

Alistair graduated from the University of Edinburgh in Mathematics and Economics and, after his early career with multinational companies, is now one of Europe's leading strategic management consultants after over 35 years in the industry. He has also had an outstanding career as a voluntary leader and consultant in sport at national level in the UK and internationally. He founded Genesis, a strategic management consulting company, in 1992 and its clients are the source of many of the chapters in *The Game Changer*.

Alistair has had a lifetime involvement in sport on a voluntary basis as a former Chair, President and Honorary President of Scottish Hockey, a member of the Board of the European Hockey Federation, and the International Hockey Federation's Development and Coaching Committee. He led the merger of Scottish Men's and Women's hockey in 1989. He was the founding Chair of the Scottish Institute of Sport and served on the board of the UK Sports Institute, the leadership group responsible for the design of

Mission 2012, the UK's successful high performance programme. He has also consulted widely in sport, especially in the modernisation of governing bodies and in the development of high performance sport strategies. He served as Chair of the Boards of British Performance Basketball and British Swimming.

He is a non-executive director of two public companies, chair of a number of Pension Trustee Boards and is on the advisory board of a number of other organisations. He is also a lecturer on strategic management on the MBA/MSc programmes at Strathclyde Business School – UK Business School of the Year in 2016.

He was a contributory author to *The Manager's Handbook*, a practical guide to successful management published in 1988 by Sphere Books, ISBN 0-7221-5754-1, and is the author of numerous articles on strategic management.

Brian MacNeice (Chapter 13)

- Academic qualifications BSc (Computer Applications), Dublin City University; Diploma in International Marketing, Chartered Institute of Marketing; MBA, Dublin City University.

Brian MacNeice is an expert in strategy, high performance organisations and change management. His career to date spans over 20 years of advising clients in multiple industry sectors globally. He has worked with senior executives and leadership teams in blue chip organisations in business and sport. Prior to founding Kotinos, he was a Director of Genesis Ireland and previously held senior consulting roles in Deloitte, Arthur Andersen and Vision Consulting.

Brian is co-founder and Managing Director of Kotinos Partners Limited – a niche advisory firm that partners with clients to deliver rapid performance improvement. Founded in 2010, Kotinos serves clients across Europe and the USA from its base in Dublin. In addition to his client work, Brian writes regularly on topics relating to high performance. Kogan Page published his award-winning book *Powerhouse: Insider Accounts into the World's Top High-Performance Organizations*, which he co-authored with James Bowen in October 2016.

Brian is an International Panel rugby referee with the Irish Rugby Football Union, regularly officiating in Pro 14, European and international matches in the professional game. He was also a national team selector for the Irish cricket team for eight years from 2007 to 2015. He chairs the high performance advisory group for Swim Ireland.

James Bowen (Chapter 12)

- Academic qualifications: BEng (Chemical Engineering), University College Dublin; MBA, Institute of Management Development (IMD), Lausanne, Switzerland.

James Bowen is an expert in strategy and organisational design and, over the course of his 20-year advisory career, has worked across geographies and industry sectors with senior executive teams of companies ranging from start-ups to blue-chip multinationals. Prior to founding Kotinos, he was a Director of Genesis Ireland and Genesis Consulting in Glasgow and London. Before that, he worked in London, the USA, Asia and Ireland with Marakon Associates, Andersen and Deloitte. James' career started in operations, where he held management roles in sales, manufacturing and purchasing in Smurfit Kappa manufacturing companies in Ireland, Venezuela and the UK. He is a committee member and former President of the IMD Alumni Association of Ireland.

James is co-founder and Managing Director of Kotinos Partners Limited – a niche advisory firm that partners with clients to deliver rapid performance improvement. Founded in 2010, Kotinos serves clients across Europe and the USA from its base in Dublin. In addition to his client work, James writes regularly on topics relating to high performance. His award-winning book *Powerhouse: Insider Accounts into the World's Top High-Performance Organizations*, which he co-authored with Brian MacNeice, was published in October 2016 by Kogan Page, ISBN 978-0-7494-7831-5.

Fiona Gifford (Chapter 5)

- Academic qualifications: MA (Hons) Sociology and Social Policy, University of Edinburgh; Postgraduate Diploma Human Resources Management, Edinburgh Napier University; MBA Edinburgh University Management School.
- Professional qualifications and membership: Fellow Institute of Personnel and Development; AOEC Accredited Executive Coach; Member of The Neuroleadership Institute; MBTI Accredited Practitioner.
- Co-operative Development Scotland: Advisory Board Member (2012 to 2015).

- Harvard University and IMD Business School: Alumnus of Executive Leadership Development Programmes (2004 and 2009).

After graduating from The University of Edinburgh, Fiona completed her postgraduate studies at Edinburgh Napier University and gained a Masters at The University of Edinburgh Management School. In the 35 years since then she has led and delivered strategic change, performance and personal development in the complex environment of global corporations and SMEs. She developed a passion for creating and developing the conditions for performance excellence through coaching and working with leaders, teams and individuals.

For the last 13 years Fiona has pursued her passion for the power of purpose. She was a director of Genesis Consulting Ltd prior to founding The Performance Collective. Her personal purpose is 'To grow leaders and leadership teams who create Human Spaces where human potential can be realised'.

Fiona is the author of several workbooks for leaders including: *Purposeful Leadership, Turning Strategy into Work, My Board of Directors, Building a Strategic Influencing Plan, Leading Change, Building Effective Relationships, Difficult Conversations* and *Personal Development Planning*.

John Bull (Chapter 20)

- Academic qualifications: BA in Agriculture Economics, Massey University.
- University of Oxford: Member of Institute for the Study of High Performance.

A specialist in leadership and organisational performance, John has spent 20 years studying, and in many cases working with, the leadership behind some of the highest performing organisations in the world – in business, science, the performing arts and elite sport.

He is Head of High Performance of Management Futures, an organisation dedicated to bringing together thought leaders on high performance, furthering research in the field, and working with organisations to help them improve their performance culture.

He is also a member of the University of Oxford's Institute for the Study of High Performance; a long-term project set up to study both examples of organisations that have transformed their performance for a period of time and those that have been able to sustain their dominance over competitors for more than 50 years.

1 Introduction

The grand strategist and the Focus Framework

The evolution of executive concerns – from Adam Smith to the Focus Framework

When I entered the management consulting industry in 1982, one of the most used jibes about consultants was that they 'borrow your watch to tell you the time'. The jibe reflected the 'them' and 'us' position of client and consultant, something still 'achieved' by many large consulting firms, who 'do strategy' to their clients.

Throughout my consulting career I realised that many client watches were set at the wrong time (usually some time in the past reflecting former glories or a point in the future unlikely to be reached on the basis of current or projected performance). I was fortunate to work with many clients who realised that the 'doers are the planners'. Only then could the ownership – and thus the success – of any strategy be ensured. The role of strategic managers and consultants is to be guides for the journey of strategic management, to facilitate and integrate the outcomes and ensure that resources are deployed for advantage.

In this opening chapter I outline my own journey through my early career and the 36 years in strategic management consulting with Arthur Young, PA and my own businesses – Genesis and Renaissance & Company. In each chapter of The Game Changer *I introduce a key topic in strategic management that brings what I hope is a useful and contemporary perspective. This introductory chapter also introduces the Focus Framework – one of the cornerstone processes of our approach to developing our role as 'guides for the journey' with our clients.*

Adam Smith and the objective observer

In my research for this book it became clear that many of the concepts currently exercising our clients were first addressed by Adam Smith, one of the forefathers of modern economic theory and an early advocate of the use of 'consultants' to resolve key strategic questions, even in the 18th century.

When I joined the Adam Smith Club[1] in 2000, to some extent in awe of the academic excellence with which we 'townies' were surrounded, little did I imagine that, 18 years later, I would be in a position where part of my portfolio of work is to be a leading lecturer and tutor on the Strategy,

Analysis and Evaluation module of the MBA programme at Strathclyde Business School, the UK's Business School of the year in 2016.

It is right that we ground our research and theories, from time to time, in the amazing insight and perspective into productivity, entrepreneurship and innovation delivered to society by Adam Smith, much of which is still relevant today. Indeed it might even be argued that he invented management consulting, extolling the virtues of the 'objective observer' in the development of institutions and businesses within the system in which they operated.

The students on the Strathclyde MBA (and also many client teams) debate whether, with all the benefits of greater education, endless management theories and increased globalisation, all fuelled by technology driven by the internet, Google and big data, life in business and institutions is more or less complex and uncertain than it was in 1970 when I started my management journey after graduating from the University of Edinburgh.

This question is at the heart of *The Game Changer*. In light of increased competitive intensity and globalisation, one might expect emerging strategies themselves to be more complex and sophisticated. In the chapters that follow the evidence shows this not to be the case. The strategies are often more simple, with the focus on effective implementation of initiatives that will lead to achieving an inspiring vision of success articulated through a suite of strategic goals or outcomes that will ensure the 'game is changed'.

In the beginning

I entered full-time paid work in 1970. As part of the baby-boomer generation I have been incredibly lucky to have had the chance to gain a university education; to expect to receive at least one job offer on graduating from university; to have had the opportunity to buy early into property; and to have enjoyed year-on-year increases in salary and associated benefits. There were recessions, usually followed by relatively quick recoveries, and particular crises such as the one that struck the UK on entry into the single European market in 1987, but gains have been made in both property and equities. As a result of all this, my generation, now in our mid-to-late 60s, is relatively debt free (though some pension pots were severely dented in the 2008 recession).

I was privileged in my early career to work for two great companies – Unilever nv and the John Wood Group plc, after a brief introductory spell with British American Tobacco (Wiggins Teape). Unilever gave me a solid grounding in management and the responsibility to apply this learning in practice from a young age. The John Wood Group was a thriving family business in the 1980s, whose Chair, Sir Ian Wood, gave me the opportunity to apply the 'big company' theory to a more entrepreneurial style of management, as well as running my own business areas in the group.

Strategic management consulting

I entered management consulting in 1982, on the advice of good family friend Peter Saunders (Founder of MSL, the recruitment firm), joining Arthur Young (now Ernst & Young), where I was privileged to be selected to be part of Arthur Young's International Strategy Consulting Group, a collection of 30 individuals like myself from across the world, who brought experience and capabilities from large multinational corporations and added consulting experience from the likes of McKinsey, Booz-Allen, Bain, BCG and Arthur D. Little – all global leaders in their fields. At the time we realised that many of our competitors were applying research-based approaches and tools to consulting and effectively 'did strategy' to their clients. We recognised, as a relatively small firm, that simply to imitate the market leaders and add ourselves to the 'red ocean'[2] was not a winning position. We recognised that successful execution of strategies required the planners to be 'doers' (the company executives) rather than the consultants. In too many cases well-researched, elegant, extensive and expensive strategies failed in many ways due to the complexity and comprehensiveness of their recommendations, and particularly as a result of the lack of ownership by the company and its executives.

In the 1970s 60% of the work done by consultants was in cost analysis. Achieving and exploiting a sustainable cost advantage became the core idea on which most business strategy was developed. The previous era had concentrated on efficiency of operations as the primary source of profitability and the allocation of resources as the way to reduce risk. Efficiency was the first dimension of strategic management and the total focus of early strategy as a management discipline.

In Search of Excellence

The 1980s saw confusion and disillusion with the profusion of management techniques that had emerged during the previous decade, but then came the publication of *In Search of Excellence: Lessons from America's Best-Run Companies*,[3] published by two former McKinsey consultants. It brought a new list of eight features to management's vocabulary:

1 A bias for action
2 Close to the customer
3 Autonomy and entrepreneurship
4 Productivity through people
5 Hands-on, value driven
6 Stick to the knitting
7 Simple form, lean staff
8 Simultaneous loose–tight properties.

In Search of Excellence legitimised the 'soft' stuff and allowed us to start talking about beliefs, values and how to deal with people. These ideas were known but simply not legitimate subjects in the previous era of hard-nosed, cost-focused, by-the-numbers management.

Of course the authors' work identifying and extolling the virtues of companies such as IBM, General Motors and Avon was discredited within two years, as many of their champion companies failed to cope with the pace of change and the increased complexity and uncertainty of markets and especially the changing needs of customers. I myself had been introduced to 'Management by Objectives'[4] in 1970 and part of my first role in business was to be an MBO Catalyst. The three decades since then saw a further proliferation of management fads and theories, no doubt accelerated by the development of business schools and the thirst for knowledge of the emerging global population.

We have had, for example, Theories X, Y and Z, Experience Curve, Zero-based Budgeting, Quality Circles, TQM, TGroup training, business process re-engineering, customer relationship management, Y2K, One-Minute Managing, Kanban, Kaizan – the list is endless (Figure 1.1).

It is salutary to remind ourselves of the words contained in the very first *Harvard Business Review*, published in 1922, where they found:

> It is surprising to observe to what extent able, intelligent businessmen have turned, and are still turning, to the methods and counsel of the quack with his boasted, ready-made, dogmatic and infallible methods of dissecting the mental and moral qualities of persons in relation to a given task.[6]

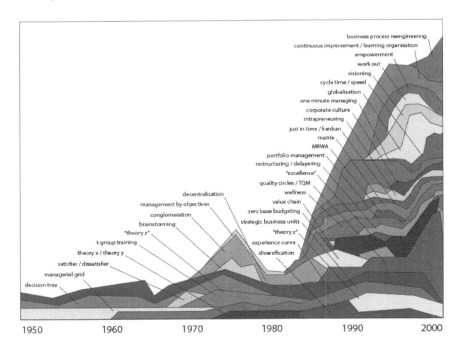

Figure 1.1 Management fads and theories. Source: Richard Tanner Pascale.[5]

To what extent do these and other fads or tools equip tomorrow's executives and consultants with the capability to address the challenges of a world that is increasingly complex and uncertain? As an example, 75% of quality circles begun with enthusiasm in the US in 1982 had been discontinued by 1986. In 2017 a McKinsey survey found that only 7% of CEOs believed they had achieved a good return on the investment made in a number of leadership 'sheep-dip' programmes, rather than building leadership through the challenge and support of executives in the execution of strategically important projects.

One of the acronyms I never tire of sharing with clients reflects the truism of planning in the age of uncertainty and exponential change:

MTBD>MTBS

The 'Mean Time between Decisions' is greater than the 'Mean Time between Surprises'. In other words, by the time your fad or tool has been applied as part of your strategic planning process, something has changed in the outside world that makes the apparently well-thought-through decision irrelevant. Consider applying traditional tools to forecasting the price of oil. The major oil companies and governments invested many millions of dollars each year, only to find some external event rendered their planning useless. It would have been far better to invest more time and less money in scenario thinking to consider different futures and develop alternative strategies that could enable organisations to respond and renew more quickly and effectively. In other words deploy real-time strategic management.

Strategy – make love, not war

Conventionally, all of the major frameworks of strategy start by assuming that the essence of strategy is to achieve superior competitive advantage. I believe that this as a concept, and more importantly as a mindset, is extremely dangerous because it puts competitors firmly at centre stage. In doing so there is the tendency to watch competitors and try to imitate them. Recent examples from the banking and utilities industries would reinforce this view.

Imitation creates sameness. Sameness will never bring greatness and the final result is something that is often the worst thing that can happen to a business – becoming a commodity. More and more young postgraduate students and young managers study for their MBA and most businesses these days are well populated with well-qualified graduates of those programmes. Commodity strategies are often the outcome of the same or similar people, with the same qualifications, in the same environment, supported by the same consultants – coming up with the same strategies. Commodity strategy means no differentiation in your product or service and consequently all you can do is fight on price, rather than commanding a premium – the true outcome of real differentiation. The consequence is aggressive rivalry. In order to win you have to defeat someone else. It is the strategy of war, with many military analogies being used to determine what is a 'good' strategy.

If competitors are not at the centre of strategic thinking, who is? The answer is obvious. The customer. The customer is the focal point and the driving force for strategy. The key is to develop a deep understanding of customer requirements and how you can help your customer in the most effective way. So, rather than imitate a competitor, you are trying to separate yourself from the pack by producing something of value that is unique, that adds value to the customer and expresses real care and concern for the customer. Value comes from mutual trust and respect, mutual benefits, transparency of transactions and a genuine and strong relationship between people in the organisations. Strategy is more about love than war.

In reality the search for the latest fix or fad represents a genuine search for new answers to new management challenges. The exciting aspect of the management consulting industry over the last 30 years has been to apply the best and most appropriate approach to solving our clients' increasingly complex challenges.

Strategic management

At Arthur Young we realised that strategic management as it was evolving in the 1980s must include and integrate not only competitive strategy but also excellence and innovation, with the customer at the centre of our strategic thinking. Importantly we agreed with Rosabeth Moss Kanter when she said: 'The challenge is not to invent more tools, but to use the ones we have more effectively' (*The Change Masters*, Rosabeth Moss Kanter, Simon and Schuster 1984).

This aligned perfectly with our belief that the 'doers have to be the planners' and gave birth to our process-based approach to developing strategy *with* clients. This approach represented the highest form of strategy, since its scope is the total organisation and its focus is the totality of designing and delivering real advantage with our clients and their customers.

As such, our 'Grand Strategy' is not just a broader definition of strategy or a new approach to planning. Its focus is on how organisations are run and it delivers a new agenda for management. Its goal is a pre-eminent and better way to run a business or organisation. Faced with unpredictable and accelerating change, it is the ultimate and only reliable source of competitive advantage. Grand Strategy is the art of achieving such an advantage.

Fundamentals of strategic management – becoming a Grand Strategist

One of the most influential people I had the privilege to work with, especially in my consulting life, was Mike Davidson, Arthur Young's leader of the International Strategic Management practice. His published works include *The Grand Strategist*.[7] It lays out in a brief, easily readable way the difference between the approach we developed in Arthur Young and more traditional approaches to strategic management consulting. In our work together we began to design a new paradigm and approach that would enable us as consultants to be the 'guides for the journey'. His 'Grand Strategist's Credo' gave a framework in which to determine one of the most difficult questions facing businesses (Figure 1.2). What is our mission?

Mission: determine it

- Shared purpose provides FOCUS by driving strategy
- Shared values provide CONTROL by guiding behaviour.

The Grand Strategist's role is to manage the mission on the basis that he should be able to rely on everyone else to run the business. Before he makes any decision he should ask himself:

- In what way will this action contribute to our purpose?
- In what way will this action reflect and enhance our values?

Davidson goes on to suggest there are three main tasks for the Grand Strategist:

1 **Strategy: plan it** – success is the reward for excelling at a set of distinctive capabilities that have a special value to a particular segment of the market place. Profitable growth comes from exploiting strengths, while avoiding our competitors to satisfy emerging customer needs.
2 **Implementation: do it** – organisations do not take action, people do. People only implement what they are involved in creating. Grade A execution of a Grade B plan always beats Grade B execution of a Grade A plan.
3 **Renewal: change it** – experimentation is the best way to find and test new ideas. One cannot dictate that there will be innovation. One can only create the climate that fosters it.

Choice of consultants

At Genesis we realised it would be folly to compete head-on with the likes of McKinsey and other major firms (especially those consultant practices in the large accounting firms). At the same time we recognised that we offered greater value than sole practitioners and less experienced competitors. One of the most successful processes, deployed as part of client engagement, was to illustrate through the use of a matrix (see Figure 1.3) how best we might be of value to the client and their management group.

Another strategic positioning decision was to deliberately work for only one player in a particular industry sector. Others took an industry-wide position, e.g., McKinsey in energy, banking and brewing where the power

The Grand Strategist's Action Plan

Strategic Vision of Success

My people know more about their business than I do. I will challenge and support them to succeed by ensuring they take into account key principles of strategic management

DIRECTION

1. How clear and achievable are their goals? Are they aligned with our vision of success?
2. Are they exploiting emerging trends quickly and effectively?

FOCUS

3. Do they love our customers? Are they building real capability in critical resource areas?
4. Are they using these resources in a sustainable way?
5. Have they built flexibility of resources into their plans?

IMPLEMENTATION

6. Are our people effectively engaged to gain everyone's commitment?
7. How well are they building competitive advantage?
8. How original and innovative is what they plan to do?
9. How simple are their plans to understand and implement?

High Quality Implementation

Selection, evaluation and training are the most powerful tools for achieving our Vision. I will:

- Recognise and reward people taking responsibility and showing initiative.
- Pay close attention to detail that matters in my strategy, and not pick my people's plans to pieces when it does not.
- Learn from our mistakes quickly and be objective in my evaluation. Encourage the practice of regular de-briefing of our performance.
- Allow no exception to our vision and values and go to any lengths to be true to it.

Effective Renewal

How I spend my time. What I reward … and punish, who I promote and where I allocate resources will determine the real climate in my team and my organisation. I will:

- Conduct all our affairs in a spirit of play, and ensure everyone else does the same.
- Model and reinforce the ability to work in teams and groups.
- Encourage constructive feedback and help my people to enjoy the process, remain open to criticism and never shoot the bearers of bad news.
- Create an environment where everyone feels able to fulfill their potential and become the best they can be.

The Doers are the Planners

The Evolution of the Grand Strategist

Vision – Sense of Mission
Shared Goals provide the GOLD MEDAL – the reward for our hard work together
Shared Purposes provide FOCUS by driving strategy
Shared Values provide CONTROL by guiding behaviour

If I lead the way to our Vision I can rely on everyone else to run the business.

Before I make any decision I ask myself:

- In what way is the proposed action aligned with our Vision and its Purpose as well as building stronger competitive advantage?
- In what way will this action reflect our Values?

Strategy: Plan It	Implementation: Do It	Renewal: Change It
Success is the reward for excelling at a set of strategic capabilities that have special value to a particular part of the market place. Profitable, sustainable growth comes from exploiting these capabilities, while avoiding out competitors to satisfy the current and emerging needs of our customers.	Organisations do not take action, people do. Only people implement what they feel they own and are involved in creating. Grade A execution of a Grade B plan always beats Grade B execution of a Grade A plan.	Experimentation is the best way to find and test new ideas and is the catalyst of true innovation and real change. I cannot dictate that there will be innovation and change. I can only create and sustain a climate that fosters it and enables my people to fulfill their potential.

Make Love, Not War

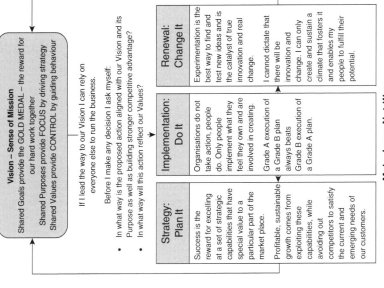

Figure 1.2 The Grand Strategist's Credo. Adapted from *The Grand Strategist* by Mike Davidson (1999). Figure created by Alistair Gray (2017).

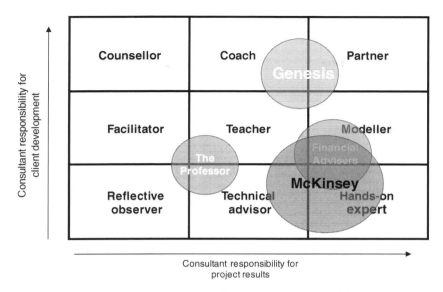

*We work personally and uniquely with one
client organisation in each sector*

Figure 1.3 Role of consultants. Model created by Alistair Gray and Kevin Parker
(2005).

of their analysis and sector know-how could be delivered, in their view, by
erecting 'Chinese walls' between clients and internal teams.

This is not possible with a smaller practice and the subsequent apparently restrictive practice proved most valuable to us over the years, though
it did mean we had to decline a number of opportunities to bid for work.
In our own strategy we aimed to develop a position as the 'Stella Artois' of
the industry – being 'reassuringly expensive'[8] relative to other providers our
size, and positioned just below the majors. True differentiation in action.

Game changer – The Focus Framework

The need for a strategic framework

Over my years in consulting I developed with colleagues and deployed with
clients the Focus Framework – a one-page articulation of a strategy from
Vision (Mission and Goals) into Action Plans, with execution monitored by
means of a scoreboard and all departmental plans aligned to the strategic
goals. Essentially a template for the design of a competitive strategy, the
Framework is also a simple way of aligning resources behind the strategy.

It provides the basis for increased focus and intensity of investment of time, assets, materials, technology and money, with the ultimate aim of achieving stronger positions with customers and greater profitability for the company and its people.

The framework illustrated in Figure 1.4 is a generic example. The Framework is an invaluable tool when communicating the strategy, as well as for engaging executives and other key people as to how they might align their roles or strategies behind achieving the strategic goals.

The Framework is also a very useful 'audit' tool to apply to any existing strategy and it enables the following questions to be asked:

- What is our current vision of success? Is it clear in its aspiration, the purpose of the desired change and does it relate to our mission? Is the view worth the climb?
- What are our strategic goals – outcomes in terms of position, capability, performance and value?
- Are our goals few in number and strategic in intent?
- Are our goals measurable and does our scoreboard have the right metrics to help us understand how we are performing on our route to the goals?
- To what extent do our actions – where we allocate resources – align and focus on achieving our goals?
- Do all our departmental strategies and plans align themselves with achievement of our strategic goals?

The Focus Framework came to represent the process by which Grand Strategy was developed and executed and the final document is the

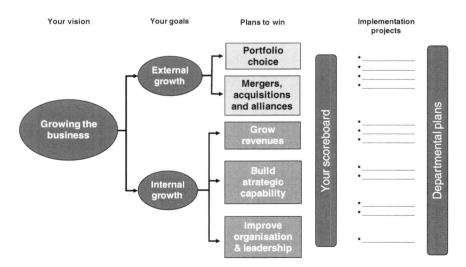

Figure 1.4 The Focus Framework. Created by Alistair Gray (2012).

summary output. The purpose of the process was not only to develop a better strategy; it would determine the extent to which it was actually implemented, having engaged a critical mass of leaders in the process. In this way an effective, time-efficient, team-based process was aimed at more effective execution and implementation, not more elegant planning.

At Genesis we developed our own version of the Focus Framework, linking it to our unique set of strategic capabilities and values that enabled us to compete with major firms over an extended period of time (see

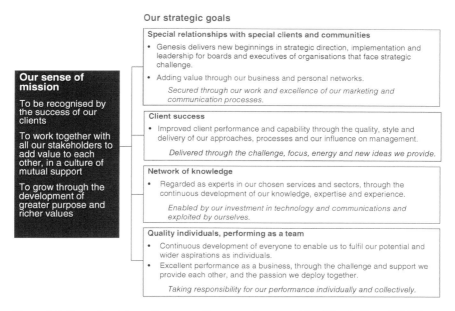

Our strategic goals

Special relationships with special clients and communities
- Genesis delivers new beginnings in strategic direction, implementation and leadership for boards and executives of organisations that face strategic challenge.
- Adding value through our business and personal networks.
  Secured through our work and excellence of our marketing and communication processes.

Client success
- Improved client performance and capability through the quality, style and delivery of our approaches, processes and our influence on management.
  Delivered through the challenge, focus, energy and new ideas we provide.

Network of knowledge
- Regarded as experts in our chosen services and sectors, through the continuous development of our knowledge, expertise and experience.
  Enabled by our investment in technology and communications and exploited by ourselves.

Quality individuals, performing as a team
- Continuous development of everyone to enable us to fulfil our potential and wider aspirations as individuals.
- Excellent performance as a business, through the challenge and support we provide each other, and the passion we deploy together.
  Taking responsibility for our performance individually and collectively.

Our sense of mission

To be recognised by the success of our clients

To work together with all our stakeholders to add value to each other, in a culture of mutual support

To grow through the development of greater purpose and richer values

Figure 1.5 Genesis: vision of success. Framework created by Alistair Gray (2006).

Figure 1.6 Where we offer uniqueness and value. Model created by Alistair Gray (2006).

Choice of consultants above) to reach a top-50 position in the industry (see Figures 1.5 and 1.6).

The process involved in developing the Framework ensures the key ingredients of strategic management:

- An engaged and aligned team.
- An agreed strategy.
- Effective execution and implementation.

No process will achieve success if the leadership does not accept this responsibility. It is not the process that brings about the change, it is the leadership. Conversely, it is not the process that fails, it is the leadership. Process is a tool of leadership. Leadership is not a component of the process.

What is useful is to utilise the Focus Framework to enable you, as a strategist or consultant, to be the 'guide for the journey'. It will provide a degree of structure and evidence of genuine commitment by the client to the eventual outcome. The confidence of those engaged in the process will increase.

The end result of a successful effort is the most exciting experience anyone who has ever been part of a winning team has known: 'The right people . . . fully engaged . . . working together . . . to build commitment . . . to achieve a shared vision of success' (Mike Davidson, *The Grand Strategist*, 1985).

Ultimately, for those involved, it comes down to a personal decision – compliance to an obligation or commitment to an opportunity? The choice is theirs.

The game changing framework

Throughout the book there are real live examples of completed strategic frameworks that bring the theory into practical reality. Many of our clients have found the process incredibly valuable in securing better strategic outcomes and, at the same time, developing their people. Each chapter is stand-alone though there are consistent themes that are relevant to business, sport and not-for-profit organisations in the private and public sectors. In addition, at the end of each chapter, there is a summary of the key areas where each of the case study organisations focused their game-changing strategies. One of the first examples was how NCR changed the game, wrong-footing IBM and others, to secure global industry leadership in the manufacture of ATMs (Figure 1.7).

In the public sector the Framework was used to underpin major change in Scotland's Food & Drink, Energy and Life Sciences industry clusters, and to transform the performance of a number of cities and local councils. In the private sector it guided NCR (Chapter 2) to a position where it dominated the ATM (automated bank terminals and ticketing machines) industry, knocking IBM off industry leadership. In addition it supported

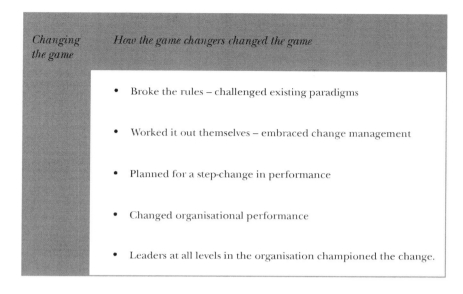

Figure 1.7 How the game changers changed the game. Framework created by Alistair Gray (2017).

Rolls Royce (Chapter 7) through the process of selling the car maker and enabled the management of UPM Kymmene (Chapter 3) to become profitable paper makers.

In sport it helped develop performance sport in England, Scotland, Ireland and Saudi Arabia, to create and implement the first ever corporate strategies for the football associations of England, Scotland and Ireland along with Irish Rugby and Cricket, Cricket Australia, England Netball and Scottish Rugby. The International Cricket Council, World Rugby/ Rugby World Cup and the European Hockey Federation also deployed our approach to strategic management. Part of their journey to success is described in the book.

Clients in multinational corporations, small business start-ups, high growth technology businesses, public sector agencies and not-for-profit organisations have all benefited from the focused approach by deploying the strategic framework. I have focused on real-life examples of 'how to change the game' through reflection on case studies, rather than simply researching from afar. At the end of each chapter there is a summary framework highlighting the key change areas addressed in each case study.

Now, drawing on my experience from 36 years of consulting, I have the privilege and pleasure to pass on this learning and insight to generations of MBA students at the Universities of Strathclyde and Loughborough, as well as to the emerging generation of strategy consultants and executives.

They have embraced the approach with great enthusiasm alongside the many tools and techniques on their way to their Masters qualifications. In *The Game Changer*, through the use of case studies, my aim is to offer inspiration to students, consultants and executives alike on their journey to becoming Grand Strategists.

I hope you find the journey, and the steps along the way, truly rewarding.

Notes

1 The Adam Smith Club was founded in 1868 at the University of Glasgow where Smith spent the most formative and productive years of his academic life. The club is made up of 12 leading academics from the university and 12 leaders in business, the arts and the private and public sectors (the 'townies'). It meets six times each year and at each meeting a member presents a topic of interest to the group, informing the topic, if possible, through a link to Smith's original research and teaching.
2 *Blue Ocean Strategy*, W. Chan Kim and Renee Marbranque, Harvard Business School Press, 2005.
3 *In Search of Excellence*, Thomas J. Peters and Robert H. Waterman, Harper & Row, Publishers Inc., 1982.
4 *Management by Objectives*, John Humble, Gower Press, 1975.
5 *Managing on the Edge*, Richard Tanner Pascale, Penguin Books, 1991.
6 *Harvard Business Review*, 1922.
7 *The Grand Strategist*, Mike Davidson, Macmillan, 1995.
8 'Reassuringly expensive' was the Stella Artois' advertising slogan in the United Kingdom from 1982 until 2007.

Part I

Changing the game in business

2   NCR Manufacturing

Challenging Michael Porter's generic strategy theories

Introduction

Choosing the first chapter for The Game Changer *was a simple task. In 1986 Arthur Young was commissioned by NCR Dundee (the maker of computers and office equipment based in Dayton, Ohio) to transform their manufacturing operation. They planned to move out of their original factory to greenfield sites – but the end result of our work together turned out differently. In the end, the decision was taken to transform the old cash register facility into a world-class manufacturing plant that enabled NCR to secure ATM industry leadership, consigning IBM to a clear second place. This was achieved by challenging the very principles of competitive strategy as devised by no lesser a thought leader than Michael Porter. Not only did it transform NCR, it changed the consulting careers of those who worked with them on the 'SuperPlant' project.*

In this, the first chapter, the story of 'The wee outfit that decked IBM'[1] is referenced, as well as the case study of 'SuperPlant'– the project through which NCR achieved industry-leading performance and 'changed the game'. Through the design and execution of 'SuperPlant', NCR Dundee successfully challenged Michael Porter's generic strategy theory that to achieve an industry-leading position, low cost and differentiation are incompatible. In this case such differentiation was essential and led to a sustained period of industry leadership. 'Do both, every day' became the new mantra and paradigm for world-class manufacturing.

The assignment Jim, should you care to accept it . . .

James (Jim) Adamson joined NCR in Dundee in 1980, newly hired from a subsidiary of ITT. Dundee, a city of 193,000 on Scotland's east coast, was at that time famous mainly for what it used to be: the poet William McGonagall,[2] jute, jam, journalism, marmalade and cake. The city's Member of Parliament from 1908 to 1922 had been Winston Churchill. Adamson's initial assignment was simply to save an old plant, but many of the employees viewed the newcomer with suspicion.

The Gourdie plant had been built by NCR to supply the British and Commonwealth markets with cash registers, but it had since become a secondary manufacturing source for other global plants that needed more modems or sorters. It was an old, decaying and inefficient facility without a mission, almost begging to be closed – and NCR planned to do just that in six months if Adamson was not able to turn it around.

The challenge for Adamson was to succeed in the competitive automated teller machine business, which included IBM, with their large established worldwide sales force and their already dominant force in personal computing. The main prospective customers would be banks, most of whom were established IBM customers. The NCR product was not very reliable, requiring a lot of re-work, and workforce morale was low in the 40-year-old plant, adjacent to the strike-ridden Timex facility along the road.

The recently installed chief executive of NCR, Charles (Chuck) Exley, decided that all plants would be profit centres with responsibility for particular products. Adamson saw this as a great opportunity, personally and corporately. He just had to figure out the best product to make. Whatever decision he made had to help him improve the plant's depressed morale. With little of substance to tell workers, he engaged everyone in his sense of mission.

The challenge he presented to the workforce was clear, readily bought into and is described in the 'SuperPlant' case study later in the chapter. While remarkable, their achievement was no miracle. This success story proved the inadequacy of previously held sacred principles of management[3] and leadership in a way that can work for anyone.

In conjunction with NCR's US operations, Dundee had developed an ATM (Automated Teller Machine) and NCR in Dayton asked the Dundee facility to supply big orders from two major British banks, National Westminster and Barclays. Dundee delivered the orders but the machines were out of specification. The finishes were poor, the software full of defects and the overall quality awful. The banks returned them to NCR.

Back to basics

This humbling experience taught Adamson and his team two lessons they took to heart and which became the foundation for their future success:

- Keep improving quality.
- Stay close to the customer.

Adamson asked his design engineers to develop a machine twice as reliable as that of the competition. Eventually they found a way to more than double the reliability and that performance was eventually achieved through a complete re-design of the product and the range.

Adamson visited customers constantly, traveling the world as NCR's Dayton headquarters turned over more of its ATM business to Dundee. He asked customers which features their customers most wanted and when they would want a new generation of machines. Slowly things started to change positively. The product line began to broaden and improve.

In 1980 Gourdie made only about 1,000 ATMs, placing it ninth world-wide, after IBM, Diebold, Docutel and others, including NCR's main production facility in the US. By 1983 Dundee had improved so much that NCR's US plant stopped making ATMs. The move made sense in part because Diebold had a strong grip on the US market, while the most exciting growth opportunities for NCR were in Europe. The Dundee plant, now exclusively making ATMs, installed over 4,000 in 1984, putting it in third place behind IBM and Diebold.

By 1985 IBM were feeling the pressure. Believing the ATM market was maturing IBM introduced a new model it thought would increase sales opportunities. The machine could read the magnetic coding on bank cheques. It could cash cheques to the penny, on the spot. Trouble was, almost no one wanted it. Banks sought an incrementally better low-cost machine to replace their old units and IBM did not have one. IBM's installations dropped 36% in 1985. Diebold's fell too, and the industry as a whole lost volume and revenues. However, NCR installed 11% more machines, making it the industry leader for the first time.

Historically the size of the installed base determined leadership in the ATM industry, i.e., the total number of your machines in the market should place the leader in pole position to replace installed units and yield additional profits through after-sales service. NCR continued to worship and engage with the customer. Adamson began bringing new customers to Dundee every working day of the year to be interviewed by marketers, engineers and executives. The company kept on emphasising quality and reliability. At a US trade show in 1985 NCR introduced a new ATM by having a demonstrator take it apart, put it back together, switch it on, and show that it worked over 50 times.

Changing the game

There were other initiatives taken by Jim Adamson that resulted in the game-changing performance:

- **Relentless pursuit of competitive advantage** – faced with an investment proposal or new product development Adamson (according to staff) had only one question – 'How does this add to our competitive advantage?' If this was not answered the proposer was asked to go back and think again.
- **Creating the bank in the factory** – a banking centre that displayed current and future products. Not only was it there for customers, it also demonstrated their future to the workforce. They were 'working for customers'.
- **Trust in me** – he introduced a new philosophy that the unions bought into: 'Here is how we will help you to work with our customers' – mutual

trust and desire to win: win compared with the previous culture of attrition that existed in other plants in the city (notably Timex) and other parts of NCR.

- **Securing 'investment' by customers** – Adamson allocated 6% of costs to advanced development. In return customers were given a commitment to be paid on time and have their inventory turned 3–4 times in return for prices that enabled NCR to invest in development. It was unlikely that NCR Corporate would have backed him to that extent at the time.
- **Making new customers an offer they could not refuse** – he offered new customers five ATMs – free on loan – for six months if they bought 1,000 at the end of the trial. No one gave them back.
- **Challenging the traditional NCR Manufacturing paradigm** – essentially our project brief. The story of our project, which ran from 1986 to 1988, follows later in the chapter.

At the time NCR sold ATMs in over 100 countries – more than anyone else. Adamson met representatives of over 600 financial institutions from 22 nations in the first two years.

Despite its vast resources, IBM was never able to recover. Diebold increased its dominance in the US but failed elsewhere. NCR became No. 1 worldwide in 1987. By the end of 1990 NCR's base was 43% bigger than Diebold's, 63% bigger than IBM's. Jim Adamson's outstanding leadership was recognised in the latter half of the 1980s by his elevation to the position of global Vice President of NCR in charge of all financial services and ticketing products. NCR Dundee remained part of his global portfolio, with George Munro[4] taking charge of the Gourdie operation.

Then IBM retaliated. In September 1990 IBM and Diebold formed a joint venture, InterBold, to make ATMs. Diebold owned 70% and Diebold's president headed the business. In other words, IBM contributed technology, patents and a global IBM sales force, which counter-balanced Diebold's weakness abroad. However, IBM sales forces had little enthusiasm for selling product other than computers. InterBold's installed base was now bigger than NCR's.

This move infuriated and energised Adamson. Being No. 2 may be nobody's goal, but it has its uses. Addressing senior managers in Dundee, Adamson briefed his staff that this was a survival issue for NCR that had to be addressed. This time round the NCR operation was large, well organised and strong in a market that a Nilson Report predicted would not be saturated for the next 20 years (1990 forecast). If NCR just kept installing units at the previous year's rate, and if InterBold did the same, NCR would be No. 1 again in three years. The new challenge had been established.

In 1990, a decade after Adamson arrived in Dundee, the revenue out of the Dundee plant exceeded the rest of NCR's revenue globally. They had the capability to produce products that were ten times more complex than that of rivals, e.g., IBM, Fujitsi, Phillips, Interbold, within the same cost parameters – adding real value to their love affair with their customers. In 1990 the Dundee factory won a prestigious competition as 'The Best Factory in the UK', something that is valued by Adamson to this day.

SuperPlant – new beginnings

As a result of the strategy and the impact of the 'SuperPlant' project the five times target for ATM production was smashed through the existing facility supported by a cadre of dedicated out-sourcing suppliers of components and sub-assemblies. The heavy cumbersome safe that had been positioned at the beginning of the line to transfer all the defects through the process was now assembled at the end, together with defect-free product assemblies. Defects were down to a few/million as against some/hundred.

Design engineers worked together with their manufacturing counterparts to create ATMs designed for economic and efficient manufacture. The engineer/blue collar ratio changed in an environment where the number of jobs associated with the manufacture of NCR's ATMs increased. However, they were not all shop-floor jobs based in Gourdie.

Over the first three years of execution of the strategy the number of product and manufacturing engineers increased five-fold, with a reduction in the number of blue-collar members of the workforce. Significant re-training was carried out to enable employees to develop themselves to fulfil their potential. The whole culture of NCR at Gourdie was changing. Staff were encouraged to come up with ideas that would add to NCR's competitive advantage. Inevitably a number were not only entrepreneurs inside the business, they were inspired to set up their own enterprises. Chris van der Kuhl and Ana Stewart were two such employees. Their story is told in more detail in the Appendices at the end of the book. The examples of Chris and Ana were an inspiration to future generations of entrepreneurs, in NCR and throughout the industry. In addition, Jim Adamson fostered many entrepreneurs inside NCR Gourdie who flourished in a culture of innovation and entrepreneurship and the new way created by the 'SuperPlant' project.

Not only would Jim Adamson refuse to 'kowtow' to NCR's corporate executives, he refused to relocate to the US as a Vice President. In 1991 NCR succumbed to an ill-fated merger with AT&T. Four years later NCR emerged as an independent company with Jim Adamson as Vice-President of financial delivery systems. Despite his having been given global responsibility as a Vice President of the new NCR, the relationship was not going to last. Adamson left NCR in 1998 and in 2005 NCR transferred manufacturing of ATMs to Hungary, breaking the local supply chain and the close integration between product engineering and manufacturing. He has always felt that Scotland did not make the most of the potential from inward investment of technology companies, citing IBM as an example of major investment to simple 'screw boxes together', something that was easily transferred to lower cost economies.

In 2009 NCR closed the Dundee manufacturing plant producing the ATMs. The business, one of Dundee's biggest employers, had slowly reduced the workforce in the city while moving some operations to Hungary where wages are traditionally lower. The company shed 650 jobs at the factory in 2007. The rationale to make high volume products had disappeared.

In its place were NCR's remaining business activities in Dundee, with a focus on higher value jobs in engineering, research and development, services support operations, solutions management, marketing and new product introduction.

The company still sells 50,000 units worldwide. In 2017 NCR's state-of-the-art manufacturing facility in Budapest achieved the unique distinction of manufacturing its 350,000th ATM in a record period of just 11 years. The Budapest facility remains NCR's largest manufacturing facility in the world, with over 750 employees, and manufactures ATMs for the US, Europe, Middle East and Africa markets. In addition to ATMs, NCR also produces self-checkout and point-of-sale (POS) solutions for the retail and hospitality industries.

The Dundee research and development arm of NCR received a major investment after landing a £30 million order to supply next-generation cash machines to RBS. In his first major public speech at the Business in Parliament event at Holyrood, RBS's new chief executive Ross McEwan confirmed RBS was working with the American technology firm's Wester Gourdie Business Park-based Centre of Excellence. The contract runs through beyond 2017 and will see NCR supply and install more than 2,000 SelfServ ATM units at locations across the UK.

'SuperPlant' – the project. How NCR re-defined world class manufacturing

By 1985 NCR had 15% of the world market, selling nearly 5,000 machines that year. At that stage Adamson recognised the need to change his strategy away from the conventional approach developed over years of manufacturing cash registers. In 1986 Julian Gray (no relation) and I successfully bid for a project being commissioned by NCR. The project (entitled 'SuperPlant') not only resulted in significant performance improvement for the Dundee facility, taking NCR to leadership in the ATM industry, it also transformed our lives and careers as consultants.

Background and context

It all began with a telephone call from Alan Murdoch, then Head of Personnel at NCR's Gourdie facility in Dundee. He explained the background to an assignment where the proposal was to radically change the size and shape of NCR's manufacturing facilities in Scotland. They proposed to close the one large cantilever-roofed factory, move into four plants at separate strategic locations in Scotland and achieve a step change in manufacturing capacity. The benefits would be to remove the dependency (and potential threats) from a 2,500 strong workforce in one site (no doubt in danger of being influenced by the poor industrial relations at Timex, a few hundred metres along the Kingsway – Dundee's ring road), and move to more cell-based forms of manufacturing.

We were asked to present our proposal to review current strategies (though not explicitly stated) and endorse management's proposal for change for onward presentation to the parent company. Our proposal was successful and we began a review that was to prove to be one of the most challenging in our careers and also transformational in the performance of NCR's Gourdie facility to deliver their financial services and ticketing product charters.

Not quite all it seemed to be

We carried out a full strategic review of the operations and the proposals that were emerging from the senior Dundee executive. Unlike many other multinational 'branch plant' facilities in Scotland (and indeed in the rest of the UK and Ireland), NCR's Gourdie facility had been granted a product-line charter by their US parent to develop the ATM business. This meant a special role in sales and product development, rather than simply being a manufacturing plant. In summary we found:

- Lots of individual processes, including casting their own components, with little use of sub-assemblies of outsourced manufacturing.
- Designs created without world-class manufacturing in mind – 'try this one for size' was the philosophy as part-assembled product was passed on – each department claiming their bonuses for output along the way almost irrespective of quality.
- Highly complex processes backed up with inaccurate forecasts resulting in many changes to plans.
- Management and planning information based on the high labour content processes to manufacture cash registers rather than high material content ATMs.
- Making a step change in output and productivity is not a workforce issue alone. It is about the strategy for the business and world-class manufacturing. Moving to individual plants was not the solution.
- Manufacturing in a new way, through the existing facility, would increase ATM capacity by 4–5 times.
- The new way required embracing Total Quality Management (TQM), Just-in-Time manufacturing (JIT) and Computer Integrated Manufacturing (CIM), and a real change in culture from the 'just-too-late' outcome of existing practices.

We fed back these findings to Jim Adamson, recently promoted to a Vice President role in NCR at global level, with leadership of the financial and retail services product charter. After some discussion and no little debate, the principles of our feedback and recommendations were accepted.

In any change initiative there are three fundamental steps to take:

1   **Face reality** as it is, not as it was, or how you would wish it to be – agree the status quo is not an option for the future (including the nil-action forecast).
2   **Build an inspiring vision of success** – the view has to be worth the climb.
3   **Demonstrate early wins** for the future strategy to build confidence that positive change can be achieved quickly.

A series of communication sessions was set up with all levels of management and workforce representatives. The outcome was ringing endorsement for the need for change. This was an important first step to develop a new approach to strategic management that was to transform the performance of the business.

Changing the game

We presented our thinking behind our belief that NCR could no longer employ the methods used to manufacture cash registers to achieve leadership in the ATM industry. It was summarised as in Figure 2.1.

The **old way** of looking at manufacturing – The Value Chain

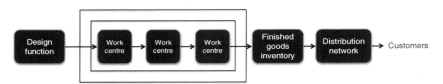

The **new way** of looking at manufacturing – Total System

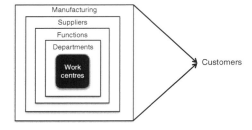

Figure 2.1 The old way . . . the new way. Model created by Alistair Gray and Julian Gray (1985).

The manufacturing system was based on three pillars or fundamental concepts of modern manufacturing, which differed significantly from Porter's initial theories. We were supported in our approach by our Arthur Young colleague Thomas Gunn[5] (National Director of Arthur Young's Manufacturing Consulting Group); an approach later encapsulated in his book. The three fundamental tools are:

- **Just-in-Time** – at the time NCR struggled to deliver customer orders on time or to specification, caused by the complexity of the manufacturing process and the uncertainty of sales forecasts.
- **Total Quality Management** – NCR focused on inspection or quality control. The end result was that most defects were only confirmed at the end of the process, resulting in considerable levels of rework.
- **Computer Integrated Manufacturing** – NCR's control and reporting systems focused mainly on labour – another legacy from their cash register days.

The Focus Framework – winning Grand Strategy

Any manufacturing strategy has to be developed in response to the overall corporate strategy for the business and has to address the opportunities and threats from the external environment. Taking input from the assessment stage, the following Grand Strategy was developed for the ATM business. We deployed what was to become the cornerstone of many future strategic projects – The Focus Framework to strategic management. It provided the pointers for the manufacturing strategy, and is illustrated in Figure 2.2.

Product leadership – the best products for the best customers – was right up front in terms of what would deliver industry leadership. The unique approach of NCR was one of the first examples of 'product plus' strategy where world-class service, strong customer relationships and other key elements were added to the basic product offered.

The company planned to dominate the global market through the capacity and strategic capability to manufacture the low-cost entry model for banks and other finance and retail institutions. At the same time they offered high performance ATMs that were multi-functional – to sell insurance, mortgages and other products and services. This they achieved through a new configuration of their manufacturing organisation.

The new goals formed a vision of success. The NCR people engaged for the first time and, with our support, developed the vision. Implementation was led functionally behind the strategy through a planned and integrated approach to changing the fundamentals of manufacturing ATMs – to a cell-based rather than line-based approach. The process also ignited the entrepreneurial spirit of NCR's people.

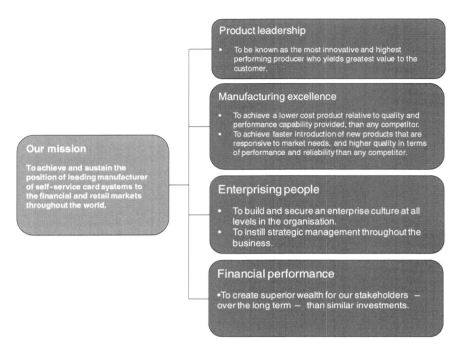

Product leadership

- To be known as the most innovative and highest performing producer who yields greatest value to the customer.

Manufacturing excellence

- To achieve a lower cost product relative to quality and performance capability provided, than any competitor.
- To achieve faster introduction of new products that are responsive to market needs, and higher quality in terms of performance and reliability than any competitor.

Our mission

To achieve and sustain the position of leading manufacturer of self-service card systems to the financial and retail markets throughout the world.

Enterprising people

- To build and secure an enterprise culture at all levels in the organisation.
- To instill strategic management throughout the business.

Financial performance

- To create superior wealth for our stakeholders – over the long term – than similar investments.

Figure 2.2 NCR: our strategy – mission and goals. Framework created by Alistair Gray and Julian Gray (1985).

Manufacturing excellence

Excellence can be defined as above average performance in the long run, relative to competing organisations. Our initial work confirmed that the historic 'cash register' culture and approach to manufacturing was not going to achieve the desired outcome.

This was recognised by Jim Adamson, but not universally shared by other senior management. They were wedded to existing methods, approaches and practices. Some were fearful and suspicious of change, while others welcomed the freshness of the approach that appeared to focus on the big issues that needed to be addressed. It was evident when presenting the findings of our work to the wider management group that there was almost universal approval for the direction of travel and the degree and type/ extent of change required.

Throughout the design of the strategy execution process we formed high performing teams of second-level executives working with consultants and engaging with their directors to provide evidence of the scope of change required. This process was not bypassing the first-level leaders. It was an essential way to get them to see the strategic situation and future challenges through a different lens. The level of ownership of the strategy was higher than in many traditional consultant-led planning assignments and was a feature of the NCR project. Our role as consultants was to facilitate and integrate the work of the teams. Though we were also given a special role by Jim Adamson to be the 'corgi'[6] to ensure the pace of change was maintained.

Time-based management

Time-based management (later renamed Rapid Response) was used as a key theme to underpin the change in culture. Rapid Response is a strategic package that gives a particular flavour and purpose to a manufacturer's competitive strategy. A process for creating a Rapid Response operation has to include all the elements for developing a normal manufacturing strategy with an overlay of Rapid Response. It is important to break down this process into digestible chunks that follow a rigorous logic, a path that ensures that decisions are made progressively.

The process that enables client organisations to break out of traditional approaches has four main stages. The sequence of stages is illustrated in Figure 2.3 against a typical six-month timescale.

Strategy pointers

The overall strategic direction can then be broken down into a number of strategic pointers that articulate the direction in which the strategy will

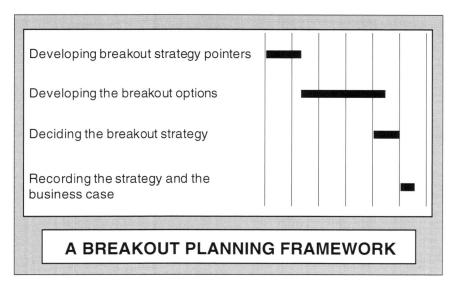

Figure 2.3 Breakout planning framework. Created by Julian Gray (1985).

drive the whole business, the pace of change and the framework of the mission, goals and actions.

The process started from the market-facing competitive positioning and financial objectives already determined – these define the goals that must be secured to achieve competitive advantage (see Focus Framework above). Developing the manufacturing strategy involved:

- Deciding on the scope and scale of the response from manufacturing and expressing these as manufacturing objectives.
- Working out the performance required from manufacturing to meet the objectives.
- Developing a 'strategic thinking framework' – a 'one-page strategy' – that encapsulates all these fundamentals.
- Creating and building a coarse financial model that illustrates the potential profit effect, the cash effect and key business ratios during and after breakout implementation. Normally a large number of assumptions and approximations are perfectly acceptable at this stage. However, the model must produce reasonable comparisons of possible options to enable the top team to distinguish the most-likely best from the rest – the differences are usually quite dramatic.
- One of the key catalysts at NCR was to produce and share the 'nil-action forecast'. This helped to provide the rationale for change and the futility of continuing to approach manufacturing in the traditional way.

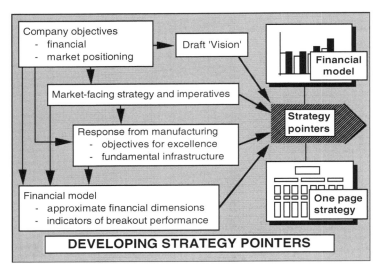

Figure 2.4 Developing strategy pointers. Process created by Julian Gray (1985).

The next stage was to create a vision for world-class manufacturing that was aligned to the business strategy. It stimulated innovation and creativity by imagining what might be achieved and, at the same time, helped to distil a huge spectrum of ideas into a coherent and straightforward framework. Its purpose was to enable the top team to distinguish their preferred development path without going into exhaustive detail (always a time-consuming trap to avoid), and to describe the way forward. Here was the vision developed by the now-energised top team at NCR Dundee:

> Our customers prefer to do business with us because our ATMs are better than anyone else's (more easily programmed, more flexible, easier to install, easier to maintain), they cost less than anyone else's and they NEVER break down. We always deliver and install on the day we promised, anywhere in the world. Our customers trust us to give them the best ongoing advice and support. If we can do that we can be No. 1.

The key document was the 'one-page strategy', building on the initial Focus Framework – a strategy framework that integrated the business and manufacturing strategy. The missing link between the conventional manufacturing strategy and the particular theme – Rapid Response – needed to be introduced as a set of distinguishing features. One way to do this was to add a second dimension to the 'one-page strategy' that highlighted the relationships between the conventional strategy, illustrated above, and the Rapid Response components.

A key feature that drove the change at NCR was the move from line-based manufacture to a cell/work centre-based approach where each cell took responsibility for their performance and the quality of their product passed forward. In management's original proposals the cells were to be separate factories.

The second feature was to make decisions about what to manufacture at Gourdie and what should be bought in as sub-assemblies or components. The foundry was closed (evidence of consigning the past to history) and the Gourdie factory only made the products that had regular demand patterns and offered high margins and degrees of difficulty.

The starting point was to add the five distinctive features of a Rapid Response operation and link Rapid Response goals and actions to the conventional structure. This produced a matrix of strategic thinking that combined the two types of distinctive features of the vision:

- Strategic goals – industry position, strategic capabilities, performance goals, people and organisation goals, as well as the financial goal.
- Rapid Response goals – rapid product and process development (sometimes abbreviated to rapid technology), rapid production, rapid logistics, rapid information and rapid management.

A document like this can encapsulate the essence of the Rapid Response strategy pointers on a single piece of paper, helping to make the whole vision easy to understand, to share and to communicate. Its development as a team effort provided the all-important glue among top management and the document became their means of focussing further work, in the next stage, only on the key issues and solutions.

Breakout – working out the detail

The top team developed its 'one-page strategy' to organise the work that needed to be done in this stage. First, they segmented their plan into 'Rapid Response foundations' and 'Rapid Response bricks', and then organised parallel working on a broad front (by a project team). The main components of the process are illustrated in Figure 2.5.

The world's best manufacturing strategy

As a consulting team we dug deep to devise the best possible manufacturing strategy for NCR, bringing together the best of good practice business strategy, rapid response and world-class manufacturing approaches. Julian Gray and Alan Stanger,[7] the latter a specialist in stock segmentation and manufacturing planning, developed a unique approach to which I hope this chapter does justice. It was certainly transformational in its impact and laid the foundations for the game-changing outcome.

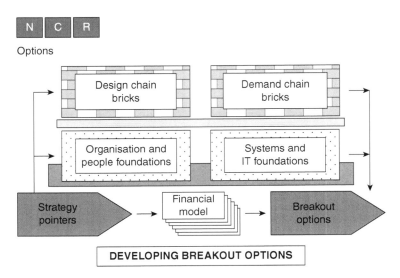

Figure 2.5 Developing breakout options. Process created by Julian Gray (1985).

They began by asking a number of critical questions that provided the framework or rules for developing a unique approach to building competitive advantage in the manufacture of ATMs:

1   Asking the right questions in the right order and not trying to develop solutions until the right answers are established are vital stages.
2   Do not copy competitors, as imitation creates sameness that stifles greatness.
3   In manufacturing, adopt a new and dynamic process to 'unwind' the current, very traditional, manufacturing methods.
4   Change from a line-based to a cell-based approach to manufacturing.
5   Decide what to make in-house and what to purchase on the basis of the future factory logistics.
6   Make only those components that have regular demand profiles with high margins that are difficult to make.
7   Commit to redesigning products in detail in order to take full advantage of opportunities to streamline manufacturing.

The next step was to initiate project teams to:

•   Decide on core product technologies.
•   Decide what should be made and where.
•   Provide support to the design engineering teams for the initiation of product-part rationalisation.
•   Reduce supply and production defects to a few parts per million.
•   Produce design-for-manufacture parts.

From a new manufacturing model to a new era

To answer the key questions about the logistics of manufacture, a computer-based method of analysis was used that examined the demand profiles of every part. This was a tried and tested method called Stock Segmentation Analysis, which had been used for both merchanting and manufacturing companies, and had been proved successful in many situations before being used at NCR. The situation prompting the use of the model was:

•   **Volume and value** – the traditional Pareto or ABC analysis graphs neglected many logistics issues. A measure of **variability** should be incorporated in the analysis.
•   Only parts or assemblies with stable profiles, that have a normal demand distribution, and only those that have usable forecasts.
•   Unstable demand cannot be forecast with any degree of confidence, but such parts need to be identified.
•   There were many different forecasting methodologies but there is a need to identify which are the most effective.

- An operational research-based mathematical approach on live data was identified to determine the best options. The actual data profile is more important than the forecast methodology.
- Comparisons could then be made on a **volume**, **value** and **variability** basis. As a result all parts would be classified into 12 sector codes, each of which share similar demand characteristics.

The start of the analysis was to generate demand information using the existing MRP (Material Requirements Planning) system. A total 'tear down' was applied on a gross-only basis down to the individual parts. This used the existing master production schedule for the previous year's shipments. The current stores stock information was used to identify current imbalances. The model created a summary, for each of the 12 sectors, of the total values of part count, sales value and stock value. The model was run to determine the *Volume, Value* and *Variability* (of demand) for each part.

The results were then examined to determine the level of variability, and then to make the relevant key findings known. Reports were produced to support all the project teams for the examination of specific classes of parts, such as those that would be candidates for cell production.

The design team used the list of parts that had been identified as targets for rationalisation. The production engineers used the reports of stable-demand parts to consider the design of the cells, methods of manufacture and cell layout. From this the future necessary flow of parts to the cells and final assembly could be defined.

Reports showing the parts with high variability were examined to define which parts were to be considered for outside purchase. Sourcing decisions could begin to be finalised with consideration of supply parameters. In addition, high cost and high variability parts were shown to be special make-to-contract components for bespoke customer orders. Standardisation in product design would eliminate the need for these parts. Product as well as part rationalisation eliminated much of the variability and made for more stable production operations.

The creation of this stock segmentation model and the subsequent analysis made an enormous contribution to the company's manufacturing strategy and provided the implementation teams with the information that helped them to focus their development work, making informed decisions with a high degree of confidence.

As the subsequent results showed, the manufacturing strategy completely transformed NCR's supply and production systems. The company projected itself into truly world-class status from which it achieved and maintained its dominant position as the premier manufacturing company in its global market.

The Big V – advanced development of the Volume, Value and
Variability analysis

No software product is immune to innovation and enhancement. Development of additional features and options for different industry sectors prompted the tools and technique of stock segmentation analysis to be modified as the needs arose. The first enhancement was to prove which forecasting technique produced the best demand forecast in a particular situation. Better and more reliable forecasts help to determine the optimal operational parameters.

Analysis of forecasting methods was achieved with modern operational mathematical research techniques in simulation mode, using computer-based algorithms. Comparisons were made in a variety of industry sectors for both manufacturing and merchanting companies before deciding upon the best approach. Modern software tools and computers speeded development.

Many successful applications provided the impetus to add more useful parameters that contribute to the design of the solution. These are *Vulnerability*, *Variety* and *Versatility* (three more Vs), as well as the margin and turn/earn ratios. All this builds the model into a 'hypercube' of data from which information can be generated that helped to design an optimum solution.

- **Vulnerability** (highlighting opportunities to reduce the risk of running out).

  These were the low-cost parts that were required in each cell as part of the build of sub-assemblies. Special consideration was given to both higher stock levels and JIT (just-in-time) replenishment. Kit-marshalling played a part in this replenishment cycle as did cell consolidation, supplier selection, goods receiving and movement to each cell.

- **Variety** (highlighting opportunities to reduce the need to add features to standard parts).

  These parts were identified during the manufacturing cycle as an effect of the design of the part. This occurred where parts reached a stage where extra machining changed the part from a common to a specific configuration by, for example, drilling a special hole to accommodate an additional feature. These situations were rare and, if found, were referred to the design department.

- **Versatility** (highlighting opportunities to add features as late as possible and only on demand).

  Parts were machined to a standard up to the point where they could be configured by a final process due to design considerations. This drastically shortened the lead-time, increasing the batch size, reducing the cost and lowering the stock levels required to meet the desired service levels.

The contribution made by our colleague Alan Stanger was fundamental to securing the change. What underpinned the *entire* transformation, and the actual design of the cell manufacturing in particular, was the unique combination of his knowledge, his ability to see the big picture as well as the finest detail, and the quirky leadership he provided that made the Stock Segmentation Model so entirely powerful and effective.

The fully developed Stock Segmentation Model (in 2017) now had the 'six Vs' as well as optimised forecasting modules, and it provided the core facilities to optimise manufacturing methods, merchanting stock parameters and customer service levels (Figure 2.6).

Companies planning to change the game through manufacturing strategy used this powerful analytical process to support their projects based on reliable and detailed supply and demand information. In addition, the model would be used to audit stock and service levels.

This comprehensive approach identified opportunities to solve critical questions of what stock, where and how much to order to achieve higher service levels and enhance bottom-line results. The model can also be

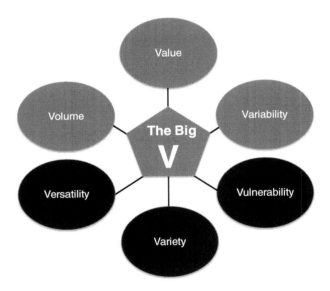

Figure 2.6 The Big V: the catalyst for change. Model created by Alan Stanger (1986, modified 2017).

used to simulate various options to evaluate the effects on commercial results.

At NCR the top team supported by the project teams defined strategy execution in detail by developing:

- **The 'foundations' – people and systems** – designing organisational developments and deciding how to change culture, attitudes and skills; planning systems developments, possibly developing a fresh strategy for information technology. These are 'foundations' because implementation of everything else depends on having both people and systems in place to enable the other changes.
- **'Design chain bricks'** – working out how to make fundamental and radical reductions in complexity of products, processes, services and logistics. This involved deciding on core product technologies, planning the product development programme to meet the market-facing imperatives, and working out how product development can be accelerated permanently. Decisions on critical competences and manufacturing capabilities followed – deciding what to make and what to buy; working out where things should be made, which factories should be opened, maintained or closed, and what methods and layouts to use; determining the requirements for technical and engineering services to support the design and manufacturing facilities of the future; designing the flow of materials and value through manufacturing – from suppliers, through the factories and on to customers. In a nutshell, the 'design chain bricks' represented the building blocks of the foundation on which to build Rapid Response as a strategic capability.
- **'Demand chain bricks'** – working out how to put in place the optimum means of managing operations so as to counteract uncertainty – developing the ground rules and methods for planning and controlling all activities (assuming reduced complexity). This achieved the levels of internal and external service required at minimum cost. The 'demand chain bricks' were about how operations would be managed in a Rapid Response environment.
- **The financial model** – supporting exhaustive analysis of the options for 'foundations' and 'bricks' so that the potential impact on profits, cash and implementation costs were clearly understood at all times during the strategy development process and its execution.

This part of the process led to a progressively refined set of 'foundations' and 'bricks', a 'Blueprint for the Future' for NCR Dundee. While it was in progress it was important to maintain the commitment and understanding of the top management team by involving them in appropriate ways. In particular, the team continued to use the Focus Framework as a means of preserving the cohesion of the various parts of the emerging strategic plan. It formed the basis of personal performance planning and development.

Finalising the breakout strategy

Initially, a large number of packaged proposals emerged from the project teams. These were evaluated as to their contribution to achieving Rapid Response and determining the preferred way forward. The top management team did four things at this stage to agree the detail of:

- The Focus Framework and 'one-page strategy', which confirmed the rationale for the required change and basis for Rapid Response. It also provided a very useful tool in wider communication across the business's stakeholders.
- The plans for developing the 'foundations' and 'bricks'.
- The validity of the financial model.
- The balance between opportunities and risks.

The company achieved Adamson's goal for 'SuperPlant' – to reach the position of becoming the No. 1 in:

- ATM manufacturing.
- The financial services industry.
- The electronics industry.

At the end of the process we produced a 'book of the film' to record the key findings, the business case and rationale for the way ahead and business plan (application for funds). Presentations were made to leading executives in NCR, Dayton and the workforce. 'SuperPlant' was launched with real ownership of the executive and workforce and future competitive advantage was secured.

The outcome

We were an also-ran in our industry. We are that no more. I have no doubt that, when we really get our act together, we can be No. 1 again in five years from now. I am not totally clear how we are going to do this. I am clear we will achieve our goals. We will need to work out for ourselves, supported by Julian and Alistair, and cement our position in the world class.

George Munro, General Manager,
NCR Dundee, 1986

Changing the game	How NCR changed the game
NCR	• **NCR broke the rules – challenged existing paradigms** 　○ Challenged and re-wrote Michael Porter's generic strategies. 　○ Offered the customer an outstanding range of ATMs and ticketing products. 　○ While at the same time achieving low cost leadership, relative to the competition. • **NCR worked it out themselves – embraced change management** 　○ Faced reality as it was in 1980, taking full responsibility for their performance. 　○ Developed together an exciting vision of success (in the Focus Framework) that was shared with all and by all. 　○ The 'SuperPlant' project achieved 'breakout' performance through planning to achieve clear short-term goals that aligned a previously dysfunctional organisation and gave a plan, purpose and confidence to their people that success was possible. • **NCR planned for a step-change in performance** 　○ The vision was simple, clear and inspiring, yet it was underpinned by a detailed plan (The 'one-page strategy') that drove the change. 　○ The move from 'line-based' to 'cell-based' manu-facturing removed many of the cash register practices that were getting in the way. Embracing a new model – 'The Big V' – provided a way to deal with the 'make or buy' dilemma. • **NCR changed organisational performance** 　○ The company engaged a critical mass of executives and their workforce in pursuit of competitive advantage – cross-functional teams worked out what to do. 　○ Everyone knew how their role would deliver the goals of the strategic plan. 　○ Success was celebrated as milestones were achieved and barriers broken down. 　○ They kept it simple – in the early years relentlessly focusing on improving quality and keeping close to their customers. • **Leaders at all levels in the organisation championed the change** 　○ Many people fulfilled their potential, not only in NCR but also in other industries, e.g., computer games and other areas of electronics.

Notes

1 *Fortune* magazine article by Geoffrey Colvin and Rebecca Lewin, 19 November 1990.
2 Sir William Topaz McGonagall was a Scottish weaver, poet and actor. He won notoriety as an extremely bad poet who exhibited no recognition of, or concern for, his peers' opinions of his work. He wrote about 200 poems, including 'The Tay Bridge Disaster' and 'The Famous Tay Whale', which are widely regarded as some of the worst in English literature.
3 *Competitive Strategy: Techniques for Analysing Industries and Competitors*, Michael E. Porter, The Free Press, 1980.
4 George Munro rose from a manufacturing role to become General Manager of NCR Dundee. A real 'Level 5 leader' (*Good to Great*, Jim Collins, Collins Business, 2001), with a distinctive and completely different style to Adamson. Tragically he died in 1990 after a long illness, and before he saw the eventual results of his leadership.
5 *Manufacturing for Competitive Advantage: Becoming a World Class Manufacturer*, Thomas G. Gunn, Ballinger, 1987.
6 From Wikipedia: The Pembroke Welsh Corgi (/ˈkɔrgi/; Welsh for 'dwarf dog'), is a herding dog breed, which originated in Pembrokeshire, Wales [1]. The herding instinct will cause some younger Pembrokes to nip at their owners' ankles [15].
7 Tribute should be paid to our colleague Alan Stanger – his perhaps quirky yet infectious enthusiasm for changing from line to cell production was probably the fundamental energiser for many of the changes made in manufacturing. His understanding of 'logistics' was and is truly exceptional and his enthusiasm and ability to get his message across was a critical foundation for many achievements that led to NCR's status as a World Class Manufacturer. The 'Three Vs' and his other gimmicks sold the approach to the NCR people.

3 Scenario thinking
The answer to future uncertainty

Introduction

1970. One of the early tasks in my first job as assistant to the manager at one of the largest and most complex papermakers in the world was to prepare a discounted cash flow for a major (>£500m) investment in a new paper-making machine. The machine was to make the backing paper for leather cloth (wet-look boots and fashion accessories were in vogue at the time and championed by Mary Quant) and other similar release papers.

I prepared a detailed analysis of the net present value of future cash flow projections for the investment with great certainty, armed with slide rule, logarithmic tables and calculator. Afterwards, with similar authority, I forecast the investment would produce a yield of 15.753% over the following 15 years.

At that time, in the early 1970s, many sectors found traditional investment appraisal and strategic tools, which forecast the future to three-decimal point certainty, to be totally inadequate. The strategic planners at Royal Dutch Shell pioneered scenario thinking in the early 1980s as an answer to the Yom Kippur war (1973) and other major uncertainties that were influencing the price of oil. I originally wrote the first section of this chapter in 2009, in the wake of the financial crisis (and pre-Brexit). Given the current price of oil (below $60 per barrel and falling), similar approaches would help hedge against future uncertainty.

The three case studies that follow outline how local subsidiaries of multinational corporations used scenario thinking to change the game, relative to established models and paradigms in their industries, to extend and enhance their mandate, not only to survive in the harshest of trading environments, but to attract additional investment as well.

Scenario thinking – the answer to uncertain times

November 2009 – for 12 months the world has been in turmoil. The global collective overdraft is €2,300,000,000,000 and many banks have been effectively privatised and become part of the civil service. In the past there have been smart people who said 'I told you so'. Not this time. The size and scale of the turmoil in the world's financial markets has been unprecedented and beyond all forecasts. Is there an analyst or forecaster who can ever trust their models and frameworks again? And now, one year on, every news-reader is seeking to be the first to identify the green shoots of recovery. Will the media fuel the recovery as they did the recession?

We are often struck by the apparent certainty with which our leaders predict the future, as if events are following some path developed in the past. In reality, few of these pre-determined outcomes actually come to pass. Yet even the most recent strategic planning approaches focus more and more on systematic, quantitative forecasts of an increasingly uncertain world. In essence they make the wrong choice between 'roughly right and precisely wrong'. In this section I contend that these approaches will be found increasingly wanting, and that alternatives such as scenario thinking will be more appropriate to address the big issues of our world. The end result is not a more accurate picture of tomorrow, but a basis for better decisions about the future – whatever the outcome. Who knows the likely outcome if the post-Brexit scenarios had been provided to the electorate prior to the 2016 referendum in the UK?

In 2004 few would have predicted the four years that followed:

- The unprecedented ease of access to capital, leading to the unprecedented crisis in capital markets.
- The impact of sub-prime meltdown in the US – failing to make the connection between equity write-offs and the impact on capital availability at the banks.
- The impact on commodity prices and currency through the activity of the hedgers and speculators.
- The speed of emergence of the BRIC nations (Brazil, Russia, India and China) and the sheer size of their potential economic power.
- The continued unrest and unease across the world, with global war or civil unrest arriving on every doorstep.
- Talented people and their skills become the new global currency and source of competitive advantage with the rapid impact of immigrant workers from Eastern Europe.
- The impact of pensions on the ageing workforce and the balance sheets of companies.
- The rapid changes and development in telecommunications and the use of the internet, especially the growth of mobile and wireless communication, and social networking.
- Environmentalism no longer 'nice to have' in a resource-starved world.

What prospects do the next five years hold? Will Asian-Pacific and Russian economies prosper at the expense of the West? Will the cost of the demographic changes cripple many of the so-called developed countries? Will the newly industrialised countries' labour-cost advantages be eroded through a return to inflation and higher welfare costs? Will the European Union break down amid squabbles about monetary policy and immigration, and continued low growth (or even prolonged recession) prevail in the major economies? Will there be another major collapse in equity markets, asset values and pension funds?[1]

Who knows? Why bother forecasting? The truth is, almost everything we predict about the future will be proven wrong, even if endorsed by ever-increasing amounts of fresh data. What does this mean for strategic choices in the future?

Too many executives when considering the future spend excessive time on a relatively useless question: what will happen to us? They try to forecast the future with increasing precision and certainty – to no avail. Managers who perceive change early should spend more time on a far more useful question: what will we do if such-and-such happens? Only this latter question can lead executives to make changes inside an organisation that will allow it to survive and thrive in the new uncertain future.

As you would expect, management groups take action to counter these uncertainties. Some build in flexibility by developing one or two quantitative scenarios around their official future prediction, e.g., +/– 10% revenue growth. That would have been really useful when oil prices were at $50 per barrel, 18 months before they reached $100.[2]

In my experience too many boards of directors and their senior management spend most of their time together:

- Reviewing historical performance.
- Managing short-term performance.
- Planning to hit operational targets.

Once a year they go through the ritual of updating a three-year plan or extended budget. This exercise is often carried out a few days before the deadline, following guidelines prepared by the finance or planning departments. I would not wish to condemn these laudable efforts to improve the bottom line. However, frequently they do not allow the time and space to enable the most senior (and able?) managers in the enterprise to consider the future, its certainties and uncertainties. Nor is the process carried out in an environment conducive to developing a winning strategic direction, shared by a critical mass of those charged with delivering the results. Few strategic conversations of consequence take place to open up fresh future perspectives and create a vision of the future. Can management afford not to think about the future together?

Help is at hand. It comes in the form of 'scenario thinking' – building, often divergent, visions of the future and developing strategies around them and their implications. Scenarios are stories from tomorrow. They enable an imaginative insightful leap into the future. They are crafted in a creative environment and are carefully constructed stories, full of rich relevant detail, oriented towards real-life decisions. They are designed to bring forward surprises and unpredictable leaps of understanding. They are also (when properly used) helpful in creating insights around 'cause and effect' connections to customer attitudes and behaviour, operating paradigms, etc., that might not have been immediately or previously evident.

The key is not to pick one preferred future, hope it comes to pass, adapt to it, or 'bet the company' on it. Strategic decisions should be crafted around a number of futures. At the same time, the early indicators of an emerging scenario should enable management to exploit any opportunity more effectively than competitors. In the past, the term 'scenario' was used to consider alternative results of what might happen, often within a narrow range of parameters. Now scenario thinking can be used to create strategic options or alternatives, as well as to test any emergent strategy.

Perhaps the most famous example of where scenario thinking has been used successfully is in Royal Dutch Shell. Historically the planners in Shell, along with colleagues in other oil majors, predicted the future price of oil with great certainty. The futility of this was clear at the time of the Middle East war. Plans based on slow and steadily increasing prices were sent spinning in 1973 by Yom Kippur and other global changes.

They had reached the point where the ever-increasing numbers of forecasts, made over shorter and shorter timeframes, were increasingly less accurate. Shell replaced their expensive stochastic[3] modelling with more qualitative scenario building and assessment of the likely outcomes and potential strategies that might address the scenario outcome.

The energy crisis burst upon the world. Similar chaos occurred in 2005 with the almost uncontrollable increase in commercial gas costs. Who knows what ranking will be afforded to the global financial crisis of 2008 and the collapse of associated sub-prime markets?

To make the best use of scenario thinking means instilling it as an integral part of the strategic management process. Scenarios are not one-off exercises to be replaced as quickly as possible by 'business-as-normal'. Scenarios are never-ending stories developed by your people, for your people. They take time to develop and cannot be built during part of the annual planning day. Those privileged to be involved in the process need to be briefed and to engage themselves in the external and internal environments that will influence the outcome.

It will be useful to engage other 'remarkable people', at some stage, to enrich the scenario story. They may be experts in related fields, but are more likely to be people respected for their skills and knowledge elsewhere. They may include actors, authors, musicians and artists to bring extra creativity. Frequently they add unique insights to an internal team (themselves often weighed down with the baggage of the organisation's past), taking them to new and spectacular heights of strategic thinking. The quality of engagement can also be influenced by the provision of information on the future – however crude or sparse.

Staff must feel genuinely empowered to develop scenarios and implement the resultant strategies and plans. This first requires building capabilities in people. The next step is to establish a charter between the individuals and the company where the taboos are as clear as the can-do's. Individuals must be free to innovate and act because they are clear as to their role, responsibilities and contribution to implementing the emerging strategic direction. As a result, organisations can manage the present and the future in complementary ways, allocating resources for sustained advantage.

The scenario-thinking process enhances an organisation's capacity to be innovative. It ensures that a strategic dialogue takes place to build greater ownership of the outcomes. This leads to greater competitive advantage, by building barriers around the unique strategy that will emerge. How different from following the 'off-the-shelf' process out of a history book written by yesterday's guru.

In an increasingly uncertain world, it will be wrong for organisations to:

- Carry out more market and competitor research in isolation.
- Intensify their planning processes.
- Increase the demands for data in the quest for greater certainty.

Instead, management teams should be given time, space and resources to build rich scenarios of the future – good, bad and ugly – using their knowledge and insight. They will be able to consider the implications of these alternative futures before they occur. By increasing the quantity and quality of strategic thinking in conversations together, leaders have a greater chance of success, or even just survival. The process through which these views of the future will emerge will also do much to prepare and develop the management team for the intense fight ahead; to secure the high ground in the battle for the future.

Tales of three local subsidiaries of multi-national corporations: Polaroid, National Semiconductor and ScottishPower PLC

The following case studies illustrate the impact that external forces can have, not just on companies but also on whole industries. In any event, all industry players can do is to respond more effectively than the competition. In some cases an industry is wiped out, as experienced by the likes of Kodak, Ilford and Polaroid in traditional photographic markets. Another example is the papermaking industry in the UK and other countries, where the business models developed by the fully integrated producers in Finland gave them ultimate competitive advantage in everything other than very fine speciality niche markets.

Scenario thinking can enable business teams to address the future and develop alternative strategies through which to prosper and, in many cases, to simply survive. Going through the process develops visions of success in a number of divergent scenarios. This in itself generates a number of options or alternative strategies for the future. They also provide base material as to how to 'change the game' should particular scenarios emerge.

Examples of these processes carried out with management teams at Polaroid (UK manufacturing facility), National Semiconductor and ScottishPower are exemplars of where competitive advantage can be gained and enhanced to assure a sustainable future, at least in the short to medium term.

1. Polaroid Inc – the ultimate double whammy scenario

The challenge

Polaroid Corporation was formed in 1937 by the US scientist and inventor Edwin Land. The new company acquired the assets of Land–Wheelwright Laboratories in the field of light polarisation to develop this field technically and professionally.

From 1937 until 1946, Polaroid focused on developing glare-reducing polarised materials that were incorporated into various enhanced products for the US consumer market such as sunglasses, TV filters and lamps, as well as solutions for use by the US military in the Second World War, such as anti-glare filters for fighter aircraft windows and specialised goggles for airmen.

On 21 February 1947, Land announced another major technological innovation, this time in the field of imaging, when he demonstrated instant photography to the Optical Society of America. Soon after, the first commercially-available instant camera, the Polaroid Land Camera Model 95, was produced by Polaroid and reached the shops before Christmas 1948.

Instant photography took the market by storm and in 1949 sales of Polaroid's film and cameras, at five million dollars, accounted for over 80% of the company's annual turnover. Polaroid's pace of growth from that point was dramatic and, by 1965, the company's annual turnover was $230 million, of which 90% was from US sales and 10% from international sales.

As part of a comprehensive strategy to rapidly increase international sales of Polaroid products, the company opened a small factory in 1965 in Scotland (at the Vale of Leven – known locally as 'the Vale') to manufacture instant film for selected European countries. The factory also produced, along with a sister plant in Mexico, cameras, sunglass lenses and industrial hardware products. Prior to 1976 the cameras had been manufactured by Timex in Dundee, Scotland.

From an initial production capability of some three million packs per annum, the Scottish factory progressively became a vital multi-product international manufacturing facility for Polaroid. By 1993, sales from the Scottish factory, to over 50 international markets, had grown to $300 million for the year. Over the years the factory had expanded and diversified to become the biggest multi-product site in Polaroid, with a total Vale workforce of some 1,200 people. Annual production of instant film had increased to over 80% of Polaroid's traditional peel-apart instant film packs for the consumer and business cameras (40 million packs), and the Vale factory was also producing, annually, some four million instant cameras, 14 million sunglass lenses and a wide range of specialised instant-imaging hardware devices for business and medical applications.

1994: recognising the need for change

In 1993, Mike Fitzpatrick,[4] a Scot from the local area who had joined Polaroid in 1977 as a young finance manager, was appointed General Manager of Polaroid's Scottish operations. At this time the Scottish manufacturing site appeared to be secure and successful, serving the parent company well as a highly efficient subsidiary and as an essential link in the company's global supply chain.

However, Fitzpatrick was conscious of underlying potential threats, both external and internal to Polaroid, that could put the long-term sustainability of Polaroid's manufacturing facility in Scotland at risk and jeopardise the jobs of the largest private sector employer in his home town. These potential threats to the Vale's security included:

- Competition for the manufacture of Polaroid's products from new Polaroid factories being opened in far lower-cost countries such China, India, Mexico and Russia.
- The Scottish factory being viewed as efficient and dependable, but now high cost and low tech, with skill levels that could equally be created in the emerging market sites.
- The Vale not being particularly considered by Polaroid headquarters for any involvement in the manufacture of new products or the installation of new technologies.
- In effect, the complete absence of any long-term plan for the future of the Vale site.

Historically, Scottish leadership had assumed that the plant's security lay in constantly improving its efficiencies, by being creative locally at a tactical level and by being highly cooperative and responsive, as a subsidiary, to the parent company's requirements and instructions. However, it was apparent to Fitzpatrick, as he took up his new role as General Manager, that continuing in this mode could seriously jeopardise the site's long-term prospects.

His first response was to get on the road and visit the leaders of other Scottish-based subsidiaries of international parent companies such as IBM, NCR and Compaq, to learn from them about how they were responding to threats to their businesses, many of which were as a result of globalisation. Several important lessons were learned from those visits, the most important being that the local leadership needed to be proactive and effectively seek to take some control of their site's own destiny.

This insight led to the next major response by Fitzpatrick to enlist the support of Genesis in 1994 to help the Vale site develop a strategy for its long-term future within the Polaroid family, which, although not conceived of at corporate level, would be a real win–win for both the Scottish subsidiary and the US parent company.

Forward to a better future – identifying future scenarios

I worked intensively with Fitzpatrick and his leadership team to understand the strategic situation faced by the business. We started by understanding the parent company's longer-term strategy, including where the current research and development efforts were leading and the potential products coming out of that process, and which ones the Vale could bid for to manufacture in Scotland. As the Scottish team gained greater understanding of the Vale's current exposed situation and of the likely future road map of Polaroid's technologies and products, it was able to create scenarios where the Vale could continue to be a vital international asset for the corporation in the long term.

The output of this intense activity at the start of 1995 was the following focused strategic framework for the Scottish facility:

> *Vision*: We will be an outstanding centre of excellence within the corporation's global operations and the best company in Scotland in the primary areas of manufacturing and innovation.

> *Aim*: Provide our Polaroid corporate customers with a manufacturing and support services centre of excellence giving superior added value in the existing business, consumer and commercial imaging products and in the next generation of products and services.

Goals:

- **Manufacturing excellence** – achieve manufacturing excellence assessed against key internal and external performance measurements.
- **Partnerships** – form partnerships with customers, suppliers and Polaroid colleagues worldwide for continuous improvement and innovation.
- **Flexibility** – gain excellent customer and market knowledge to enable us to anticipate needs and respond quickly to market changes.
- **Customer value** – provide value (product and service quality as measured by our internal and external customers) that is clearly superior to alternatives available in the marketplace.
- **Product development** – have product development capabilities to support locally manufactured products and to support new business development, complementary to the corporate development resources.

- **Service development** – become a key source of a range of international services, of importance to Polaroid, wherever we can add significant value.
- **Skills/knowledge** – develop overall skills, know-how and technical capabilities that clearly differentiate the Vale from the competition.
- **Personal responsibility** – each take personal responsibility for our own development and for the continued success and wellbeing of Polaroid.

As part of their deployment of this strategy, Fitzpatrick and his team enlisted support and networked extensively. They built bridges with their international Polaroid sales and marketing colleagues, liaised with UK governmental enterprise agencies, sought the support of their local and national politicians, worked closely with their European suppliers and created valuable links with Scottish universities, colleges and design centres.

To begin with, the Vale leadership did not explicitly tell Corporate about this new integrated win–win strategy. When they began to do so they were initially met with polite lack of interest and, sometimes, accusations of parochialism. There was pressure from some just to stick to overall company policies, to the extent that some Scottish managers felt reluctant to rock the boat.

Early in this process the importance of effective corporate influencing became very apparent, and this became a key area of developmental support from Genesis to the Scottish leadership.

Over time, however, the Vale's reputation grew strongly during 1996 and 1997, to the extent that the Vale was increasingly viewed positively, became the best performing site in the corporation and was building valuable relationships with influential Polaroid colleagues internationally. New skills were developed and, although the Vale started to lose significant parts of its traditional manufacturing business to new Polaroid factories in emerging markets, it began to acquire new products for Scottish manufacture and new service responsibilities. These service responsibilities included, in 1997, the creation at the Vale of the first Polaroid product design centre outside of the US and the setting up of a major European centralised services operation in Glasgow, providing back office and IT support to the whole of Polaroid's European sales and marketing network.

The scenario thinking carried out with local management enabled new propositions to be presented to and accepted by the corporation that resulted in:

- Substantial investments secured in new plant and products.
- The creation of a major design and development centre.
- A European shared services centre located in Glasgow.
- China/Mexico expanding – exited from Russia/India.
- Scottish job numbers now in higher-value activities.

- The Vale plant now the sole supplier of certain key products.
- A number of worldwide roles entrusted to the Vale.
- Technical capabilities greatly enhanced and performance up with the best in the corporation.
- Reputation and corporate relationships very positive.

By 1997 the streamlined Scottish business was much more robust and appeared far more sustainable. Scotland was supporting the corporation more profitably and was the sole global source of several important products and worldwide roles located in Scotland. The workforce, though reduced, was becoming more knowledge-based and was totally engaged in supporting the new direction. The Vale was becoming increasingly valued for its drive, enhanced technical capabilities and its entrepreneurial mindset.

In a visit to the Scottish site in 1997, the head of Polaroid's sales and marketing operations said to the workforce: 'I love coming to the Vale. You are can-do and more!'

1997 and beyond – welcome to a new world

Polaroid (UK) still faced a number of corporate risks in the late 1990s. Sales of the traditional camera and pack-film were declining at an increasing rate. The lack of sales growth was driving the need for further reduced manufacturing costs and rationalisation of facilities. The corporation began discussing supply possibilities with low-cost third-party manufacturers.

Gary Di Camillo had joined Polaroid in early 1996 from Black and Decker, following a long spell as a senior executive in GE. He challenged the manufacturing strategy for retail cameras and film. There were three things in the minds of global executives in the mid-1990s:

- Shareholder value.
- The new global economy – driven by e-commerce and the internet.
- The free agent – loyal, entrepreneurial people.

He was in favour of relocating camera production to the Far East, as he had done with Black and Decker, and, as cost and profit pressures increased on Polaroid, the company did begin exploring the outsourcing of camera manufacture to a Taiwanese toy-making company.

Six-Sigma had been the single largest component of GE's incentive compensation – the first change in over six years when introduced to Polaroid facilities. The competition was not between products or manufacturing locations. It was between business models that work in the eye of the customer. The internet and e-business were changing the way the global economy operated.

The GE executives had arrived from relatively low complexity manufacturing operations and had developed a successful outsourcing strategy with suppliers from Taiwan. The same suppliers indicated they would produce the 1997 version of the basic camera for less than $20, adding pressure on historic manufacturing operations around the world, where factories (especially the Vale) were integrated manufacturers of the camera and associated film products.

Their 1997 agenda for local management focused on identifying the best opportunities for the Vale (and Polaroid) and the capability to exploit these. This involved enlisting key partners (e.g., Locate in Scotland – the Scottish Government's inward investment agency – and European Marketing in Polaroid and their suppliers) in addition to closely monitoring corporate developments and strategies.

Our next phase of work with local executives produced a proposition to reduce the cost of manufacture below $20 (potentially $15). It was also clear that this would only slow the decline in manufacturing rather than stop it.

There was a realisation that the journey to a sustainable future was still uncertain.

Agreeing the new mandate

It became obvious that the likes of Kodak and Polaroid were facing not just a wave of change but a tsunami driven by two global turbo-charged forces:

- penetration of the use of digital cameras;
- use of the internet for acquisition, sharing, storage and display of photographic images accelerated by the adoption of Twitter, Instagram, Facebook as personal lifestyle applications.

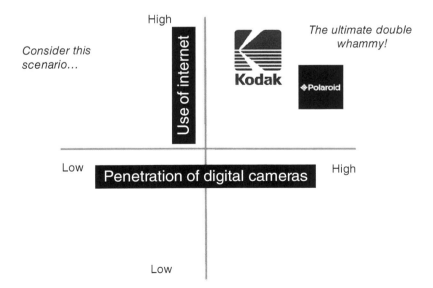

Figure 3.1 Sayonara Big Boys. Scenarios created by Alistair Gray (2007).

To inform the future debate Genesis consultants worked with local management, led by Fitzpatrick's successor as General Manager, the energetic and entrepreneurial Jim Hall, to develop and consider four divergent future scenarios that are illustrated in Figure 3.1.

Simply to look at a number of scenarios based on the current situation would not deal with the drivers of change in almost all the scenarios. The preferred scenario was clearly diametrically opposite to the most likely emerging scenario. Simple incremental improvements in productivity or the performance of the existing portfolio would not be sufficient. The scenario thinking process explained the implications of the emergence of each scenario – who would be the winners and losers in the industry? What would be the implications for Polaroid? What would be the implications for the Vale?

It was clear. Polaroid UK needed to negotiate a new mandate for their role as a manufacturing subsidiary in the new environment. Such mandates are never permanent and, in the ever-changing world of the digital and global economy, they are likely to change faster than ever (Figure 3.2 and Figure 3.3).

The end of manufacturing as they knew it was at hand, other than for high-end professional photographic and security markets. The second phase of influencing the corporation established an enhanced product design and development operation (eventually employing 20 engineers) at The Vale, not only carrying out projects for Polaroid but also for third-party customers. The local executive had become skilled at influencing the

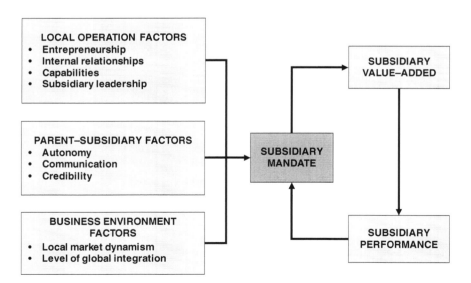

Figure 3.2 Factors influencing subsidiary mandates. Source: Professor Neil Hood, Strathclyde Business School (1995).

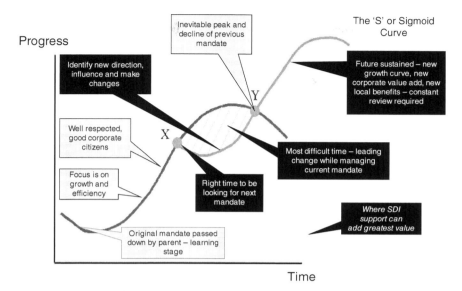

Figure 3.3 The life cycle of mandates and roles. Source: Mike Fitzpatrick, Director of Genesis (2002).

corporation by their active involvement with and support of the regional and at times international marketing management. The Vale developed the reputation of delivering solutions for marketing and product management. Gone were the days of mass manufacturing, to be replaced by much more high-value engineering and service areas. At no point did they seek pity or sympathy for their position – the declining volumes of cameras and pack film.

The final outcome

In 2001 Polaroid filed for Chapter 11 in the US. Polaroid Corporation's last recorded share value was 28 cents compared with a ten-year high of $60.31 back in July 1997. Polaroid owed almost $1 billion in total ($600 million to bond holders, $350 million to two groups of banks). Polaroid Corporation was effectively bought out in 2002 and over the next decade there were a number of changes of ownership.

By the early 2000s the workforce in the Vale was down to about 750 people and voluntary redundancies had been replaced by compulsory redundancies on reduced packages. In 2006 employment levels at the Vale were down to 350, and that figure included staff at a multi-lingual service centre that was established in Glasgow in 1997. In 2005 Flextronics of the US acquired Polaroid's manufacturing operations. In 2007 camera manufacture ceased and Polaroid was bought by the Stylemark corporation. All that was left on the Vale's site was the sunglasses lens manufacturing business, now known as Polaroid Eyewear. It was acquired by Safilo, an Italian eyewear company, in 2012. In 2016 Safilo closed the Dumbarton facility, transferring production to their site in China. There are currently only 100 employees.

The 'New Polaroid' declared itself bankrupt in 2008. In May 2017 the brand and intellectual property of the Polaroid Corporation was acquired by the largest shareholder of the Impossible Project, which had originally started out in 2008 by producing new instant films for Polaroid cameras. Impossible Project was renamed Polaroid Originals in September 2017. New pack film and a new instant camera have subsequently been launched. A huge range of Polaroid products are still being sold in over 100,000 retail stores in over 100 countries around the world.

Change in global markets is continuous, and there is no better example than manufacturing industry. The markets for the Vale's products were either supplied by countries with a far lower cost base, or they disappeared completely because the products became obsolete. Most unusually, none of the corporate entities that manufactured at the Vale's business park/industrial estate is still in existence. A number of the brand names are still around, but the companies no longer operate.

The performance of the local management had become an exemplar to other subsidiary operations of multinational corporations. They took control of their own destiny (recognising that if they did not, someone else would) to extend the life of the Vale and its employees and, by doing so, increased the employability of their staff and their surrounding communities.

2. National Semiconductor – how Greenock's diet of chips has bred health and efficiency[5]

In 1998 National Semiconductor was one of the world's leading suppliers of analogue integrated circuits. Headquartered in Santa Clara, California, it had revenues of $1.7billion, 10,000 employees worldwide and five manufacturing sites globally, including a major wafer fabrication plant in Greenock, Scotland.

At this time, the corporation's CEO had recently gone off to work for Apple, the global business was under pressure, and the new team at headquarters in Santa Clara had embarked on a major strategic review. As part of this review it was decided that the Greenock facility should either be closed or sold off, with its production capacity being transferred to National's US plant or sub-contracted to a low-cost wafer fabrication foundry in China.

National had opened the Scottish facility in the Greenock hills overlooking the Clyde estuary at the start of the 1970s. The business had survived a disastrous fire towards the end of that decade before growing successfully in the eighties, employing over 2,000 people by the mid-1990s. However, it had become an ageing, costly, inefficient arm of the global business and 'had lost its way' according to the recently appointed managing director of the Greenock plant, Gerry Edwards. Edwards had arrived with a strong track record in the electronics industry, having worked with Motorola in Scotland, Wales, Holland and the United States. Faced with the corporation's instruction that he oversee the cessation of National's manufacturing involvement in Greenock, he and his management team conferred urgently and decided instead to fight for the future of the Scottish operation.

Edwards and his colleagues knew that if the facility at Greenock was to have any chance of survival it would have to be radically restructured, and they immediately started to work on what that restructuring should look like, as a viable alternative to closure or sell off. Meantime, the corporation sought to find a buyer for the operation and this process actually bought the Greenock management some time to put together their proposals. 'We knew that, as a going concern, nobody would buy it', recalled Edwards, so he asked National to support, in the meantime, a proposal to rapidly close their two old 4-inch production plants from the 1977 era and roll investment into the more modern 6-inch production line built around 1987.

Edwards and his team pressed ahead with the closure of the two ageing 4-inch plants, cutting the site headcount progressively from 2,000 to 600 employees in the process. The implication of moving over completely from 4-inch to 6-inch geometry was massive, resulting in the ability to produce twice as many chips from each wafer. Productivity on the Scottish site soared by some 200% and 'in the time it took us to restructure and for National to complete the sales prospectus, we had become the most cost-effective factory in the corporation'. Within a year, 'we had gone from worst to best'. Edwards was full of praise for those employees who had to leave progressively during that restructuring phase, yet supported the site strategy. 'We had to keep the whole factory running while we moved to 6-inch. I cannot speak highly enough of the people who left us, because they helped us move forward'.

In September 1999 the corporate decision to exit Greenock was officially reversed. The site had become highly cost effective and manufacturing lines, processes and equipment had been rationalised and consolidated to be able to concentrate solely on the latest wafer configuration. On the people side, the workforce had been streamlined down to some 550 highly skilled employees, of whom over 40% were graduates and qualified technicians. So strong was this restructured operation in Greenock that Edwards and his team were actually in favour of a buy-out option, had Corporate not reversed its decision.

At the start of the new millennium, then, the future should have been looking very good for the Greenock facility. However, a new threat now emerged as a result of the semiconductor industry hitting its worst ever recession, resulting in increased global consolidation of resources within the sector. Having just come through what local management had coined its 'near death' experience, Edwards and his team were even more determined to remain proactive and act strategically in how they would respond to the threats that this renewed turbulence might present.

It was around this time, in April 2000, that one of Edwards' colleagues, Graeme Dixon, attended a Scottish Enterprise-sponsored seminar on corporate influencing run by Genesis. He came back and showed Edwards part of the presentation given by Mike Fitzpatrick.

'Everywhere it says "Polaroid, Vale", put "National, Greenock" and it seems to make sense. Let's talk to these guys', said Dixon. With some funding from Scottish Enterprise, they climbed a new learning curve with help from Genesis and my colleagues Mike Fitzpatrick (the former leader of Polaroid at the Vale) and Kevin Parker. As a result they moved further, from the survival mode of working of the nineties to a much clearer strategic focus on how one satellite plant within a global corporation can influence its own destiny, by understanding better where the whole enterprise is headed and seizing opportunities as they arise. They aptly named this effort 'Project Bullet-proof'.

Reporting on this work undertaken by Edwards and his team in conjunction with Genesis and on what it was achieving, Alf Young, Business Editor of the *Sunday Herald*, wrote the following: 'Cynics say consultants simply tell you, at great expense, what you want to hear. National's experience challenged that prejudice'.

The scenario thinking process was built around axes focused on the extremes of potential semiconductor technology within the context of future computing and the strategy to become a leading world-class manufacturer. In Figure 3.4 we illustrate the Focus Framework developed by the team at National.

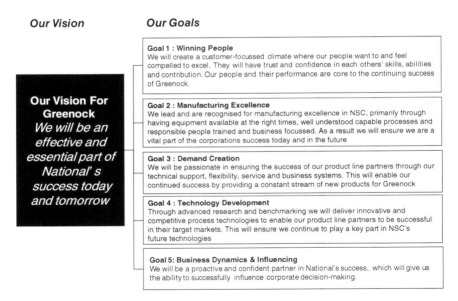

Figure 3.4 National Semiconductor: our new diet of chips. Framework created by Alistair Gray and Kevin Parker (2002).

At the heart of this strategy, technologically, was the realisation that, counter-intuitive as it may sound in this digital age, National's focus on analogue devices was a valuable differentiator that could be especially well leveraged at Greenock. Analogue chips had avoided the commodity fate of DRAM memory chips and were continuing to play a vital role in everything from flat-panel displays to extending the power life of batteries in mobile devices like cellular phones. Here is another example of changing the game rather than simply incrementally developing an existing product range.

Edwards and his team committed themselves totally to implementing their holistic strategy and, as a result, the progress by 2003 was remarkable. This progress included record levels of performance on all key operational metrics (such as cost, yield and cycle time), the attraction of substantial new investment in technology and processes (over $70 million in new funds by 2003), the building of enhanced technical capability in Scotland, and the rapid growth of a product design centre on site.

In 2003 Don Macleod, CEO of National Semiconductor, said the following:

> In 1998 we made a corporate decision to eliminate what was then excess capacity by seeking a buyer for our Greenock facility. The facility is now our most cost efficient wafer fabrication facility. The leadership team now has tremendous credibility with corporate management. They grasped the 'for sale' reality check and transformed the downward spiral that was the previous destiny of the facility and made it into a world class wafer fab that is now a candidate for future capital investment.

Postscript – when the chips are down, in an increasingly globalised world

In April 2011 Texas Instruments acquired National Semiconductor for $6.5 billion and in January 2016 TI announced the phased closure of its Greenock site, despite rating its Greenock workforce very highly:

> Our employees have done everything they can to keep the site cost-competitive, and we strongly considered ways to improve the site's efficiency, such as upgrading or expanding the facility. However, even with a considerable investment, Texas Instruments' factory in Greenock would be far less efficient than our other larger, more efficient fabrication facilities which have open capacity available to absorb what's produced in Greenock.

It is planned to complete the closure process in 2019.

3. ScottishPower (part of Iberdrola)

The challenge

The UK government privatised the English and Welsh electricity industry in 1990 by splitting the market into 12 regional electricity companies (RECs) and two power generators. However, in Scotland, the industry was already organised on an integrated generation, distribution and supply basis, and this integration survived the privatisation to become a model for the rest of the United Kingdom.

ScottishPower was largely formed from the larger of the two Scottish electricity boards – the South of Scotland Electricity Board. The effective privatisation and deregulation of the industry in the UK left these former institutions with the challenge of embracing entrepreneurship and new business models. Amongst the wide-ranging strategic issues and questions they faced were:

- How do we (Power Operations UK) break out of our constraints, be they regulatory, geographic, financial and cultural, to become a real investment opportunity?
- Should we remain in this business as asset managers or as a development company seizing growth opportunities through new capabilities in building portfolios of business and managing synergy across these businesses?

Of special interest at the time was the development of renewables and particularly fuel cell technology. Should ScottishPower invest in this technology and to what extent was there synergy with existing businesses? At the time, for many executives in ScottishPower, the ideal scenario was one large coal-fired power station delivering 100% of Scotland's electricity.

A team of ScottishPower executives, along with some external specialists supported by Genesis, created and explored a number of alternative futures. By 'living in these futures' the team developed a creative range of options for the future, as well as testing the current strategic direction of the utility.

The approach

In considering possible future scenarios it is important to establish the focal question that needs to be answered, and also what the current 'official future' is for the newly privatised business. The latter might be described as follows:

- UK brand – developing in the United States as a network business – power wires, water pipes and not telecom (then). Continuing to own the public supply with little replacement planned.

- Mass domestic – separate 'Ltd' businesses, not focusing on synergy, with corporate making portfolio decisions.
- Driven by the city, betting the company and make the numbers work and grow. Profits will be under increasing pressure.
- Old assets – need to be held together and sweated in fortress Scotland.
- Growth in 'brown-outs' (power cuts) in the US, pushing the price up.

The ScottishPower team refined the focal question, in the context of the official future, and developed two axes on which to base their scenarios. The needs of key stakeholders were reviewed and consultation carried out across the stakeholder group. The axes were:

- The extent to which 'green matters' and sustainability would dominate the competitive and public sector environment into the future?
- The degree to which there was a genuine global village served by large corporates?

The divergent scenarios outlined in Figure 3.5 were developed and articulated out to 2020.

- Environment dominates
- Pace of change accelerated
- Zero growth
- Energy efficient

ENVIRONMENT
Sustainable

Reclamania

GLOBAL VILLAGE
Industry Structure

Jolly Green Giants

- One world
- Few global players
- Legal radicals

Sod'em Today, Sodum Tomorrow

- Fragmented
- National/Regional
- Isolationist
- Fortress Scotland

Gas Guzzlers

- Never takes off
- Self interest
- Continued consensus
- Inefficiency acceptable

Figure 3.5 Our alternative futures: divergent scenarios for ScottishPower. Scenarios created by Alistair Gray (images purchased from Shutterstock 1995).

The team immersed themselves in each of the scenarios and considered:

- What would be going on? Who would be the winners and losers?
- What strategies would lead to a good outcome in each future?
- How might major risks be avoided?

The group considered which scenario was most likely to emerge, and which strategy would best exploit the opportunities presented in the most likely scenario. How would the focal question be answered? The team also considered what metrics or analytics should be gathered that would represent indicators of the most likely future.

The team reported to the board that 'Jolly Green Giants' was the scenario most likely to emerge and their vision of a good outcome for ScottishPower was:

- Global alliances in place with the right brands and winners.
- ScottishPower has taken the environmental high ground and has become a world leader in green energy generation.
- ScottishPower had acquired skills and capabilities in acquisition and marketing of new technologies of which fuel cells may be one.
- Old assets had been sold before others realised change.
- ScottishPower had entered leading environmentally conscious markets, e.g., Sweden/N. Europe.

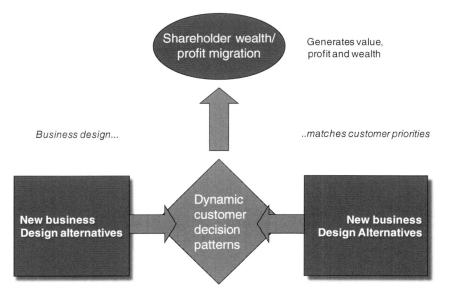

Figure 3.6 Building future value in uncertain times. Model created by Alistair Gray (1995).

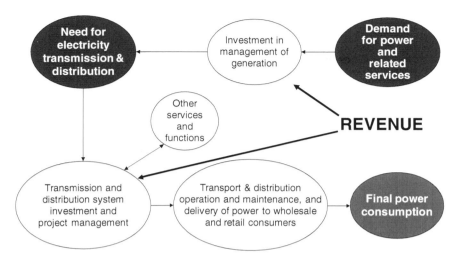

Figure 3.7 'Jolly Green Giants': the business system. Model created by Alistair Gray (1995).

In terms of answering a specific question relating to fuel cells, it was agreed to continue to monitor the development of the technology but to avoid any early investment into the sector. The logic was that the industry would reorganise and consolidate into larger competitive groups to attract and generate capital to support investment in a 'greener' system. Consideration was also given to any strategic pointers from the other divergent scenarios that might be reviewed to reduce risk and contribute to the final integrated strategy to enhance shareholder value (see Figure 3.6 and Figure 3.7).

The final outcome

The result was a better-informed decision and changed strategic direction, with an enhanced ability to anticipate and react with confidence to future changes in the external environment. A new business group was formed outside the reformed generation and power systems/utility businesses to focus on acquisition of new technologies and businesses through joint ventures and alliances, adopting more the position of a venture capitalist. In 2006 ScottishPower became a subsidiary of Iberdrola, the Spanish utility, and through that alliance became a leading global player in renewable technologies. Through scenario thinking ScottishPower succeeded in anticipating future market changes in time to tailor effectively its strategic plans for power generation, distribution and supply. The process enabled them to embrace renewable technology faster and more effectively.

- **Break the rules: challenge existing paradigms**

  - Consider more than the official future.
  - Build divergent scenarios for the future based on the most important factors and greatest uncertainties.
  - Establish *the* focal question that needs to be answered.

- **Work it out together**

  - Create conversations that lead to better options and decisions about the future.
  - Use cross-functional teams, supported by remarkable people from outside the organisation to bring fresh perspectives.

- **Plan for a step-change**

  - Consider the scenario that will emerge, not the preferred future.
  - Spend your time at the extreme point of each scenario, develop a vision of success and the strategies that will lead to a good outcome.
  - Do not focus on strategies that will work in all scenarios as that delivers lowest common denominator strategies and outcomes.
  - Instead, focus on the most likely scenario and how ideas from the other scenarios can strengthen your plans in the eventual integrated strategy.
  - Develop 4–5 options for the integrated strategy and evaluate to develop the optimum strategy. Do not just choose what appears to be the best option. (See the appendices for how to develop and evaluate strategic options.)

- **Change organisational performance**

  - Using scenario thinking can provide an effective way of checking future strategies.
  - Gather data in key metric areas from the most likely scenario to confirm it is near and clear (or otherwise if it is emerging).
  - Utilise scenarios at each stage of your annual strategic/operating planning process. Wind-tunnelling of major initiatives with the help of scenarios will strengthen their focus.

- **Engaging leaders at all levels in the organisation**

  - Engage leaders at all levels in the process of scenario thinking.
  - The use of external 'remarkable people' also yields surprising and positive results.

Notes

1 This section was originally written as an article in 2009. It is interesting to reflect on these questions now.
2 The price of a barrel of Brent crude in May 2017 is $50, 20% higher than it was in 2016 and half the price for most of 2014 (NASDAQ.com).
3 From *The Chambers Dictionary*: Stochastic /stə'kastɪk/ having a random probability distribution or pattern that may be analysed statistically but may not be predicted precisely.
4 Mike Fitzpatrick served as a Director of Genesis Consulting. He left Polaroid in 2000.
5 The *Sunday Herald*, Alf Young, 2003.

4 The new age of strategic management

Introduction

> What's my return on investment on e-commerce? Are you crazy? This is
> Columbus in the New World. What was his ROI?
> Andrew Grove, Intel Chairman, *Fortune* magazine, 2016

*The global recession of 2008 changed the world order, and the longest, slowest recovery
in history (of recessions) has changed the nature of competition and the way organisations strategise, plan and run their operations. Having lived and worked through
four recessions I endured, both directly as an employee and indirectly as a consultant and non-executive director, the challenges faced at each downturn and in the
subsequent recovery. As a result I came to realise that traditional approaches to
strategic management were and would be found wanting. In Genesis, Kevin Parker
and I developed an approach to strategic management that has enabled many of
our clients to address the future with confidence. The principles of this approach are
outlined in this chapter.*

*UPM Kymmene, one of the world's leading manufacturers of paper, is one example
of where 'new age' strategic management has been applied. During the last decade we
worked in partnership with them at a number of their locations from Irvine in Scotland
to Helsinki, London and Chicago. The case study that follows outlines the changes
that took place to improve their collective performance and position in the industry.*

Historical perspective

Every organisation has competitors. Businesses compete to sell their
products and services. Cities and states compete to attract new industries,
contracts or government funds. Schools and universities compete for students and to attract and retain a talented faculty. Start-up ventures and
small companies compete for scarce resources to ensure their very survival.

For a whole generation after the Second World War, a healthy growing economy left room for many competitiors to prosper alongside each
other. Then, in one decade – the 1970s – the advent of a global market,
scarce resources, expensive money and the end to steady growth changed

the rules of the game. Achieving the absolute goals of an organisation now depends on relative success. The search for the competitive edge and management of the whole organisation to achieve and sustain it are the central operating tasks of our time.

Over 30 years ago, Tom Peters and Richard Waterman (*In Search of Excellence*),[1] revolutionised the strategic management paradigm through their '8S' Framework. However, in the last two decades, many excellent companies that were inspired by their Framework have fallen from grace, as they failed to reinvent themselves in the face of rapid changes in technology and an increasingly customer-oriented environment. The last two decades have seen the emergence of Apple, Amazon, Google (Alphabet), Facebook, GE, Microsoft and Cisco Systems at the top of the corporate value league. Recently Alibaba and Tencent (both Chinese corporations) have joined them. The latter half of the 1990s saw a surge in entrepreneurial activity, driven by blind belief in the potential of all that is '*e*'. In the year 2000 we witnessed the spectacular failure of a number of these new-age organisations and, although large corporations are today committing increasing amounts of investment to major IT initiatives, its impact on shareholder and economic value is often questionable. Apple now hold a leadership position with a market value of \$800bn in 2017.

Early indications are that success or failure has more to do with effective strategic management of these new-age corporations, rather than investment in major IT-led initiatives. Leading service standards, excellent product design, marketing and distribution are still more important for corporate success than the espousal of the latest technology.

What does this new age hold? How should we respond to the challenge of *e* and the digital economy? In one of Bill Gates' recent epistles, he promotes three key management themes for the new age.

- Seeking a fundamental new approach to the development of knowledge work, underpinned by significantly higher levels of information availability and communication, and investment in a digital nervous system to raise the corporate IQ of the organisation.
- Redefining business operations to improve responsiveness and efficiency, by personalising products and services and encouraging greater levels of customer feedback.
- Developing new forms of commerce through reduced cycle times, elimination of middlemen in the supply chain and greater focus on higher value customer needs.

Many corporations reach out for *e*-solutions, such as ERP, CRM, BPR and Analytics/Big Data-driven knowledge management, apparently ignoring the lessons from the last two decades. Over that period the number of management fads and systems-driven 'solutions' has grown disproportionately to the value added to the client organisation.

Surely a new age demands a new management paradigm? But what form should it take? Do we replace our current system with *e*-based business, analytics and management systems? Do we use the potential that *e* undoubtedly provides to underpin and enhance best strategic management practice? We certainly must not ignore the emergence of *e*, but should it be the be-all and end all?

The Genesis Framework

The digital age, the knowledge economy, the experience era – call it what you will – is now a reality of life in the future. As corporate leaders we cannot afford to respond to it in an ad hoc way. We must harness information and IT as a strategic resource. As managers, we must chart our course to the future, and implement these strategies with confidence, striving for continuously improving performance. The use of *e*-based business practice, technologies and learning will be fundamental to success in the future. All organisations – large or small; new or mature; listed or private; corporate or public – should apply *e*-thinking to their strategic management in five key areas, as illustrated in Figure 4.1.

Strategic direction

Any business must have a vision for the future, a goal to which the organisation aspires and that will bring enhanced value to all stakeholders. In the new

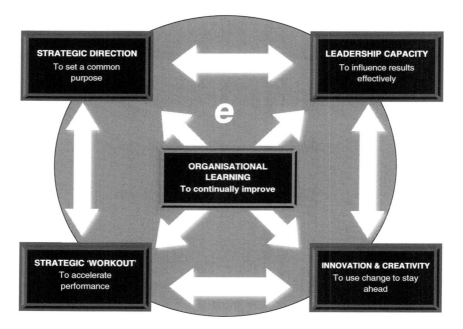

Figure 4.1 Genesis Framework: new beginnings. Model created by Alistair Gray and Kevin Parker (1994).

age more of what brought success in the past will not suffice. The new competitive environment requires management to apply new context and content to strategy development and, more importantly, to adopt more innovative conduct of the strategy development process. Real strategy innovation requires:

- New voices.
- New process.
- New perspectives.
- New experiments.
- New passions.

New voices can be brought in to stimulate the process and the participants, bringing new perspectives to inform potential alternative futures: betting the company on one emerging future, however apparently certain, is the worst approach to the management of risk. There must be a willingness to experiment and a passionate approach to innovate. The potential for *e* to inform the strategy development process is enormous, with access to global trends, data and information now transformed through the use of electronic databases, analytics, technology searches and competitor intelligence. It is an immensely powerful tool.

Strategic workout

The energy required for successful implementation requires acceleration of the actions of a critical mass of managers to a speed capable of sustaining its own momentum. This momentum will carry the organisation through periods of difficulty and challenge and carry its people to build future success.

Creating organisational change seems a daunting task because of the number of variables involved, so as leaders we must concentrate on the things we really need to control from the top, and on leveraging the areas of greatest benefit. We should encourage subsidiarity throughout the organisation and empower those further down to make appropriate decisions.

So what is needed to initiate and maintain momentum? Adopting the following core approaches, which provide real potential for successful implementation and performance improvement, would be a good start:

- Step change thinking.
- Using the PDCA (Plan:Do:Check:Action) cycle approach with a difference that makes the difference.
- Building real commitment to, not mere compliance with, compelling goals.
- Delivering short term but sustainable performance breakthrough.

The potential for *e* is significant – through improved process effectiveness, enhanced information flows and shifting people into higher value work. A new set of business metrics is also necessary for this new era, with emphasis on market and customer information, rather than on the past financial performance of the enterprise.

Leadership capacity

> I do not see IT as a stand-alone system. I see it as a great facilitator. It's a reason for me to keep asking – why, why, why?
>
> Paul O'Neill, Chairman and CEO of Alcoa, quoted in
> *Business @ The Speed of Thought: Succeeding in the Digital Economy*, Bill Gates, 2014

Most organisations regard leadership as the province of the board and senior management team. Few approach the development of leadership capacity throughout their staff with any serious intent, yet continually increasing that capacity and capability is critical to competing effectively in the new age. Everyone is capable of searching for and finding the hero inside themselves, and of striving for higher levels of performance. With the collective benefit of a critical mass of staff leading with enthusiasm, the potential for change or development is dramatically increased. All staff should be encouraged to:

- Discover the leader in themselves.
- Adopt a mindset for excellence.
- Develop speed and flexibility.
- Manage the delta – the continuous improvement in performance.

People must have information at their fingertips, and *e* has a significant role in this area. The communication environment can be transformed through the use of e-mail, and the corporate IQ raised through fostering knowledge and learning via the digital nervous system. Training and learning should be available online, at the employee's desk as well as in the classroom. This should begin with senior management embracing *e* with enthusiasm, rather than regarding it as something for others. (How many CEOs have their PA print out their e-mails each morning?)

Innovation and creativity

Innovation is based on an organisation's ability to come up with ideas *and* implement them successfully. Too often the focus is on the creation of new ideas for products, services or working practices, with little attention being paid to the more difficult areas of 'successful implementation'. Of the barriers to innovation, fewer than 20% are accounted for by 'coming up with the idea'.[2]

Technology has a role to play in both areas. The new ways of accessing information, the source of ideas, can provide organisations with the stimulus for creativity. But it can also provide the HOW – the implementation.

The flexibility of new systems allows the creation of many business units or profit centres to empower groups to behave as businesses within the enterprise. The new-age entrepreneurs will flourish.

Organisational learning

> An organisation's ability to learn, and translate that learning into action rapidly, is the ultimate competitive advantage.
>
> Jack Welch, Former GE Chairman, 2012

Knowledge management was a short-term fad in the mid-1990s, and many organisations implemented extensive and expensive systems to develop data-based knowledge. The effective management of knowledge workers will be crucial to success in the new age, where people are empowered, equipped and enthused to learn from the past and apply that learning to future opportunities. The potential for *e* in this area of strategic management is huge. For example, organisations can:

- Foster knowledge through policies, rewards and projects to establish a knowledge-sharing culture.
- Enable work teams to act with the same unity of purpose and focus as a well-motivated individual.
- Ensure every new project builds directly on the learning from any similar project undertaken anywhere else in the world.

How to gain advantage

The new millennium should be a great launching pad for any organisation. If plans rely solely on a major company-wide implementation of an IT-based system, recent history would suggest that failure is imminent. Without addressing the five areas outlined above, in a systematic way, better data management simply monitors the decline more effectively. However, by using technology in the ways suggested, there is the chance of real success.

In endeavours to change the game and developing a new paradigm for the new age, we should ask ourselves:

- Do we have a clear strategic direction for the next five years, calling for a step change in performance, irrespective of the market or industry conditions? Have we considered the potential for *e*-business?
- Are our people engaged and committed to enthusiastic and accelerated workout of that strategy? Are they empowered and equipped to carry out the task?
- Do we plan to increase the capacity of our leadership, through the development of new core competencies, skills and higher levels of performance?

- Are we confident we have plans in place to secure higher levels of creativity and innovation to improve continually?
- Do we plan to develop a digital nervous system – to facilitate organisational learning and translate that learning into action?

Relying on annual plans, budgets and hope will offer little prospect of survival in the 21st century. Simply seeking to improve incrementally on past performance will only result in real-term decline and decay. Equally, to throw out the lessons of the past would also be a mistake – many of the good practices in the last two decades still apply. The new technologies provide the means of creating a new and better way of doing business and enhancing best practice. The new century heralds a new age for strategic management, with the *e*-economy providing a great opportunity for innovation.

New age strategic management at UPM Kymmene

Though based in Scotland, Genesis was privileged to work for a number of global corporations including NCR, Hewlett Packard, National Semiconductor, Polaroid, Oki, Genzyme, Exxon Mobil, Banta Global Turnkey, W L Gore, DTZ and Aberdeen Asset Management. In many cases our work began with the local subsidiary and spread to other locations and often to the global parent itself. A case in point was UPM Kymmene, one of the world's largest manufacturers of paper and board products.

Our work with UPM Kymmene represents one of the longest consulting relationships during our firm's history; it also provided the vehicle that drove the development of many of our most innovative processes and tools. Our consultants worked with UPM Kymmene over a period of ten years to transform the performance of a number of their mills, functions and operating divisions. The strategy framework contained in the first section of this chapter is a case in point. I confess its first conception was by Kevin Parker and me during a long flight from London to Helsinki, partially fuelled by Finnair's in-flight bar service.

Our first project – 'Making Money, not just Paper' – was with Caledonian Paper located at Irvine, Scotland. We then facilitated the 'Kymmene Means Business' programme prior to merger with UPM, and our work across the newsprint and magazine papers division enabled the management teams to make a step change in their performance in one of the most competitive global industries.

In the beginning – Caledonian Paper changed the game

In 1993 I sent an article entitled 'Managing innovation' (one of a series on strategic management), on the need for renewal, to David Gray, then CEO of Caledonian Paper. He was faced with a history of loss-making at a one-machine mill commissioned in 1989 at a cost of £220m. Established as a strategic location near to Scotland's forestry resource, Caledonian was a fully integrated mill that literally digested trees and produced a range of coated art papers on a single large paper machine producing over 500 tonnes/day operating 365 days a year on a four-shift system of working.

At that time Kymmene deployed a global strategy to optimise the output of each machine (through a universally applied tonnes/day metric). Most of the successful units in the group operated two machines (as at the newsprint facility at Shotton in North Wales). Caledonian, despite many good operating practices, had continued to pile up losses, without the prospect of the additional investment in a second machine.

The theme of the article stimulated Gray to get in touch and from that flowed a stream of projects that were successfully delivered over a long and mutually beneficial relationship. The projects included:

- **Strategy for Caledonian Paper** – 'Making Money not just Paper' – the executive of this previously loss-making mill focused on the light-weight coated paper segment of the magazine paper market globally. This, coupled with a new approach to customer service and client management, transformed the performance of one of UPM Kymmene's most important production units. This radical change enabled them to change the game in the magazine paper sector.
- **Kymmene Means Business** – we designed and facilitated a major change process with Kymmene's senior executive team. Working in Finland and across Europe, we led a number of work groups (cross function/location) in a process of change to create a step change in performance.
- **UPM Kymmene USA** – we worked with the sales organisation of UPM Kymmene's US division to achieve a $1m profit turnaround through refocusing and raising the game of the sales force activity and performance.
- **Planning in Magazine Papers** – we established a new planning system in UPM Kymmene's most successful division, that enabled profits to be increased through a more strategic focus across European markets.
- **Tilhill Forest Products** – UPM Kymmene acquired Tilhill, one of the largest and most successful forest management companies in the UK. Our role was to work with the senior management team to integrate the business into UPM Kymmene and its overall forest strategy.
- **UPM Kymmene UK** – we designed and facilitated the strategy for UPM Kymmene's UK business, especially focusing on the performance of the UK sales force, resulting in improved sales and contribution in an ever-challenging market.
- **UPM Kymmene UK Forestry Strategy** – the two dominant mills in the UK were Caledonian Paper (Magazine Papers) and Shotton (Newsprint). Each had different forestry strategies for the procurement of wood supplies. We worked with the leadership of both mills to produce an integrated strategy reducing the overall cost of wood procurement significantly without affecting supply continuity.

In this case study we highlight three particular projects where we took on the 'official future' of UPM Kymmene's management philosophy and worked with a number of management groups to secure higher levels of performance within a discernable change in culture. Together we changed the game of one of the giants of the paper and forestry products industry.

'Make Money, not just Paper'

The first project, carried out by Margaret Dewhurst (a valued Genesis Associate for nearly two decades), was to determine the relative attractiveness of potential product segments in coated magazine papers. At the time Caledonian produced a wide range of paper substances (weights or gsm – grams per square metre – on their machine, which had an in-line coating facility), making efficient manufacture and machine changeover difficult and expensive. Opportunities were identified in lighter weight papers (lower than 50gsm). This market segment was growing by 30% per annum, fuelled by the internet and other media where almost every website resulted in the production of a magazine. So much for the decline in paper in the internet age! The cheaper newspaper-like supplements were a declining and low profitability segment of the market with a depressing value:price ratio.

Having decided on the market focus, the next challenge was to develop the strategic capabilities to underpin the new strategy, identify the key customers in European markets and where strategic partnerships might be established to secure a profitable future for the business. How could profits be increased to secure future profitability, yet still retain the competencies developed at the Irvine site?

Working together with the management group, Genesis reviewed the competitive environment, including a number of alternative futures. This creative insight was necessary, given the impact of wood pulp prices on the market for coated art papers. Several options were developed for the future and an integrated strategy emerged to cope with the most likely future, as well as hedging against future market discontinuities. A new focus on service levels and key account management enabled the business to focus on the most valuable customers. Profits were sustained during hostile periods in the future and the mill became the most productive in the group. The model outlined in 'The new age of strategic management' was used to review the business and its functionality. Interestingly, in 1994, the question was asked 'how many of the management team had internet access?' and the answer was one. How things have changed! In developing the future strategy the model ensured we established, together:

- Strategic direction – to set a common purpose.
- Strategic 'workout' – to accelerate performance.
- Innovation and creativity – to use change to stay ahead.
- Leadership capacity – to influence results effectively.
- Organisational learning – to continuously improve.

The energy required for successful implementation required acceleration of the actions of a critical mass of managers to a speed capable of sustaining its own momentum. Creating organisational change seemed a daunting task to some because of the number of variables involved. The senior leadership at Caledonian practised and encouraged true subsidiarity throughout the organisation and empowered those further down to make appropriate decisions.

So how was momentum achieved? Adopting the following core approaches kick-started what was to prove successful implementation and performance improvement:

- Step change thinking.
- Using the PDCA (plan:do:check:action) cycle approach with a difference that makes the difference.
- Building real commitment to, not mere compliance with, compelling goals.
- Delivering short term yet sustainable performance breakthrough.

The potential for *e* (use of information/internet/ebusiness) was significant – through improved process effectiveness, enhanced information flows and shifting people into higher value work. A new set of business metrics evolved for the new era, with emphasis on market and customer information, rather than on the past operational and financial performance of the mill.

One of the new innovations was to form cross-functional teams at the mill, pulling in resources from the Kymmene's sales and marketing divisions, and to develop customer service propositions associated with sales development strategies. Each team had clear terms of reference that led them to develop specific outputs to make change happen and move the business from the current position. The groups considered:

- A statement of the current position relative to the goals.
- Prioritising existing and proposed initiatives and projects.
- Outlining the change required.
- Implications for change:
    - Identify intermediate islands and define risks.
    - Quantitative – analytical, structural, barriers.
    - Behavioural – progress through people, constraints.
- Scope and pace of change – including opportunities for test;
- Transition plan programme and resources required.
- Immediate improvement measures.

The other approach we deployed was corporate influencing to engage effectively with Kymmene's headquarters-based executives in Helsinki, committing them to the process of execution of the strategy. The approach, developed by my colleague Kevin Parker, was effectively key account management in reverse. The work in Kymmene subsidiaries pioneered a business stream that was extended to the likes of National Semiconductor, Polaroid, OKI and Hewlett Packard subsidiaries in the UK in subsequent projects. Figure 4.2 shows the strategic framework developed at Caledonian Paper including the resultant action plans that delivered profitable growth to what was in danger of becoming a 'white elephant' facility on the Ayrshire coast of Scotland.

In Figure 4.2 it is interesting to note the strategic goals and the extent to which they reflect a business more than a paper manufacturer. The early (almost only) focus was on optimising the throughput (tonnes/day) from the paper machine. The vision for the future encapsulated the focus and the strategic outcomes to enable Caledonian to dominate the UK LWC (Light Weight Coated art paper – below 50gsm) market. This would only be achieved by the mill leadership engaging with Kymmene's corporate management and the UK sales operation, based in London. The vision of success contained a new sense of mission – purpose and values and strategic goals that reflected the new external positioning and the need to instill a culture of innovation and customer service in the mill.

New sense of mission

Our purpose

Our purpose is to develop the unique opportunity of being the first UK producer of LWC paper.

Our values

- We care for our customers, personally.
- We care for individuals, and achieve results through teamwork and innovation.
- We seek commitment through involvement.
- We honour our commitments to our stakeholders and recognise successful achievements.

Strategic goals

- Strategic customer relationships:
    - Acknowledged by key customers as the preferred supplier who adds greatest value through the performance of our products and the service we provide.
    - Secure and special, long-term relationships with major publication paper customers in our priority markets.
    - Marketing excellence – previously unheard of in the industry!

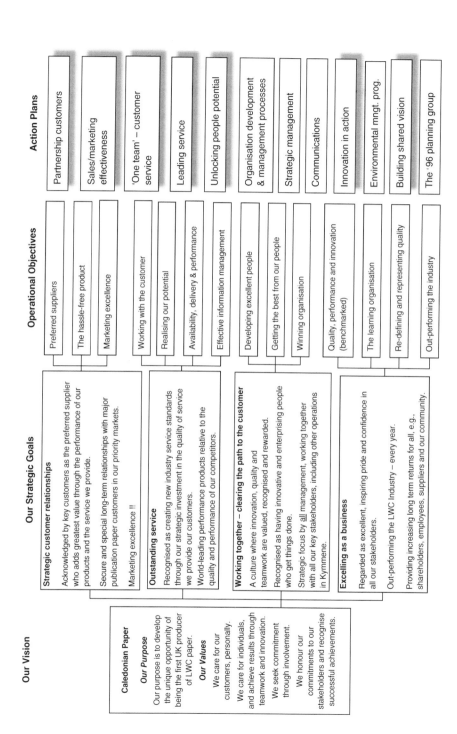

Figure 4.2 Caledonian Paper: Grand Strategy. Framework created by Alistair Gray (1996).

Our Vision

Our Strategic Goals

Operational Objectives

Action Plans

Caledonian Paper

Our Purpose

Our purpose is to develop the unique opportunity of being the first UK producer of LWC paper.

Our Values

We care for our customers, personally.

We care for our individuals, and achieve results through teamwork and innovation.

We seek commitment through involvement.

We honour our commitments to our stakeholders and recognise successful achievements.

Strategic customer relationships

Acknowledged by key customers as the preferred supplier who adds greatest value through the performance of our products and the service we provide.

Secure and special long-term relationships with major publication paper customers in our priority markets.

Marketing excellence !!

Outstanding service

Recognised as creating new industry service standards through our strategic investment in the quality of service we provide our customers.

World-leading performance products relative to the quality and performance of our competitors.

Working together – clearing the path to the customer

A culture where innovation, quality and teamwork are valued, recognised and rewarded.

Recognised as having innovative and enterprising people who get things done.

Strategic focus by all management, working together with all our key stakeholders, including other operations in Kymmene.

Excelling as a business

Regarded as excellent, inspiring pride and confidence in all our stakeholders.

Out-performing the LWC Industry – every year.

Providing increasing long term returns for all, e.g., shareholders, employees, suppliers and our community.

Preferred suppliers

The hassle-free product

Marketing excellence

Working with the customer

Realising our potential

Availability, delivery & performance

Effective information management

Developing excellent people

Getting the best from our people

Winning organisation

Quality, performance and innovation (benchmarked)

The learning organisation

Re-defining and representing quality

Out-performing the industry

Partnership customers

Sales/marketing effectiveness

'One team' – customer service

Leading service

Unlocking people potential

Organisation development & management processes

Strategic management

Communications

Innovation in action

Environmental mngt. prog.

Building shared vision

The '96 planning group

- Outstanding service:

  o Recognised as creating new industry service standards through our strategic investment in the quality of service we provide our customers.

  o World-leading performance products relative to the quality and performance of our competitors.

- Working together – clearing the path to the customer:

  o A culture where innovation, quality and teamwork are valued, recognised and rewarded.

  o Recognised as having innovative and enterprising people who get things done.

  o Strategic focus by all management, working together with all our key stakeholders, including other operations in Kymmene.

- Excelling as a business:

  o Regarded as excellent, inspiring pride and confidence in all our stakeholders.

  o Out-performing the LWC industry – every year.

  o Providing increasing long-term returns for all, e.g., shareholders, employees, suppliers and our community.

The team at Irvine embraced the new strategic direction and especially the goal to 'make money, not just paper'. Increased motivation was secured by working in cross-functional teams, not only in the mill but together with other business units and functions in Kymmene (the parent company). Customers were also involved in the process and new service standards emerged that generated real win:win outcomes for the mill and its key customers.

The key projects were all designed, scoped and executed by a cross-functional/business unit team and objectives set in a scoreboard that was regularly reviewed by the Executive. The flagship projects that emerged were:

- Customer service – 'one team', meeting customer expectations, quality.
- Partnership in action, key customer relationships, 'hassle free' products.
- HR strategy – organisation development, unlock unfulfilled potential, reward and recognition, motivation, communications.
- Leading service.
- Sales company alignment, marketing function review and marketing plan.
- Shared vision and strategic objectives.

After two years of implementation Caledonian Paper not only secured sustainable profitability, it performed in each of the strategic goal areas to enable the mill to dominate not only the UK market but further afield in Europe.

'UPM-Kymmene Means Business'

Finland has a disproportionately high number of major global companies relative to the size of its economy and population – none more so than in the paper manufacturing and engineering industries.

When the CEOs of these global corporations go to their homes on the archipelago each summer they frequently return having agreed a merger with one of their neighbours. The second half of the year is spent executing the mega-merger. In such a way UPM-Kymmene was formed through the merger of Kymmene Corporation and Repola Ltd and its subsidiary United Paper Mills Ltd in 1996. UPM consisted of six business groups. The group employed around 21,000 people and had production plants in 14 countries around the globe. UPM is the only paper company that is listed in the Dow Jones Sustainability Indices and the only forest industry company invited to the United Nations Global Compact LEAD sustainability leadership platform. A number of Caledonian executives secured senior positions in the new group.

We had just commenced a culture change project, entitled 'Kymmene Means Business', deploying many of the techniques and processes introduced at Caledonian Paper, when the mega-merger was announced.

Following the creation of the new company, Douglas McArthur, a member of the original management team at Caledonian Paper during our initial project, was appointed to head up UPM's Catalogue and Retail Papers in Europe. He had seen the power of our approach and the thinking models and frameworks we had deployed. Having taken leadership of the pan-European division he was keen to accelerate the performance of his new leadership team and develop a 'plan to win' over the four years from 1998.

The first team session was held at Brands Hatch, the FI racing circuit in Kent, England. The two-day session combined strategic thinking with the inevitable racing on the track in Formula Ford cars. The focus was on lessons from 'peak performing organisations' and setting the goal for 2002 – what would be a gold medal winning performance? The sporting analogy worked for the team. Out of interest, Figure 4.3 is the agenda we followed for the two-day session. It represents a particularly effective structure for a strategic session of this type.

One of the other global projects was to work with the US sales team, based in Chicago. At the time they were losing around $10m each year. Working with the team and agreeing challenges for the future, they developed a Focus Framework (their work-in-progress is illustrated in Figure 4.4) that enabled them, through focused execution, to turn round the performance over two years.

Over a period of ten years engaging with executives in UPM Kymmene we helped business units change their game from a centralised manufacturing culture into modernised organisations focusing on executing a strategy that fully demonstrated the 'New age of strategic management'.

Race for Performance

Day 1

- Introductions
- Setting the Context - Mapping the Circuit
- The World we face - Changes to Grand Prix 'Regulations'
- The Winning Position
  - see ourselves as others see us
- The Win-Win for UPM-Kymmene by 2002
- Our Gold Medal in 2002 - Our Stretch Objective
- Priority Opportunities and Issues to be addressed
  - in mixed discipline groups (3-4)

Race for Performance

Day 2

- Reflections on Day 1
- Peak Performing Organisations
- Getting on the Grid
- The Race Plan - Planning to Win
- Getting to the First Bend, First
  - action in the next 6-12 months
- Business Group and Personal Commitment
  - next week
  - next month, quarter etc
- The Next Race - when we meet again

Figure 4.3 Race for performance: UPM UK sales force. Workshop design created by Alistair Gray (2004).

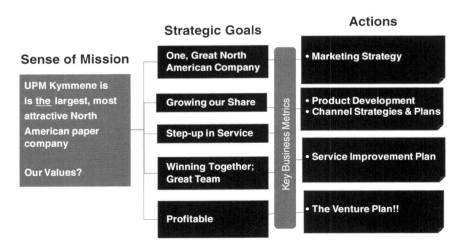

Figure 4.4 UPM US strategic framework. Created by Alistair Gray (2004).

UPM

- **Broke the rules; challenged existing paradigms**

  - Developed scoreboards that were richer than tonnes/day.
  - Focused on market share and optimisation of paper machine performance, e.g., profit and productivity rather than just volume.
  - Empowered their people.

- **They worked it out themselves – embraced innovation management**

  - Developed together an exciting vision of success (in the Focus Framework) that was shared by all.
  - Achieved performance through planning to achieve clear short-term goals.
  - Worked out through cross-functional teams that transformed the performance and commitment of a previously siloed organisation, ruled by the manufacturers.

- **Planned for a step-change in performance**

  - The vision was simple, clear and inspiring – 'Make Money, not just Paper', yet it was underpinned by a detailed plan (the 'one-page strategy') that drove the change and aligned everything behind achieving the outcomes of the strategic goals
  - They had the courage to take on the corporation and their strongly held beliefs. This was done not by confrontation but by careful influencing over a period of time.

- **Changed organisational performance**

  - A culture of innovation encouraged empowered executives to take planned risks rather than monitoring and evaluating performance against a budget or production plan.
  - A critical mass of executives and their workforce were engaged in pursuit of competitive advantage – cross-functional teams worked out what to do.
  - Everyone knew how their role would deliver the goals of the strategic plan.
  - Keeping it simple – in the early years relentlessly focusing on improving profitability and keeping close to their customers through new forms of account management – sales and manufacturing working together despite being at remote locations.

- **Leaders at all levels in the organisation championed the change**

  - Critical numbers of staff were engaged and empowered in cross-functional projects.
  - Significant investment in leadership development and promoting a culture of entrepreneurship and innovation.

Notes

1 *In Search of Excellence*, Tom Peters and Robert H. Waterman, Harper and Row, 1982.
2 Ernst & Young Survey 2001.

5   The power of purpose

Fiona Gifford

Introduction

We have long understood the psychological importance to humans of having purpose. Purpose creates cognitive connection, enables learning and motivates action. More recently, with the development of our knowledge of the neuroscience of leadership and performance, we have been able to identify clearly the dominant drivers of motivation.

The neuroscience and psychology agree. When leaders co-create a clear and meaningful purpose with their teams, and talk about purpose instead of key performance indicators and objectives, when they connect people's personal values to purpose – they get truly amazing results.

For 15 years I have been helping leaders to understand the 'Power of Purpose'; to unleash the potential of their teams. What follows is a summary of the psychological and neuroscientific features that explain the 'Power of Purpose', and three case studies from my work with leaders in the field where they changed the game.

In the three case studies that follow the first is from a heavy engineering company whose CEO used the 'Power of Purpose' to transform performance, culture and leadership over a period of several years. The second demonstrates how Purpose grew collaboration in a leadership team of a pharmaceutical company and the third describes how a financial services team used Purpose to foster improved and more effective teamwork and found a simple way to motivate and measure team performance.

Purpose as power

The 20th-century US anthropologist Margaret Mead is quoted as having said 'Never doubt that a small group of thoughtful committed citizens can change the world; indeed, it is the only thing that ever has'.

Every change in our world has been the result of (initially) small groups of people who have bonded over a common purpose and, as a result, released an unstoppable human energy.

These movements can create positive transformation in society; think about the Grameen Foundation.[1] The Foundation grew from the bold vision of Muhammad Yunus to end poverty. It gives micro-loans to people who are excluded through poverty from the banking system. It now serves over eight million people in Bangladesh and 25 million worldwide.

Muhammad Yunus was an Economics Professor and in the 1970s he tried to influence various national and international organisations to provide small loans, particularly to women, to set up sustainable small businesses. His ideas were universally rejected, so he decided to set up the Grameen Bank.

Another powerful example is embodied by Malala Yousafzai. Born in 1997 in Mingora, Pakistan, she became an advocate for girls' education, which resulted in the Taliban issuing a death threat against her. On 9 October 2012 a gunman shot Malala when she was travelling home from school. She survived, and continues to speak out on the importance of education and women's rights, becoming the youngest person to receive the Nobel Peace Prize.

Where does this type of energy, passion and resilience come from? How is it sustained against the odds, resistance and fear of failure – or worse?

The same kind of power can be harnessed to the great detriment of humanity. We only need to think of the Nazi movement or Apartheid South Africa in our recent history. All of the examples that come to mind have one very important ingredient at their core – *Purpose*.

Neuroscience and purpose

The SCARF model (David Rock, www.neuroleadership.com) describes the five strongest neurobiological drivers of the threat and reward response:

Status is about our relative importance.

Certainty concerns being able to predict what is going to happen.

Autonomy involves a sense of being in control over events.

Relatedness is a sense of security with others.

Fairness is a perception of fair exchanges between people.

The threat and reward response is at the core of human motivation. We know that purposeful people and teams are highly motivated, resilient and high-achieving. So what might be the link between the neuroscience and Purpose?

Remember the story about President John F. Kennedy visiting the NASA space centre in 1962? He walked over to a janitor with a broom, introduced himself and asked what the man was doing. 'Well, Mr President', the janitor responded, 'I'm helping put a man on the moon'. That janitor could see the link between what he did every day and the *Purpose* of NASA.

When people have a clear and meaningful purpose – it feels important for them to do and, as a result, they feel important and valued. This fuels the *Status* driver.

Purpose stays relatively stable over time, unlike business plans and metrics. Purpose also therefore fuels the *Certainty* driver; everyone knows exactly where we are going, what outcome we are trying to deliver and their personal contribution to achieving it.

When the boss is not around and problems or dilemmas occur, Purpose signposts what to do next: 'If that is our Purpose, what will move us towards it?' Purpose enables teams and individuals to be self-managing – more *Autonomous*.

Purpose also creates a collective focus and a culture of collaboration and 'I can't win if you lose'. This fuels the *Relatedness* driver – the sense of being a part of a community.

Employees often experience the decisions made by managers without any context. In Purposeful organisations, decisions are made *because they serve our purpose*. Employees are more likely to see them as *Fair*.

The psychological impact of purpose

When we have a sense of purpose, we tap into the full range of our personal power. We are capable and confident. We challenge boundaries and received wisdom. We are infinitely resourceful, resilient and creative. Our motivation to act and to change is integral to our being, and the source of our energy to keep going when otherwise we would be exhausted. What's more, we excite and engage others with our passion; they find themselves making connections with our purpose and, if there is sufficient overlap between us, we join together.

The 'Power of Purpose' is why humans achieve amazing things that may seem to most of us to be exceptional or even impossible. The power that purpose releases is therefore important for us as leaders to understand. Imagine if even half of your people presented the behaviour described above. How would your organisation be different? How would it be performing?

The good news is that the power of purpose is very fundamentally human – and we may be leaders, but we are human first. So why do we find it so very hard to tap into this great source of energy and creativity?

Purposeful leadership

Purpose is fundamentally different from the goals and objectives we use to try to align the organisation because it connects with us emotionally.

Leading with the power of purpose involves having very different conversations with our people; engaging in human dialogue about what really *matters* and making our working lives *meaningful*.

Leading with the power of purpose also involves *clarity*. Clarity is not the same as detail; in fact detail is the arch enemy of clarity; just re-read your strategy and business plan if you don't believe me.

Examples of Purpose statements

'To lead the way to the future of mobility; enriching lives around the world with the safest and most responsible ways of moving people.'

Toyota

'To push the leading edge of aviation, taking huge challenges doing what others cannot do.'

Boeing

'To supply products that do exactly what they say on the tin.'

Ronseal

'Medical aid where it is needed most. Independent. Neutral. Impartial.'

Doctors Without Borders

'To make natural, delicious food and drink that helps people live well and die old.'

Innocent

'To connect millions of people in real life all over the world, through a community marketplace – so that you can Belong Anywhere.'

Airbnb

Clarity and meaningfulness

Our team's performance is the result of levels of alignment and engagement (Figure 5.1).

Alignment and clarity

Clarity of Purpose is the foundation of good alignment. In order to get to clarity, however, we often need to get into details, explore metaphors, examples and scenarios, and test assumptions.

Once we get back to clarity, we can express our purpose with simplicity and in a way that anyone would understand. With this level of clarity of purpose, people do not need to be told what to do:

- The purpose drives their focus and goals.
- When they are stuck or lost, revisiting the purpose signposts the best options and actions.
- Teams therefore become self-managing.

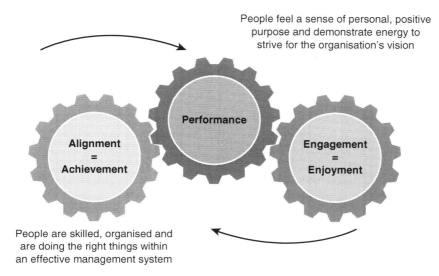

People feel a sense of personal, positive purpose and demonstrate energy to strive for the organisation's vision

Performance

Alignment = Achievement

Engagement = Enjoyment

People are skilled, organised and are doing the right things within an effective management system

Figure 5.1 The Performance Engine. © The Performance Collective Ltd.

Furthermore, when the purpose is shared, team members are more likely to both support and challenge one other effectively.

Engagement and meaningfulness

> Motivation is a fire within. If someone else tries to light it, it will burn very briefly.
>
> Stephen Covey

Meaningfulness of Purpose is the foundation of high engagement – there has to be a 'why' and it has to connect people's emotions. When our purpose is meaningful to the individuals in the team, levels of engagement are significantly higher. Think about it. Have you ever been asked to do something in which you cannot see any purpose? How motivated and engaged were you in the task?

David Rock, the founder of the Neuroleadership Institute, summarises what the science is telling us in his book *Quiet Leadership: Six Steps to Transforming Performance at Work* (HarperCollins, 2006). He says that to be committed, people need to think things through for themselves. Having an 'aha moment' stimulates the chemistry in the brain that creates the energy and motivation to act.

So, leading with goals and objectives may get you compliance. However, leading with purpose allows the autonomy for people to make their own connections, to innovate and tap into their personal passion, thus delivering of their absolute best.

Transformation is made possible through dialogue – the search for ever-increasing levels of clarity, meaning and purpose. These are the tools of tomorrow's leadership – the ones that unleash the amazing potential and power of people.

Three examples of the 'Power of Purpose' at work

Purposeful leadership at work

Mike was the MD of a large, global, heavy engineering company with huge opportunities in the growing economies of China, India and South America. However, unpredictable changes in the competitive environment were putting huge pressure on the company's performance. Quality and cost issues dominated the leadership team discussions, resulting in finger pointing and conflict between the functional directors. Mike was struggling to maintain morale and team working:

> The demands on the business just keep growing and we are always behind plan. It's like herding cats trying to get every team focusing on the right things and morale is starting to suffer. My team is becoming demoralised. We have a documented and prioritised plan and communicate constantly, so why are we not aligned? Something has to change, and soon.

Mike showed me the 'documented and prioritised plan'. It was in fact printed on A3 paper in font 6! With so many key 'priorities', it was little wonder that people were not focused. Mysteriously, each function had almost the same number of priorities on the plan. This seemed very unlikely to reflect the true critical path to the business's success.

Something really did need to change the game. We turned to The Performance Engine (see Figure 5.1) for insight and it became clear that the levels of alignment and engagement were low, both in the leadership team and the wider company. We started with the leadership.

Mike and I brought his leadership team together to work on developing a clear and meaningful purpose for the business. They started with: 'To become a £10bn business by 2020'.

While this is a clear intention, it is not 'purposeful'; it won't drive alignment or engagement. Most employees will have little perception of how what they do every day relates to the value of the business. Also, what did the team imagine will be employees' interpretation of this statement? 'I am going to work a lot harder to make someone else richer.'

After a long and often painful dialogue, the team agreed on: 'To be the customers' first and only call for quality, engineered-to-order solutions'.

To co-create this purpose through dialogue, the team had to rigorously explore the 'why' of the organisation. That dialogue, and the shared meaning and understanding it generated, was every bit as important as the statement.

Each of the functional directors then repeated this process with their teams – aligning their purpose to that of the organisation. This cascade continued until every employee in the company had a role-purpose statement aligned to their team and company purpose.

The company and functional purpose statement was reproduced on a wall at the employee entrance. The projects aligned to delivery of the purpose were also posted on Velcro®-backed tiles along with their red/amber/

green status. This acted as a constant reminder of what is truly important. No new project could be added until a project was delivered and its tile could be removed (unless new resources were also added to deliver it).

As a result of this activity of dialogue, communication and focus, Mike and his leadership team significantly increased both alignment and engagement. The functional teams used their purpose to prioritise and focus their projects and work and everyone could see how their personal contribution added value. Performance improved significantly over time and dialogue about purpose became embedded in the culture.

After five years of leading through purpose the company was routinely delivering on time and on quality to customers. Mike also observed that the leadership team was more collaborative; leading to faster decisions, problem solving and less upward delegation.

The results attracted the attention of a larger global corporation, which acquired the company to increase its global reach and market share.

Transforming a leadership team with purpose

Pharmaceuticals is a demanding business; capital and operating costs are high and patients and clinicians are rightly demanding. Leading a €500 million multi-phased biopharmaceutical facility in Europe would be a challenge for any leadership team. In this case, the business unit had the global license to supply a drug for a rare disease. The drug is essential for quality of life and life itself. The pressure was high and the leadership team often found itself in conflict.

The three process managers reported to the Operations Director and were focussed purely on meeting output goals. The Quality Manager reported to a Corporate Vice President and was seen as getting in the way with constant compliance challenges and auditing. The Financial Controller also reported into Corporate and was always challenging and squeezing cost. These reporting lines undermined any sense of 'one team' or collaboration, with significant impact on leadership team effectiveness. This lack of collaboration and the constant conflict were also affecting performance and perceptions of the team's competence.

The team agreed one thing. One of the process managers summarised: 'If we carry on like this we will fail and if we fail, we all fail'.

What was clear was that each of the managers was working to different goals and outcomes. So the obvious first step was to co-create a common purpose that transcended the functional goals. The starting point was clearly desirable, but not purposeful: 'To meet the output plan at or better than the quality and cost targets'.

During the working session that I facilitated with the team, the conflict of the previous 12 months was fully aired and the team co-created a purpose for the whole operations team: 'Our purpose is to ensure no patient anywhere in the world goes more than 24 hours without their medication'.

We also discussed how differently people would behave under this purpose as contrasted with the original. The team concluded that this purpose meant they needed to adopt the mind-set of 'I can't win, if you lose'. They even requested that the boss stop measuring and rewarding them individually. So a team bonus was implemented to replace individual performance rewards.

The team also rolled out the purpose to the whole business unit and had 1:1 dialogues about what the purpose meant for each individual and the purpose of their role.

From that moment the team began to collaborate more effectively and they also noticed that people were solving more issues and problems without involving their leaders; they had simple clarity of what was expected of them.

This outcome was only possible because the leaders committed the time to have very difficult, and different, conversations. They lifted their sights from the daily operational issues to explore what the real purpose of their business was. They found a purpose that was both meaningful and shared. This resulted in their finding the energy and courage to do things differently.

As a result of subsequently engaging their people in an exploration of purpose, they built trust and gave people the autonomy to make decisions. The leaders could be confident in those decisions, because purpose guided the thinking that led to them.

The new spirit of one team and one purpose was sustained because they chose to be measured and rewarded only as a team.

Using purpose alignment to create focus

A customer proposition team in financial services set out to use purpose to create focus on their deliverables. As a result they also fostered increased team-work and found a simple way to motivate and measure team performance.

My first meeting with this team was at their weekly check-in tele-meeting. Five people were in the meeting room and three joined by phone. After each gave a short update against their deliverables, it was clear that things were not going well. It was not due to lack of effort or commitment. However the team found their attention and energy constantly pulled in different directions. 'We seem to start the week with a clear to-do list and get to the end with a longer one and the realisation that several really important things have slipped', Angela, the team manager, told me.

The team then co-created a team purpose statement and aligned their personal role-statements to it.

At the subsequent weekly check-in tele-meeting they created a 'if we do nothing else this week we must . . .' list. These were the top five most critical deliverables that were aligned to the purpose. The list was sent to everyone to write on their team whiteboards for the whole team to see.

This created focus, as teams could see that they needed to prioritise these deliverables, even if they were not on their personal to-do list. People offered help and resources across team boundaries, thus increasing collaboration.

This was such a simple change to the teams' ways of working, but it truly changed the game. Each week the teams took great pleasure in wiping the delivered priorities from the board on a Friday afternoon. The whiteboards had accidentally created a source of team motivation; no one wanted to get to the weekend and not clear the board. To enhance the potency of this source of motivation, the managers started to publish the number of consecutive 'clear' weeks as a team performance measure.

Fiona Gifford
Genesis Director (2006–2010)
Founder and Director of the Performance Collective

Changing the game	*How embracing Purpose changes the game*

	• **Aligning the whole organisation**
	
	  ○ Leaders co-create and communicate a clear and meaningful Purpose for the whole organisation.
	  ○ Teams and individuals co-create and communicate a clear and meaningful Purpose for themselves.
	  ○ Processes are in place to constantly check alignment.
	
	• **Increasing engagement**
	
	  ○ The process of co-creating alignment through dialogue is in itself highly engaging.
	  ○ Every person can see how their role serves the purpose; they feel more important.
	  ○ Purpose also breaks down functional silos and drives greater collaboration between teams.
	
	• **Teams become more self-directed**
	
	  ○ Knowing Purpose allows people to make better decisions and problem-solve without delegating upwards to the boss.
	  ○ Purpose allows for creativity and innovation because it focuses on outcomes and not tasks; people have more choice and scope about 'how'.
	
	• **Teams and individuals have greater focus**
	
	  ○ Purpose cuts out 'white noise' with the simple question 'How does that serve our purpose?' If the answer is negative, stop wasting time on it.
	  ○ Individuals can focus more clearly and spend their time and energy predominantly to deliver Purpose.
	
	• **Motivation and change are fuelled by Purpose**
	
	  ○ Purpose fuels the five known neurological drivers of motivation, resulting in high energy and performance.
	  ○ Because of this high motivation state, change becomes easier to effect.

Note

1 The mission of the Grameen Foundation is to enable the poor, especially women, to create a world without hunger and poverty. It is a global not-for-profit organisation that brings innovative and sustainable solutions to the fight against poverty and hunger. Together with local partners, they equip families, women and small-holder farmers with resources and services that expand financial inclusion, strengthen resilience, enhance health and improve livelihoods.

6 Innovation management and MTBD>MTBS

Introduction

Over the last two decades management has been dealing with increasingly turbulent times by increasing the amount of time planning and developing budgets, often at the last moment. In my work with clients in the private and public sectors I find most management teams plan principally to improve on the audited certainty of the past, incrementally over a typical time frame of three years. These strategies are inevitably found wanting, as, by the time their carefully crafted strategies and plans are executed, something has happened in the external environment that makes the basis of the strategic plan no longer relevant. I am sure all readers can remember something that has happened in the last five years that would never have been forecast five years ago.

As described in Chapter 2, embracing scenario thinking is one way of thinking the unthinkable and therefore of testing assumptions underpinning strategies and plans. The other response is simply to be better at innovating, ahead of turbulence or as a rapid response to events. This means building strategic capabilities – assets, skills and systems – that enable organisations to get and stay ahead of competition.

One example of building real capability in innovation was the 'game changing' strategy developed and implemented by Taunton Cider, one of the leading cider manufacturers in the UK around the year 2000. Faced with the mighty H.P. Bulmer – the industry leader and low-cost producer – Taunton developed strategies that delivered double the profitability of Bulmer on half the volume. The story of how they broke out of the Cider Box is outlined in the second half of this chapter.

Innovation management – the way to cope with increasing change and uncertainty

A new algorithm to describe life in the millennium beyond 2000 is MTBD > MTBS. It is an acknowledged truism that in any aspect of corporate life *the mean time between decisions (MTBD)* is greater than *the mean time between surprises (MTBS)*.

Many organisations have adopted a bottom-up approach to innovation management in the belief that staff will feel more committed and involved.

Sometimes this is guided by corporate requirements from the top. There has been more planning by executives themselves than by planners and accountants – in itself a good thing – but still we find many management teams cannot gain lasting advantage in the ever-changing competitive environment outside the organisation. In truth, by the time their carefully crafted plans are in place, something has often happened in the external environment to change the whole basis on which many of these plans were made. They are surprised that MTBD>MTBS.

Perhaps the best example of the type of shock in store for many traditionalists is the current price of oil, after a period of stability at a price double the current level. This is similar to the impact of the six-day war in 1974.

At that time, and over the next ten years, the apparent certainty of the future was thrown into disarray, despite extensive planning systems. A decade later, when prices fell well below $10 per barrel, the industry had a sharp reminder of the futility of conventional planning and management approaches. The Swiss watch and international computer industry have faced similar seismic turbulence through the impact and uptake of quartz watches and electronic technology.

In the digital, knowledge and consumer economies we have to address markets about which there is incomplete information due to the nature of their life cycles and the speed of change. Traditional research and planning approaches, building forward from the certainty of the past, are found wanting when predicting the future.

As considered more fully in Chapter 2, it is no longer sufficient to consider +/– 10% scenarios on key metrics. The scale of impact faced by Cisco Systems in 2000 when US treasurers stopped spending on IT systems after Y2K, or the consequences for industries such as tourism and security of the tragedy that was 9/11, mean that we have to consider scenarios that are more divergent from the official future.

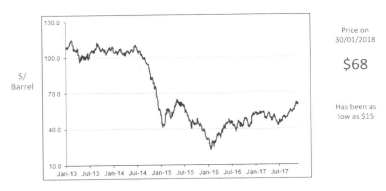

Figure 6.1 The price of oil today. Chart created by Alistair Gray (2018).

Over the last 20 years I have advised clients to imagine a business environment that features low economic growth, shorter product lifecycles, increasingly tough domestic and global competition – and that was before the world's worst recession in 50 years in 2008. Innovation is a global game – you have to fight global competition before it starts. Shifting demographics, lifestyles, online purchasing and increased deregulation will create new and intriguing blends of potential customers and new competitors.

It will become more and more important to make rapid decisions, frequently on incomplete information, and to stop waiting for other people to show the way. Many of today's companies appear to be building new corporate offices, rather than new organisations and businesses. In a previous chapter I highlighted the importance of 'vision', helping to achieve across-the-board understanding and agreement to the way ahead, even in hostile times. The second key dimension to successful strategic management is to instil innovative capabilities in the organisation. Why? Simply to cope with the unprecedented pace of change and the competitive intensity in all markets and industries.

Taking the lead in innovation or achieving success in renewing your company does not come from putting a few bright people in a secluded room, pouring in some money and hoping something will happen. Most attempts to plan systematically and in detail for 'breakthrough research' fail. Equally, being innovative once, either in developing a new product, process or business, will not win the battle in the short term, far less the long run. Fleet-of-foot competitors across the world mean products can be copied and distributed faster than ever. It is easy to become intrigued with the prospect of innovation, it is quite another matter to find and implement appropriate courses of action. In our experience, most organisations from small to large, and across most sectors, are poorly equipped. There are common fundamentals underlying the success of innovation management in companies and other organisations, however much they may appear to be unique on the surface.

What is innovation management?

Innovations occur in all organisations, most frequently as one-off random events. However, no one can leave innovation to chance in the environment towards and beyond 2020. It must be purposeful, considered and above all *managed*, but not in the traditional way. Innovation management establishes the sources, resources, organisation structures, culture and management practices required to spawn, nurture and bring about increased innovation – and to do this not only in new products and services, but internally as well.

Business schools and corporate career paths concentrate almost entirely on training executives for managing the on-going business, i.e., an extrapolation of the past. Consequently, the structure, culture, policies and practices that have evolved over the years work very well for managing the day-to-day business. However, they are typically inadequate for managing the new, or for managing innovation.

In general, managing innovation properly ensures faster response to customers, competitor action and changing markets, values, lifestyles and opportunities. It also ensures that ideas for change are encouraged, and invariably implemented successfully and profitably. The problem with successful innovation is not a shortage of ideas, but the ability to commercialise and implement these ideas effectively.

The innovative organisation

The innovative organisation should be described as an interactive network and not a hierarchy. Many manufacturing organisations, especially those in financial services, exist by the rule of the hierarchy, where the career banker or actuary rules. In this situation innovation is stifled at every level as it appears threatening to the upper echelons of management. Indeed many senior executives save a 'good negative' on a good idea until it is well into development rather than in its embryonic state. In our experience organisational and political structures in business are the most common causes of lack of innovation. Great benefit can be achieved through enabling organisations to be creative and innovative, without losing control. Here are some checkpoints:

- Always talk about your organisation as a network, not a hierarchy. Then people will think about it in this way and use it accordingly in mutually supporting teams.
- See it as a multi-project organisation, with reducing focus on reporting relationships and increased focus on working together to solve increasingly complex problems.
- Let 'small short-life crews' flourish. Set them up for specific missions and disband them at the end. Do not perpetuate their state as committees. Some regrettably are 'shot down' before completing their task.

The major difference between growing innovative organisations and their mature static counterparts is that managers in growing organisations make deliberate, substantial and frequent use of the informal systems. Instead of fitting people into the organisation, they create new parts of the organisation around key people, bending the structure accordingly to accommodate new formations.

In this situation, talented people are given space to develop resources around their unique capabilities. In the innovative organisation, persuasion, repaid favours and shared interests are the key levers for change rather than instruction or command. Informality and change are integral parts of the response to competitive pressure.

The paradox of innovation is that you require stability in which to implement change

Stability does not require organisational hierarchy. Stability is nurtured through the acceptance of the organisation as an interactive results-oriented network of people, not jobs and titles.

The key difference is that in the average company or organisation you engage and develop people who are fact-oriented, cautious and relatively passive, while the innovative organisation encourages people to be entrepreneurial and intuitive, with control coming from a clear and well-articulated vision, understood by all.

The Growth Action Programme – success through innovation

Finding innovation 'critical mass' requires a systematic approach. Programmes that emerge must represent an integrated, comprehensive, coordinated chain – with no weak links. The Growth Action Programme must be designed, assembled and implemented around the needs and nature of the individual business unit – no 'standardised' plans are possible.

To achieve real gains from a structured approach to innovation requires more than simply setting up a few programmes. Innovation management comprises:

- Enabling people to become innovative by accessing sources of information that will stimulate new ideas.
- Setting goals, or longer-term positions of competitive advantage, which demand greater innovation in the response from management.

Rules of the game	
Average company	**Innovative company**
Follow the rules and procedures	*Understand the competitive vision and take strategic initiatives*
Co-ordinate and plan	*Be flexible and react to opportunities*
Avoid mistakes – be thorough	*Learn by mistakes, develop your intuitions*
Wait until you are told or given information	*Get the information you need*
Act within your area of responsibility	*Focus on key issues, get the resources you need*
Committees preserve the status quo	*Project teams abound*

Figure 6.2 Rules of the game. Figure created by Alistair Gray (2018).

- Achieving the required balance between innovation management (managing the new) and traditional management (managing the existing) in terms of business processes, culture and incentives.
- Ensuring that the structure of the organisation enables innovation to flourish and that 'godfathers' exist to support the entrepreneurs and venture teams, rather than killing ideas at birth.
- Instilling policies that demand innovation, e.g., even in the setting of budgets, ask what is proposed for this year that is different and improves competitive advantage.
- Rewarding and recognising innovation behaviour through new people systems, backed up by new approaches to training, development and communication.
- Recognising what a more innovative culture will look like and fostering it throughout the organisation.

The only constant in business today is change. To embrace change you have to take calculated, measured, controlled risks – constantly. Once you have mastered this approach, opportunity and stability of performance will be within your grasp, because you will be nimble enough to flex and grow with change. This will be especially important in a flat economic environment.

Instilling innovation management through growth action programmes will not only introduce more new management tools and techniques to the organisation. It will become the new fundamental of corporate life in responding to the demands of today's competitive environment. The essence of innovation is discovering what your company is uniquely good at and exploiting that to the full. Most companies have unique strengths and strategic capabilities. Success comes from leveraging those strengths in the market place. Successfully implemented, it means that people at all levels with the will to implement good ideas are encouraged to do so and given the opportunity to learn and grow personally by contributing to the profitable growth of the enterprise.

Taunton Cider – success through innovation

The Taunton Cider Company was a cider producer, born and based in Norton Fitzwarren, just south of the county town of Taunton, Somerset, England. The company was best known for being the developer and producer of Blackthorn Cider and Autumn Gold. Little had changed in the manufacturing or presentation of cider since its origins in the 13th century. By the 1980s, the company was the UK's second largest cider maker
(after Hereford-based H.P. Bulmer), employing 550 people at its Norton Fitzwarren site and producing 30 million gallons of cider each year.

Major change through the MMC

In 1989 the MMC (Monopolies and Mergers Commission) produced a doorstop of a report on the brewing industry that aimed to loosen the control exerted over public houses by the industry's Big Six – the heavy battalions with 80% of beer production.

The MMC concluded that this complex monopoly operated against the public interest in that consumer choice was further restricted because of brewers' efforts to ensure that their own brands of cider and soft drinks were sold in their outlets, and independent manufacturers and wholesalers of beer and other drinks were allowed only limited access to the on-licensed market. The brewing industry felt their landscape might shift a little, but it would not be subject to too many seismic upheavals. They were quite mistaken.

Taunton Cider was owned by a combination of the major brewers including Bass, Whitbread, Wolverhampton and Dudley, Greene King and Scottish & Newcastle. The board decided to enable a management buy-out headed by Peter Adams (Managing Director) and Andy Nash (Marketing Director). A package of funds was assembled by Morgan Grenfell (part of Deutsche Bank) with the plan to list the buy-out company on the London Stock Exchange.

Given recent falling sales and margins in draught cider, and facing competition from an increasing number of lager-type brands, Taunton had pursued a strategy of diversification away from their core products. Their product portfolio included:

- Mineral water distribution rights for Strathmore Spring.
- Appletise – a sparkling apple juice.
- Piermont – a pear-based drink.
- A German orange juice.

In addition, the business acquired the Copella[1] brand of fresh Cox Pippin apple juice and developed Tapas, a range of snack products combining tortilla chips and a sauce for sale in the on-licensed trade.

The diversified strategy was to be the platform for floating the company and taking the business out of what was perceived to be a mature Cider Box. They asked PA Consulting Group to review and hopefully validate the strategy in advance of flotation. At the time they expected little change. For the second time they were quite mistaken.

Challenging the strategy

I led the PA team that carried out a full review of the external and internal environment facing Taunton Cider in 1990. This included:

- A thorough review of the markets across their portfolio of products to establish their relative attractiveness and Taunton's position relative to competition.
- Their position in the industry, especially relative to H.P. Bulmer who held a 50% market share in the UK, as well as leadership in global markets.
- The effectiveness of their value chain and where the power was held in the industry, including their former shareholders – the major brewers.
- An assessment of their stakeholders and their relative importance to Taunton in their proposed new state as a listed company.

Our conclusions

Following detailed research and a comprehensive set of interviews (internal and external) we fed back our conclusions to the buy-out board (Peter Adams and Andy Nash had been joined by Nick Pearch, Finance Director, and Brian Longstaff, the Manufacturing Director, as well as non-executive directors appointed by Deutsche Bank). We concluded:

- The draught cider market, though mature, was not dying.
- Premium lager and other alcohol products represented growing markets in which premium cider and other closely related products had a natural place.
- The industry was open – wide open – to innovation, especially in the shake-out of MMC. Bulmers were stuck in their technology-based box with real-term declining earnings.
- The current and proposed diversification portfolio represented real risks, taking the business into areas where they had no experience in terms of marketing, distribution or technology.
- Commercially the new business areas, with few exceptions, had a negative impact on an otherwise healthy core business.
- There was real potential in Taunton people to contribute to innovation in terms of their ideas and passion – this needed to be released. In general, a critical mass of the executive leadership did not own or endorse the diversified portfolio strategy.
- There was scope for real innovation, using apples as a source of alcohol, to produce an exciting range of premium drinks products.

We used the Anshoff Matrix as a tool to demonstrate the risky position[2] of the diversified portfolio (see Figure 6.3).

Another lovely anecdote was the description of the management team as 'the blancmange'! This referred to a perceived (and to a degree actual) culture where a number of change initiatives had been tried in the past but the group had the propensity to fall back into their original form, shape and practices. Something special was necessary to 'whip up' the blancmange into a more innovative and enterprising dessert.

After much discussion the board agreed with our assessment and began a process, with the management team, facilitated by us, to develop a

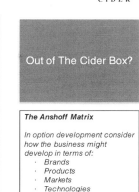

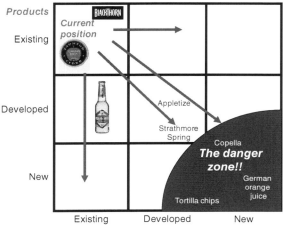

Figure 6.3 Diversify and die? Matrix created by Alistair Gray (1992).

different strategy focusing on the optimum future portfolio and focusing on building a real strategic capability in innovation – establishing the assets, skills and system required to achieve industry leadership.

Vision of success

Through a series of workshops that engaged fully the management team at Norton Fitzwarren we established a vision of success for the first three–four years of the buy-out and soon-to-be-listed company, expressed in a Focus Framework (see Figure 6.4).

The goals were expanded to provide the basis for the alignment of the actions, as follows:

Product leadership

- Recognised as the most innovative and highest performance producer of cider and other drinks.
- Acknowledged as the producer who adds greatest value to the customer.

Integrated manufacture

- Achieving lower cost of production relative to quality, range and performance of other competitors.

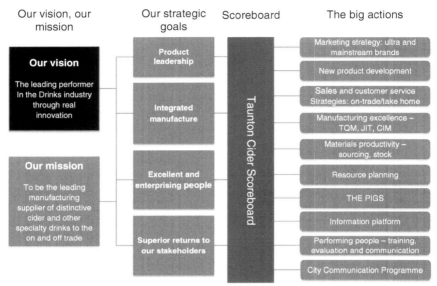

Figure 6.4 Taunton Cider: success through innovation. Framework created by Alistair Gray (1992).

- Secure, more effective relationships with key customers than our competitors.

Excellent and enterprising people

- Recognised as having an innovative and enterprising culture.
- Strategic focus by all management.

Superior returns to our stakeholders

- Out-performing the drinks industry.
- Providing superior wealth for our stakeholders.

The next step was to plan for the execution of the strategy. Many good strategies fail and indeed some never get off the starting blocks.[3] The reasons for failure or slow progress are given as:

- Limited resources.
- Limited external support available.
- Limited experience.

Therefore implementation had to be focused and simple to follow. Real investment is required to build a strategic capability – investment in assets, skills and systems. Taunton had to build on their considerable strengths as well as ensuring that initial motivation began to build momentum.

Getting it right required leadership to identify critical breakthrough performance goals and build leadership and breakthrough thinking. The first step was to go for real commitment (rather than compliance) to the new strategy and the innovation process. A strategic planning and implementation calendar was developed to ensure progress was tracked throughout the year and momentum maintained.

Having started the process, it was essential to deploy these goals in the Focus Framework throughout the business to ensure that everyone understood their role in the journey to industry leadership. A balanced scorecard was developed for the business at a number of levels. This drove the 'plan:do:check:act' debriefing process that stimulated disciplined improvements to a number of traditional methods.

As has been the case in many of our successful projects with our clients, the strategic plan was developed through a series of cross-functional teams (called 'bomber crews' in 1992, a term that is perhaps less appropriate in 2018). Each team had a main board director as the champion and one of the senior executives as the project lead. The teams were formed using team-building and psychometric principles[4] and given a mission to return with their strategic plans in 12 weeks. Each team was supported by one of our consultants and, in some cases, by specialist external input.

A joint workshop/conference was held at the end of the 12-week period and the full strategic plan prepared, ready for execution by departments and a small number of cross-functional teams.

Revising the portfolio of brands – out of the Cider Box

The earlier work with the Anshoff Matrix was reinforced by another strategic analysis that highlighted the opportunity for the proposed new cider brands to take Taunton out of the red ocean of traditional brands and beer (Figure 6.5).

The white diamond

Taunton's portfolio was made up largely of traditional brands and cider varieties, with falling margins given the mature state of the market. Having accepted the folly of a diversified portfolio of products out of alcohol, the initial period of execution was to focus on the odyssey out of the 'Cider Box'. One of the first steps was to launch Diamond White, a 7.5% abv (alcohol by volume) white cider, made not from

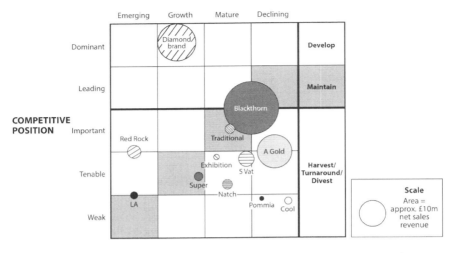

Figure 6.5 Product maturity. Model created by Alistair Gray and James Farnham (1992).

fresh Somerset apples but imported Polish apple concentrate. A few readers may remember the halcyon days of the sixties and seventies when introduction to alcohol was often in the form of cheap wine, increasingly consumed in night clubs or as a kick-starter for parties. Diamond White was born, unlike any other cider, with the following features for the consumer and the customer (pubs, clubs, hospitality outlets and retailers):

- A 'discovery' brand for the party generation.
- An interestingly high abv.
- 275 mm non-returnable bottle with a dynamic modern pack design.
- Shrink-wrapped in dozens rather than in crates on pallets.

Test-marketed in the best clubs in key cities, little more than word of mouth was required to begin what proved to be a revolution in this market segment, and it was a sustainable position until the explosion of alcopops a decade later. Diamond Blush followed, at a lower abv of 5%, all delivering an alcoholic contribution at two to three times that of premium cider. Imagine the challenge experienced by the traditional beer sales force, faced with new products on new markets and not sold in barrels or volumes of pints.

Taunton's success came from speaking directly with customers and NPD agencies, the latter specialists in areas of FMCG outside the mainstream drinks markets. Taunton Cool followed in 1.5 litre PET bottles, along with Caprini, the first champagne perry since Babycham, and Brody, a more refined and dark cider.

All of these new products flew in the face of the traditional cider business, which, though still 50% of the market, was truly commoditised. The whole marketing mix was changed. Bulmer responded with Scrumpy Jack (in cans to appeal to the take-home market) and Gaymers with 'K', neither of which enjoyed the early market advantage of Diamond White.

Excellent and enterprising people

In addition to changing the products and approach to selling, the key changes were in the ambition, attitude and self-belief of the Taunton people. Some embraced the opportunities afforded by the new direction. However, although many were happy to see the back of the diversified portfolio, many of these were also resistant to any change and struggled to cope. Inevitably there was also an influx of new talent as the company's listing and increased profile attracted executives from other companies and sectors, many of whom rose to the challenge of the new direction, embraced change and volunteered for new roles that took them up the executive ladder, in some cases passing their bosses on the way.

A significant investment was made in training of staff, especially in the sales force and the way they presented the Taunton portfolio. These were the early days of .ppt[5] presentations so, when the Taunton executives turned up in the multiple grocer boardrooms, imagine the surprise for the customer at the style and substance of these former beer salesmen.

Clearly marketing and sales staff were excited with the new direction and activity. New products were flowing under the Taunton and retailer brands. All this added to the complexity and uncertainty of the cider-making, bottling and distribution. Traditional process took a long time and ever-increasing numbers of products were putting pressure on packing lines and warehousing. How would those in manufacturing respond to the new way, from what was a safe, solid, steady 'Dry Blackthorn' process?

The Focus Framework, shown in Figure 6.4 with the 'big actions', illustrates the integrated nature of Taunton's strategy. It provided the opportunity for a critical mass of executives and staff to be engaged and involved in the execution of strategy. One highlight for me was to facilitate the formation of the *PIGs* – the *P*rofit *I*mprovement *G*roups. They were set loose on costs with a freedom to question any areas. Within the first few months of operation over £100k of savings were identified, all of which could be channelled into 'investment' in more potentially profitable areas. Many groundbreaking ideas emerged, e.g., halving fermentation time and reducing the weight of glass bottles by 40%.

The Taunton Cider scoreboard

Figure 6.6 is an example of part of the scoreboard established for each of the strategic goals.

Taunton Cider
Key performance area: product leadership
year-on-year growth Sales value (£m – % growth) Profit (PBT £m – % growth)
Advertising spend/market share %
Net profit margin/net sales value %
Discounts % net sales value
Commercial factors % net sales value

Figure 6.6 Taunton Cider scoreboard. Created by Alistair Gray and James Farnham (1992).

This data was benchmarked against others in the industry and other drinks manufacturers and distributors.

First six months – real progress

During the first six months the directors were more than occupied in the City of London putting forward their prospectus to become a publicly listed company. It was left to the management at Norton Fitzwarren to get on with the task of execution of the reformed strategy.

My role, along with my PA colleague James Farnham,[6] was to lead the scoping and early implementation of the most important projects, and those that would yield early benefits. Figure 6.7 illustrates the process we went through during this early stage.

In two iterations of the projects (first six months) substantial progress was made and at a de-brief on progress the teams were pleased to report:

- The new marketing plans for Dry Blackthorn and Diamond White were being implemented.
- The company had secured the rights to market and distribute Miller Genuine Draft lager in the United Kingdom in a joint agreement with the Miller Group as a deliberate move into other premium alcoholic drinks.
- The sales strategies and plans had a much stronger focus in terms of:
  - Key account management.
  - Service standards to the on-trade.
  - Sales force effectiveness standards set with new call controls.

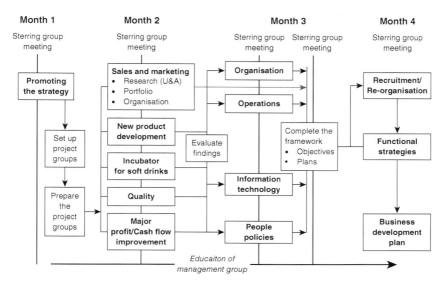

Figure 6.7 Planning the projects. Process created by Alistair Gray (1993).

- There had been a number of achievements in new product development:

  ○ The launch in regional trials of Brody and Red Rock.
  ○ The launch of Caprini, Brody and Taunton Cool.
  ○ A cross-functional brainstorming process ('ASIMOV') established and delivering results.

- The vision for integrated manufacturing was established, encapsulating total quality, computer integrated manufacturing and 'Just-in-Time'. The quality initiatives had raised their status through the creation of 'Project Lexus', removing the need for using jargon-like shorthand such as TQM, CIM, JIT and CAPP.
- The sales information management system pilot had been successful and Phase 1 was now approved.
- Internal communication activity had been significant through the use of briefing groups, 'Intercom' and CEO newsletters. In addition, the newly formed Management Forum had met and agreed a number of actions in their new state of empowerment.

In the remainder of Year 1 a new HR Director, David Fothergill, was appointed with the task of developing a function that was more than 'pay and rations'. The scope of the function included performance management, training, assessment and communication. A new management forum and briefing groups were established and further training was given to enable great value to be achieved out of hardware/software investment. Fothergill later moved to head up operations when Brian Longstaff retired. His experience in making change happen through people shone through. Key executives embraced the change and major initiatives emerged to halve fermentation times, slash changeover times, reduce stock holding and increase flexibility. Innovation workshops seemed to be everywhere and it was clear the culture was changing from the 'Flat Earth Society' of pre-MBO days. Taunton Cider was transformed.

Improved strategic management

Over the first year of implementation of the strategic plan there had been a significant improvement in strategic management capability at Taunton Cider. A critical mass of management had been engaged in the process of designing and executing the strategic plan, creating greater ownership and enthusiasm for the new direction.

Due to the pressure surrounding flotation and the sale of Copella and Piermont it had not been possible to carry out the competitor research on Bulmer or other drinks manufacturers. This was now activated and significant information gathered that helped the projects to be further refined. Taunton also instigated training in strategic management, innovation and planning skills for the executive team. The quarterly business review and planning schedule was established as an integral part of the planning calendar.

I highlighted earlier the comparison between Taunton Cider and other comparators in terms of profitability and productivity. Figure 6.8 illustrates the progress Taunton made before and after flotation in terms of profit/ employee.

The gains made by Showerings and Bulmer in profit/employee were deceptive. Showerings reduced their workforce by 16% in 1989 and Bulmer reduced their workforce by 14% in 1990. Andy Nash reinforced the benefits of keeping the overall headcount within 500 and improving the productivity and added value through adding new recruits. 'The Romans had the right idea when they made 500 the number of their cohorts', he reflected.

One interesting feature was the way in which the executive directors kept together during the flotation of Taunton Cider. Two innovative forums were established: 'Morning Prayers' as a once-a-week get together to share one another's programme and key objectives for the week; 'Evensong' – a once-a-month late afternoon/evening session on one or two topics of importance to the company during this exceptionally busy time. We were pleased to support the team in designing and facilitating this process.

Nick Pearch took responsibility for the business planning process and the development of strategic management skills across the management

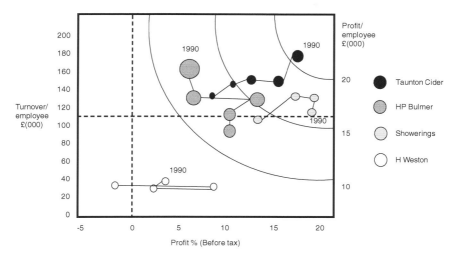

Profit/employee
1986 – 1990

Figure 6.8 Profit/employee productivity. Model created by Alistair Gray (2018).

team. He also became the 'Minister of Corporate Culture – Innovation'. One tool he used was to own and allocate a modest fund to stimulate new ideas and offer further seed-corn funding, requiring feedback on the projects and where progress was being made. Some projects were given their own bank account and 'cheque book'. Interestingly a previous culture of over-spending on projects virtually disappeared overnight.

The strategy development process engaged a critical number of staff and, through the execution of the strategy, individual and corporate performance made a step change. The 'big actions' were fully aligned to strategic goals and the cross-functional approach taken had ensured not only effective implementation, but it also brought people together in a way in which they had never worked previously. The Focus Framework provided the basis for the execution of the strategy and I was privileged to be part of this process over the first two years after flotation as their guide for the journey.

Postscript

Within the first three years Taunton Cider PLC achieved a position of double the relative profitability of Bulmer with half the turnover as a direct result of their more focused portfolio concentrating on fewer more premium products. In the words of Andy Nash, Taunton with 500 people and vastly increased sales and profits were 'too small to hide and not big enough to run'. In 1995 Taunton Cider was sold to Matthew Clark for £256m – a fine premium on the £75m Taunton paid the previous owners. A large number of employees in Taunton Cider owned shares in the listed company. The same happened to the Gaymer cider brand, which was bought by management from Allied Domecq and subsequently acquired by Matthew Clark for £105m.

Almost total control of the UK cider market was now in the hands of two companies. The deal gave Matthew Clark, which only moved into the cider market the previous year, a 45% share of the market compared with the 46% controlled by Bulmer. Matthew Clark and Taunton combined owned several leading cider brands, including Olde English, Dry Blackthorn, Red Rock, Diamond White and Autumn Gold. This clearly breached the 25% market-share rule established by the MMC but was sanctioned as cider only represented 7% of the beer market.

It did not end there. In 1998 Matthew Clark plc was acquired by Constellation Brands Inc of the United States. In 2002 the company acquired Forth Wines. In 2007 Constellation sold a 50% stake to Punch Taverns. In 2010 the cider businesses were sold to C&C Group plc of Ireland, leaving Matthew Clark as an alcohol wholesaler. The C&C Group own Magners Cider and also distribute the Bulmer brand in Ireland.

In 2003 Bulmer was bought for £278 million by Scottish & Newcastle (S&N). In 2008 it was announced that S&N had been bought out for £7.8 billion by the Heineken group. Bulmer's Australia and New Zealand business interests were sold to Australian brewer Foster's. Bulmers now survives only as a brand name, with operations in Hereford scaled back considerably to principally the production of cider.

The beer/cider industry that seemed so unassailable in 1989 had been blown apart. Large parts of the UK brewing industry are now in the hands of overseas companies such as Interbrew, Carlsberg and Coors.

It was a privilege to work with the inspiring team at Taunton during this period, to take them to a new level of performance, corporately and individually. That enabled the business to grow and secure a relatively large and short-term return for the shareholders. Flotation and sale of a business in such a short time is a feature of business that a number of people feel does little for the sustainability of businesses in the community, to which one has to agree. Equally you have to recognise this is part of today's business enterprise.

TAUNTON CIDER

- **Broke the rules; challenged existing paradigms**

  - Broke out of the Cider Box.
  - Developed and sustained a strategic capability in innovation.
  - Achieved industry leadership in premium alcohol products to catch the wave of premium lagers and beers.

- **They worked it out themselves – embraced innovation management**

  - Faced reality as it was in 1992, the inadequacy of the diversified portfolio.
  - Achieved 'breakout' performance through planning to achieve clear short-term goals that aligned the organisation and gave a plan, purpose and confidence to their people that success was possible.

- **Planned for a step-change in performance**

  - The vision was simple, clear and inspiring yet underpinned by a detailed plan that drove the change and aligned everything behind the strategic goals.
  - They had the courage to change their previous portfolio strategy that was putting the healthy parts of the business at risk.

- **Changing organisational performance**

  - The Finance Director became the 'godfather' – the minister of the new corporate culture of innovation.
  - A critical mass of executives and their workforce were engaged in pursuit of competitive advantage – cross-functional teams worked out what to do.
  - Everyone knew how their role would deliver the goals of the strategic plan.
  - Keeping it simple – in the early years relentlessly focusing on improving new product development and keeping close to their customers through new forms of account management.

- **Leaders at all levels in the organisation championed the change**

  - Critical numbers of staff engaged and empowered in cross-functional projects.
  - Significant investment leading and promoting a culture of entrepreneurship and innovation.

Notes

1 The subject of a *Troubleshooter* programme, a British reality television series produced and shown by the BBC, focusing on experienced business leaders visiting and advising small and often struggling UK businesses. Launched in 1990 with Sir John Harvey-Jones, formerly of ICI, the series ran successfully for five series.

2 We used the analogy of 'plooks' on the skin to illustrate the point – infections taking away energy from an otherwise healthy body. They can be unsightly and unpleasant, and some people devote much of their time to getting rid of them, but the plook has recently taken on two different meanings. The word plook typically refers to a spot or a pimple, and is thought to come from the Middle English 'plouke' or the German 'plock'. An affliction that has befallen teenagers from Scotland and beyond for many years, the dreaded plooks are exactly the sort of thing that people try to divert attention from and yet, at the same time, promote to show how getting rid of them would improve the overall health of the body.

3 'Strategy innovation and the quest for value', Gary Hamel, *MIT Sloan Management Review*, winter 1998.

4 Belbin/Myers Briggs.

5 '.ppt' is Microsoft PowerPoint® – the presentation software within Microsoft Office.

6 James Farnham was to join Taunton Cider as Marketing Director at the end of their first year as a PLC. He brought extensive experience from the fmcg industry as well as his consulting experience.

7   Strategic benchmarking

Introduction

Benchmarking, as a management tool, emerged in the exponential growth of strategic management tools in the 1990s. The pursuit of excellence was reflected in its definition that it related to 'above average performance in the industry in the long run'. To establish the position required competitor or comparator analysis. Benchmarking can be defined as a systematic process of continuously comparing and measuring an organisation's business processes against business leaders anywhere in the world, to gain information that will help the organisation take action to improve its performance. It grew out of commodity-based manufacturing striving to achieve low-cost manufacturer status. In increasingly service-based industries, as well as those manufacturing industries where product alone is not enough to gain long-term competitive advantage, benchmarking has taken on a more strategic role. Basic processes are superseded by strategic capabilities made up of assets, skills and systems, as well as processes.

In this chapter I give what I believe is a considered view of strategic benchmarking as a way in which organisations can develop sustainable competitive advantage. Later in the chapter I use examples of work where I supported Rolls-Royce Motor Cars prepare themselves for the sale to BMW/Audi, and how Mobil Plastics Europe benchmarked themselves not against the rest of the plastic film manufacturing industry but as an integral part of the food and drink industry.

In the beginning

Benchmarking certainly has its virtues. Comparing production time or the cost of a standard process with that of peer companies can yield important insights about your own efficiencies and, ultimately, your competitiveness. But benchmarking also has its limits. When you ignore the differentiated output that internal support or shared services groups provide, such straight-across cost or numeric comparisons become meaningless.

Benchmarking became popular several decades ago as part of the total quality management movement. An IBM executive defined it as the ongoing activity of comparing one's own process, product or service against the best-known similar activity, so that challenging but attainable goals can be set and a realistic course of action implemented to efficiently become and remain the best of the best.

In one dramatic benchmarking example, General Motors, in the early 1980s, learned that a Toyota assembly plant could change its stamping presses from one model to another in eight minutes, compared with the eight hours GM plants spent to change over the same basic equipment. Clearly a deviation of this magnitude between its current performance on a critical process and industry best practice served as a wake-up call for GM.

Benchmarking works well when the process being benchmarked is essentially the same at the multiple units (either internal or external) participating in the exercise. For example, it's useful to compare the cost of producing the same widget, taking the same kind of customer order, or processing the same type of pay cheque or benefit claim across multiple companies.

Benchmarking is less informative when it is used to compare fundamentally different processes or products. For example, knowing that a Mercedes-Benz 450SL costs more to produce than a Mazda Miata is not a meaningful, let alone actionable, comparison. Similarly, although the cost of serving a customer who is purchasing clothing from a Wal-Mart/ASDA store is likely to be far below the same cost for an Armani store, Armani would probably not benefit from studying the Wal-Mart/ASDA selling process. The value proposition offered by the two clothing retailers is so different that one cannot learn much from comparing the aggregate cost of servicing customers at the two companies.

Can support services be benchmarked?

With these simple examples in mind, we can explore the limits of benchmarking when used to assess the performance of human resources, information technology, finance, and other internal support or shared services groups. The strategy map for a support unit typically includes a financial objective to improve its efficiency in supplying services to the enterprise. This objective is usually measured by the cost of services provided and a comparison of actual costs versus authorised or budgeted amounts.

The headline numbers in surveys of HR, IT, finance and marketing functions indicate a range of expenses, typically measured by the cost of the support department as a percentage of total revenue or the number of full-time-equivalent (FTE) employees per billion dollars of revenue. A number of external organisations produce summary statistics of 'world-class' performance versus average departmental performance, using aggregate financial and personnel metrics. Marketing effectiveness can be measured through the cost relative to added value (margin) and the results of campaigns relative to spend.

Perhaps many HR, IT and finance departments do indeed strive to be low-cost suppliers of standardised services. But, if so, they are not likely to remain internal departments for very long. After all, an outsourcer of these services enjoys economies of scale that virtually no internal support unit can hope to match. An outsourcer can shift operations to the lowest-cost regions of the world, such as India or China, to supply standardised services at the most competitive rates. That is why support services find it 'mission impossible' to pursue low-cost strategies. There are just too many variables.

Differentiating support services

The question remains: how to evaluate the effectiveness of service units that offer different outputs? The cause-and-effect linkages in a service unit's strategy map and Balanced Scorecard will describe how the unit's investment in people, systems, and culture will drive improvement in processes that create specific tangible value for its internal customers, the business units. Ultimately, the effectiveness test is whether profit-oriented business unit leaders recognise this value.

Should the desire to benchmark remain, a service unit should seek counterparts at other companies that are following roughly the same strategy. They can check one another's strategy maps and scorecards to confirm that they are, in fact, attempting to offer similar services. Through site visits, the benchmarking companies can identify best practices within those processes to learn how to become more efficient and effective in them.

Although benchmarking can be beneficial, it has limitations. Be sure that when you subscribe to a benchmarking service, you limit your comparison to basic commoditised services. Do not expect to gauge what you spend on differentiating services by comparing your costs to entities that are not offering customised solutions. Spending on differentiated services is more like an investment than an expense – an investment meant to yield benefits that exceed its cost.

Strategic benchmarking

The two case studies that follow in this chapter, Mobil Plastics Europe and Rolls-Royce, concern market leaders in their respective industry sectors/ market niches – low density polypropylene packaging film and luxury motor cars. There is little point in Rolls-Royce benchmarking with Ford or Chrysler or indeed Mercedes or BMW. Mobil's films were complex laminated products manufactured to package and present confectionery in the best possible light while maintaining freshness on display.

The key question faced by both was not whether or not to benchmark, but with whom to compare and contrast themselves. Any benchmarking assignment or process should begin by establishing the optimum scope for the project. This meant:

- **Defining the benchmarks:**
  - Business?
  - Product?

     o   Process?
     o   Function?

- **Selecting the benchmark partners:**

     o   Own industry?
     o   Aligned industry?
     o   Aspirant industry?

- **Establishing the detail of the review:**

     o   Pilot first?
     o   One product line or process?

In practical terms, benchmarking means determining what operational processes to study, discovering the performance level of excellence in that process relative to your process performance, i.e., analysing your own processes and deciding how to make changes that will result in significant improvement rather than small marginal gains. The following questions arise:

- What should we benchmark?
- Who should we benchmark with?
- How do we perform the process?
- How do they perform the process?

Given that strategic benchmarking is more than assembling data or analytics, the choice of benchmarking partner is critical. In the same way, desk research alone is not sufficient. It will be useful to have a shortlist of potential strategic benchmarking partners. Short-listed candidates should be visited to establish if there is a cultural fit and a spirit of win:win that can underpin the initiative over a number of years. A benchmarking partnership is a relationship between two parties who associate in a collegiate relationship involving close cooperation to conduct benchmarking studies, under a protocol or code of conduct.

Here are questions that might be discussed at initial meetings, from the perspective of both you and the potential partner:

- What measure or measures will give us the best picture of reality in terms of what we want to know?
- Do we have the information or data needed for those measures?
- Is the information available in a measure that will meet our needs?
- Is the measure common enough among industry or business representatives that comparable measures can be found?
- How likely is it that another company will have comparable data?
- How likely is it that another company will give us the information?
- Would we give it to another company that may or may not be a direct competitor?

Instead of using a direct competitor or comparator from the same industry, it may be beneficial to widen the net to include:

- Type of business.
- Company culture.
- Organisational structure.
- Employee profile.
- Company demographics.
- Multinational representation.
- Product complexity.
- Product/process technology.
- Key financial performance indicators.

The benchmarking process will typically take a number of months to establish and will involve different groups of people from each partner. We have two clients who actually assemble businesses from along the supply chain of which they are part, e.g., premium quality packaging for retail confectionery products.

Typically joint project teams are established. Tools such as Belbin's Team Role Preference Indicator can be used to form teams working on processes. Each team, at their initial meeting, should work to a consistent framework, such as the one illustrated in Figure 7.1.

The following are examples of typical measures or KPIs:

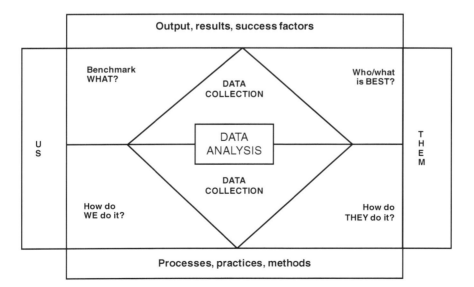

Figure 7.1 The benchmarking framework. Created by Alistair Gray (2018).

Benchmarking Measures

Finance	Earnings Quality	Return on sales (%NSV) Return on capital (ROCE) Cash flow (NPV of earnings)
Customer satisfaction	First pass yield Product quality/ performance	Yield Customer returns Completion/plan ratio
Cost	Material costs Added value Labour (direct) Indirect labour Overheads	Material cost % NSV Margin (sales – materials)% NSV Labour % NSV Cost % NSV or direct indirect %direct or % NSV
Internal operations	Business processes Support services Employee satisfaction	
Supplier performance	Inventory Delivery performance	Stock (days) % on time, cost
People	Team-working and employee involve Education	Measure e.g., 250 man years %NSV on training/education
Networks and alliances	No of licenses, JVs	

Figure 7.2 Benchmarking measures. Created by Alistair Gray (2018).

The partners may also be prepared to share their respective scoreboards. Potential criteria for partner selection might be along the lines of:

Benchmarking partner criteria
Type of business
Company culture
Organisation structure
Employee profile
Company demographics
Multi-national representation
Product complexity
Product/process technology
Financial performance indicators

Figure 7.3 Benchmarking partner criteria. Created by Alistair Gray (2018).

Strategic benchmarking in action

In the rest of this chapter I outline the strategic benchmarking approaches taken with two clients – Rolls-Royce Motor Cars and Mobil Plastics Europe. Both led their particular niche in global industries – one the ultimate luxury car market leader and the other the supplier of polypropylene packaging for chocolate bars.

1. Rolls-Royce Motor Cars

By 1980, British defence company Vickers had bought Rolls-Royce Motors Limited, producing Rolls-Royce alongside Bentley motor cars. The new Rolls-Royce Motor Cars Limited was floated on the London Stock Exchange in 1985.

In 1995 my colleague Kevin Parker and I had already carried out a major strategic review of Cosworth, the specialist engineering business famous for its work producing Formula One engines (in a joint venture with Ford Motor Company). I had also carried out a strategic review (with my colleague Margaret Dewhurst) of Vickers Pressings, the Newcastle-based business that provided specialist steel pressings for customers ranging from Vickers Tank and armoured vehicle businesses through to rear doors for Ford Transit vans. In addition, we had worked with the casting business in Worcester that produced engine blocks for performance vehicles. A major element in both cases was to change the mindset and culture of the senior teams, as well as crafting new directions for the mature businesses.

It was with surprise and delight that we received the news from Vickers CEO Chris Woodwark that he wished us to carry out a similar review of Rolls-Royce Motor Cars in advance of the proposed sale to BMW or Volkswagen, planned for 1999. It was even more pleasing to be uplifted from Manchester Airport by the company car – registration number RR2 – and delivered in style to the headquarters and main manufacturing plant in Crewe.

A manufacturing icon

Charles Rolls and Henry Royce established Rolls-Royce in the year 1906. At the time of inception, the company mainly specialised in manufacturing cars. However, that changed a few years later as the company designed and developed the first jet engine in 1914.

In order to ensure that there was no conflict in the different products that the company designs and manufactures, Rolls-Royce Motor Cars was set up as a different entity that only focused on the designing and production of cars, while the Rolls-Royce designed, developed, manufactured and serviced integrated power systems for use in the air, on land and at sea.

Strive for perfection in everything you do. Take the best that exists and make it better. When it doesn't exist, design it.

> Sir Henry Royce – one of the two founders of
> Rolls-Royce Motor Cars

Custom-built

The luxury car manufacturer had enjoyed considerable success, rising to a peak of sales of around 3,000 in the 1970s. Since then sales had been in decline and the manufacturing plant at Crewe had not been performing. Rolls-Royce separated itself as an automaker in that every single car is different from every other Rolls-Royce produced.

A fit with tanks? Not totally

The design and materials used make these cars outstanding examples of traditional British build quality. From the quality of the multi-layered paint, through the walnut facia and handstitched leather to the Spirit of Ecstasy that graces the bonnet, Rolls-Royce cars are a class apart. The customer handpicks every car, and Rolls-Royce even retire specific colour ways once they are used. Yes, that's right, no paint job is the same on any of their cars (even if it is just because it has an ounce more of gloss white). However, that is still not enough for a lot of people. Tuners have produced plenty of refreshed Ghosts and Phantoms, trying to show off their unique skill sets.

Any world-class manufacturing operation in the 1990s should be able to demonstrate real competitive advantage in three particular areas:

- Total Quality Management.
- Just-in-Time manufacturing.
- Computer Integrated Manufacturing.

We found Rolls-Royce to be failing in each of these three fundamental areas. In the late 1990s over 35% of new cars were recalled within three months of delivery to customers with a variety of faults. Many of the faults were electrical, which was hardly surprising given that the electrics were not electronic and mainly comprised wires, harnesses and switches rather than electronic sub-assemblies or panels. The quality of the legendary paintwork and Connolly leather interiors was high but the general engine build and associated parts (all made at Crewe) were the main source of defects.

In addition, planning was not a well-practised art and almost every promised delivery was not made on time. As for computer integrated manufacturing, this was almost completely absent and systems were also under-invested. All in all, this led to a manufacturing operation that was under-performing in almost every element of the process.

The dealer network was extensive and historic and frequently carried out by dealers with other franchises alongside Rolls-Royce. On enquiring why there were so many dealers, it was clear that the company was light on market and consumer research. Interestingly, from their own research, they had discovered that almost every owner of a Rolls-Royce operated an American Express account and also typically owned at least four other cars.

Benchmarking – far from strategic

Our job was to provide benchmarks to demonstrate Rolls-Royce had strategic capabilities that would persuade a future buyer of the sense and viability of the purchase. Initial interviews with management were held at which they endeavoured to assure us that they were genuinely world-class manufacturers of the world's most expensive motor cars.

Given the plentiful array of areas for investigation, it was clear that Rolls-Royce's strategic capabilities were built more on manufacturing tanks than luxury motor cars, and they lacked the assets, skills and systems required for a world-class manufacturer moving towards the new millennium. Their pricing structure was almost built on 'cost-plus', other than in Mulliner Park Ward, their specialist car subsidiary.

One of features initially stressed by Rolls-Royce management was the importance of their customers coming to Crewe and enjoying the 'Creweness' of the Rolls-Royce experience – unfortunately this often meant understanding how your 'about to be cherished' Rolls had the faults built in and the delivery date pushed back.

We asked the senior team who they benchmarked themselves against and the answer came back – Ford, Chrysler, Daimler Benz. When challenged, they stressed it was vital to perform as the best car manufacturing companies in order to keep costs of manufacturing low.

We agreed it was useful to compare not only performance but also practice – in other words, what do the different organisations do to enable that performance to be delivered? Applied in this way it should be a powerful tool in process innovation to provide clues for changing the way processes operate. Process benchmarking of this kind can operate at several levels:

- Between similar processes in the same factory or service branch.
- Between different factories or service branches.
- Between different competing organisations.
- Between different sectors using the same process.

While it offers a significant learning opportunity, benchmarking between competing organisations is harder than the other three because competitors do not want to disclose their process information since it is a source of competitive advantage to them.[1] So benchmarking of this kind often involves a third party who can collect the data, make the comparison and provide feedback but all on a confidential basis.

A good example of this was the Automobile Industry Benchmarking Study at the heart of a long-running programme organised by MIT with other academic partners around the world called 'The Future of the Automobile'. This programme was co-funded by most of the major auto industry players and explored a variety of aspects of the industry including product design and innovation, service delivery, retailing and supply chain management. Its results appeared in many books and articles and over a sustained period of time provided a powerful stimulus for change in the sector. The original project involved a systematic benchmarking study of 68 car assembly plants around the world using a standard structured framework to ensure direct comparisons were made. Researchers from the various university teams looked in detail at all aspects of productivity and compared performance factors like:

- Labour hours to produce a car.
- Number of defects per car.
- Inventory levels per car.
- Factory space utilisation, etc.

Their findings were significant and challenging for the industry.

> The Japanese plants require one-half the effort of the American luxury-car plants, half the effort of the best European plant, a quarter of the effort of the average European plant, and one-sixth the effort of the worst European luxury car producer. At the same time, the Japanese plant greatly exceeds the quality level of all plants except one in Europe – and this European plant required four times the effort of the Japanese plant to assemble a comparable product.[2]

This massive difference in performance provided a powerful incentive for the lower-performing firms to explore how the best plants were able to deliver these different productivity levels. Various studies began to focus on trying to understand the process innovations involved and gradually it became clear that the differences were not down to levels of automation or other physical investments but rather in the underlying organisation and management of production.

The successful plants had an integrated philosophy backed up by an extensive toolkit of approaches that focused on eliminating or reducing waste in all areas and activities. They achieved this through a mixture of team working and employee involvement in innovation. This focus on waste and its reduction led the researchers to think of the successful systems as being 'lean' – rather like an athlete who carries no extra weight or fat and is therefore able to perform better. The term stuck and became a label for an approach that has had enormous impact on process innovation around the world. Benchmarking remains an important tool within this framework and continues to provide the motivation for change in many sectors.

Relevant to Rolls-Royce?

Our challenge to Rolls-Royce was to question the relevance of this at the ultra-luxury end of the market. We asked them how much it cost to build a Rolls-Royce and the answer was around £130,000 with a sales price that might be between £250,000 and £1m.

Their specialist division Mulliner Park Ward made bespoke bodies in London for Rolls-Royce and Bentley motor cars. For example, they produced beach-buggies (Rolls-Royce modified cars) for the children of Middle East sheiks and armour-plated limousines for politicians, where the selling price could be in excess of £1m. To worry whether the average cost of manufacture was £110,000 or £150,000 would make little difference to profitability, especially within such a flexible pricing environment. Rolls-Royce customers are effectively immune from recession. Luxury brands, in general, have remained resilient through even the most recent recession. Luxury customers do not follow the traditional purchasing or operating behaviours of even premium car customers. For example, Rolls-Royce owners typically own at least four other cars, as well as yachts and other forms of transport.

We respectfully suggested that strategic benchmarking should pitch Rolls-Royce against the likes of Sunseeker yachts, Rolex watches, Shangri La hotels or other luxury brands, as well as the manufacturers of top quality cars, e.g., Maybach and Ferrari.

Forward to a new future – what we did together

After the initial feedback sessions we ran a number of workshops with the management of Rolls-Royce. Within a short period of time the executive carried out further benchmarking studies along the lines suggested, which revealed new data around:

- The ideal customer and their buying needs and processes.
- Effectiveness of the dealer network and the purchasing process from the customer's perspective.
- Definition of quality at the luxury end.
- Customer relationships – marketing, communication, service levels.
- The journey – the experience from purchase to delivery and after-sales service.
- Customer profitability.

This led to a revised pricing structure, new ways of assembling the cars and especially a radical review of how the cars were sold, customised, manufactured and delivered to clearly identifiable potential customers. This included addressing the three focus areas of world-class manufacturing: just-in-time/cell-based manufacturing, that brought in sub-assemblies and cable harnesses to replace spot welding; total quality management to replace the inspection processes; and new levels of planning and computer integrated manufacturing.

The Focus Framework prepared was an integral tool used to align resources and communicate the strategy to all stakeholders, including future purchasers, and staff who, for the first time in almost a century, were engaged in the process. It also provided the basis for the prospectus for sale. The scoreboard associated with the revised strategy and plan was one of the features that convinced BMW and Volkswagen to conclude the deal and enabled Vickers to make a good return on their investment.

Sale of the century

In 1998 Vickers decided to sell Rolls-Royce Motors. The most likely buyer was BMW, who already supplied engines and other components for Rolls-Royce and Bentley cars, but BMW's final offer of £340 million was beaten by Volkswagen's £430 million. Rolls-Royce Motor Cars Limited is now a wholly owned subsidiary of BMW, established in 1998 after BMW was licensed the rights to the Rolls-Royce brand name and logo from Rolls-Royce PLC and acquired the rights to the Spirit of Ecstasy and Rolls-Royce grill-shape trademarks from Volkswagen AG.

A stipulation in the ownership documents of Rolls-Royce dictated that Rolls-Royce plc, the aero-engine maker, would retain certain essential trademarks, including the Rolls-Royce name and logo, if the automotive division was sold. Although Vickers plc sold the vehicle designs, nameplates, administrative headquarters, production facilities, Spirit of Ecstasy and Rolls-Royce grill-shape trademarks to Volkswagen AG, Rolls-Royce plc chose to license the Rolls-Royce name and logo to BMW AG for £40 million, because Rolls-Royce plc had recently had joint business ventures with BMW.

The BMW contract to supply engines and components to Rolls-Royce Motors allowed BMW to cancel the contract with 12 months' notice. Volkswagen would be unable to re-engineer the Rolls-Royce and Bentley vehicles to use other engines within that time frame. With the Rolls-Royce brand identification marks split between the two companies, and Volkswagen's engine supply in jeopardy, the two companies entered into negotiations.

Volkswagen agreed to sell BMW the Spirit of Ecstasy and grill-shape trademarks and BMW agreed to continue supplying engines and components until 2003. Volkswagen continued to produce Rolls-Royce branded vehicles between 1998 and 2003, giving BMW time to build a new Rolls-Royce administrative headquarters and production facility on the Goodwood

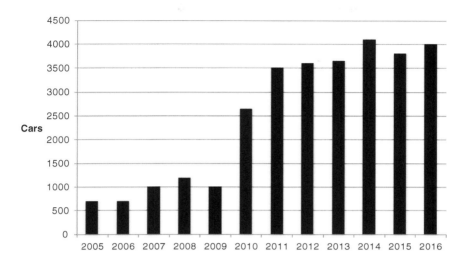

Figure 7.4 Rolls-Royce luxury car production. Chart created by Alistair Gray (2018).

Estate near Chichester, West Sussex, and to develop the Phantom, the first Rolls-Royce from the new company.

Rolls-Royce Motor Cars Limited became the exclusive manufacturer of Rolls-Royce-branded cars in 2003. Rolls-Royce opened a new technology and logistics centre close to the main headquarters in Bognor Regis. Mulliner Park Ward is now located at the former Rolls-Royce factory in Crewe.

The all-time-high record of sales was achieved in 2014, at 4,063 cars, beating 2013 sales by 433 cars. In 2011 Rolls-Royce Motor Cars Limited sold 3,538 cars, an increase of 31% compared with 2010, beating the previous sales record from 1978. In 2014 sales increased by 13% in the UK, 40% in Europe as a whole, 30% in the USA and 20% in the Middle East. Australian sales were up 75% in 2014 and Japan's rose 60% (Figure 7.4).

The most successful individual dealership was in Abu Dhabi in the United Arab Emirates. The USA is now the company's largest market, followed by mainland China, the United Arab Emirates, the UK and Saudi Arabia. Sales were boosted by strong orders for the newly developed Ghost Series II and the Wraith.

The change of ownership and established service excellence delivered by BMW will alter these features in the long term, just as much as the location right slap bang in the middle of their UK target market in Goodwood and exploiting the proximity to Heathrow airport.

A significant investment in the brand has been made by BMW, adding a new and special brand of luxury to the new range of Rolls-Royce motor cars.

That investment requires nothing other than to enhance and improve on the basis acquired at the time of sale and should ensure a successful future for the unique marque.

2. Mobil Plastics Europe

Mobil were the No. 1 supplier in Europe of plastic packing films to the food and drink industry. They recognised that this position was under continuous attack from the competition and wished to underpin recent performance.

They asked Genesis, in partnership with our partners Generics,[3] to assist the development of unique strategic capabilities to build, deploy and grow in the near future. Working closely with management, four core competencies were identified that would build on the established capabilities, as well as new ones to secure future market leadership.

Competencies are often confused with skills and personal capabilities. The Genesis approach identifies those organisational capabilities that are critical for future investment. The result has been a strengthening of their competitive position as industry leaders, as well as increased management focus. Turnover and margin gains have been a direct result of the project. In addition a unique model – 'The Committee' – was developed. Replicating the supply chain in which Mobil played a key role, representatives of key members of the supply chain met twice each year to compare their capabilities and build a more effective value chain.

Our approach

Our approach was to identify the strategic capabilities that existed in Mobil, then challenge them to agree those capabilities that would be required in order to deal with the highly dynamic environment they faced in the industry.

By strategic capabilities we meant the combination of assets, skills and systems that they brought to their manufacturing operations (Figure 7.5).

Following the research stage and interviews with key external and internal stakeholders, we established the Focus Framework for Mobil with the working group and the board (Figure 7.6).

The next stage was to identify the top-down strategic capabilities that would enable Mobil to dominate the market and consolidate their industry-leading position. Four strategic capabilities were identified (Figure 7.7).

- Market interfacing
    We have a strategic capability in offering our most important customers exclusivity in the creation of cost-effective, global, plastic films solutions.

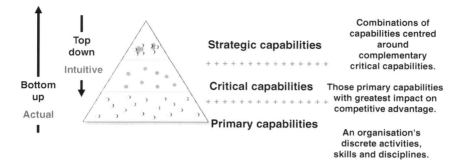

Strategic capabilities belong to the organsiation asa whole. They provide a
set of unifying principles for the development of all strategies.
They ensure these strategies have continuity, are robust and are flexible
to changing circumstances.

Figure 7.5 Levels of capability. Model created by Alistair Gray (1996).

- Technological (1)

  We have a strategic technical capability in managing innovation to develop environmentally responsive coating and orientation technologies for the future.
- Technological (2)

  We have a strategic technical capability in the manufacture of low-density homogeneous opaque film through the application of cavitation technology.
- Technological (3)

  We have a strategic technical capability in the formulation and high-efficiency processing of coatings for customised functional films applications.

The market interfacing strategic capability represented the basis on which the emotional response of the market is developed. The technological core competencies built the functionality on which this emotional response is based. Technological 2 and 3 are at the core of Mobil – they represent what the external 'world' recognises as being unique and central to Mobil's success. Technological 1 is what will sustain Mobil's ability to maintain the recognition as a technological leader and will enable Technological 2 and 3 to be protected and regenerated.

Following further development of the statements it was felt that Mobil needed to develop an additional capability. The status of Mobil as an

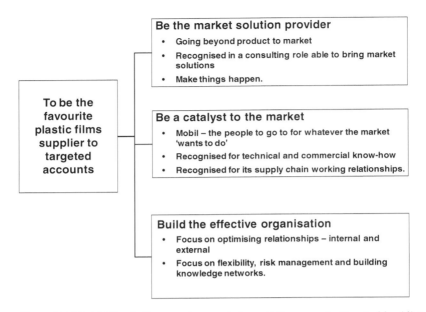

Figure 7.6 Mobil Plastic Europe: 'strategic intent' framework. Created by Alistair Gray and Dr Caroline Vance, Genesis Consulting (1996).

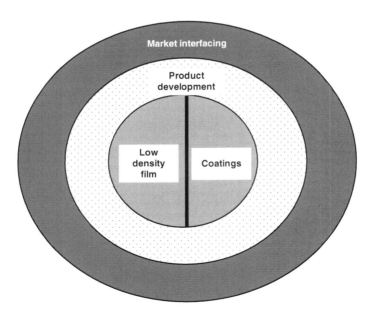

Figure 7.7 Mobil's unique signature: strategic capability model. Created by Alistair Gray and Dr Caroline Vance, Genesis Consulting (1996).

international company with different cultural and creative inputs from diverse sites with opportunity to form strategic rather than tactical supplier alliances was added as a fifth strategic capability.

Action planning

A profile of each strategic capability was detailed and the gaps between 'desired position' and 'where we are' established. The performance of each strategic capability was detailed in a customised database built specifically to provide an accessible inventory of insight into the capabilities within Mobil. This provided the foundations for taking the project into the stage of implementation.

The next key exercise in the project was to 'benchmark' or calibrate the capability performance using external sources. This was designed to stimulate and challenge thinking on whether Mobil had the appropriate components to represent capabilities. It gave them a gauge on the current status of their performance and provided insight as to what was required to develop towards 'world-class' performance. These findings fed into the next stage of the project that was to:

- 'Use' in strategy development.
- 'Build' to fill gaps.
- 'Deploy' in business development.
- 'Protect' by nourishment.

The Committee

One of the questions that provided additional insight was asking 'what industry are we in?' Mobil decided they were an integral part of the wider food and drink industry rather than packaging or plastic films.[4]

Mobil's supply chain was examined in detail and key members of the supply chain – up and down the chain – were identified. They included ingredient suppliers, sources of staff and, at the other end, packaging manufacturers, retailers and wholesale distributors.

Around 20 representatives of the chosen companies attended the first workshop, held on the shores of Lake Geneva. Mobil shared their strategic capability work and discussion took place on where cross-company projects might add to the strength of the capabilities, not only of Mobil but others as well. As a result, a number of projects were identified and were reviewed at subsequent meetings of The Committee.

The game changer framework below summarises where both organisations developed more strategic approaches to benchmarking than the traditional approach.

Rolls Royce

Exxon Mobil Chemicals

- **Where and how to break the rules; challenge existing paradigms**

    o Challenging the industry you are in, e.g., motor cars or luxury goods? Plastic film or food and drink?

- **Establish how to work it out – embraced the 'world class'**

    o Facing reality as it was, especially relative to world-class standards in the real world, not their own 'internal' world.
    o Developing together an exciting vision of success (in the Focus Framework) that was shared by all.

- **Planning for a step-change in performance**

    o The vision was simple, clear and inspiring, yet it was underpinned by a detailed plan, e.g., Mobil's strategic capability diagram that drove the change and aligned everything behind achieving the outcomes of the strategic goals.
    o Achieving 'breakout' performance through planning to achieve clear short-term goals that aligned a previously dysfunctional organisation and gave a plan, purpose and confidence to their people.

- **Changing organisational performance**

    o The Mobil Committee added a cross-company/sub-sector insight team to their cross-functional teams, adding a new dimension and innovation potential.
    o Everyone knew how their role would deliver the goals of the strategic plan. Giving responsibility for developing the strategic capabilities to promising young executives with a senior mentor or 'champion'.
    o Keeping it simple – in the early years relentlessly focusing on early wins, underpinned by evidence from the benchmarking process.

- **Leaders at all levels in the organisation championing the change**

    o Critical numbers of executives, staff and the workforce engaged and empowered in cross-functional project teams to build the new strategic capabilities.
    o Significant investment in leadership development, gained through project work and promoting a culture of entrepreneurship and innovation.

Notes

1 Interestingly, around that time Toyota invited many of the US manufacturers to visit their plants. They had no problem sharing their current process information. They were already well on the way to designing the processes to halve the cost of manufacture of future models.
2 *The Machine That Changed the World: The Story of Lean Production*, Daniel Roos, James P. Womack and Daniel T. Jones, Harper Perennial, November 1991.
3 I was supported by my colleagues Dr Caroline Vance and Dr David Coates of Generics. David subsequently became a director of Genesis.
4 Another example is Walker's Shortbread, one of the most profitable food manufacturers in the UK. Though they produce baked goods (especially shortbread), they see themselves as part of the gift industry as their attractive boxes are much sought after in travel and duty-free outlets, rather than on supermarket shelves.

8 *Braveheart 2*
Future lessons from yesterday's leaders

Introduction

In business education we regularly hear of the relevance of military strategy and tactics to the way we plan our businesses or organisations.

In times of unprecedented competition and uncertainty, within the ever-increasing pace of change, it is more and more relevant to consider how better to defeat our enemies or competitors, though the priority has always to be the way we reflect the love for our customers. Most organisations have to compete with apparently inferior resources against international competitors.[1] Tomorrow's markets and industries will be more and more global, and the success of businesses will depend on their vision and ability to achieve lasting competitive advantage. Many CEOs search for instant success formulae or tools off the shelf – often to no avail.

We need look no further – in the battle of Bannockburn in 1314 (and to a lesser extent Stirling Bridge in 1297) we have outstanding examples of excellent competitive strategy and successful execution. We can take the lessons directly into the battlefields of the corporate jungle. 'Now is the Time, Now is the Hour' was Bruce's exhortation to his troops. Do we, today, have leaders who share his vision and are prepared to follow his example with passion? The successful outcome at Bannockburn was determined not by the relative numbers on each side, but by the superior strategy, generalship and followership of Robert Bruce, King of Scots, over Edward II, King of England.

This chapter is based on one of the first articles I published in Genesis. It is followed by a case study on the spectacular success of The Famous Grouse brand, building sustainable competitive advantage over the mighty Diageo (formed in 1997) through a number of brave decisions to change the game and take it from being number one in Scotland to a position of global leadership in premium blended Scotch whisky.

Braveheart 2

Prelude

In William Wallace and Robert the Bruce (Image 8.1) Scotland provides two examples of outstanding leaders who somehow galvanised apparently inferior and inadequate resources to secure famous victories. They and their achievements contributed to the development of a culture that has

Image 8.1 Robert the Bruce. Source: National Trust for Scotland (2018).

spawned many leaders of successful enterprises across succeeding generations of Scots. A decade after the movie *Braveheart*,[2] based (loosely) on the
character of Wallace, scooped the major awards at the Oscar ceremony in
Hollywood, it is reasonable to reflect on his success as a grand strategist
and, in particular, on the achievement of his successor, Robert the Bruce,
who secured his place in history through the emotional victory over Edward
II at Bannockburn on 24 June 1314; on that hot sticky midsummer day.

Key success factors

On the face of it, Edward should have won easily (Figure 8.1):

- **Edward**: 17,000 archers and spearmen and 2,000 heavy cavalry.
- **Bruce**: 5,000 foot soldiers and spearmen, 500 light cavalry and 2,000
  reserves.

Day 1   Day 2

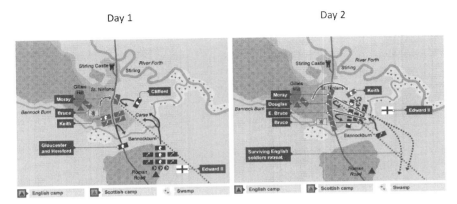

Figure 8.1 6 to 1 against: no chance – Battle of Bannockburn. Source: BBC
BiteSize.[3]

Bruce, on the other hand, had spent time meticulously planning a strong
defensive position, and through teamwork and a carefully thought-out formation of spearmen and cavalry was in a position to minimise the potential
impact of the superior numbers on the other side. Edward's troops were
tired after the long journey from England, but they were also complacent
about the outcome, having committed themselves to a frontal assault with
their heavy cavalry and superior numbers. Bruce's generals had spent
months in training and shared totally their objectives and a vision of what
might transpire. Edward's generals frequently argued about the best way
ahead in their council of war.

Choose where to fight and the basis of engagement

After a long hard journey, and on the day before the main battle, the
English went for a quick victory hoping that the result of an early skirmish
might dispirit the Scots. Poor planning forced Edward to go for the instant
direct approach and he was to pay the penalty. He chose the worst possible
position for the fight – where his strength, the heavy cavalry, could not
manoeuvre effectively. Realising his numerical superiority, he opted for the
frontal assault in a position that trapped him between the river and broken
ground. His strengths were thus rendered impotent.
    Bruce, on the other hand, had prepared well and planned his strategy.
Recognising his weaknesses, he minimised their impact by choosing his
ground carefully. Outright frontal assault by Bruce and his 7,500 troops
against the might of the English would have yielded one result – defeat for
the Scots. To secure the victory Bruce followed carefully the principles of
successful strategy development and execution.

Strategic principles

Direction: Bruce had a single and *clear objective* in mind – to prevent the relief of Stirling Castle. On the other hand, Edward became confused between storming the castle and inflicting a heavy defeat on the Scots. Bruce also seized the initiative early on with his risky but influential duel with Sir Henry de Bohun on the day before the battle. Bruce, unarmoured and mounted on a sturdy Scottish pony, was riding in front of his troops, encouraging them for the fight. Recognising the Scottish king, de Bohun charged him in full armour. Bruce skilfully avoided the charge and, rising high in his stirrups, cleft de Bohun's helmet and skull with his axe. What an inspiration and symbolic action this turned out to be, and what a devastating blow to the tired and weary English army.

Focus: Bruce's limited resources were concentrated, ensuring that his defence was secure. He had built his position, confident that the weeks of training had instilled in his troops discipline, commitment and values superior to those of the opposing army. He built on and exploited his strengths, which were defensive, by digging camouflaged pits and caltrops[4] to maim the mounted cavalry, just as Wallace had done years before. Bruce was careful to take a flexible approach, giving him a number of options should one fail. His shield-like formation gave strength to any attack and was readily transformed into hedgehogs of spearmen in defence. Edward, on the other hand, was committed to the success of the initial charge of heavy cavalry, a tactic that came to grief on Bruce's superior defence.

Leadership in action: there was no questioning the unity of leadership and shared values of the Scots. Bruce led from the front, not from the hill behind, and was a leader highly visible to his troops. His policies and strategies were well understood and deployed throughout the engagement. Edward's army had no such leadership. His council of war ended in bitter disagreement. Bruce ensured the battle was fought from a position of maximum security, created by careful planning, which forced the English to fight on a narrow front, just as Wallace had done at Stirling Bridge. By being innovative in tactics, he took the early initiative and made the enemy less able to interfere with the execution of his strategy. Through his innovative approach he ensured that his plan was full of surprises for Edward – from the careful positioning of his troops (schiltron formation) and cavalry traps (caltrops), to the deployment of the 'small folk' or supporters at the crisis of the battle. What a menacing horde they must have appeared to the English, as their King fled the battle to safety.

Overall, Bruce's strategy was excellent in its simplicity – simple to communicate to his leaders and their troops, and simple to implement after the success of the initial skirmishes and the fatal mistake made by the English in crossing the water at Bannockburn.

Indirect approach: Bruce's approach to planning for the battle was excellent, as was his decision to adopt a more indirect approach to securing a successful outcome. Success was assured through the quality of his planning and by:

Image 8.2 Leadership in action. Source: National Trust for Scotland (2018).

- Communicating his strategy to everyone involved and gaining their commitment.
- Symbolic actions to inspire his troops and convince them that victory was possible.
- Developing excellence, through recruitment of courageous people who would perform, and a concentrated training and discipline programme.
- Allowing innovative ideas to flourish and be implemented.
- The strength of the Scottish culture, and the shared values amongst a critical mass of the leadership.

The lessons for business

Frequently in business, well-conceived and designed strategies and plans fail to be implemented successfully, despite the elegance of their theory. Successful implementation is not about the headlong rush of the heavy cavalry, backed up by the resources of corporate planning or a cohort of consultants. We see many examples of 'armies' seeking to increase their percentage market share, in headlong attack, discounting obsolescent product ranges as their apparently major tactic for the battle of the supermarket lanes. Real profitable success is achieved through the careful deployment of resources, in strategically important areas, by people (and their coaches) armed with the necessary skills, capabilities and commitment.

As businesses, will we rise to the challenges thrown down by global markets in the years ahead, or continue to stagnate in the belief that the home market will sustain our future prosperity? Will we take the opportunities afforded to us by Brexit,[5] the growth in India, China, South America and further globalisation of markets, or complain about the influx of unfair competition? Will we continue to assume that today's products and services will satisfy tomorrow's customers, or will we embrace the commitment to excellence, innovation and learning necessary for market and industry leadership?

As business leaders, we are faced frequently with positions where the odds are stacked against us, and we have no divine right to survival, far less victory. We could all do worse than imitate the approaches used by William Wallace and Robert the Bruce on those memorable days 700 years ago. These lessons from the past are of relevance to our future. They are:

- Develop a competitive and compelling strategic direction and proposition based on sound principles that have stood the test of time.
- Avoid direct confrontation with the enemy, and seek positions of relative strength that can be defended.
- Deploy and promote real strengths in areas of opportunity provided by the external environment. Spend less time worrying over risks and weaknesses and avoiding every threat.
- Strive for excellence – better implementation results and higher performance levels than competitors in the long run – in strategically important areas, especially if market- or customer-focused.
- Develop innovation and learning skills within our organisations to improve continually and cope with change, rather than suppressing them.
- Build in our people, at all levels, leadership capability that is superior to that of our competitors, supported by shared values, commitment and motivation.

'Now is the Time, and Now is the Hour'[6]

The key challenge of the first 20 years of this millennium and beyond, for all corporate leaders, is to address their markets with courage, real ambition and vision. Wallace and Bruce proved themselves at Stirling Bridge and Bannockburn to be superb leaders of men as well as great generals. Meeting with Sir Tom Farmer, the entrepreneur who built Kwik Fit[7] as a leading brand, to discuss his contribution to the book (the Foreword), he endorsed the importance of the passionate following achieved by Bruce and Wallace as integral to their victory against the odds. They adhered to and followed closely all the principles of developing competitive strategy and assuring successful execution. Their handling, timing and deployment of limited resources were decisive and masterly. Their places as heroes are assured for all time.

Local hero – The Famous Grouse soars to global success

Background

The Highland Distilleries PLC[8] (renamed Highland Distillers PLC before being acquired by Edrington, their major shareholder, in 1999)[9] was one of the most significant independent Scotch whisky distillers, much sought after by many of the major international drinks companies. Matthew Gloag and Sons was the main trading business of the company and, in 1896, they had developed the Grouse brand as the principal product of the original family business 'to appeal to Victorian sporting gentlemen'.

What is The Famous Grouse?

The Famous Grouse is a premium quality blended Scotch. In 1973 Matthew Gloag shipped 180,000 cases globally, at the same time as Nike were founded and Sony launched the Walkman. By 1979 the business shipped 1.3m cases of which 17% was sold outside the UK. By 1996 Highland PLC had grown The Famous Grouse brand into Scotland's No. 1 blended Scotch whisky, with sales in excess of 1m cases each year in the UK and by 1989 sales approached 2m cases, with 27% to export markets. It was No. 2 behind Bells (Diageo) in the UK, a position that was to be reversed by 2000.

The global challenge

A successful joint venture had been formed with Rémy Cointréau to help stimulate sales in the US and a number of other export markets. The initial vision was to make The Famous Grouse globally famous by becoming a 5m-case brand by 2011. This venture increased export sales to 37% in over 100 countries, with Greece being the largest export market. This left the Far East and other emerging global markets, where the local economies were expanding at double-digit growth, as unconquered territory. It was estimated that the market for blended Scotch was growing fast in these markets and around £150m would be required to achieve good penetration levels in the main markets of the Far East (Figure 8.2).

The board was uncertain as to where the solution lay, as there were other demands for the investment. The decision was complex and required consideration of a number of scenarios to test where the next tranche of investment should be made and whether it should be behind the recently acquired Macallan[10] or The Famous Grouse, the principal cash-generating brand in the group's portfolio. Here was an opportunity to develop insight into the future, while Highland's executives plotted the global expansion for that 'famous' bird and its brand.

The scenarios

Strategies are normally based on a number of assumptions about the future. In many cases the board of a company determines the 'official

Image 8.3 Perfectly balanced: advertisement for The Famous Grouse. © The Edrington Group (2018).

future' on which strategies and plans should be developed. Frequently, not enough consideration is given to alternative futures and, more often than not, the official future does not come to pass. Scenarios are stories. They are works of art, rather than scientific analyses. The reliability of their content is less important than the types of conversations and decisions they spark. Scenario thinking is one of the most creative ways to develop strategy around a focal question articulating the strategic challenge. In Highland's case that question was 'Should Highland Distillers invest £150m in the emerging Asia Pacific markets for Scotch whisky over the next 10 years?'

mn. cases

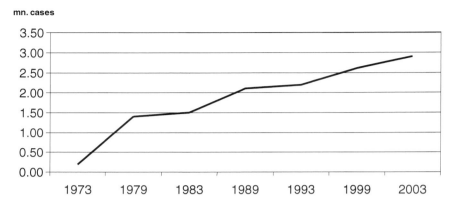

Figure 8.2 The Famous Grouse's first international flight. Chart created by Alistair Gray from Edrington Group data (2018).

Two major factors were important to the future strategy as well as representing big uncertainties:

1   The overall performance and continued high growth of the Far East economies.
2   The quality of distribution of spirits in the Far East, and where the power of distribution lay.

These factors or ones similar would be used to develop four alternative and divergent futures. In any scenario-thinking project the following questions need to be considered and tested in each of a number of divergent scenarios:

• What events would be going on? What would be the media headlines?
• Who would be winning or losing?
• What would be the implications for the industry? (In this case the spirits industry.)
• What would be the implications for Highland, and for other competitors (such as Diageo)?
• What would be the best possible outcome for Highland – the vision of success?
• What strategies would deliver that outcome?

Four divergent scenarios provided differing perspectives on the future. These could be summarised as follows (Figure 8.3):

1   **Deng's Children** – where the equivalent of the nouveau riche society of the West emerges in the Far East, reinforced by the one-child strategy, especially in China. This emerging generation aspires to emulate the best of the West. In general there is political stability and free trade is encouraged.

2   **Scotch Swatch** – here profits are challenging due to trade restrictions and protectionism by local distributors. Difficult for incoming brands to either develop or exploit the existing infrastructure. Low prices dominate and brand look-alikes are plentiful and available, other than in luxury segments.

3   **Into Africa** – as in Africa, profit opportunities are low and the ideal infrastructure does not develop. Major brands limit their investment in new markets in the region. Prices are low and low quality brands fill the basic fragmented distribution. Poor quality of demand with local spirits dominating.

4   **Apocalypse** – a relatively austere regime continues to dominate the region, in which China is increasingly influential. Austerity prevails, restricting the development of a new distribution network and incoming brands find it difficult to communicate with consumers who remain loyal to local brands. Anti-west sentiment continues.

In scenario thinking it is wrong to try and identify the best or optimum scenario. Each should be explored deeply and evenly, using the questions above. The scenario that is most likely to emerge will then be identified. In this case, Deng's Children appeared the most likely to develop over the following decade (by 2013).

The emerging strategy

The scenario-thinking project concluded that it would be too risky to focus penetration into the Asia Pacific region with The Famous Grouse as the flagship brand. The key considerations were as follows:

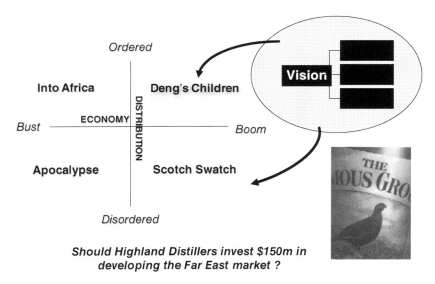

Figure 8.3 'The Famous Grouse Flies East'. Scenarios created by Alistair Gray at Global Business Network (1996).

- Premium malts would outperform blends as the Far East became more aspirational, with China and Japan in the lead.
- Singapore and Hong Kong represented two niche markets where Scotch presence was already established – at the premium end.
- Off-trade outlets such as cigar/spirit bars would be the focus for initial penetration rather than retail distribution.
- 5m millionaires in China represented a major premium market by 2000.
- The risk of counterfeit in malts is much less than in blends.

Soaring to success at the premium end of a declining market

The Highland board[11], armed with this insight, agreed to invest further in the emerging strategy, adding the Far East dimension to the overall strategy being developed for the brand by the executive team. This new global dimension was only a small part of the story behind the rise and rise of one of the world's most successful drinks brands.

The key ingredients of the strategy to penetrate the Far East markets were to:

- Work closely with a major partner in the region, e.g., building on their relationship with Suntory.
- Focus on the best mix of malts and blends aimed at the most attractive segments, e.g., whisky bars/clubs and top hotels and other locations – The Famous Grouse would effectively 'piggy-back' on the planned growth of The Macallan.
- Limited theme and scheme advertising and promotion.
- Premium price position – top quartile.
- Establish a strategic business unit in the region – Shanghai chosen, to move later to Singapore.

Shrinking global markets

For most of the late 1990s premium malt whiskies grew at three times the rate of premium blends (like The Famous Grouse). This factor reinforced the logic behind Highland's successful acquisition in 1996 of Macallan-Glenlivet to add to Highland Park, Tamdhu, Glenturret and Bunnahabhain, the remaining malt whiskies in the company.

The top five markets for premium blended Scotch were Spain, UK, France, USA and Greece. As can be seen from the chart in Figure 8.4, blended Scotch sales globally have been in decline for some time, especially in the UK. Why promote The Famous Grouse in this situation? Although the main global growth was in the single malt category, the *premium* blended Scotch segment of the market was still doing well. Brands such as Johnny Walker (Red, Black, Blue variants), along with Buchanan's, J&B, Cutty Sark and The Famous Grouse, still enjoyed premium positions, especially in global markets, and the segment, though delivering lower margins, was still attractive, particularly as part of a global spirits portfolio (Figure 8.5).

One of the most important features of Grouse's growth strategy was the choice of markets. A number of principles were established. The brand would:

- Not fight on all fronts – indeed there were only nine priority markets.
- Have a basket of low- to high-risk market options, i.e., emerging to mature.
- Set rigorous criteria for market priority, e.g., macroeconomics, drinks/ Scotch market size, growth trends and price points, concentration of distribution, cost of entry.
- Not be afraid to pull out.

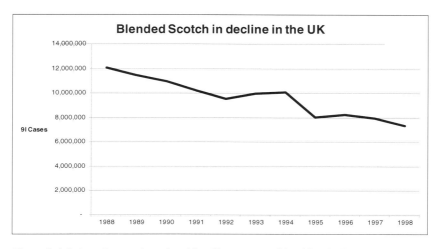

Figure 8.4 Swimming against the tide. Chart created by Alistair Gray from data provided by The Scotch Whisky Association/The Edrington Group.

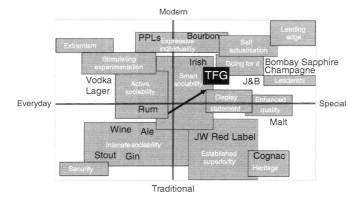

Figure 8.5 Consumer insight needs map. Model created by Ken Grier, Highland Distillers PLC from data provided by The Scotch Whisky Association/ The Edrington Group.

The global strategy was to concentrate sales in nine key growth markets. Sales grew to 3.5m cases (nearly £50m in sales) by 2011, short of the initial objective of 5m, but the growth in contribution ended up exceeding the original objective, so more than compensating for the shortfall in case sales. Importantly, exports now represented 52% of total case sales (from 22% in 1998). The Famous Grouse and its brand extensions now account for over 6% of the global market. Recent initiatives have seen significant growth in key markets, especially in the USA. Sales in the UK fell to 1.5m cases in 2015, but the market share of The Famous Grouse increased to maintain its No. 1 position (Figure 8.6). Export sales now accounted for more than 1.6m cases, of which the top ten markets delivered 1.1m. The lead markets are the US, the Netherlands, Nordic countries, Portugal, Greece, Russia, Germany and South Africa, representing a major shift from the dominance of Spain and Greece who between them had dominated export sales.

This focused sales strategy is a great example for other fmcg (fast moving consumer goods) companies aiming to develop export markets for their brands and product portfolios. In exporting the 80:20 principle works, i.e., 80% of sales tend to come from 20% of potential markets. Focus is key – both for people and resources.

Modernising the brand

A new marketing strategy was required to support the focused sales strategy. The original positioning 'to appeal to Victorian sporting gentlemen'

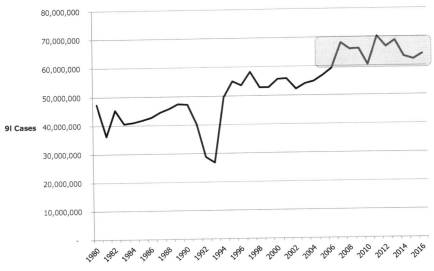

Figure 8.6 UK decline compensated elsewhere. Chart created by Alistair Gray from Scotch Whisky Association data.

clearly was not relevant to the post-millennium consumer, especially within a global strategy for Scotland's No. 1 blended Scotch. Research into consumers' changing needs showed clearly the direction of travel that was open to the Famous Grouse and produced examples of the changing consumer trends. The theme advertising would need to re-position a 'traditional' blended Scotch so that it more closely met the needs of modern consumers. The qualitative research established that The Famous Grouse had a good opportunity to achieve a position not open to other competing brands.

To modernise The Famous Grouse meant creating the ICON platform that focused on the grouse in various catchy situations. This provided the brand with instant recognition, creative excellence, and outstanding recall and, as a result, removed many barriers to its future growth. The advertising and promotional spend in 1994 was £1.3m each year, rising to £4.5m by 2002, a level that has been maintained since. The early television advertisements can be viewed at The Famous Grouse on TV on YouTube. Some of the early imagery used in the advertisements is illustrated in Image 8.4.

Global partners

In 1999, in advance of the acquisition by Edrington/William Grant, Highland had formed an innovative joint venture (MaxxiuM) with Rémy-Bols, Absolut Vodka and Jim Beam brands in response to the creation of Diageo as the super-industry leader. MaxxiuM[12] operated in 60 countries with 1,700 staff and a turnover then of €1.8bn, ranking three in global spirits worldwide. This opened up many new markets for The Famous Grouse, as well as substantially reducing the distribution cost/case.

In addition to market expansion the portfolio of products under The Famous Grouse brand increased, e.g., Famous Grouse Vintage Malt is on track to be in the top ten malt (not blended with grain whisky) whiskies in the world.

After the successful 'privatisation' of Highland, Edrington decided to launch their own business unit in the Far East, based in Shanghai, and focus penetration on The Macallan, their premium malt whisky. Market penetration was managed carefully over the next five years and resulted in the malt becoming the market leader in premium malts in the region. In 2007 The Famous Grouse was added to the portfolio through its brand extensions – The

Image 8.4 ICON advertisements for The Famous Grouse. © The Edrington Group (2018).

Famous Grouse Malt, 18-year-old blend and The Famous Grouse Gold – to compete directly and successfully with Johnny Walker (Diageo) through their own distribution network.

By 2003 The Famous Grouse was the No. 8 blended Scotch (in all categories) in the world and No. 1 in Scotland. From a single expression in 1990 the full Grouse range now included:

- The Famous Grouse 12yr, 18yr and 30yr blended Malt Scotch;
- The Famous Grouse 15yr, The Famous Grouse Gold Reserve 12yrs, The Famous Grouse Mellow Gold, The Famous Grouse Prestige, The Famous Grouse Smoky Black Scotch, The Famous Grouse Bourbon Cask Finish and The Famous Grouse Port Wood Cask Finish;
- The Black Grouse (with higher peated malt content) and The Snow Grouse.

In summary

The story of The Famous Grouse's success mirrors many of the strategic principles outlined in the *Braveheart 2* section earlier in this chapter. The very traditional way of positioning premium brands and marketing had been changed by one of the most traditional of all blended Scotch whisky brands. The Edrington/ Highland team believe their success was based on the following:

- **Consumer insight** – based on solid research and relationships throughout the supply chain (communication, direction).
- **Differentiated proposition** – breaking the mould of traditional marketing of Scotch whisky and the use of effective tools to promote the brand (innovation, surprise).
- **Geographic focus** – concentration on a limited number of priority markets (focus).
- **Market access** – innovative ways to secure a significant share (indirect approach).
- **Modus operandi** – the new way to take a traditional brand global (excellence).
- **Bravery, belief and flexibility** – change in culture (unity of leadership/ shared values).

True *Bravehearts* indeed!

Image 8.5 Welcome to Grouse Country: banner advertisement for The Famous Grouse. © The Edrington Group (2018).

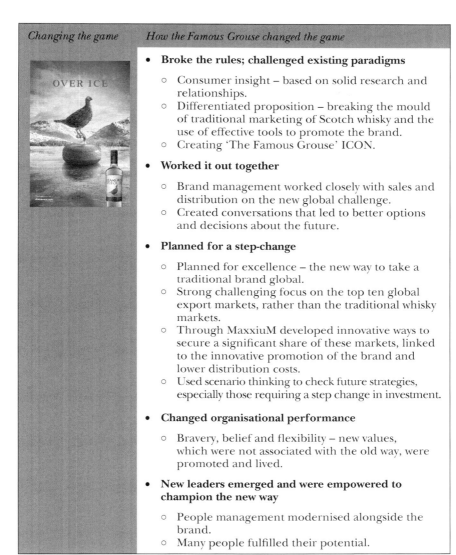

Changing the game	How the Famous Grouse changed the game

- **Broke the rules; challenged existing paradigms**

  - Consumer insight – based on solid research and relationships.
  - Differentiated proposition – breaking the mould of traditional marketing of Scotch whisky and the use of effective tools to promote the brand.
  - Creating 'The Famous Grouse' ICON.

- **Worked it out together**

  - Brand management worked closely with sales and distribution on the new global challenge.
  - Created conversations that led to better options and decisions about the future.

- **Planned for a step-change**

  - Planned for excellence – the new way to take a traditional brand global.
  - Strong challenging focus on the top ten global export markets, rather than the traditional whisky markets.
  - Through MaxxiuM developed innovative ways to secure a significant share of these markets, linked to the innovative promotion of the brand and lower distribution costs.
  - Used scenario thinking to check future strategies, especially those requiring a step change in investment.

- **Changed organisational performance**

  - Bravery, belief and flexibility – new values, which were not associated with the old way, were promoted and lived.

- **New leaders emerged and were empowered to champion the new way**

  - People management modernised alongside the brand.
  - Many people fulfilled their potential.

Image 8.6 Over Ice: advertisement for The Famous Grouse. Permission granted by The Edrington Group (2018).

Notes

1 Boston Consulting Group: Growth Share Matrix. The Boston Consulting Group 1973.
2 *Braveheart* is a 1995 American epic war film directed by and starring Mel Gibson. Gibson portrays William Wallace, a 13th-century Scottish warrior who led the Scots in the first war of Scottish independence against King Edward I of England.
3 BBC BiteSize – National 5 History www.bbc.co.uk/education/guides/z9hk7ty/revision/5.
4 Caltrops are spiked weapons used against men and horses since at least Roman times.
5 Brexit is a commonly used term for the United Kingdom's planned withdrawal from the European Union. Following the 2016 referendum vote to leave, the UK government triggered the withdrawal process on 29 March 2017, setting the date for the UK to leave by April 2019.
6 Quote attributed to King Robert the Bruce.
7 Kwik Fit was acquired by Sir Tom Farmer in 1970. Farmer opened the first Kwik Fit centre in Edinburgh in 1971. In 1973 the first centre was opened in the Netherlands and, with the acquisition of Speedy in France, the company operated over 600 centres in the UK and mainland Europe. In 1995, Kwik Fit Insurance, part of Kwik Fit Financial Services, was formed and has since grown to become one of the United Kingdom's leading car insurance distributors. In October 1999 Farmer sold the company to the Ford Motor Company for US $1.6bn.
8 Alistair Gray joined the board of The Highland Distilleries PLC in 1991 as a non-executive Director.
9 Edrington makes some of the world's best-loved Scotch whiskies. including The Macallan, The Famous Grouse, Cutty Sark, Highland Park and Glenrothes. The portfolio is complemented by Brugal, the leading golden rum in the Caribbean, and by Snow Leopard vodka. Edrington is owned by The Robertson Trust.
10 In 1996 Highland Distillers merged their 26% shareholding in Macallan-Glenlivet with the 25% holding owned by Japan's Suntory, who owned the Bowmore and Auchentoshan brands, to take control of the business.
11 Alistair Gray was a Director of Highland Distillers PLC from 1992–2000 and currently chairs the Edrington and Highland Pension Trustee boards.
12 MaxxiuM – formed with other independent spirits companies including Jim Bean brands, Finlandia and Rémy Cointréau.

9   Clusters are cool!

Introduction

Why do some social groups, economic institutions and nations advance and prosper? This subject has fascinated and consumed the attention of writers, universities, companies and governments for as long as there have been social, economic and political units. Many have tried to explain the questions posed by the progress of some entities and the decline of others.

For companies 'competitiveness' meant the ability to compete in world markets with a global strategy. To economists it often meant low unit costs of labour adjusted for exchange rates. Whatever the definition of competitiveness there is no generally accepted theory to explain it. Nor has there been a shortage of recommendations for improving it.

Michael Porter in The Competitive Advantage of Nations[1] *developed the argument that the national environment does play a central role in the competitive success of firms. With striking regularity firms from one or two nations achieve disproportionate worldwide success in a particular industry. Examples included Swiss watches, Scotch whisky, New Zealand dairy, Danish meat, Finnish paper-making and Italian fashion. After research into these successful industries it can be argued that in each case a cluster exists.*

Industry clusters are groups of similar and related firms in a defined geographic area that share common markets, technologies and worker skill needs, and which are often linked by buyer–seller relationships. The end result is the strategic capability for a critical number of firms to achieve and secure sustained competitive advantage over their peers.

Over my consulting career I have been privileged to lead and facilitate the development of cluster strategies in Scotland, Ireland, England, Finland and Australia, as well as developing key strategies for firms in food and drink (see the case study that follows), paper manufacture, Scotch whisky, technical textiles and performance sport.

In the chapter below I outline the key learning from this experience as well as outlining the main steps in developing a cluster-based strategy for the Scottish food and drink industry. This is perhaps one of the best examples where the industry leaders took ownership of the future growth strategy alongside other key stakeholders to change the game.

Clusters for competitive advantage

Most readers will be familiar with Michael Porter's work as it appears in the publication of *Competitive Strategy*[2] and *Competitive Advantage*.[3] Here he outlines his theories around five forces, generic strategies of firms and the strategic advantage that can be gained from development of a value chain. He argues that the competitive intensity of an industry is determined by the relative strength of the five competitive forces. The more competitively intense the industry, the lower the returns to the players in the industry.

Porter also argues that firms should decide where they compete in an industry and then choose between three generic strategies – either industry-wide or focused on a specific niche or segment (see Figure 9.1). In Chapter 2 we contest this theory, using NCR's strategy to dominate the ATM market as an example. The basic principles of Porter's theories are still valid in developing and evaluating strategic options, and in encouraging firms not to get stuck in the middle, halfway between true differentiation and low cost.

Firms create competitive advantage by conceiving or discovering new and better ways to compete in an industry and bringing them to market in what is ultimately an act of innovation. In Genesis we defined innovation as ideas implemented successfully.

The value chain – at the heart of cluster formation

Porter introduced the concept of the value chain to business management in *Competitive Advantage* (1985). Illustrated below in Figure 9.2, it enables executives to understand which elements of the business process add value and which elements are those that erode value.

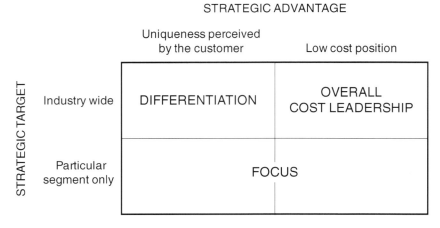

Figure 9.1 Three generic strategies. Source: Michael Porter, *Competitive Strategy*.

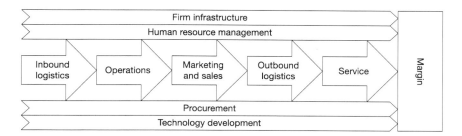

Figure 9.2 Value chain. Source: Michael Porter, *Competitive Advantage.*

In a more cooperative environment, firms can establish which aspects of their value chains can form the basis of cooperation or development through the industry cluster.

Vitality of innovation

Innovation is not invention or valuable for its own sake. Real innovation means bringing these ideas to market and delivering a commercial success. It results as much from organisational learning as from research and development efforts. The most typical causes of innovation that shift competitive advantage are:

* New technologies.
* New or shifting buyer needs.
* The emergence of a new industry sector.
* Changes in regulation.

The vitality of innovation in a location is shaped by national innovative capacity. National innovative capacity is a country's potential – as both a political and economic entity – to produce a stream of commercially relevant innovations. It is not simply the realised level of innovation but also reflects the fundamental conditions, investments and policy choices that create the environment for innovation in a particular location.

A framework was developed by MIT Sloan[4] to identify the sources of innovative capacity that enable a nation to innovate at the global frontier. Although the framework was created for application at the national level, managers can also use it to evaluate innovative capacity at the regional or local level. The framework includes three broad elements. Together, they capture how location shapes a company's ability to innovate at the global frontier.

What drives innovation in an industry cluster

Many things matter for competitiveness. Successful economic development is a process of successive upgrading in which the business environment improves to enable increasingly sophisticated ways of competing. This environment is embodied in four broad areas as captured in the diamond model (Figure 9.3).

Clusters offer potential advantages in perceiving both the need and the opportunity for innovation. Equally important, however, is the flexibility and capacity that clusters can provide to act rapidly to turn new ideas into reality. This is often derived from the quality of the linkages between various players in the cluster's value chain or system. A company within a cluster can often more rapidly source the new components, services, machinery and other elements necessary to implement innovations. Local suppliers and partners can and do get involved in the innovation process; the complementary relationships involved in innovating are more easily achieved among participants that are nearby. Reinforcing these advantages for innovation is the sheer pressure – competitive pressure, peer pressure, customer pressure and constant comparison – that is inherent within a cluster. We focus on clusters (e.g., information technology) rather than individual industries (e.g., printers), then, because of powerful spillovers and externalities across discrete industries that are vital to the rate of innovation.

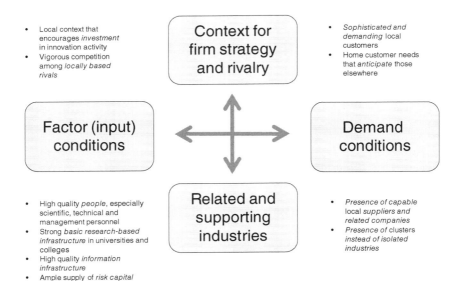

Figure 9.3 MIT Sloan: the diamond of competitiveness – what drives innovation in an industrial cluster. Figure created by Alistair Gray (2018).

The competitiveness of a cluster and its innovativeness depend on the quality of the 'diamond' in a country. For example, the Finnish pulp-and-paper cluster benefits from the twin advantages of pressures from demanding domestic consumers and intense local rivalry, and Finnish process-equipment manufacturers are world leaders, with companies such as Kamyr and Sunds leading the world in the commercialisation of innovative bleaching equipment, and Jacko Puryi who are specialist consultants to the sector. A strong innovation environment within national clusters is the foundation for global competitive advantage in many fields, from pharmaceuticals in the United States to semiconductor fabrication in Taiwan.

The quality and importance of linkages

The relationship between the common innovation infrastructure and a nation's industrial clusters is reciprocal: strong clusters feed the common infrastructure and also benefit from it. A variety of formal and informal organisations and networks – which we call 'institutions for collaboration' – can link the two areas.

A particularly important example is a nation's university system, which provides a bridge between technology and companies. Without strong linkages, upstream scientific and technical advances may diffuse to other countries more quickly than they can be exploited at home.

For example, although early elements of VCR technology were developed in the United States, it was three companies in the Japanese consumer electronics cluster that successfully commercialised this innovation on a global scale in the late 1970s. Of course, taking advantage of the national environment for innovation is far from automatic, and companies based in the same location will differ markedly in their success at innovation. Nevertheless, sharp differences in innovative output in different locations suggest that location exerts a strong influence.

Californian Wine Cluster

The California Wine Cluster comprises of wine-making and grape-producing companies in the form of networks. The various network firms involved are in the form of suppliers of grapes, irrigation and harvesting equipment, public construction and various advertising firms. The cluster also contains wine publications that are a source of promotions and information. Local institutions of California are also involved on a large scale.

The graphical representation of the California Wine Cluster is shown in Figure 9.4.

Apart from the disadvantages of facing competition within the cluster, the California Wine Cluster provides the following advantages:

- **Significant contractual relationships**: The buyers of grapes are usually the wine makers. The grapes market is usually an 'on the spot' market where buyers and sellers enter into on the spot transactions. But the California Wine Cluster provides a place for grape producers for an assured demand for grapes and a place for the wine makers where they can get an assured supply of grapes at predetermined quality standards.

- **Providing an additional source of revenue**: A vital segment of revenue comes from tourism in the California Wine Cluster that was evident from the data of the year 2005 where tourism generated revenue of $1.3 billion per annum and accounted for 15 million visitors. The main reason for tourists visiting the Wine Cluster is that numerous wine makers can be visited in a particular location, thus providing time and cost advantage to visitors.

- **Reduction in cost per transaction**: In the California Wine Cluster shipping cost accounts for $11 to $17 per case, whereas in other states the cost is comparatively high, ranging from $13 to $54 depending on the destination. In this way the cluster is providing advantage to California wine makers.

- **Intensive social networking**: Social networking platforms are provided by numerous networks, such as the Wine Institute, and the Napa Valley or the Sonoma Valley vintners associations. For example, an annual golf tournament is organised by the Napa Valley Economic Development Corporation. In 2005 it had the distinct punch line 'Networking in Napa', thus providing a promotional and relationship-building platform to cluster firms.

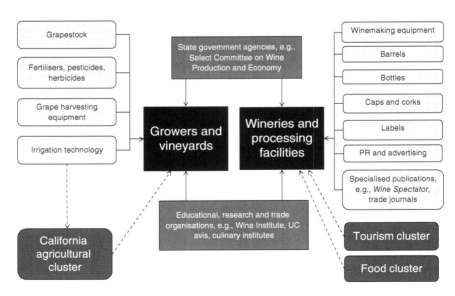

Figure 9.4 MIT Sloan: the California Wine Cluster. Figure created by Alistair Gray (2018).

The relative strength of the linkages is as important as the cluster elements themselves. They provide the basis to develop strategies that can strengthen the clusters. Cluster-based strategies are an excellent example of a relatively new management term – co-opetition – where companies who compete in the market place with their final products co-operate in other value-chain activities to secure competitive advantage for one another and the industry. Examples of this include the southwest chicken industry in the US and the Scotch whisky industry in Scotland. The latter encourages economies in the malting of barley that are shared between players, as well as supporting education and skill-based training at various universities and colleges.

The California Wine Cluster provides a simple and useful example of how clusters prove to be advantageous, outweighing the shortcomings.

The broader agenda

Building a foundation for competitive advantage requires a clear understanding of the role location plays in both innovation and competitiveness. Reduced communication costs and more open borders actually enhance the importance of location as traditional sources of advantages are 'competed away'. Managers can no longer simply manage the innovation process within their companies; they must also manage the process of how their companies enhance and take advantage of opportunities in the local environment. Indeed, long-term competitive advantage relies on being able to avoid imitation by competitors. Ironically, then, location-based advantages in innovation may prove more sustainable than simply implementing corporate good practice.

Scotland – land of food and drink

One of the best and most recent examples of cluster-based strategy is that developed and deployed in Scotland by the food and drink industry over the last two decades. Yet, in 1990, things could not have been further away from the outcome that has been delivered over the succeeding 20 years.

Early in my business career I secured a senior management position in the food industry with Unilever and Birds Eye Walls and was selected for Unilever's management development programme. Over three years this gave me the opportunity to work with fellow executives from different functions and nationalities on corporate issues, and especially introduced the young manufacturing executive to the much-admired marketing philosophy of the great fmcg corporate.

My first introduction to industry strategy was in 1985, when (as a consultant with Arthur Young) I was asked by Grampian Regional Council to review the performance and future prospects for the fish-processing industry in the northeast of Scotland. This was triggered by the Council's controversial funding of the sale and leaseback of Clipper Seafood's premises[5] following the firm's sale by Unigate and acquisition of Macfisheries to form Scotland's largest fish-processing company. The resultant review and strategy pointed the way forward for the industry. One of the key recommendations was for greater integration between the processing industry and the producer sector (representing the catchers). In many ways this and subsequent direct landings, bypassing ports and traditional fish markets, marked the beginning of a transformation in Scotland's food-processing sector and through that the reformation of food as a sector integrating processor and producer – be they farmers or fisherman.

By 2015 the Scottish food and drink industry had grown five-fold to become one of the foremost food-producing nations in the world, with the development – by the industry working together – of a cluster-based strategy at its core. I was privileged to work with the Leadership Group of Scotland Food & Drink over a ten-year period to create what has been an industry-transforming initiative. Here is their story.

In the beginning

Scottish Enterprise was formed in 1991 out of the Scottish Development Agency and, early on, a number of sector groups were formed, of which food was one of the most important. Farming, fish catching and other primary-producing sectors lay at the heart of the Scottish government's interventions in support of the food industry. The processing sector was generally ignored, other than as a source of SME (small and medium-sized enterprises) start-ups and employment statistics. Processors were formed in processor organisations and catchers/farmers in producing organisations or cooperatives.

Output and therefore value added was measured through landings of fish and animals processed without a £-sign in sight. Representations had been made to Scottish Enterprise by a number of leading processors for the agency to develop a strategy for the sectors. In the early 1990s Scottish processing firms were finding favour and therefore listings with major multiple grocers and significant value was being added to the basic 'landed' value of the raw ingredients. The industry contribution to Scotland's GDP was around £7bn (including £2.3bn of whisky sales). Exports totalled £0.5bn of non-whisky sales (exports of meat products were decimated post-1996 due to the BSE outbreak) and the industry employed 52,000 people (17% of the Scottish workforce).

In Genesis we had carried out significant work in the food industry from the introduction of plastic boxes to the fish-processing sector through to a nation-wide survey of the same industry for Seafish. The negative 'double-whammy' of BSE and Foot and Mouth disease (the latter in 2000) meant a turbulent and worrying time for the food sector in Scotland, even though there were no confirmed cases of either in the region. We had supported the red-meat industry from 1996 and in 1998 we were commissioned by

Scottish Enterprise to support a recently formed Industry Strategy Group, made up of representatives of the processing industry, to develop a cluster-based strategy for the food industry in Scotland.

Cluster-based strategy

Our approach to the first stage of the project was to review the large amounts of data collected by the agency and other stakeholders, which had the following features:

- 1-2-1 company visioning interviews.
- Global trends and opportunities for the industry.
- Mapping the cluster.
- Comparing the Scottish industry to other successful food clusters.

Following the synthesis of information and data,[6] we carried out a number of consultation workshops to develop the future direction.

At its simplest, a cluster-based approach takes a more holistic view of an industry, concluding that, in a rapidly changing and complex global economy, success for individual companies will increasingly rely on networks with (and the performance of) suppliers, customers, research institutes, education, utilities, and even competing companies. This provides an environment where information, ideas and solutions flow quickly and to best mutual advantage. Figure 9.5 indicates what was necessary for the industry to develop and move forward.

The industry Leadership Group was formed to review the findings under the chairmanship of David Kilshaw, a leading entrepreneur in the food

Drivers and dynamics   Four themes

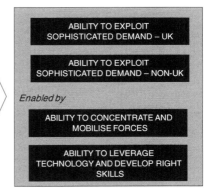

- Consumer is King and now truly international
- Instant food
- Food as a need becomes food as a want
- Tighter, fewer, bigger, faster, fitter
- People, people, people
- Comparing us to the best.

ABILITY TO EXPLOIT SOPHISTICATED DEMAND – UK

ABILITY TO EXPLOIT SOPHISTICATED DEMAND – NON-UK

Enabled by

ABILITY TO CONCENTRATE AND MOBILISE FORCES

ABILITY TO LEVERAGE TECHNOLOGY AND DEVELOP RIGHT SKILLS

Figure 9.5 Focus for the future: the themes for the cluster. Model created by Alistair Gray (2005).

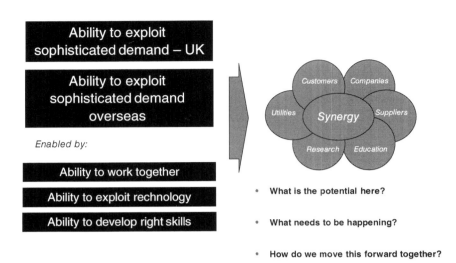

Figure 9.6 The way ahead: the cluster framework. Created by Alistair Gray (2005).

industry. He had led a management buy-out of one of Scotland's leading meat-processing firms from Grampian Country Foods, and had now started what was to become one of the UK's largest suppliers of sandwiches and snacks to the burgeoning lunchtime and food service markets. A group of 13 processors (later to be christened the Kinfauns13, after Kinfauns Castle – which became our spiritual home over the next four years working together) was established (Figure 9.6).

Working groups were set up to explore the potential synergy in a number of areas:

- Premium markets.
- Innovation and technology.
- Leading processors.
- Communications quality, safety and service.
- Developing people.
- Responsive infrastructure.

From the work of the groups four strategic themes emerged to develop future market opportunities and competitive advantage. These were:

- Excellence in raw materials.
- Healthy, natural and organic.
- Food service.
- Meal solutions.

Following discussion, the Leadership Group recommended the following focus for future strategy.

Our first priority

- Excellence in raw materials (red meat and seafood):
  - Premium market segments in key European markets.
  - Growing through healthy sustainable products (post organic).

Our next priority

- Value-added meal components:
  - Food service in key European markets.
  - Meal solutions in retail.
- E-business.

The focus for the cluster strategy was tightened, using an innovative tool that evaluated the various product categories against two basic criteria:

1 The most attractive markets for Scotland's food and drink.
2 The relative competitive advantage enjoyed by Scottish produce and processors.

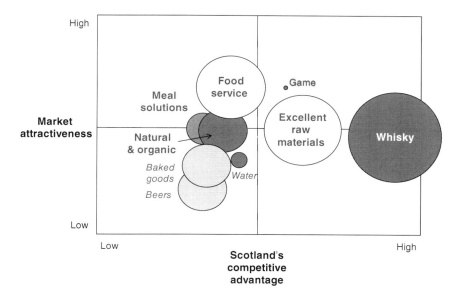

Figure 9.7 Focus for the strategy: the winning portfolio. Created by Alistair Gray (2005).

The resultant matrix (Figure 9.7) gave real focus for the development of the cluster strategy.

A number of strategic goals were set for the first four years of the development plan for the industry. The strategic goals were:

- To develop and grow leading suppliers and processors of food and drink.
- To build our reputation as suppliers to the premium sophisticated retail and food service markets of the UK and Europe.
- To grow advantage through innovation, including our exploitation and application of technology.
- To build an efficient and competitive supply chain.
- To develop the capabilities of our people, working together, active in local and global networks.
- To foster excellent communication between all stakeholders.

Mapping the cluster

One of the most important outputs from the initial work of the Leadership Group, supported by Genesis and Scottish Enterprise, was to develop real meaningful data about the cluster's performance and to map the various sectors and sub-sectors and the linkages between them. The original map of the cluster is illustrated in Figure 9.8. Note the weak sectors and linkages between key areas of the cluster.

Since 1999, a number of changes have been significant. A major review was undertaken in 2004 to establish if the focus and strategy for the development of the industry was relevant. Here are the key findings.

- The impact of BSE (1996) and Foot and Mouth (1999/2000) continued to adversely affect the competitive position of red-meat breeding, processing and marketing with dramatically reduced exports. The cost of compliance with revised regulations effectively ruled out most of the red-meat sector from meaningful export activity. In addition, abattoirs and rendering capacity and capability did little to add to Scotland's competitive position.
- Quality Meat Scotland (QMS) and similar schemes were having a positive but limited effect in the face of the negative impact of the two devastating events of the late 20th century. Scotland was yet to capitalise on the 'clean and natural' image possibilities.
- Agriculture was emerging from the crisis in better shape, with farmers facing up to the future reality (new CAP) and investing in a number of developing areas, e.g., prepared vegetables, fresh and specialist fruit. Fishing too had continued to suffer under increasingly tight quotas and decommissioning. The quality of a reduced fleet had improved and fish markets had declined in their importance in the value chain.
- On a more positive note, Grampian Country Foods continued to dominate the UK poultry sector and processors like Kettle Produce were now established suppliers of prepared vegetables and salads. Wiseman

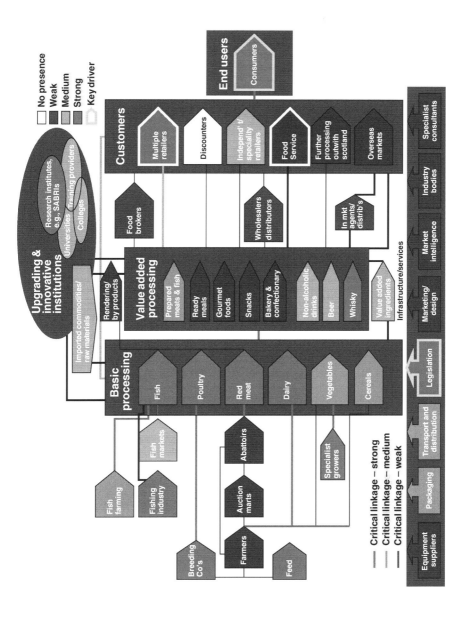

Figure 9.8 Scotland's Food and Drink Cluster: the cluster map. Created by Alistair Gray (2005).

also dominated milk distribution in the north of the UK and smaller players, e.g., Graham's Family Dairies were following their example. Scotland's position in snacks, prepared meals and meal solutions had strengthened and Baxter and Walkers continued to do well as leading brands, extending their ranges in key areas. Lightbody Cakes (the M&S Celebration Cake range) and Tunnocks represented rays of light in a segment that was being livened up by the major retailers.

- If anything, the strength of the upgrading and innovative organisations had weakened since 1999. The collective industry position had been strengthened by the development of food forums throughout Scotland.
- The location of the Food Standards Agency in Scotland should have a positive impact on the industry cluster with little change in the quality and capacity of the packaging, design and marketing agencies.
- There was still a feeling that the provision of capital to food and drink companies was risky.

Clear progress had been made as the recovery continued from the impact of BSE, Foot and Mouth disease, quotas and other constraining factors. The Leadership Group set its sights on 2010 and their vision of a successful cluster.

Priorities for the public sector

One of the main features of Scotland Food & Drink as it emerged was the level of empowerment afforded the industry Leadership Group by Scottish Enterprise and the rest of the public sector. It was quite incredible how this fledgling organisation brought together not only the industry and its various sectors but different public sector agencies as well. For example, in Scotland, Scottish Enterprise deals with most areas of economic development but Scottish Development International deals with inward investment and major export initiatives. A good example of the influence of Scotland Food & Drink was to establish priorities for public-sector investment in the industry, as Figure 9.9 indicates.

Post-2004 review

The implications for the industry were significant. The group realised that, to succeed further, they needed to consider their market as the newly enlarged Europe, not the UK, and not even the EU15 (the number of member countries in the European Union prior to the accession of ten candidate countries on 1 May 2004).

Marketing of Scottish product had to be demand driven (what the consumer wanted) not simply supplying what is produced. Scottish processors needed to be responsible for what they produced and how it was processed. Food service was fast becoming a growing opportunity outside retail and the industry had to embrace this trend. The strategy had to be integrated and

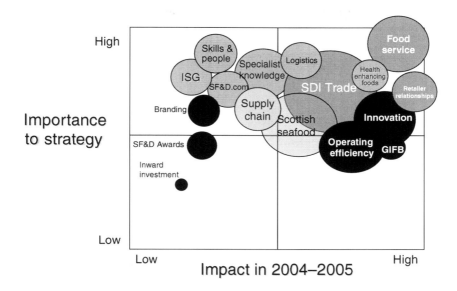

Figure 9.9 Scottish Enterprise/SDI new priorities. Chart created by Alistair Gray (2005).

flexible, and not risk-averse. There needed to be even closer integration with producers (farmers and catchers) and the drinks industry (including whisky). A number of challenges were identified.

- The industry had to be pan-European and global in its focus. This was especially true to secure sustained profitability and growth in fishing and fish products with an increased importance in the role of fish farming.
- Radical change and action in the red-meat industry was necessary to develop a Scottish brand that could be competitive in the premium sophisticated markets of the UK and, where possible, in Europe and elsewhere.
- The growth sectors of the meal solution, ready meals and food service segments required to be addressed, taking basic processors into the added-value segments of the food and drink markets.
- A step-change response and performance was required from the upgrading and innovative organisations in support of the industry. They would have to revise their strategies to align with the priorities for the industry. A similar change/performance was required in the infrastructure supporting the industry, e.g., specialist service providers.
- Implementation of the 'doubling value' recommendations contained in the review, embracing marketing and branding, new product development, along with world-class efficiency. These were specific targets to enable the step change in performance.

The Focus Framework – a first for cluster strategy

The Leadership Group warmed to the idea of building a framework to guide the execution of the next phase of development of the Scottish Food and Drink Cluster. The Focus Framework provided the ideal tool to display and communicate the strategy to key stakeholders and integrated with leading plans behind a number of strategic goals. The framework is illustrated in Figure 9.10.

Integrating farming and drinks with food

After the 2004 review by the Leadership Group, considerable efforts were made to bring the producer sector to the table. The key tipping point came, interestingly enough, at an Industry Strategy Group meeting at the home of the Scottish Malt Whisky Association in Edinburgh. There was a realisation that by working together towards increasing the GDP (output) of the whole industry this would benefit both producers and processors. By openly discussing the reality of their respective performances there was much common ground and the producer representatives gained much and contributed much to the working groups.

The Scotch whisky industry is perhaps one of the best examples of an effective industry cluster. What possible advantage might there be for them to cooperate with the rest of the food and drink industry? After a number of exploratory discussions a number of areas for initial collaboration included:

- Skills and learning.
- Quality.
- Innovation.
- Environmental and other areas of legislation.
- Health and safety.

A Food and Drinks 'Cabinet' was established with leading players and there was joint activity at the Scottish Food and Drink conference in 2003.

The spirits industry is now well integrated with Scotland Food & Drink and the growing craft-beer industry, e.g., BrewDog and Innis & Gunn, is also making its presence felt as the industry develops. Scotland Food & Drink had become established as a company with a board of directors. Directors were appointed from the industry sectors and, in addition, Scottish Enterprise and the Scottish Government were represented on the board. The latter was a key intervention and change from previous government policy to remain remote and detached from industry initiatives.

Our challenge, together

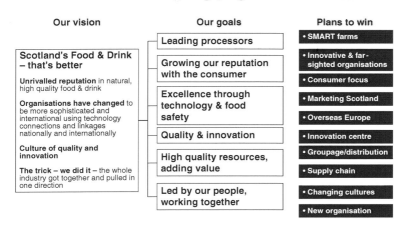

Our vision	Our goals	Plans to win
Scotland's Food & Drink – that's better **Unrivalled reputation** in natural, high quality food & drink **Organisations have changed** to be more sophisticated and international using technology connections and linkages nationally and internationally **Culture of quality and innovation** **The trick – we did it –** the whole industry got together and pulled in one direction	**Leading processors** **Growing our reputation with the consumer** **Excellence through technology & food safety** **Quality & innovation** **High quality resources, adding value** **Led by our people, working together**	• SMART farms • Innovative & far-sighted organisations • Consumer focus • Marketing Scotland • Overseas Europe • Innovation centre • Groupage/distribution • Supply chain • Changing cultures • New organisation

Figure 9.10 The Focus Framework. Created by Alistair Gray (2007).

Image 9.1 Scotland's leading industry. Source: Scotland Food & Drink.

Towards 2017

At the 2012 Review a new business plan was established for Scotland Food & Drink. The next four years saw considerable progress towards achieving the original objectives of the cluster strategy. An industry that in 2000 was fragmented, fractious and dominated by noisy farmers and catchers riding roughshod over weak uncoordinated processing companies in a fragile sector, had been transformed. In the early days the food and drink industry had few linkages and many committees. The public sector was continually under pressure.

Stretching objectives were set for 2017 and, as we write this, the industry is on track to delivery double the performance in 2019.

In 2016 the top ten facts about the industry's performance (as published by Scotland Food & Drink) make impressive reading.

- The food and drink industry is worth £13.9bn to Scotland's economy, on track to the 2017 objective.
- 360,000 people are employed in the industry.
- Exports are worth £5.1bn to the Scottish economy, on track to deliver their 2017 objective of £7.1bn.
- Scottish food is exported to 100 countries.
- £600m of salmon and seafood is exported each year.
- 517m bottles of Scotch whisky were exported in the first half of 2015.

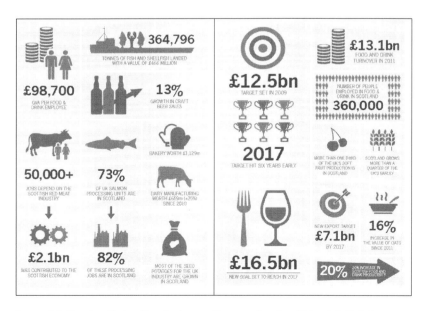

Image 9.2 Scotland's leading industry. Source: Scotland Food & Drink.

There was also huge endorsement for Scotland Food & Drink as an organisation from the members of the industry. This was mainly because there was the opportunity to take control of its own destiny. There were attractive features of the proposed structure to government. They were impressed with the longevity, commitment and continuity provided by the Leadership Group working in public/private partnership with Scottish Government involvement.

In particular, there was strong engagement of firms on the Leadership Group and growing engagement with the firm base outside the membership of the wider strategy group. In a short space of time there had been tangible achievements (notably the food skills group, retail account management, Scotland Food & Drink). Importantly there was a sense of reinvigoration, growing momentum and success in an industry sector that had felt disgruntled and disenfranchised.

Scotland Food & Drink is now established as a business that has taken on the task of delivering a step change in performance of one of Scotland's most important industry sectors. In its empowerment from government it is quite unique and has provided a model for the development of other industry clusters. Energy and Creative Industries have followed their example.

Scotland's food and drink industry is led by a membership organisation whose mission is to drive sustainable business growth for the industry as a whole, and to provide competitive edge for its members. It facilitates the

Image 9.3 Support network. Source: Scotland Food & Drink.

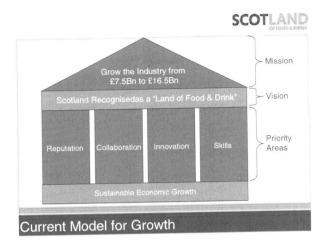

Image 9.4 Developing the organisation. Source: Scotland Food & Drink.

whole industry coming together, from farm to fork, to work more effectively. It has ambitious, long-term objectives, while being in tune with current business needs. The Executive Group is drawn from the membership of a number of organisations and their strategy is clear (see Images 9.3 and 9.4).

Genesis' role in support of the industry

Over ten years from 1998, our role was to facilitate and deliver a project where the overall purpose was to turn the Scottish food and drink industry vision into actions, delivering real impact on performance; to create a new leadership organisation, Scotland Food & Drink, led by industry and supported by the public sector and other stakeholders. In addition, we were charged with designing the optimum organisation for the body to lead the development of the Scottish food and drink industry in Scotland and to prepare the business plan for the organisation to 2013.

What we did

We assured full engagement with the industry Leadership Group, made up of senior executives from Scottish Government and major companies – processors, representatives of the agriculture industry, research institutions, other trade associations and Scottish Enterprise. We also facilitated engagement with a wider stakeholder group for the purposes of industry consultation. We designed and led the process to determine the optimum organisation over a period of 12 months, including hosting eight events during this period.

Two Genesis directors, supported by Genesis staff and other specialists, supported the Leadership Group. The process was designed to ensure there was full engagement and, through a number of one-to-one meetings with Group members, areas of agreement were identified and differences resolved.

We provided a number of additional services to assist Scottish Enterprise, in particular to prepare the justification behind the business plan for Scotland Food & Drink. These included work to establish the economic impact of the industry and a revenue generation model for the new company. We also sourced information on comparator organisations worldwide, e.g., Australia, Denmark and New Zealand.

How did we manage this project to achieve a successful outcome for the client?

We prepared an overall process approach, following one-to-one interviews with a number of the Leadership Group, and agreed the required milestones and key outcomes. At the end of each event we debriefed the session, confirming areas of agreement and issues to be resolved. We prepared the Group for each event, issuing briefing papers in advance and quickly providing a paper summarising key agreements and actions after each event. We also reviewed progress with Scottish Enterprise after each event, noting progress against milestones and performance against budget and timescale.

What were the outputs of this project?

The organisation for Scotland Food & Drink was agreed and endorsed by all stakeholders. This included roles of directors and senior executives and the make up of the board and other forums to support the company.

Contribution levels from the public sector and other organisations to provide the start-up capital for the company were included in the revenue model for income generation for Scotland Food & Drink.

A business plan for Scotland Food & Drink from 2008–2012 was prepared like a prospectus for investment, with key chapters:

- Background.
- Prospectus for the new leadership organisation.
- Making a difference.
- Organisation and structure.
- Sources of funds and financial model.
- Various supplementary papers, e.g., economic analysis, comparator reviews, income generation for Scotland Food & Drink.

What were the outcomes of this project?

The company was formed within the planned timescale and the initial funding commitments met by the public sector. Key decisions were taken as to the strategic priorities for the industry over the next four years. The organisation was a public/private sector partnership, with core funding from industry and the different stakeholders. From the start there were to be substantial contributions from industry, the public sector, levy organisations and trade associations. Contributions from the private sector increased as the organisation developed. Over time, revenue was generated from other sectors (e.g., financial institutions) and from delivering projects.

The Scottish food and drink industry, one of the most important to the Scottish economy, is definitely led by the industry with strategic goals in line with the government's agenda. There is now a plan in place to particularly increase GVA (Gross Value Added) and exports along with three major strategic projects to change attitudes and behaviour in the industry's organisations. Scottish Enterprise was able to transfer a number of its functions to the new organisation.

In 2017 Ambition 2030 was launched. These are exciting times for the industry and Scotland Food & Drink (the organisation) moves from strength

Image 9.5 Ambition 2030. Source: Scotland Food & Drink.

to strength. Earlier in 2017 the First Minister announced an innovative government/industry partnership funding agreement where Scotland Food & Drink's private and membership income would be trebled with government funds to create a £10m fund to support the industry leadership and development work through 2020.

Food and drink has become a star of the Scottish economy (44% rise in turnover, 56% rise in food and drink exports, 110% rise in food-only exports and a 71% rise in R&D investment).

Many opportunities and challenges are still in front of the industry, especially with the uncertainty of Brexit, hence the need to aspire to even greater heights and to further deepen the collaborative activities, as outlined in Ambition 2030,[7] the new strategic plan.

And finally

When I was first involved in the food and drink industry the sector was relatively static. It would be wrong and inappropriate to conclude this case study reflecting only on our engagement with the project without paying tribute to the leaders of the industry, Scottish Enterprise, the Scottish Government and other organisations involved in the creation and development of Scotland Food & Drink. Their collective foresight and commitment has ensured Scotland Food & Drink and all our partners have worked collectively to make a huge difference.

They truly changed the game of Scotland's most important industry. They are all true 'Bravehearts'.

SCOTLAND OF FOOD & DRINK

- **Broke the rules; challenged existing paradigms**

  - The traditional approach of government departments and agencies towards industry sectors was consigned to history.
  - Scottish Enterprise and their colleagues empowered the Industry Leadership Group to take on many of their roles.
  - A new not-for-profit organisation was set up to take collective leadership of the industry.
  - For the first time, farming and fishing came together with their processing colleagues, and eventually with the whisky industry, to lead the way.
  - Volunteers queued up to join the Leadership Group.

- **They worked it out themselves**

  - The Leadership Group developed into a formidable vehicle to take the industry to new levels of performance.
  - The supporting process, well designed and facilitated, was important. Previous meetings had been complaint sessions with the public sector in the processors' firing line.
  - The Leadership Group took responsibility for the performance of the industry and provided resources for the work of the Group.

- **Planned for a step-change in performance**

  - The development of a vision for success with which everyone agreed was critical.
  - It enabled big ambitious goals to be set, planned for and progress reviewed on a regular basis.
  - Scotland Food & Drink was responsible to its shareholders and stakeholders, held business-like meetings and produced an annual report demonstrating their accountability.

- **Changed organisational performance**

  - Engaged the whole industry in the development of the business, offering the opportunity to be shareholders.

- **Development of leadership and the workforce**

  - Skills development was at the heart of the industry's improved performance.
  - The Leadership Group and Scottish Enterprise, providing possible future leadership capacity, championed leadership development.

Image 9.6 Scotland Food & Drink logo. Source: Scotland Food & Drink.

Notes

1 *The Competitive Advantage of Nations*, Michael E. Porter, Free Press, 2005.
2 *Competitive Strategy*, Michael E. Porter, Free Press, 2004.
3 *Competitive Advantage*, Michael E. Porter, Free Press, 1998.
4 'Innovation: Location Matters', Michael Porter and Scott Stern, *MIT Sloan Management Review*, 15 July 2001.
5 Grampian Regional Council acquired Clipper's premises in Aberdeen for £0.9m. The local processing industry was up in arms at this apparently specialist treatment of one of the largest firms in the sector.
6 Largely carried out by my colleagues Caroline Vance and Margaret Dewhurst.
7 Ambition 2030 – the latest strategy for the company and its Leadership Group.

10 Making mergers work

Mixing spirits

Introduction

In this chapter I have drawn from 2012 research from MIT Sloan[1] *in Boston to gain insight into how mergers and acquisitions succeed, or fail. The harsh reality is that a majority of mergers, alliances and acquisitions are demerged or sold within five years of the original deal. According to collated research and a recent* Harvard Business Review *report, the failure rate for mergers and acquisitions sits between 70–90%.*

Executives too often overlook the vital question of identity when seeking synergies from mergers and acquisitions. Respective identities and egos all too often get in the way of making a success of the merger or alliance. During my early business career I was fortunate to be involved with a number of strategic initiatives with the John Wood Group PLC (UK/US) and, in my consulting work, especially with Low & Bonar PLC (UK), UPM Kymmene (Finland) and Royal Neverdahl Ten Cate (Netherlands).

The case study in this chapter focuses on the merger of Rémy Cointréau and Bols, the international drinks companies. Genesis facilitated the early stages of the post-merger integration and it provides another example of the success and failure factors to be considered when trying to change the game in an industry sector.

Making mergers work

1+1>3?

Mergers or alliances (M&As) are often proposed on the basis of the certainty of the synergy potential. Synergy can be defined with the algorithm '1+1>3'. Unfortunately this outcome is hardly ever achieved.

It illustrates why we need a new merger/alliance algorithm. For 1 plus 1 to make more than 3 at the economic level, 1 plus 1 must make at least 1 at the psychological level. When M&As fail to deliver promised levels of performance, as frequently occurs, it is likely due, at least in part, to a lack of psychological and personality synergies. Psychologically, the new entity is often a house divided. The goal of a merger is to have the component parts add up to more than what they are worth individually. The MIT research and extensive work in this field has convinced me that this will only happen if you are able to merge the two companies into one on a psychological level. The challenge lies in the implementation of a simple idea: *people can-not achieve better results if they do not come together as one entity and pull in the same direction.*

This may sound simple, but identity integration is often overlooked as the merger unfolds. Planning for post-merger integration typically focuses on operational issues such as harmonising product lines and financial and human resource information systems, or determining which employees are retained and which ones are let go.

Attention is also paid to the identity of the merged enterprise in a superficial sense. The name of the acquirer may be retained, a new logo created, or new name found. For the psychological synergy principle to operate, though, executives need to attend to a more complex and deeper set of identity issues; those that define the essence of the entity and give employees a clear answer to the question 'Who are we?' and give exter-nal stakeholders a clear answer to the question 'Who are they?' The first question refers to members' view of what makes that organisation unique among others. The second question captures what external audiences believe is the essence of the organisation. Left unattended, these deeper identity issues will diminish engagement and will inevitably affect the per-formance of the merged entity.

Operational integration post-merger is a necessary but not sufficient con-dition for successful performance. Careful attention to identity integration is also essential for success. Lack of attention to identity issues was largely responsible for the persistent performance problems encountered by many

There are four paths that managers can follow to achieve identity integration in a merger or acquisition: assimilation, federation, confederation and metamorphosis. Each path addresses two crucial questions: what should be done with the parties' historical identities, and how a common identity for the future should be built.

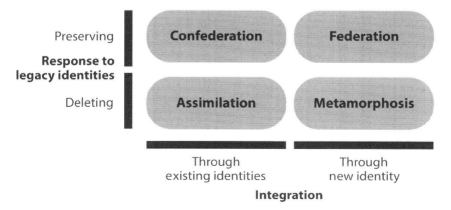

Figure 10.1 Four approaches to identity integration. Adapted from *MIT Sloan Management Review* (2012).

mergers. It is amazing how much time and money companies spend on this problem after the fact, when they could have eliminated it with a little pre-merger planning. There is no 'one best way'. Rather, consider four distinct paths to follow and achieve identity integration: assimilation, federation, confederation and metamorphosis.

Each of these paths represents a particular combination of the answers to two questions that managers must confront in anticipation of a merger or acquisition:

1   What should be done with the identities that the parties to the merger bring with them (their historical identities)?
2   And how should a common identity for the future be built?

Specifically, managers must answer these questions:

- Can we, or do we want to, preserve the identities of each party in the merger, or do we need or want to delete some of them?
- Do we pursue a common future through the creation of a new organisational identity, or should we integrate through legacy identities?

Assimilation

Assimilation occurs when the identity of an acquired company is deliberately dissolved into the identity of the new parent. The acquired company is stripped of its name and visual identity (logo, letterhead and so on) and adopts those of its new parent. The acquired company's management structure is dismantled, and employees who are not let go are distributed across the parent's organisational units. The process sends a clear signal to the members of the acquired company that they are expected to adjust and be loyal to their new employer. It also sends a clear signal to the company's external stakeholders that they will henceforth deal with a new organisation.

Although this description of the process might sound brutal, the members and other stakeholders of the acquired company do not necessarily experience it that way. The reactions of employees and other stakeholders depend on the depth of their psychological commitment to the dissolved identity and on the perceived desirability and superiority of the identity of the new parent. For example, when a small technology company is bought by Cisco (for example), its founders, employees, investors and customers are likely to see the acquisition as a positive event on the whole and not to see the trading of its identity for that of Cisco as a serious loss. Because becoming a Cisco employee has many benefits, members of the acquired organisation have little reason to mourn their defunct identity.

Assimilation is less effective when the merged organisations are perceived as equals or when the identity of the buyer is less valued than that of the acquired firm. When the new parent and its acquisition target are comparable in size, profitability or reputation, members and stakeholders of the acquired company may feel that their organisation's identity is at least as valuable as that of the new parent and may bristle at losing it. The problem is compounded when the acquired company has doubts about its new parent. For example, European and Japanese companies have had difficulty with the integration of their acquired subsidiaries in the United States when the US managers did not think highly of the management skills and effectiveness of their European or Japanese 'owners' and resented dissolution of the identity of their company into that of a foreign-based company. A similar challenge is faced now by multinational companies from emerging markets such as China and India as they are making acquisitions abroad.

Confederation

Confederation is the extreme opposite of assimilation. Here, the merged organisations preserve their historical identities and are not expected to blend in order to create a new one. Each organisation keeps its name, legal independence, management structure and autonomous decision-making. Coordination in this setting is kept at the minimum level necessary to achieve synergies in particular and limited areas.

The Renault/Nissan and Air France/KLM combinations are good illustrations of the confederate approach to integration. Instead of pursuing a fully-fledged merger with Nissan, which some might argue would have maximised economic synergies, Carlos Ghosn consistently emphasised that he was trying to fix Nissan's strategic and operational ills and preserve its core Japanese identity at the same time. He did, however, create a purchasing organisation jointly owned by Renault and Nissan, and also created ad hoc taskforces to encourage new product managers and engineers at Renault and Nissan to use common parts and platforms.

The Renault/Nissan design served as a template for the implementation of the Air France/KLM combination. Although Air France formally acquired the Dutch airline in 2004, the deal explicitly specified that KLM would keep its name, management structure and operational autonomy for eight years. Here the agenda was more about coordination. In sectors such as freight, where branding is less important, there was more integration. The passenger side of things was more complicated, so rushed integration in this area could have led to disaster.

Confederate integration should be considered when a satisfactory level of synergies, on the revenue or cost side, can be achieved without tying the organisations closely together in day-to-day operations. In this case, broad strategic guidelines and a few coordination mechanisms are enough to ensure that the merged organisations pull in the same direction while maintaining their autonomy and respective identities.

The economic calculations should be supplemented with serious consideration of the psychological distance between the merged organisations. In the case of Nissan/Renault, while both make cars, the two companies have unique identities established through several decades and have grown in countries with very different cultures. Their people do not know one another, do not speak the same language and deal with different suppliers and business partners.

Furthermore, although Nissan was in deep trouble when Renault took over, the stakeholders of the Japanese company were not prepared to let Nissan's identity be dissolved into that of a French automaker. In hindsight, the approach achieved the best possible trade-off between the benefits of tighter integration and the cost of ignoring the psychological distance between the two companies.

Similarly, the psychological and cultural divide between Air France and KLM was and is still wide, even though both organisations are European. The CEOs of both companies were careful to use the French word *rapprochement*, meaning 'gradually bringing together' – thus giving people on both sides time to get to know one another and to begin informally to forge a common identity. Eight years after the merger the CEO of Air France/KLM announced in an interview that the time was ripe for deeper integration of the two airlines. The plan outlined suggested that integration was shifting to a federalist configuration with a stronger common corporate centre. It is interesting to compare this with the case study of the merger between Rémy Cointréau and Bols, where the top executives pushed through the integration in less than a year on the basis of perceived harmony between the top teams.

For the confederate model to work, people on both sides must understand how far down the integration path top management is willing to go. In the Renault/Nissan case, it was important that Renault managers, at all levels, refrained from adopting a 'conqueror' attitude toward their Japanese counterparts when Nissan was struggling to recover from near death. Now that Nissan has recovered and is reconnecting with its glorious past, it is equally important for Japanese managers to avoid arrogance toward their French counterparts. Much of the burden for maintaining mutual respect falls on the shoulders of the senior managers who bridge the two organisations.

Federation

The key difference between federalist and confederate integration lies in preserving the identities of merged organisations while, at the same time, developing an overarching identity to which each member organisation can relate, identify with and thrive within. The image that comes closest to the federalist model is Russian nesting dolls: *each has its own existence and face and, at the same time, contains dolls with their own faces and beings.*

The federalist approach seeks to develop a new layer of identity and identification on top of the existing layer. In the business world, the Paris-based luxury brands conglomerate LVMH has successfully and consistently implemented federalist integration.

Bernard Arnault, chairman and CEO of LVMH, has consistently reinforced the federalist model as a way to balance two contradictory imperatives:

1 Preserving the uniqueness of the organisations supporting luxury brands while achieving economies of scale and scope in selected areas. The federalist model has enabled Arnault to maintain the identities of a galaxy of highly autonomous organisations supporting high-end companies and brands including Louis Vuitton, Moët & Chandon, Hennessy, Parfums Christian Dior, TAG Heuer, Céline and Sephora.
2 At the same time, the LVMH Group identity has enabled Arnault to put a recognisable face on this diverse portfolio of organisations and brands, enabling LVMH to achieve economies of scale and scope in distribution, advertising, human resources management and efficient access to financial markets.

Metamorphosis

Metamorphosis is the process by which the identities of merged companies are dissolved and fused into a completely new identity. The key benefit of this approach is the avoidance of uncertainty and anxiety among people on all sides about who are the winners and losers of the merger. Efforts by top management to establish a new identity for the combined organisation are intended to create a neutral terrain. The process enables members to 'forget' the identity of their original organisation. This, in turn, permits the development of a common shared identity, in which all parties ideally feel they have voice and contribution.

An example of metamorphosis is the creation of SSL International. This resulted from the merger between Seton (maker of tubular bandages and pharmaceuticals) and Scholl (maker of orthopedic footwear) in 1998, followed by the merger of that company in 1999 with London International (maker of Durex condoms and disposable products used in hospitals). Instead of using the identity of one of the companies to integrate the others, or keeping the merged companies at arm's length within a confederate or a federal structure, the chief executive sought to create a new organisational identity for the merged company.

To build the new identity he set up an integrated corporate strategy and organisational structure, picked a leadership team from the three merged companies and contracted with a business school to design an executive training programme, in which we were asked to facilitate the identity part. Interestingly, SSL International was acquired in 2010 by Reckitt Benckiser, which has followed the assimilation approach and has dismantled the SSL organisational structure and identity.

Symbolic and substantive levers of identity integration

Managers can shape and reinforce an organisation's identity through effective use of two different and complementary levers: symbolic and substantive.

Symbolic identity management develops what the merged organisation stands for or should stand for. It includes crafting a mission or identity statement, defining organisational goals and values and developing corporate branding (name, logo, slogan and visual identity). It can also include creation of an organisational saga to celebrate the defining moments in the company's history or strategic use of a sponsoring budget to express the identity of the organisation through identification with an area of human activity, such as a humanitarian cause, a sports discipline or a cultural movement.

Our experience suggests that there is a tendency for senior managers to think of identity management largely in terms of symbolic initiatives. Cosmetic work on the surface of the organisation has to be connected to substantive actions that embody and give meaning to the cosmetic symbols.

Substantive levers of identity management refer to acts and decisions about the organisation. They include decisions regarding ownership, governance structure and leadership team composition. They also include recruiting people who can embody and promote the new organisational identity; letting go of people who are not in line with the new identity; changing organisational structures and management systems; and perhaps ensuring consistency between the company's business strategy and the new identity.

When a merger involves the creation of a new identity, swift symbolic initiatives (mission statement, name or logo) enable managers to communicate the new projected identity fairly quickly. For these efforts to be fruitful, however, they need to be followed by substantive decisions regarding people, business strategies and operations that are aligned with the symbolic initiatives. Problems arise when managers fail to realise the importance of supplementing symbolic initiatives with consistent, and often more difficult, substantive decisions regarding people, business strategies or operations, or undertake divergent symbolic initiatives and substantive decisions.

Recommendations for successful identity integration

The four paths to identity integration described offer alternative approaches to making one organisation out of many. Each model represents particular trade-offs regarding how to deal with legacy identities in building a common future. The cases used to illustrate each model show that all four can be successful when they are a good fit with the context and objectives of a merger. The research and our experience lead us to the following conclusions.

First, there needs to be recognition that in order to have an effective merger, executives must recognise both the economic *and* the psychological synergies that need to occur. Too often, the psychological issues tend to be either overlooked entirely or underappreciated as mergers are contemplated and consummated.

Second, there should be some assessment in the pre-merger phase of the extent to which identity issues might preclude successful fusion. By including an identity audit in the due diligence process, managers might in extreme cases decide that, despite potential economic synergies, a merger should not be pursued because psychological synergies would be very difficult to achieve (see 'The identity audit', Checklist 7 in Appendix 1). In less extreme cases, the identity audit would enable managers to identify the issues and obstacles that would need to be addressed in order to achieve successful identity integration.

Third, it is dangerous to use language from one model while pursuing integration through a different model. Although it may be tempting to use language from the metamorphosis or federalist model to disguise what is really assimilation – especially when the architects believe that open admission of assimilation might derail the transaction or increase the price tag – the longer-run credibility price is steep. For example, by joining the two companies' names in DaimlerChrysler and using the 'mergers of equals' phrase, the leaders of the ill-fated merger raised the expectation among Chrysler people of a federalist design in which the US automaker would retain its autonomy, US-born leadership and identity. Two years later they admitted they had never taken seriously the 'merger of equals'. Such an open admission is rare. But discrepancies between espoused and actual integration practices are a common fact of business life and can cause senior executives of acquired companies to feel they have been lied to in order to secure their agreement to a merger. The long-term effects are likely to be highly toxic.

Fourth, managers should be pragmatic with regard to the four integration models and not fall into a 'one-size-fits-all' trap. The approaches followed by Unilever with regard to its acquisition of ice-cream maker Ben & Jerry's suggest that the uniqueness of an acquired organisation can justify an exception to a standardised post-merger integration template. Unilever, a successful practitioner of assimilation, acquired Ben & Jerry's in 2000 and has made a set of formal commitments to maintain the ice-cream maker's independence and unique identity. References to Unilever are not plentiful on Ben & Jerry's website. Cisco has developed a hybrid identity integration model, with *assimilation* applied to targets operating in the company's historical core business and *federation* applied to firms operating in new areas of diversification.

Fifth, we stress that, although they have access to powerful symbolic and substantive levers by which they can shape identity, defining the identity of an organisation is not the province of senior managers alone. Identity is shaped, owned and reinforced by the organisation's key stakeholders. Failure to acknowledge this can lead managers to promote definitions of their organisation that are disconnected from, and sometimes at odds with, how other stakeholders perceive them. To avoid divergence and contradictory claims about what the merged company stands for, managers should include an initiative designed to monitor how employees, customers, government, shareholders and other relevant stakeholders perceive the merged company in the post-merger plan.

Finally, we underline the importance of the time dimension in identity integration. With the goal of maximising psychological synergy as a priority, managers should remember that, in contrast to strategic and operational alignment, identity alignment is not a 'one-off' task but a process that can take several years. The Renault/Nissan case provides a good example of gradual identity integration. Given the globalisation of the car industry and the size of potential synergies and economies of scale, full-fledged integration of the two automakers would probably have been the most optimal economic solution. However, neither Nissan nor Renault was prepared for assimilation (of Nissan by Renault) or for metamorphosis (full integration of the two automakers into a new identity). The wide geographical and psychological distances would not have allowed a federalist scenario, which would have meant the creation of a new identity and common management structure above the historical identities of Renault and Nissan. Therefore, the confederate model provided a good starting point for the two companies, but it is clearly not the end of the story. After the federalist phase has allowed for the creation of enough bonds and sense of common purpose, the time could be ripe for a fully-fledged metamorphosis, in which Renault and Nissan would cease to exist as separate organisations and would be promoted as mere brands.

Integration is a long-term process. The returns from combining the resources of more than one organisation under a common ownership structure will be enhanced only when the importance of identity integration is fully recognised – and when the same careful planning and execution that tend to accompany the economic aspects of a deal simultaneously accompany the psychological dimensions.

The merger of Rémy Cointréau and Bols – mixing French and Dutch spirits

In 2000 Rémy Cointréau acquired Lucas Bols, the leading Dutch manufacturer of a unique range of spirits, to complement their main brands and counter the consolidation going on elsewhere in the spirits industry. At the time I was also a director of Highland Distillers PLC with a board colleague in Mme Dominique Hériard Dubreuil, then chair of Rémy Cointréau. She asked me to facilitate a workshop with the executives of both companies to prepare for the future venture. She was anxious to treat the acquisition as a 'merger of equals'. She assured me both parties were committed to the merger and passionate about the prospects for the future growth of the businesses and their people.

At the first event together, in Paris in November 2000, it soon became clear that though there was a strong rationale behind the merger from a business perspective, a number of issues were potential barriers to the successful execution of the merged companies. In addition to those outlined earlier in this chapter, there were additional challenges, mainly related to the national cultures of France and the Netherlands and the management style and orientation of the French and Dutch leadership and management. It all led to a fascinating and unique cocktail of events that was to unfold during the early months of the merger.

In the beginning – home alone

Rémy Cointréau is a French alcoholic beverage company (€1bn revenue) that produces cognac, liqueurs and spirits. The company is a result of a 1990–1991 merger between Rémy Martin and Cointréau. The Rémy Cointréau Group, whose charentaise origins date back to 1724, is the result of the merger in 1990 of the holding companies of the Hériard Dubreuil and Cointréau families, which controlled E. Rémy Martin & Cie SA and Cointréau & Cie SA respectively. It is also the result of successive alliances between companies operating in the same wines and spirits business segment. Rémy Cointréau's portfolio of global brands is sold primarily through its own distribution network, which comprises subsidiaries in the United States, Asia, and Western and Central Europe.

There was a strong philosophy behind Rémy Cointréau and their stated strategy that goes a long way to explaining the culture of the business, over its long history:

The power of authenticity

Far from being artificial, the Rémy Cointréau Group's brands derive their strength from a unique authenticity, which is our most valuable asset.

Each one of them has been, in some cases for several centuries, deeply rooted in the terroir in whose traditions they remain steeped: Petite and Grande Champagne vineyards for cognacs, the vineyard on the island of Samos for Metaxa's Muscat wines, the Isle of Islay for Bruichladdich and The Botanist and, further afield, Barbados for Mount Gay.

We recognised the opportunity to be the heirs of these terroirs, of this legacy of the founders, and of this expertise handed down through the generations. Whilst competition is intensifying, and no market is ever truly won, it is up to us to manage this absolute authenticity without sacrificing the creativity which sets it apart.

More than ever before, it is up to us to assert our identity by continuing to select the best the land has to offer, to meticulously transform what time provides, and to give new meaning to each of our brands by doing very little to them, because it is our authenticity that remains the key deciding factor for our consumers. It justifies the amount that they are willing to pay to buy our products, to give them to others or to savour them themselves. In other words, it is priceless.[2]

Lucas Bols might best be described as an old soul making new spirits. The company, founded by its namesake, Lucas Bols, in 1575, mastered the art of distilling, mixing and blending old recipes with new flavours for their portfolio of premium and super-premium brands. They make Genevers (the national liquor of Holland, which is also called Dutch Gin), Damrak gin, Bols vodka and a variety of Bols liqueurs. It also offers the Italian liqueur Galliano and the green-coloured banana-flavoured liqueur Pisang Ambon. The Dutch distiller's products are distributed in more than 110 countries across the globe. In the 1970s and 1980s Bols continued to build up its diverse and unique portfolio of drinks, even entering into non-alcoholic variants as part of their diversification away from their core spirits business.

By 1993, competition and consolidation in the industry had become cutthroat. Heineken decided to retrench to its beer business, and sold off its stake in the joint venture (wines and spirits with Bols) for 58.6 million Fl. Dutch foods giant Royal Wessanen and Bols saw a natural fit for horizontal integration and a merger was completed, creating a new company – Bols Wessanen. From the beginning, integrating the two lines of business was difficult and so led to profit pressures. The 1995 annual shareholders meeting was contentious and the company decided to focus its growth efforts toward the food sector. In 1997 the company moved to a new headquarters and production facility in Zoetermeer.

By 1999 it was obvious that the partnership was not working. The Bols side of the business was being neglected and management wanted to unlock its potential for growth and profitability. A private equity firm, CVC Capital Partners, agreed and a management buyout by the executive board was engineered forming Bols Royal Distilleries. Immediately thereafter, Bols acquired a number of brands from British drinks conglomerate Diageo including Asbach, a German brandy, and Metaxa, the world's biggest-selling Greek liquor.

In bed together – acquisition or merger?

Almost immediately after the buyout, it became clear that Bols did not have the scale to compete effectively in the rapidly consolidating drinks industry, led in many ways by Diageo. CVC Capital had an existing relationship with Rémy Cointreau, so it seemed natural to combine the two companies. In

Strategic rationale	
Rémy Cointréau	Bols
Reinforce our distribution muscle (MaXXiuM)	Improved distribution through the MaXXiuM and Rémy networks
Complement the liqueur and spirits portfolio	Become part of a complementary premium brand portfolio
Strengthen our financial structure and resources	Shared philosophy – brands and people
Use the complimentary strengths of Bols management to support our growth plans.	Combined acquisition power.

Figure 10.2 Strategic rationale. Created by Alistair Gray (2000).

August 2000 an agreement was reached and Rémy paid CVC €510 million for Bols – at a multiple of more than ten times earnings – which retained a 9% equity stake in the enlarged group. The merger (or was it an acquisition?) was perceived as greatly helping both companies and delivering '1+1>3' (Figure 10.2).

The question of national cultures

There is now well-established research and knowledge[3] (ironically much of it centred in the Netherlands) that shows that one of the biggest influences on the likely success of global acquisitions or mergers can be found in addressing the differences between the cultures in the home nation of the companies involved in the transaction.

This was further complicated in Rémy Cointréau and Bols leadership and management in that both 'camps' exhibited relatively extreme positions of their national cultures, e.g., Bols' management was especially task-orientated – doing deals, getting on with the job – while Rémy management was more focused on building the correctness of actions and the relationships for the long run, as had been their history over many decades.

It did not take long, using Fons Trompenaar's model (see Figure 10.3), to realise the challenges of addressing the cultural issues facing Rémy and Bols in their desire to merge. It is also ironic that the theorist is himself Dutch-French.

Deploying good practice

Building on the lessons of good practice, many of them outlined in the first section of this chapter, it was clear that to be successful there needed to be consensus across the new executive around areas such as:

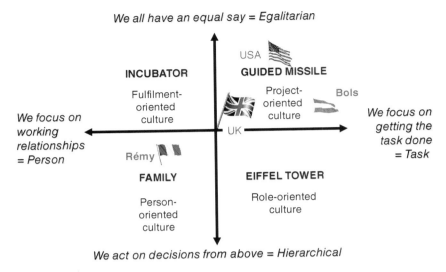

Figure 10.3 The problem with cultures. Scenarios created by Alistair Gray (2000).

- Establishing clear objectives and a workable game plan as early as possible for the new business.
- Customising the post merger integration process to fit the new organisation and initial goals.
- Running a tight implementation process (especially over the first six months).
- Executing decisively for swift integration.
- Keeping pressure on through continuous management.
- Building an experienced team.

We were mindful that many factors line up to get in the way of successful execution of a merger-based strategy. These had been clearly identified through research from MIT's Sloan School of Management[4] (Figure 10.4).

As a result, any implementation has to concentrate on securing commitment rather than compliance to the overall goal of the acquisition/ merger, and conducting any review of the businesses and their people in a professional way to stay on course. In times of change, positive direction and leadership is even more vital and of particular importance is the recognition that communication is a two-way process. Getting staff feedback is more important than broadcasts from the top.

After the initial skirmish in Paris, Genesis[5] was retained to work with the top 120 executives in the business, and we planned to deploy the above principles in our work with the top team.

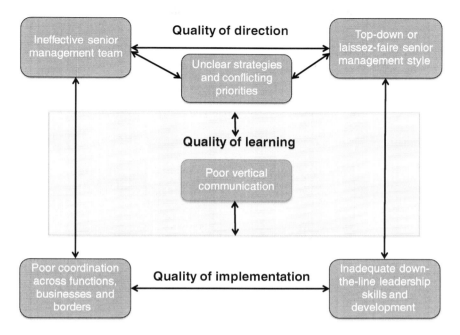

Figure 10.4 The silent killers of implementation. Figure created by Alistair Gray (2000).

Project blending – the development of a winning strategy

The leadership of both companies assembled soon after the acquisition and we led the facilitation of the conversation to establish the strategy for the new merged business.

Many changes had happened in the drinks industry in the latter half of the 1990s. The year 1998 saw the first mega-merger with the creation of Diageo,[6] followed quickly in 2000 by the second with the merger of Pernod-Ricard and Seagram. Both organisations eased quickly to a global distribution cost/case significantly below that of their competitors. More mergers were expected and, in addition, new alliances were being formed through major players buying and selling their brands, e.g., Diageo selling Dewars to Bacardi Martini. Rémy and Bols had been involved in the creation of MaXXiuM, a strategic alliance between the Highland Distillers, Rémy, Finlandia and Jim Beam brands. All these were designed to bring the distribution costs more into line with the big players.

The feeling was that champagne would follow spirits in this direction and such a move would mirror the concentration in the on-trade (pubs and clubs). Pressure would be double-edged – larger and more dominant brands against increasing buying power and distribution savings offset by higher marketing costs.

Both Rémy and Bols felt they needed to play in this game of chess if they were to prosper. The following illustration (Figure 10.5) of where the consolidation was heading in 2000 reinforced the new team's thinking.

'Project Blending' was chosen as the title of the post-merger integration process. A theme that not only reflected the drinks business but also the aim to regard the acquisition by Rémy of Bols as a merger rather than a takeover.

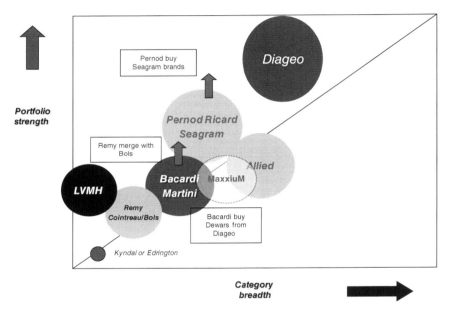

Figure 10.5 The developing world of spirits. Matrix created by Alistair Gray (2000).

Performance metrics	Next 3 years
• Sales • Organic sales growth • Merger & acquisition • Profitability • A&P/margin • Cost/net sales.	• 1.2M€ rising to 3M€ • 5–6% pa • 1.5M€ to 2M€ additional turnover • >20% EBIT on net sales • Maintain 35% • Reducing year on year.
Our objectives for post merger integration • Earnings/share • Cost synergies.	• 3€ • 10–15M€.

Figure 10.6 Performance metrics. Created by Alistair Gray (2000).

The senior management group was charged with the task to consider what the objectives should be for the 'merger' and to report back to the new board (Figure 10.6).

Clear priorities were established, especially for sales and marketing (Figure 10.7).

Mergers and acquisitions are potentially destabilising. The faster issues can be resolved the better. The focus on the early stages of any merger should aim to be reasonably right rather than perfectly wrong. Working at speed also creates a feeling of momentum and achievement and forces people to overcome problems creatively, as well as building a feeling of excitement and challenge. Early wins, especially those that can be tagged as a result of the merger, are vital in the first six months after tying the knot.

The directors set about the task of developing their vision of the new company at a number of sessions that Genesis had the privilege to facilitate. In quick time they determined the strategy and goals that would represent the route map to securing a successful first island of stability for the new company. The resultant Focus Framework is shown in Figure 10.8.

The combined leadership team then moved on to consider how the acquisition/merger might be successfully delivered in two themed phases:

- Phase 1: planning to win – key processes, capabilities and structure.
- Phase 2: focus on value.

There was early recognition that there needed to be substantial change, not only in the strategy, structure and systems of both businesses, but also mental change, as illustrated by the overview of the first phase (Figure 10.9).

Market	Priority	Growth
No. 1 Priority		
• USA – Portfolio	√	√√
• EU (The 15) – Portfolio	√	-
• Asia – Rémy Martin	√	√
• CE Europe – Bols, Metaxa	√	√
No. 2 Priority		
• Scouting Opportunities		√
• CS America		√
Principles for market development		
• Brand: market groups make choices based on brand evaluation model, for all brand development proposals		
• Aim for minimum 5% market share in 3 years (new markets) or for an exceptional business case		
• Invest in advertising and promotion		

Figure 10.7 Market priorities. Table created by Alistair Gray (2000).

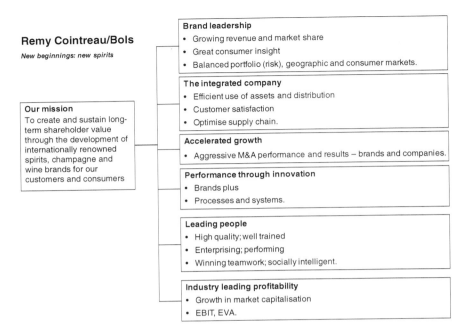

Figure 10.8 Our strategic framework. Created by Alistair Gray (2000).

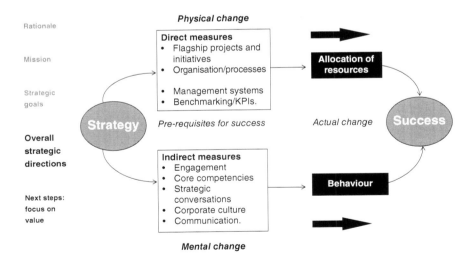

Figure 10.9 First phase: planning to win. Created by Alistair Gray (2000).

The 'soft' issues and mental change challenges (psychological) were identified and debated at an early stage. The senior leadership team themselves recognised the need for openness and trust to debate potentially sensitive issues. There could be no room for the elephant in the room. Here is an illustration of what was shared.

- **Good so far:**

  o   Shared understanding.
  o   Few threats – in the top team.
  o   Due diligence – well executed.
  o   Positive feel in the leadership team with few politics.

- **What we admire in each other (Rémy of Bols):**

  o   People had vision.
  o   They had the guts to undertake the MBO.
  o   Speed and proper management.
  o   People were greater than the brands.

- **What we admire in each other (Bols of Rémy):**

  o   Marketing and innovation competence.
  o   MaXXiuM[7] was a brilliant move.
  o   Our potential as people.

Nine cross-business/function project teams were established, facilitated by Genesis consultants, and a plan prepared for the first six months. The projects were all led by a senior director and formed using team-building techniques such as those researched and promoted by Belbin.[8] The projects were:

1   Brand group strategies.

   - Business/market units – three-year strategies and the interface with MaXXiuM.

2   The integrated company.

   - Purchasing; supply chain management; customer service.

3   Business development.
4   Improved business reporting.

   - Business Balanced Scorecard; financial/management reporting.

5   Secure and monitor synergies.
6   New synergies.

7   Managing distribution – MaXXiuM and own distribution.
8   Organisation and management processes.
9   Communication, communication, communication.

   •   External and Press Association; internal.

The emerging structure for leading and managing the new company

The final step of the first phase was to establish the initial leadership and management structure for the new business (Figure 10.10). A matrix approach was used to ensure optimum integration across the new business. The main business streams were brand/market-focused business units. Interfacing with them were the key business functions – the specialists – each focused on building the strategic capabilities to run the new business.

   The key focus for the brand groups was profit responsibility, design and implementation of brand strategy, optimising the MaXXiuM relationship and development of key markets such as the US. The specialists and the analysts supported each brand group. The specialists were in functions such as people development, marketing services (planning and market intelligence), innovation, quality, business development, strategic management, corporate communications and information. The analysts were primarily in finance, administration and legal functions.

The integrated company

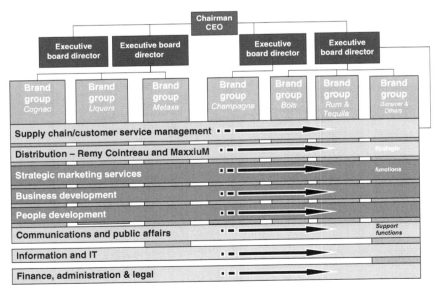

Figure 10.10 The integrated company. Structure created by Alistair Gray (2000).

Forward to phase 2

Having established the building blocks and a basic plan for accelerated change over the first six months, the next phase was to focus on adding value in three key areas:

- Shareholders.
- Customers.
- People in the new company.

New performance indicators were set for the delivery of increased value in the long term. Three principles were established at an early stage by the leadership team:

1 Focus rewards on the ratio between profit (not revenue) and cost of equity will ensure the improvement of employees' productivity.
2 Putting customer satisfaction at the core of RC's values implies a closer proximity with customers' and consumers' needs and wants.
3 Well-treated, well-led, well-trained and well-managed employees add long-term value through commitment and loyalty. Strategic thinking is required to look inward as well as outward.

The leadership team was confident they had now put in place processes/structure ensuring that Rémy Cointréau/Bols' values, mission and goals were coherent with the expectations of the market and the customer/consumers.

They believed they had established Rémy Cointréau/Bols' value proposition and market position relative to competitors and revised the business system and leading projects to out-perform the market in the long term. There was commitment to build and enhance the strategic capabilities (assets, skills and systems) that would deliver a winning position that, in turn, was needed to generate a competitive value position.

The next stage was to empower people to add value in their everyday tasks and reward them on the basis of their value added to the new enterprise. The leadership group now felt ready to communicate the position they had reached and the way ahead. It was now time to roll out 'Project Blending'.

The directoires session

The leadership of the new company had established the vision and goals for the new business as well as establishing the principle and structure for how the new business might be organised – all within the first 12 weeks after the acquisition was announced. The next step was to engage with the top 120 executives to stimulate their input and contribution to post-merger planning, as well as ensuring that the projects were truly aligned behind achieving the strategic goals, as articulated in the Focus Framework.

One of the key principles of our work in Genesis was to be able to articulate to clients what drives performance. Three overall principles apply:

1   Engagement of a critical mass of the executives in the process.
2   Alignment of plans to the vision and strategic goals.
3   Having a clear and agreed plan to win.

The top 120 executives in the new business were initially gathered together in Reims, France, for a session where the leadership shared their vision of success for the merged business.

It was clear from the initial leadership sessions that the cultural difference between the two companies was significant and the desired new culture would take some working out. It was therefore imperative to engage a critical mass of management to understand how they felt about the merger and build commitment (rather than compliance) to the merged company.

Questionnaires were issued to the 120 in advance of the session (see Checklist 7 in Appendix 1) to solicit their hopes and concerns for the new merged company. Here are their views.

Hopes

Almost everyone wanted to be part of a more significant international player in the industry. They also wanted to succeed in the integration of teams and brands so that they became a more competitive and profitable enterprise.

There was a strong desire to go beyond the family-organisation in order to embrace an international reality without losing the former value, and at the same time to keep an open-style management approach. By exploiting both companies' skills and best practices they would make a difference in the marketplace

Fears and concerns

At the same time, a majority wanted to remain a medium-sized player in terms of volume and financial strength. They feared the integration process would be too long and momentum would be lost.

They also recognised the strength of respective national cultures and that these might jeopardise the positive growth of those brands deeply rooted in their territories. The two cultures might not work effectively because of selfish interests and the willingness to dominate each other.

There was also a fear that, in the short term, a brand investment and strategic approach would jeopardise longer-term investment and that the larger merged business would become more administrative and political and lose the effectiveness of action.

This reinforced the need for continuous engagement in the process of integration of this critical mass of management. Sharing the leaders' vision of success and engaging the top 120 had a positive impact on the planning process. As a direct result of this and subsequent sessions the list of integration projects changed. The new beginning for Rémy Cointréau and Bols had been established and they embarked on their new journey in March 2001.

Post-merger performance

After the acquisition of Bols, Rémy Cointréau stopped acquiring and began consolidating. This strategy differed from the industry trend but helped focus Rémy Cointréau's champagne and wine portfolio and tripled the operating profits of its four key brands in just two years. The synergies of the combined company were immediately felt. Remy reported a string of strong earnings and profit growth, until a weakening dollar and a temporary drop in sales of Bols Vodka in Poland due to taxation and counterfeiting issues hurt 2003 results. Results in 2004 remained weak, but strong growth of the vodka brand was noted throughout Eastern Europe, and MaXXiuM committed considerable resources to modernising the Bols image, including new packaging and refocusing on a youth-driven market. Bols was awarded 'Best Brand Re-Launch' by *Drinks International Magazine*, the trade publication.

Although Rémy Cointréau was becoming more efficient, the company had opened itself up to be acquired by a larger group. In 2004 Dominique Hériard Dubreuil restructured the company's upper management. Jean-Marie Laborde became CEO. Mme Dominique Hériard Dubreuil continued her tenure as executive chairman but no longer handled the day-to-day operations. She also continued supporting Rémy Cointréau's investor relations and ongoing business strategy. Even though sales had dropped at the start of the year, they had rebounded by July. Analysts were giving Dominique Hériard Dubreuil credit for reviving a company in which she also held a considerable stake.

Streamlining the company even more, in June 2005 Rémy Cointréau sold the rights to distribute and produce Bols vodka in Russia and Poland. In 2005, Rémy struck a complex deal with Central European Distribution Corporation NASDAQ:CEDC, wherein CEDC took ownership of the Bols production facilities in Poland and licensed various trademarks for use in Poland and Russia in exchange for a 9% equity stake. The deal gave each company access to the other's distribution networks. Rémy also received a seat on CEDC's board of directors, and CEDC would later buy Bol's Hungarian subsidiary and trademarks.

Another management buyout

In 2005, Rémy, having decided to focus on its premium brands, put the entire Bols brand up for sale. In March 2006 Rémy Cointréau announced that it had completed the sale of not just Bols but also its other Dutch brands, including Bokma, Coebergh, Corenwyn and Pisang Ambon. It had also sold off its two Italian liqueurs, Galliano and Vaccari. Rémy Cointréau's key brands – Heidsieck Champagne, Piper Heidsieck, Cointréau liqueur and Rémy Martin cognac – continued to grow.

A number of the Bols senior management prior to merger had left the company within a year of merger. Huup van Doorne, a director of Rémy Cointréau prior to the merger, became CEO of the joint company. He led the team that revitalised the Bols brand under Rémy's aegis. Fast forward to 2004 and van Doorne decided to leave Cointréau. Looking for a new challenge, and with Cointréau looking to focus on their premium brands, he asked whether Rémy would potentially sell one of their Dutch brands and 2005 saw him begin to look into a buyout. On 16 March 2006 Rémy announced the sale of Bols, returning it to Dutch ownership through European investment fund **ABN AMRO Capital** (75%), together with a management group led by van Doorne (25%), and mezzanine capital was provided by GSC Group. As a proud Dutchman, he just had to see it come home. Lucas Bols is now a successful focused company operating in its unique niche and van Doorne has guided it to this position over a decade on from securing the buy-out.

The new company is named Lucas Bols B.V. and is headquartered in Amsterdam. Its assets include the production facilities in the Netherlands, along with the brands Bols, Galliano, Vaccari Sambuca, Pisang Ambon and Damrak Gin, plus leading Dutch Origin spirit brands such as Bokma and Hartevelt genevers and Coebergh. Distribution is still mostly done by MaXXiuM, although the United States is handled by new partner William Grant & Son, USA, a wholly-owned subsidiary of William Grant & Sons.

In April 2006 Rémy Cointréau reported that its consolidated sales jumped 6.4% for the fiscal year in 2006 over the previous fiscal year. By focusing on its top-shelf cognacs, champagnes and wines that had made Rémy Cointréau famous, the enterprise was still one of the largest drink groups in Europe.

Learning from the MIT research

Essentially Rémy Cointréau/Bols is a good example of a 'failed' acquisition/merger that got stuck in the middle – describing the acquisition as a 'merger of equals'. The egos of a number of the Bols senior management probably prevented Rémy taking the 'assimulation' or 'metamorphosis' approach to which it eventually had to revert. Unlike LVMH in the first section of this chapter, the leadership never managed to allow the merged companies to operate in an empowered way.

Rémy Cointréau

Lucas Bols

- **Breaking the rules; challenging existing paradigms**

  - Always a challenge in a 'friendly acquisition', the egos of senior management of the individual companies failed to recognise the cultural and psychological challenges.
  - The 'federation' or 'confederation' approaches did not work.

- **Working it out themselves – embracing change management**

  - They did this and launched off with great commitment to implement the post-merger integration projects.
  - The project teams were formed with staff from both companies.
  - Many senior Bols staff left as it was clear who was running the company.

- **The six killers of strategy implementation were alive and well**

  - Ineffective senior management team – not in terms of talent and experience, but in terms of functionality.
  - Unclear strategies and conflicting priorities.
  - Top-down senior management style inconsistent.
  - Poor vertical communication.
  - Poor coordination across functions, business and borders.
  - Inadequate down-the-line leadership skills and development.

- **Changing organisational performance**

  - This was the key area where the cultural differences played out, getting in the way of effective implementation, leading to the eventual buy-out.
  - The 'soft stuff' is often the 'hard stuff' in terms of achieving lasting and positive change. Efforts and resources required to address the issues often need to be doubled relative to other areas of capability.

Notes

1 Originally published in the *MIT Sloan Management Review* in 2012, the research won the Richard Beckhard Memorial Prize in 2015. Its authors are Hamid Bouchikhi, a professor of management and entrepreneurship at ESSEC Business School in Cergy-Pontoise, France, and John R. Kimberly, the Henry Bower Professor of Entrepreneurial Studies and a professor of management at the Wharton School of the University of Pennsylvania in Philadelphia, Pennsylvania.
2 Rémy Cointréau website: www.remy-Cointréau.com.
3 Fons Trompenaars; Alfonsus Trompenaars is a Dutch-French organisational theorist, management consultant and author in the field of cross-cultural communication. He is known for the development of Trompenaars' model of national culture differences. Geert Hofstede is a Dutch social psychologist, former IBM employee and Professor Emeritus of Organisational Anthropology and International Management at Maastricht University in the Netherlands.
4 'The Silent Killers of Strategy Implementation and Learning', Michael Beer and Russell A. Eisenstat, *MIT Sloan Management Review*, Summer 2000.
5 My colleagues Kevin Parker and Raffaella Cardarelli Mitchell joined me in the Genesis team.
6 Diageo was formed in 1998 and, after two years, shed 50% of turnover and profit and 25% of its market capital value.
7 MaXXiuM is a strategic alliance formed from the sales, marketing and distribution alliance between Beam, Suntory and Edrington. They have a world-class whisk(e)y portfolio and a broad range of premium liqueurs and speciality spirit brands. Rémy Cointréau and Finlandia were original members of the alliance but subsequently withdrew.
8 The Belbin Team Inventory is a behavioural test, also called the Belbin Self-Perception Inventory, Belbin Team Role Inventory, SPI or BTRSPI. It was devised by Meredith Belbin to measure an individual's preference for one or more of nine team roles; he had identified eight of those whilst studying numerous teams at Henley Management College.

11 Managing in (and out of) recession

Introduction

My business career began in 1970 and, within a year, I was part of a team closing a major paper mill and removing a layer of supervisory management. Welcome to the real world, Alistair! Through the nearly five decades of my career I have lived, worked through and survived four recessions, including the mother of them all in 2008 as a result of the global financial meltdown.

In this chapter I reflect on the lessons learned from working through and surviving these times of crisis. The initial review of these lessons is followed by a practical example of how to succeed in such an environment through the case study of Donald Russell, a supplier of top-quality meat products to the premium European horeca market (hotels, restaurants and catering), when the business almost disappeared during the BSE crisis of 1996. It is a story of courage and innovation and an inspiration to others.

Doom and gloom

The current economic, political and social climate has never been more intense – even ten years since 2008 and the real start of the last global recession. The impact of external forces is different this time:

- The scale and frequency of increases in oil and gas prices, their subsequent fall and the impact on energy and fuel costs.
- The size of losses and write-downs from major banks and lenders caught out by the reckless funding of property loans that were never going to be paid back.
- The impact of Brazil, Russia, India and China and the new world economies, not only on consumption of commodities such as steel and oil, but on the global markets, stock markets and industries in which they play an ever-increasingly important role.
- Increasing uncertainty and unprecedented competitive intensity in most industries, fuelled by news channels and net-based business and social media.

- Traditional market cycles are irrelevant and business models found wanting in the internet/experience economy.
- The reality of the pensions burden facing the G8 economies dawning on younger generations who assumed there would not be a problem in the future.

The 1980s was a decade of corporate restructuring on an unprecedented scale. Foreign competition became established on a global playing field. Without doubt the competitive intensity of most industries increased, particularly through the bargaining power of customers, the pace of innovation and change, and an increasing strategic stalemate in many industries. The early 1990s in Europe saw recession bite but commentators were soon talking about the golden decade of prosperity and growth as the new millennium dawned. Traditional labour economics were irrelevant for businesses where finance and materials became the key economic factors in many industrial economies due to advances in technology and design. Many companies, perceived as successful, fuelled their expansion through increased debt, offered by profligate banks repositioning themselves in the revolution within the financial services industry. In 1990 26% of corporate finance was debt funded, compared with 18% in 1984 and 9% in 1974.

The debt-laden crisis that we have undergone since 2008 has been unprecedented. Perhaps the best example of what good, then bad, then ugly looks like has been in Ireland, where the nation is now in hock for a generation of repayment of international loans. To its credit, Ireland took the medicine early and, unlike Greece, there are now signs of real recovery for the former Celtic Tiger.

The 2008 recession was quite different from any of the previous three I had experienced, and it lasted longer, much longer than observers predicted. It caused years of frustration to news channels eager to be the first to sight early green shoots of recovery. They started the 'hope' broadcasts before 2008 was out. The chart in Figure 11.1, published in the *Economist* in 2009, was one of the most accurate and level-headed assessments indicating it would be well into 2014 before recovery would be evident. In reality, even by 2017 there were few signs of single-digit economic growth other than fractional swings between quarters.

In many of the previous so-called recessions organisations adopted losing responses to recession or reduced growth:

- Costs were cut unilaterally, and accountants rose in importance to measure the decline better.
- This time round there have been pay cuts, salary holidays and other measures to reduce previously spiralling payrolls.
- Companies hung on to shares of markets that simply disappeared, in hope of an upturn.
- The meek were fired rather than the evil; often the best people left subsequently and irreparable damage was done to morale and enthusiasm. Even accountants and bankers were fired this time.

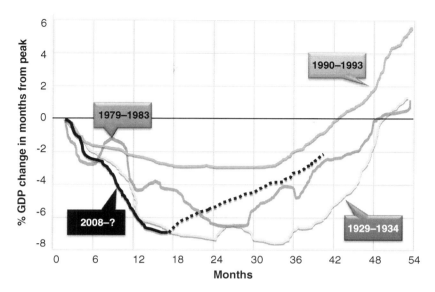

Figure 11.1 Recessions compared. © *The Economist* (2012).

- Many companies reduced their management to below critical mass, with marketing and R&D being the first functions to suffer the largest and deepest cuts. Competitive advantage being thrown away at a stroke.

You will probably recognise many of these actions, all of which are focused on internal operations of the business. Companies stopped looking outside – they were either frightened of what they might find, or bewildered at the amount and volume of change influencing their industry. Too many companies rode through recessions lean and paralysed.

In recent conversations with CEOs it is clear that many consider the business model that has served them reasonably well over decades is now inadequate to face up to the current and forecast competitive intensity of their industry.

Hope for the future

Not all companies lost during this recession. Companies who succeed in or even survive a protracted period of recession must develop new approaches that include:

- Choosing and implementing a positive *offence* or initiative.
- Cutting costs strategically, not unilaterally, to build the *defence*.
- Developing *creative and radical solutions*, through new business models and methods of managing the business, as well as instilling new improved behaviour in their people.

Taking the offence

It takes courage to develop and implement offensive strategies during recession. But what is the alternative – continuing to rely on revised targets and objectives that will never be met as the only way to manage or change business performance?

First, *enhance your strategic thinking* by focusing hard on customers and their needs, rather than on competitors, and establish how to maximise customer satisfaction and product/service profitability. Often product ranges are sustained in a state of proliferation that has built up over the years. I have seen a number of organisations lose more money the more they sell.

Replace SWOT analyses, and other annual rituals, with strategic management, where a critical mass of management run the business according to clear goals, all the time, not once a year. The ultimate in offence is to redesign the value chain in your industry as Dell and latterly HP did in hardware supply for the information industry. Get out of that deep red ocean of price-cutting and discounting. Focus on developing leadership and implementation skills in the management group and support this with management information that delivers fast feedback on a range of measures rather than historical management accounts. Objectives and milestones must be set and achieved quickly.

Second, *increase real marketing.* Develop new or extended markets rather than following the pursuit of the last percentage point of share in existing markets. There is often plenty of scope within existing or extended products to enable significant growth into new markets, e.g., the development of online service by the major retailers, while at the same time reducing the risk of continuing recession in one market or economy. Revisit some of your old market/product research for ideas, re-focus advertisements through new media or on new customer needs in recession. Product development can be expensive, but significant progress can be made through adding services to basic products or adding value to existing services – all at relatively low risk.

Paradoxically, recession is often the best time to *increase R&D activity* to lead a step change in innovation. This does not mean throwing money and resources in an unfocused search for the golden fleece. It does mean improving R&D effectiveness through increased focus, commercialisation of existing ideas and incubation or euthanasia of dormant developments. Improve the insight into emerging key technologies, making sure you have the technologies to enable you to compete, and seek advantage through converging or complementary technologies. Research and development effectiveness can be catalysed by the release and distribution of information through open networks and a common understanding of the business needs, rather than by being kept secret in locked offices and laboratories. Finally, innovation should be rewarded and entrepreneurs empowered to achieve successful implementation quickly.

The final element of the offence is to focus on *adding value to existing resources*, rather than waiting until you can afford the new. This can be achieved through the relentless drive to fill under-utilised capacity, a real investment in productivity of all resources, not just labour, and in rapid return projects. Value analysis of products, people and functions can also prove effective at this time.

Building the defence

Too frequently in recessions the foundations of businesses are undermined at the very time when they need to be most firm. *Cutting work, not jobs* seems to be the opposite of what companies implement in recession, expecting a smaller number of the same old staff to achieve more. Life is hard enough.

A clear *focus on quality* is proven to reduce cost, remove waste and result in simpler products with fewer parts. Avoid the lemming-like rush into TQM (Total Quality Management) programmes that are often offered as panaceas for flagging management morale, but invariably fail after the initial hype. Your people are your greatest asset, and they need *power rather than protection*. A recent client saved over 18% of overhead by turning loose a group of managers on overhead expenses with no constraints and few accountants.

Following staff cuts you need to *look after the survivors*, and the process starts with regular and effective *communication* on how the business and its customers are developing through difficult times. In particular, during strategic change, clear communication and explanation of role change is essential to maintain the momentum of change.

Creative and radical solutions

Now is the ideal time to appraise your position and craft out your future direction. The alternative is to allow the creeping paralysis of recession the opportunity to terminate your enterprise. Not one of the abundant selection of management tools will provide the quick cure. 'The problem before us is not to invent more tools, but to use the ones we have more effectively' (Rosabeth Moss Kanter[1]).

Examples of what may appear radical solutions are in fact well qualified to deal with recession where there is increasing pressure on prices, costs and resources. These solutions lie in:

- Focus, rather than diversify or cut.
- Develop alternative scenarios for the future to stimulate options.
- Forge alliances, rather than acquire at a premium.
- Change style, rather than restructure.
- Create and sustain a culture of performance in your business.

Examples of these principles lie in Cisco Systems who survived the crash of the early part of this century's first decade through their focus on providing internet-based solutions; NCR in Dundee where ATM unit costs were forced down by 40% in three years through a relentless push to world-class manufacturing status; and Taunton Cider, where a serious investment in people and new product innovation produced new premium products and a profit increase of 33% in the teeth of recession. Positive high quality offence and defence.

To do this in the future will require you to address and increase the strategic thinking capability and leadership capacity of your management team. They must have the opportunity to think in competitive dimensions, to establish the small number of key goals that will deliver future success and assure value for customers and shareholders. This thinking will be long range and lateral as well as dealing with the immediate future. It will require deeper consideration of key customer segments than ever before and the demolition of hierarchies in the organisation, replacing them with a network fuelled by shared information. The 'Doers have to be the Planners', the planners and consultants facilitate and integrate.

The 2008 recession was quite different. Conventional cost cutting and strategic responses have not sufficed, while buying growth was too expensive. Success or survival came from addressing opportunities with positive courageous initiatives and stiffening the defence through strategic cost management. Creative and radical solutions were required, that required new business models and new standards for performance company-wide.

Modest adjustments to the status quo that were sufficient in times of artificially high growth will not be good enough in this post-recession period of low growth, which has only just begun. At the same time, on the other side of the world to the West, are opportunities that must be grasped.

Donald Russell Ltd – managing in (and out of) recession

Hans Baumann, the CEO of Donald Russell, was on his way to his annual vacation with his family on 26 March 1996. The call came through that the Marks & Spencer truck on its way to their Paris store with prime Aberdeenshire beef products had been turned round. News broke of the confirmed outbreak of BSE and all meat products from the UK were to be banned from export markets. The vehicle returned home and his business faced a bleak future.

Donald Russell was a start-up business founded by Willie Donald and John Stone, two giants of the meat industry in the UK who wished to capitalise by selling their quality products to niche markets in Europe – leading hotels, niche retailers in France, Germany and other premium markets. Aberdeen Angus beef commanded a premium and their approach to producing primal products gave them a significant quality edge and taste advantage over competition.

The business was 100% export-based on the day the ban was imposed. Much of the drive behind the business resided in Baumann, Swiss by birth, trained as a chef with experience in the horeca (hotel, restaurant and catering) industry and with a passion for quality in an industry dominated by mediocrity.

We had the privilege of working with Hans and his team before, during and after the BSE crisis. The challenge was to transform the business quickly to sustain the enterprise, and to develop markets and customers that would not only restore previous trading levels, but also build an even stronger enterprise into the future.

Image 11.1 The source of great beef. © Donald Russell Ltd.

Their story is one of courage, resilience and hard work, from the depths of despair through to its current position as the UK's leading online retailer of beef, lamb, pork and other products, and a valued multi-channel partner to many of the leading restaurants in the UK and elsewhere in Europe. As a business, it not only survived the BSE crisis but also the 2001 Foot and Mouth outbreak and then the recession in 2008, when customers tightened their belts to survive.

Survival

Having returned from the vacation he never started, Hans summoned me to Blairmore, his Highland home between Huntly and Aberlour, for a three-day summit. Encouraged by his pet Rottweiler Bruno, we set to the task of determining the survival strategy, suitably fuelled by the business's excellent produce, the Highland air and the occasional liquid refreshment.

Clearly export markets were not going to reappear for some time. We challenged the concept of direct retail, online sales from every direction. Such a venture needed cash and we agreed the best route to initial sales was to those establishments that would pay for quality. I happened to have my Amex Platinum Card restaurant directory with me and that database was the start of the recovery. Relationships with a number of leading hotel chains followed, including Malmaison, a long-term partner, and MacDonald Hotels. These, along with other wholesale customers, gave the business a solid trading platform in profitable markets, and a way out of the red-ocean[2] of Scotch Beef.

From zero sales in 1996 the business grew to over £20m of profitable sales in 2008, with 75% retail and 25% to the trade. Its website (www.donaldrusselldirect.com) shows how Donald Russell Direct clearly differentiates itself from competition. How was this turnaround achieved?

Taking the big first step

Online competition existed in 1997 but largely from highly fragmented farms and individual butcher businesses, mainly selling to local markets. No effective national fresh meat business existed online. Supermarkets did not display and promote fresh meat, poultry or fish well. Even in the unfamiliar area of fish, Donald Russell saw opportunities to outperform the likes of Loch Fyne and The Fish Society.

The decision was made to focus on high quality beef, poultry and lamb, adding in specialist Scottish fresh produce in areas such as fish, both shellfish and salmon. The focus was also on better taste, where Donald Russell was able to supply the highest quality Aberdeen Angus beef, aged for 25 days, to deliver real tenderness and flavour. Products were delivered fresh in quality packaging and the initial marketing material was also of a high quality. A feature in the *Sunday Telegraph* started the rush from what was to be the most important segment for the business – the Home Counties around London. Other promotional features followed, positioning Donald Russell Direct well away from competition in the industry.

The Donald Russell people were also featured, personalising the service and displaying the loyalty of staff, many employed pre-BSE. Therein lay the basis of being able to charge premium prices for the product as part of a total customer experience. Other people, leading chefs, continued to endorse the products and the service including Nigella Lawson and Olivier Roux.

The big decision was taken to promote the business heavily (relative to competitors) through direct mail and to secure repeat purchases and higher-value purchases. The initial quality of product and delivery assured a good response and subsequent research carried out amongst customers was hugely encouraging. Further investment was made in staff with direct selling experience and in further promotion. One of the early capabilities that has endured and is now embedded in the business is an insatiable desire to secure customer feedback and data.

This bred confidence that the Donald Russell experience was truly valued by customers and especially the best customers for the business.

Following wine

Always thirsty for comparative information and data, Baumann saw what Laithwaites had done to the traditional distribution of wine in the UK, growing their turnover from £10m to £100m in under a decade to 2000. He convinced the owners and fellow shareholders to intensify efforts in customer acquisition and recruitment. At this early stage investing around £1m was a

Image 11.2 Great products. © Donald Russell Ltd.

daunting prospect but one that delivered real results with over 80,000 customers acquired.

Case studies and stories that 'people like our steaks' were circulated widely and this, combined with special offers around Easter, BBQs and Christmas, fuelled the business to a new level of profitability. Space was bought in other direct mail catalogues and inserts placed in quality magazines and supplements, all carefully targeted at premium customer spending.

2008 UK in crisis

Turnover had grown to £20m by 2008, of which 80% was through the new Donald Russell Direct business. But in 2009 the phones stopped ringing (for six weeks) as customers tightened their belts, adjusting to the most severe recession in living memory. In a three-month period total sales grossed only £1m. It was clear that the current strategy of customer acquisition was not working and was also becoming expensive. In January 2010, after a review, the decision was taken to get back to the basics that had created the business.

Ready meals were added to the range, picking up on the desire of consumers for 'meal solutions'. Baumann insisted that they be of restaurant quality and customer feedback was excellent, many saying they were the 'best they had ever tasted'. These quickly added over £1m of turnover in what was to be one of the most profitable segments. The core of the business – beef and other meats – remained robust, but with greater emphasis on value packs, offering customers real value during challenging times for household budgets. Though average purchase levels fell, the relentless focus on the most profitable segments and customers kept profits up.

The focus paid off – on product, on offers (backed up with free gifts), on audience growth and timing, all backed up by industry-leading service delivering an unrivalled experience. The range of products was further extended. Twenty years on, Donald Russell is producing nearly 10,000 individually wrapped steaks a day, courtesy of 15 butchers and a further 11 on portion control, in the vast on-site butchery at Inverurie. The current catalogue includes charcuterie, fishcakes, bacon, sausages, haggis pudding, award-winning meat pies, potato rösti, cheesecakes and apple crumble.

What makes Donald Russell special?

Quality ingredients took them so far, but there is no question that the personality and profile the business generated has kept it ahead of the pack both in sales and profitability. Their products tasted better, were of a higher quality and, coupled with their commitment to delivering sector-leading service and experience, this has served them well. Sales have now broken through £30m and profits have also grown, assuring future sustainability.

Baumann brought the highest service standards from the Swiss hotel and catering industry and also embraced lessons from other businesses that had created markets, not only in food and drink but elsewhere. It will come as no surprise to readers to realise that Donald Russell's success was down to its people.

Image 11.3 Donald Russell logo. © Donald Russell Ltd.

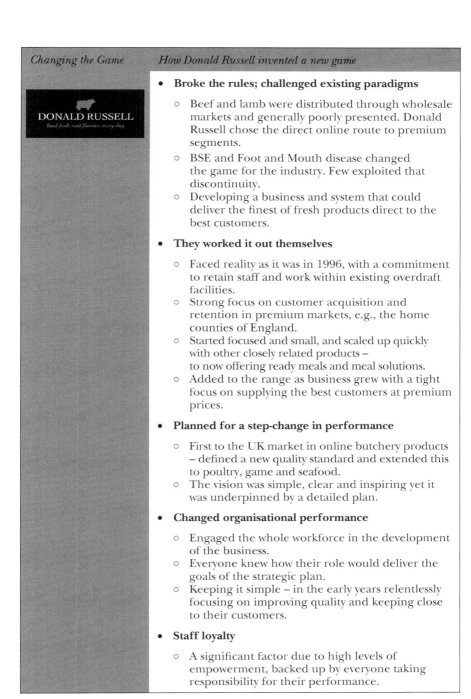

- **Broke the rules; challenged existing paradigms**

  - Beef and lamb were distributed through wholesale markets and generally poorly presented. Donald Russell chose the direct online route to premium segments.
  - BSE and Foot and Mouth disease changed the game for the industry. Few exploited that discontinuity.
  - Developing a business and system that could deliver the finest of fresh products direct to the best customers.

- **They worked it out themselves**

  - Faced reality as it was in 1996, with a commitment to retain staff and work within existing overdraft facilities.
  - Strong focus on customer acquisition and retention in premium markets, e.g., the home counties of England.
  - Started focused and small, and scaled up quickly with other closely related products – to now offering ready meals and meal solutions.
  - Added to the range as business grew with a tight focus on supplying the best customers at premium prices.

- **Planned for a step-change in performance**

  - First to the UK market in online butchery products – defined a new quality standard and extended this to poultry, game and seafood.
  - The vision was simple, clear and inspiring yet it was underpinned by a detailed plan.

- **Changed organisational performance**

  - Engaged the whole workforce in the development of the business.
  - Everyone knew how their role would deliver the goals of the strategic plan.
  - Keeping it simple – in the early years relentlessly focusing on improving quality and keeping close to their customers.

- **Staff loyalty**

  - A significant factor due to high levels of empowerment, backed up by everyone taking responsibility for their performance.

Image 11.4 Donald Russell logo. © Donald Russell Ltd.

From the belief and bravery of Willie Donald and John Stone in recruiting and empowering Hans Baumann, and the latter's charisma and relentless drive for success, they had the ingredients for success. Added to that, the recruitment of a young and ambitious team and the support of the likes of Scottish Enterprise Grampian provided the capability and capacity to grow the business.

There are many lessons that can be taken from this case study that any SME would be wise to follow. It was a privilege for Genesis to be involved at a number of points in a journey that has taken Donald Russell from the ashes of BSE to a segment-leading position in the food industry.

Postscript

The Vesty Group purchased Donald Russell from Willie Donald and John Stone in late 2012 for £30m, retaining the existing management team to take it forward.

Notes

1 *The Change Masters*, Rosabeth Moss Kanter, George Allen and Unwin, 1984.
2 *Blue Ocean Strategy*, W. Chan Kim and Renée Mauborgne, Harvard Business Review Press, 2005.

12 Adelon[1] Ireland
The road to a strategic site

James Bowen

Introduction

Foreign direct investment (FDI) is a key driver of the economies of many of the countries where we work. Taking Ireland as an example, more than 200,000 people are directly employed by more than 1,300 foreign-owned multinationals, and in 2015 these operations spent a total of €18.7bn in the Irish economy, including €1.5bn on R&D.[2]

Ireland, along with other countries including Singapore, Scotland and the Netherlands, has consistently punched above its weight in attracting FDI. Government has developed tailored policies in taxation, education, infrastructure and technology, and the IDA – Ireland's inward investment agency – has done a great job selling the country's proposition to major corporations. Looking forward, however, it appears the game will only get tougher, with outbound investment, in particular from the US, coming under significant political scrutiny, and international competition for that investment, already fierce, ratcheting up even further.

To hold on to what they have and to continue to win a disproportionate share of new FDI, countries need a multi-dimensional response. Governments need to push their policy agendas – to ensure taxation remains competitive and aligned with the investments they want to win, and also to ensure infrastructural, skills and other obstacles to investment are addressed. National investment agencies, like the IDA, need also to further raise their games as their countries' sales and marketing agencies. On their own, however, we believe these steps are not enough. Rather, we believe local leaders of many existing subsidiaries need to take a bigger hand in their own sustainability.

This chapter outlines our view of what this means, using a case study that describes our eight-year partnership with the leadership team of Adelon Ireland. It tells the story of how the leadership team of Adelon Ireland took an active role in ensuring the continued growth and sustainability of their site, and shows the positive impact of their commitment – on the levels of performance, investment and employment at the site – over time.

Adelon is a food company with a focus on developing and commercialising high-nutrition dairy-based food products primarily for emerging market customers. Originally founded in Switzerland in 1985, Adelon Limited was acquired in 2012 by BigFood Corp. – the US-based global leader in functional foods. Post-acquisition, Adelon has been merged with BigFood's own dairy products business such that BigFood Adelon exists now as a fully integrated unit of the overall Corporation.

Adelon Ireland is based near Limerick, at the edge of the 'Golden Vale' in the southwest of Ireland. Established in 2001 as a packaging facility, by 2008 – when our work with the team commenced – the scale and scope of activity on site had expanded to include high-tech development, formulation and spray-drying operations. Prior to the BigFood acquisition, as one of 24 Adelon production sites across Europe and the USA, Adelon Ireland manufactured 200+ individual items across eight different product lines, and distributed to 50+ countries in predominantly developing regions of the world. With a workforce of more than 350 people, the majority of whom were third-level qualified, Adelon was one of the local area's flagship employers.

Part 1: 2008 – the 'original' site strategy

Our initial engagement with Adelon Ireland was to work with the team to develop a site strategy. Just ahead of our project, the leadership team had completed a visioning exercise that produced as its output an articulation of what the business aimed to achieve over the medium term along a series of different dimensions. Our brief was to build on these outputs and support the team in designing a strategy to put the vision in place.

Two key challenges that we faced in taking on this engagement were (a) to define the target outcome, and (b) to create the space – in terms of share of calendar and share of mind – to make progress. Our approach was to frame the exercise as being about developing a strategy for Adelon Ireland to *compete*. We argued that the site needed to develop, and own, a strategy that would deliver competitive advantage on two levels as follows.

1   Maximising Adelon Ireland's role in driving Adelon Limited's competitive advantage, growth and performance.
2   Positioning Adelon Ireland as an integral element of the Corporation's success for the long term.

The consequences of framing the project in this way were important. In the first instance it introduced an edge to the exercise, creating a platform for arguing that over time the site *could* win, or lose, in a meaningful way, and that managing incrementally on a short-term basis was not going to be enough. Second, it forced the team to prioritise and work *across functions* to build defined agreed sources of advantage – first for the Corporation versus its competitors, and then for the site relative to others within the network. Third, it forced the adoption of a more 'outside-in' approach to the exercise, as improved understanding of the evolving market and corporate contexts were recognised as prerequisites for effective competitive strategy development.

Having agreed the target outcomes, we worked with the team to develop a purpose-built approach based on 'lenses (see Figure 12.1).

The lenses shown were identified as those we thought would bring the most insight to the exercise. Note that, of the eight chosen, five are explicitly 'outside-in' (i.e., rather than relating to the site itself, they relate to the context within which it operates) and only three are 'inside-out'. With the lenses defined, we worked off-line with the team to develop high-level answers to three specific questions as follows:

1   What are the key themes that we observe in this lens?
2   How do these themes impact on/relate to the business?
3   How might the themes play out over the course of our planning horizon?

The outputs of this research were summarised for each lens, becoming the subject matter for a leadership team strategy workshop. This approach, while involved and intense, brought two key benefits. In the first instance leaders deepened their collective awareness of what was going on in each lens, opening their eyes in particular to the changing and demanding world outside the site's boundaries. Second, and perhaps more importantly, the team was able to join the dots *across* the lenses – connecting cause and effect, and building much better clarity around the opportunities and challenges facing the site.

From here the team was able to home in on the three to four key strategy questions to be addressed and mobilise in sub-groups to make progress. Over the following three months they addressed the questions, constructed the strategy and packaged it for launch with the workforce. Along the way they identified and actioned a series of 'no regrets moves' that allowed the work to have immediate impact.

Figure 12.1 Adelon Ireland strategy lenses. Source: James Bowen (2018).

The detail of the 2008 strategy demonstrated a real step change in the attitudes, ambitions and collective focus of the team. Key elements included: (a) a commitment to achieve levels of performance 'stretch', against the most important site KPIs, that were significantly greater than had previously been contemplated; (b) a commitment in parallel to building corporation-leading capabilities in key areas of manufacturing excellence that would raise the profile and value of the site within Adelon; and finally (c) an explicit intent to extend the manufacturing mandate of the site over the horizon of the plan. Every member of the team played a 'public' role in launching the plan with the site's workforce – a move that added tremendously to their individual and collective ownership and sent a real signal of intent to their people to get energised and engaged.

Part 2: 2012 – getting ahead of the acquisition

Implementation of the 2008 strategy went really well over the period that followed its launch, with the Limerick site's performance improving dramatically and systematically, and Adelon's corporate leaders becoming increasingly aware of the quality of the assets they had at their disposal. Three years later, however, in mid-2011, the landscape changed completely. The US-based giant BigFood appeared on the horizon as a suitor for Adelon and, over the subsequent months, engaged in a process that led ultimately to acquisition in early 2012.

Adelon Ireland, having arrived at a place where it was the only site of its type in the Adelon network and a flagship site overall, now faced the prospect of being integrated into a BigFood manufacturing network which included 57 sites, employed 25,000 people and produced literally hundreds of products daily, several using similar processes to those in place in Limerick. Rather than sitting back, letting the acquisition run its course and seeing what the new world brought with it, Adelon Ireland's leadership team decided to stay on the front foot.

Ahead of the deal, indeed at a point when the success of BigFood's bid was by no means guaranteed, the team asked us to support them in thinking and strategising through its potential implications. We started by building a profile of the company and, more particularly, its manufacturing operations. To do this we trawled through publicly available information and leveraged all available contacts. We built pen-pictures of BigFood's product portfolio, its leadership, and its key sites of relevance to us. Then we pieced together recent statements, newsflow and other commentaries to build a sense of how they were thinking about business, product and especially manufacturing strategy. Finally, using this information, we developed alternative scenarios – both positive and negative – for how an acquisition of Adelon by BigFood might play out for Limerick. All of this information formed the basis for a series of briefing and strategy discussions with the team.

The consequence of this work was to give the site a head-start when it came to establishing itself in the BigFood world post-acquisition. The team updated its shared ambition, from being leaders within Adelon to being leaders within the new combined entity, and reframed its strategy – and more especially its stakeholder management – to achieve that end. They created a shortlist of BigFood corporate executives they wanted to connect with, and a narrative for how they wanted the site to be presented. They were proactive in inviting senior executives to visit, and pulled out all the stops to make sure those visits were successful – engaging and involving not only the workforce but also the local community and national government to that end.

The effect was dramatic. In January 2013, just months after the acquisition was completed, Limerick was the first Adelon site to be visited by BigFood's global CEO Art Crumb who, in describing what he saw, used the explicit and important language of 'strategic site'. In the months that followed he backed up his words by committing to a significant new investment in Limerick to develop and manufacture a new variant of one of BigFood's flagship products. This breakthrough was as important in its symbolism as its substance, in that this was the first instance of a legacy Adelon site being given an important role with regard to a mainstream BigFood product.

Part 3: 2015 – resetting Adelon Ireland's strategic horizons

For the final part of this story we roll the clock forward another two years to 2015, when we again had the opportunity to work with the Irish site's leadership team – this time on renewing the site's strategy to reflect the dramatic changes that had taken place since its last full refresh. The approach this time around was similar to 2008, and the spirit of the outcomes was also similar. However, there were two key outcomes of the process that bear being highlighted here.

The first was an explicit commitment in the strategy to *protecting the core*. This reflects an overt recognition on the part of the leadership team that the site's right to grow is founded entirely on its ability to deliver consistently and reliably on its existing mandate. Leaders in multinational manufacturing organisations – especially in highly-regulated industries like this one – have justifiably low appetites for manufacturing issues and risks. As such, over time, they become very positively disposed towards sites they perceive to be under control. Having the intent to protect the core enshrined in the Limerick site's strategy brought with it two main consequences; increased leadership focus on and ownership of performance commitments in the round and, second, increased investment in risk management – processes, technologies and people – enabling anticipation and early warning of issues as well as preventative or mitigating actions.

The second outcome we would highlight is the reiteration of the 2008 commitment to grow the site's mandate over time – specifically through a cross-site focus on *improving the rate at which we improve*. This reflects the leadership team's recognition that, in order for any proposition it might put forward for new investment to be compelling, it needed to be based on leverage – on taking advantage of available physical, infrastructural, technical and/or organisational capacity to achieve safety, quality, cost and other synergies versus greenfield or other options. The faster the team could create new capacity in key areas, the earlier and greater the opportunities it could unlock. As a result of this strategic commitment, the team homed in on organisational and leadership benchstrength, prioritising leadership development and succession to make sure it could staff new opportunities as they arose. It also channelled investment towards automation of key processes to give scalability at low levels of marginal cost.

Taken in the round, the consequences of the 2015 strategy exercise have again provided an important basis for continued performance improvement at Limerick. In parallel they have enabled further improved positioning and reputation of the site within the BigFood network. As a result the site has seen further capital investment in facilities and equipment to make more and different products, establishing an expanded platform on which to build the next phase of sustainability and growth.

Conclusion

Site sustainability in a multinational environment is a niche area of strategy that is really important for corporations as well as for local and national economies. Relying, as it does, on local management initiative, we find that, for a number of reasons – some good and others not so good – it often falls through the cracks. This brings bad consequences – mostly in terms of missed opportunities – for parent corporations. However, on occasion, the consequences at a more local level can be devastating.

The story of Adelon Ireland offers one illustration of how site leadership teams can be proactive and look, in a way that is appropriate and fit for purpose, to influence their own destinies within a corporate environment. For us, there is unequivocally no downside here – as long as local teams understand that they exist as entities of a bigger corporation, with a primary responsibility to deliver their 'core' mandate and a secondary growth responsibility that is framed by the context of where the corporation is looking to go. Rather, our story highlights the potential that exists for a win:win: a great news story for Limerick – for both the site and the community within which it exists – and also a great news story for BigFood. Most particularly it's a great news story for the developing-world families who depend for their well-being on BigFood Adelon's products.

James Bowen
Genesis Director (2004–2010);
Managing Director of Kotinos Partners

Adelon Ireland

- **Broke the rules; challenged existing paradigms**

  - They 'swam against the tide' – adopting the mindset of commercial businesses in a world where their operation was defined as a cost centre.
  - Created local unity of purpose in a world where matrix structures were working to pull the local team apart.
  - Invested local leadership time on strategy in a world where they were resourced to spend time on operations.
  - Developed local talent in a world where the focus was on cost elimination.
  - Created local opportunities for growth in a world where competition was high and politics was important. They developed clarity about the sustainability challenge they faced.

- **They worked it out themselves – embraced change management**

  - They became clear about the local capabilities required to meet these objectives.
  - Vision – real ambition for local development, anchored in real understanding of where the corporation was looking to go over time.
  - Operational competence – 'safe hands' with respect to operational basics; a focus on eliminating waste and risk; and on developing and retaining talent.
  - They embedded strategy and business development processes at local level.

- **Planned for a step-change in performance**

  - Delivered on each of two objectives in parallel – maintained a track record of delivering on all near-term performance commitments *and* increased the role and influence of the subsidiary as integral to the corporation's long-term success.

- **Changed organisational performance**

  - Stakeholder management – strong relationships with corporate executives based on multiple, regular, planned points of contact; proactive involvement of local leaders in corporate initiatives – having them become recognised for adding ideas, insight and capabilities to the mix.

Notes

1 This study is based on real experience. However, actual situations and names have been disguised throughout this chapter to protect client confidentiality – being replaced with fictitious alternatives.
2 Source: IDA Ireland, 2016 Annual Report.

Part II

Changing the game in sport

13 Ambition as a driving force for performance

Brian MacNeice

Introduction

Ambition is a vital starting point for sustained high performance. It is an essential ingredient – but by no means the only one – without which it is virtually impossible to reach the goal of excellence to which most organisations aspire.

Over the last five years we have been lucky enough to have access to some of the most successful and inspiring high-performance environments across business, sport, the arts, military and several other sectors. The research journey covered the Indian subcontinent with Tata Group and the Grameen Bank, to New Zealand with the All Blacks, into Russia with the Kirov Ballet, across Europe taking in institutions such as the Finnish State School Education System and Médecins Sans Frontières, the US with organisations like Southwest Airlines, the Mayo Clinic, the St. Louis Cardinals and the Marine Corps.[1] What became clear, very quickly, was the importance of ambition as a driving force for performance. It was one of several common characteristics repeated across the various exemplars of high performance visited.

So why is ambition so important in driving performance and how do you leverage it to deliver the impact you want?

Fly me to the moon

In 1962 John F. Kennedy delivered an inspirational speech at Rice University. In his address, he set out the rationale for embarking on the ambitious project of sending a manned flight to the moon and returning it safely to Earth again, and to do so before the end of the decade. The words he used in his speech are illuminating:

> We choose to go to the moon. We choose to go to the moon in this decade and do the other things, not because they are easy but because they are hard, because that goal will serve to organise and measure the best of our energies and skills, because that challenge is one that we are willing to accept, one we are unwilling to postpone, and one which we intend to win.
>
> President John F. Kennedy, address at Rice University, Houston, Texas, 12 September 1962. Source: *Presidential Papers of John F. Kennedy.*

In these words he captures the essence of 'unreasonable ambition'. Kennedy was clear that the reason behind this great endeavour was because it was really challenging and hard. It was such a difficult and ambitious project that this would force the nation to combine the best of its skills and knowledge to meet that challenge. It would ensure that the level of creativity and innovation would be significantly increased in order to take on the near impossible goal. People would be forced to think in different ways, work together as they had never done before, be at their best all the time and really make the most of all the talents available to achieve the unthinkable. As a result, the benefits to the nation would reach far beyond the merely vain claim of being the first nation to complete a manned moon landing. The advances in technology, new inventions, applications of existing knowledge in new ways, level of creativity and scientific development would serve to drive progress forward at a great pace. This was the real benefit of embracing this 'unreasonable ambition'.

In virtually every high-performance environment researched, we see ambition at play. It may not always be called 'unreasonable ambition', but it exists and is a critical element in delivering improved performance. The driving force of a stretch goal or the just-possible challenge lies at the heart of the performance energy within an organisation.

The antithesis of this notion is a commonly-heard phrase in companies – 'let's under promise and over deliver'. This creates a culture that promotes mediocrity and lack of ambition. If you have an entire organisation operating under this maxim where will the drive, energy, innovation and challenge to continually pursue better performance come from?

Ambition should be 'unreasonable' – challenging the paradigm and fostering a culture of continual challenge

It is important to set the bar for ambition at a level that seems, at current course and speed, to be out of reach. This creates positive dissatisfaction with the status quo and challenges individuals and teams to think differently – deconstructing 'good enough' approaches and innovating to build something fundamentally better. This challenging mindset becomes fundamental to the culture of high-performing organisations. It is omni-present.

A case in point is the culture that prevails with the New Zealand All Blacks rugby team. They are the most successful international team in any sport on the planet. However, they are never satisfied with their current standard. They are always seeking ways in which they can improve. After every game they challenge themselves to identify ways in which they can be even better. It is this constant focus on always improving that helps them sustain their performance as All Blacks, generation after generation.

The same philosophy is mirrored across every high-performance environment we have studied. It is driven by, and to some extent defined by, the presence of ambition as a core component of the organisational DNA. Without it, the continual challenge that drives performance improvement simply does not exist. When it does exist, it becomes the catalyst for continual change and performance improvement.

Ambition is uncomfortable – get comfortable with that

It is often an uncomfortable place for leaders to go. By definition, 'unreasonable' suggests a demand beyond the capability of the organisation. But therein lies the crucial point. By aiming for something that is just out of reach, it creates an energy and focus for improvement that lifts the organisation. Leaders must be prepared for the naysayers who will say it is not possible. If they don't exist, in our experience, the ambition has not been set high enough.

Reflecting on another example from the research, Dr Muhammad Yunus, the founder of the Grameen Bank in Bangladesh and Nobel Peace Prize winner, set his organisation – a profitable corporate entity not a charity – the challenge of eliminating poverty forever. In so doing, Dr Yunus unlocked the door to transformational thinking that in turn drove the success of the Grameen Bank. In his words, 'Let us dream the wildest dream and then pursue it'. This driving force helped release 100 million families from the curse of living below the poverty line. Poverty in Bangladesh is not eradicated; however the Grameen Bank, by taking on this challenge in the first instance, has made massive inroads into empowering and lifting generations of families from below the poverty line.

Ambition should capture hearts, not just minds

Good ambitions appeal to the emotions as well as the intellect. They capture the imagination and provide real meaning for individuals in organisations, inspiring them to give of their very best. Exactly what it is that captivates will reflect the specific circumstances of each organisation and its people; however, it is essential that any ambition challenge must be framed in a way that enables people to emotionally buy into it. We like to use the phrase 'The view must be worth the climb' to describe this.

When you get this right, it becomes a powerful force of engagement for staff within the organisation. People become proud of what they do and committed to it in ways you only see in organisations that have been energised through ambition. Some months after his famous speech at Rice University, when visiting the NASA Space Center, JFK encountered a janitor. He introduced himself and asked the man what he did at NASA. The janitor replied 'I'm helping put a man on the moon!' This is a perfect example of a captivating ambition that engaged and energised an entire organisation.

Ambition should be linked to the core purpose of the organisation

The Mayo Clinic, the US-based medical practice and research group, has a powerful core purpose – 'the needs of the patient come first'. This is used to define the primary value that drives everything that happens at the Mayo. Their ambition to be the best-integrated healthcare practice in the world is rooted in this core purpose. It links that ambition to the very reason the clinic exists in the first instance. By doing this it creates total alignment across the 60,000 plus staff working at the Mayo.

The route to delivering an ambition challenge should not be overly prescriptive

In the majority of cases, when leaders or organisations set 'unreasonable ambition' challenges they do not know at the outset exactly how they will achieve that goal. This is a good thing, not a bad one. One of the core reasons for setting the challenge in the first instance is that it creates a dynamic of creativity and 'game-changing' behaviour. If the journey to achieving the aim is defined explicitly, it limits the scope for new ideas, paradigms and behaviours.

Strong leaders set the challenge. They then empower the organisation to figure out how it can be realised. They unlock the full potential of the people within the organisation to problem solve, to invent new ways of doing things and to set new standards in every aspect of what they do. After all, to have any chance of pulling off the challenge, this is what it takes. Therefore, ambitions should be framed so as to leave the widest possible scope for individuals and organisations to innovate in respect of their approach.

Reflecting on the example of the Grameen Bank, establishing the simple ambition to use micro finance to eliminate poverty led to a raft of innovative actions that fundamentally challenged the status quo in Bangladeshi banking. The Grameen lent money to assetless women, introduced a set of guiding philosophies ('The 16 Decisions Model'[2]) for how the borrowers should behave, turned traditional banking practices on their head and, in so doing, changed dramatically the lives of so many poverty-stricken families.

None of this would have happened without the catalyst of the ambition Dr Yunus set and the flood of innovative thinking that followed.

Ambition does not mean 'win at all costs'

There is a danger that ambition can be mistaken for a justification to do whatever it takes, to win at all costs. This is not the case. It is essential that the core principles of an organisation are not sacrificed at the altar of unfettered ambition. Ambition, while stretching, must be clearly and overtly constrained by institutional boundaries of safety, quality, legal compliance and the core values of the organisation. Most of the time these limitations reside in the background of day-to-day activity. However, in high-pressure situations, they become absolutely critical as guides to management behaviour and decision-making.

The recent global financial crisis exposed the dangers of ambition being pursued in the absence of strong guidelines and controls for behaviours in many organisations. Leaders must be clear and strong in their determination to chase the ambition goal without compromising core principles to get there.

Ambition should be managed to build momentum and confidence over time

One of the most difficult elements of the concept of 'unreasonable ambition' is that, when set, a large proportion of the population within an organisation initially think that the challenge is unachievable. In fact, if this is not the case then as a leader you have not set the bar high enough. In our experience, and this is a rule of thumb not a scientifically proven fact, the most effective scenario is where approximately 75% of the people within the organisation think the challenge is impossible.

The job of the leader then becomes one of building momentum and confidence over time in the ability of the organisation to meet the challenge. To achieve this, it is critical to set and recognise milestones in the journey towards achieving the goal. We call these milestones 'islands of achievement'. Each time one is hit, celebrate the fact publicly. As the various 'islands' are conquered, slowly but surely the confidence of the people increases. The 75% cohort reduces over time. People start to change their minds about the plausibility of the challenge. Eventually a corner is turned when over 50% now believe it can be done. At that point momentum gathers and the speed at which the organisation drives towards its ultimate goal increases.

This is exactly what happened at the Grameen Bank. After the initial experiments on a small scale with a few borrowers proved successful, the project was expanded to other areas in Bangladesh. When these in turn delivered the results anticipated, more and more people started to believe. Eventually the momentum built to such an extent that the concept of eliminating poverty for large swathes of people in the country became a reality.

Dr Yunus said his biggest challenge was to fight the mindset that prevented people from seeing what was possible, but he met that challenge by logging and recognising each success – each 'island of achievement' – along the way. Eventually the momentum became so strong that nothing has been able to stop Grameen's progress towards its ambition.

Success is not a binary equation

It is important to set clear parameters for how you define success when taking on an 'unreasonable ambition' challenge. In some cases the organisation doesn't make it all the way. For example, poverty is still endemic in Bangladesh. The Grameen Bank has not completely eradicated it for everyone in the country. If you are to go by the strict definition of what Dr Yunus set out to achieve, he and the bank he founded have failed. However, since the inception of the bank in the mid-1970s, the Grameen has helped some 100 million families rise above the poverty line. Nobody can claim that this is failure. This is an unbridled success story. To this day, the Grameen Bank is the only profit-making corporate entity to be awarded the Nobel Peace Prize.[3]

By way of example, assume you are a leader in a business currently mid-ranking in performance in your industry. You set the organisation the challenge to become number one in your chosen market. This leads to a raft of innovation, new ideas, energy and drive across the business. Some three years later you are standing at number three in your market. That is success, not failure. The organisation has transformed from mediocre to high-performing. Your journey is not yet over, but the momentum generated by taking on the challenge has led you a long way towards that goal.

It is not just about ambition – it is also about what happens next

Ambition is only the starting point. What you do next matters just as much. The setting of an ambition challenge should mobilise a planning process that allows the organisation to determine how to get from where they are now to where they want to be in the future. As outlined above, that journey should not be prescriptive from the outset. However, the organisation should deploy planning processes that convert the ambition into action. It should spawn an on-going process of review with everyone engaged in challenging how they are doing against the stated ambition. It should result in continual re-evaluation of the best route to take and the setting of clear priorities at any point in time, consistent with the end goal.

What follows is an example of this in action. We have worked closely with Cricket Ireland as an organisation over the last decade. Their story reflects all of the principles of how ambition drives performance.

Cricket Ireland – a transformed organisation

Warren Deutrom is the CEO of Cricket Ireland. His first day in the job on a cold icy day in December 2006 is etched in his memory. He arrived at the offices of the Irish Cricket Union[4] in Dublin in a facility shared by several other Irish sports governing bodies. The cramped 10m × 10m office had room for two desks, one for him and the other for the part-time PA. The only other paid employee was the head coach, Adi Birrell. Flanking the Cricket office were larger offices occupied by staff of Mountaineering Ireland and the Irish Canoe Union. Warren, having joined from the International Cricket Council (ICC), the sports world governing body, and having relocated his family from Monaco to Dublin, reflected on the rude awakening of his new surroundings, 'Such was the HQ of the 13th best country in the world's 2nd largest sport!'

It is less than a decade ago but the contrast between then and now is remarkable. At the end of 2006 the Irish Cricket Union was an un-incorporated body overseen by an Executive Committee of 18, with two full-time staff and one part-time administrator, no contracted players, fewer than 13,000 players across the island of Ireland, revenues of less than €265,000 with the vast majority of this in the form of grant income from government bodies or the ICC. The sport enjoyed precious little coverage in the media in Ireland. It is fair to say that cricket, both on and off the field, was an insignificant player in the Irish sporting landscape.

It is worth comparing that picture with the one that exists today. On and off the field the story is very different. Cricket Ireland is now an incorporated entity. Governed by a board of 12 people with a mixture of business and cricketing expertise, the organisation employs 30 full- and part-time staff. In addition, some 18 players are contracted to play for Ireland. Turnover now exceeds €6m per annum, of which approximately 50% is generated through non-grant income sources. There are 52,000 registered players across the island of Ireland. Cricket has the 2nd largest social media profile of any sport in Ireland – second only to Rugby Union – and outstrips the traditional sports of Gaelic games and Soccer. From an organisational point of view, the entity that greeted Warren on his appointment as CEO is unrecognisable from the modern-day organisation over which he now presides.

On the field, the development in that time has been similarly dramatic. In 2006, Ireland had never played in a World Cup event. The qualification of the Irish team for the 2007 World Cup in the West Indies was to change that. A decade later, the results speak for themselves. Ireland has qualified for each of the last eight ICC Men's World events. In each of the last three World Cups Ireland has beaten major test-playing nations. They have won four of the last five InterContinental Cup competitions and, at the time of writing, they sit on top of the table in the current edition. The Irish women's team has qualified for the last two T20 World Cups, winning the qualification tournament outright last time around.

In the same way that Cricket Ireland as an organisation has developed beyond all recognition over the last decade to become one of the most admired and well-run sports governing bodies in Ireland, the Irish cricket teams have become a force on the world stage and recognised as the strongest emerging nation in the world. How did such a transformation, on and off the field, occur?

Part 1: 2007 – the pirates of the Caribbean

Sabina Park, Kingston, Jamaica, 17 March 2007 – St Patrick's Day. Ireland have just bowled Pakistan out for 132 and have an opportunity to make cricket history. The captain, Trent Johnston, gives an impassioned speech to the team of amateur players before they go out to bat. Looking each in the eye he asks a simple question. Do you want to go back to your day job or live this dream for six more weeks? The players were emphatic in their answers. Some three hours later, Ireland were victorious and one of the biggest shocks in World Cup history was complete.

Nobody was prepared for what had just happened. The shockwaves were felt back in the Irish Cricket Union headquarters too. Totally unprepared for the success of the team at the World Cup the organisation was exposed. In the short term, the problems were operational. First, there was no budget available to pay for the costs of keeping the team at the tournament for the second-round stages. Second, the organisation was inadequately resourced to cope with the demands this unforeseen success had. What followed was a chaotic period of papering over the cracks to keep the show on the road. The team went on to perform outstandingly well in the latter stages of the tournament and returned home to national acclaim.

The players had led the way. They had an inner belief backed up by a professional mind-set – in spite of the fact they were part-time amateur cricketers – and a steely determination to overcome the odds. They demanded respect. Moreover, they earned it. Warren Deutrom as CEO knew that it was time the organisation responded in kind. If this was to be something more than a fleeting success, the organisation itself had to transform. This was the moment for cricket in Ireland to grasp the opportunity. What was required was organisational ambition and bravery that matched that of the players.

The first step was a radical restructuring of the organisation itself. The part-time PA was replaced with a full-time Teams Administrator to manage the needs of the playing and coaching staff. At a more strategic level, a governance review was conducted and resulted in several recommendations including incorporation as a limited company, a slimmed-down governance model and a new brand name. The executive committee of 18 was replaced with a more focused board with a mix of cricket and business backgrounds. Independent directors were appointed, with marketing, commercial and legal experience. The organisation was re-formed under the Cricket Ireland name.

Other bold decisions were taken. At the time the Irish team played in a limited overs English County competition. The best Irish players had started to play on the county circuit and so were unavailable for the national team when playing in this competition. In spite of being competitive on the World Cup stage, the Irish team, shorn of its best players, struggled when facing county opposition. It was decided to withdraw from the English

County competition. Warren Deutrom explains the rationale of that decision: 'We wanted to be what we were, the 10th best country in the world, not the 19th best English county'. The decision was not universally popular. With no guarantees of international fixtures, many wondered when and where Ireland would play. Ireland hosted a tri-series event with India and South Africa against the wishes of the ECB, in a bold move that led to a significant arrangement being agreed with the ECB regarding future fixtures against England and the bundling of TV rights for Irish games into the ECB deal with Sky for a considerable financial consideration. These moves were a statement of ambition. In hindsight they were examples of many that helped transform the fortunes of Irish cricket.

Part 2: 2011 – an Indian adventure

M Chinnaswamy Stadium, Bangalore, India, 2 March 2011. Ireland are playing England in the ICC World Cup. England post an imposing total of 327 for 8. Ireland are in trouble chasing it at 111 for 5. Enter Kevin O'Brien. A stunning century, the fastest in World Cup history, changes the course of the game and Ireland record a remarkable victory with five balls to spare. Yet again, the Irish team have rocked the world of cricket. However, this time it is not as big a surprise as four years before. In the intervening period Ireland has established itself as a formidable team capable of testing the very best. This result is confirmation that Ireland belongs at the top table of world cricket.

Cricket Ireland as an organisation had changed too in those four years. A commercial programme had been developed that attracted corporate sponsorship, which helped fuel the growth of the game. Buoyed by the success of the 2007 World Cup and the profile it generated for the game, staff numbers had grown. Development officers were now employed, charged with increasing participation levels domestically. Players were contracted to play for Ireland. The quality of preparation for the national team was vastly improved. The Irish team were now succeeding internationally because of, not in spite of, the organisation behind it.

It was time for the next statement of intent from Cricket Ireland. They launched a new strategic plan with lofty objectives. Ireland to become a test nation by 2020 was the headline. It was backed up by other equally ambitious targets – doubling of playing numbers over the next four years, the introduction of a domestic 'first class' equivalent competition, securing more ODIs (One Day Internationals) against test nations, hosting major events including a target to attract 10,000 people to an ODI, the establishment of a National Academy programme to develop the next generation of international players, a commercial programme that generated sufficient finances to support the plan and the professionalisation of the provincial structures underpinning the domestic game.

When launched, the plan was greeted with widespread scepticism. For a start, the goal of becoming a test nation by 2020 was ridiculed on the basis that there was no pathway to achieve this in the first instance, and how could 'minnow' Ireland be so bold as to announce publicly such an 'unreasonable' ambition. However, there were enough people within the leadership of the sport that believed in the plan. They set about taking the necessary steps to fulfil the targets. They focused on each step in the journey, emboldened by the sheer scale of thinking that lay behind it. Warren Deutrom summed it up well when he said:

> We were sure of one thing. We needed to embrace a vision for the sport in which our reach exceeded our grasp. We believed that in doing so the shame would not be to fail but rather being afraid to try.

Four years later, yet again, the results spoke for themselves. Player numbers had doubled. A multi-format inter-provincial competition was successfully launched, acting as a bridge between the club game and the international side. The number of ODIs Ireland played increased. When Ireland played England in their new international venue at Malahide in September 2013 they played to a capacity 10,000 attendance. The National Cricket Academy was established, underwritten by a ten-year sponsorship agreement from an Indian company. The commercial programme flourished, with a host of major companies investing in the game, providing a sustainable revenue base for the expansion of the development programmes undertaken by the increasing staff numbers working within the organisation.

Most important of all, the ICC announced a pathway, through the InterContinental Cup, that ultimately could lead to test cricket status for a nation such as Ireland. There is no doubt that the bold statement that was the headline of the Cricket Ireland strategic plan was a critical factor in forcing this change within the world governing body.

The doubts expressed at the announcement of the ambitious plan were silenced as the milestones were knocked off one by one. Irish cricket was now admired, not just for what the players were doing on the field but equally for what the organisation was achieving off the field. As one leading sports administrator in the country remarked to us, 'Cricket Ireland is the standard which all other governing bodies in the country are benchmarked. They are the envy of many for what they have achieved in such a short space of time'.

Reflecting on the progress made since 2007, Warren Deutrom is clear that one of his key roles as CEO, and that of the organisation in general, has been and will continue to be the alignment of the domestic game and the buy-in of the multiple stakeholders within the sport.

We have instigated a period of radical change for cricket in Ireland. We always have to ensure that we bring those within the game along with us on that journey. That takes considerable effort and planning, but put simply we could not have achieved all we have without the support and commitment of those within the game.

The various changes, at a domestic level, such as the governance re-structure in 2007/2008, the introduction of eight-team domestic leagues in the three strongest unions, the re-introduction of the Inter-Pro competition and the provincial union organisational capability development are some of the steps that the volunteers, who are the lifeblood of the sport, have helped implement.

Part 3: 2015 – the road to mainstream

Saxton Oval, Nelson, New Zealand, 16 February 2015. Ireland are taking on the West Indies in the ICC World Cup. Pre-game, the predictions are that this game will be too close to call. Many pundits predict an Ireland win. Others call it for the West Indies. The fact that opinion is divided in this way is a sign of just how far Ireland's standing in the game had grown since 2007. As it happens the game goes Ireland's way. Chasing a formidable total of 304, the Irish side cruise to victory with almost five overs to spare. The result does not send shockwaves through the game in the way it might have done some eight years before.

Cricket Ireland had come to the end of its strategic plan cycle and it was time to refresh it. In reflecting on the previous four years, the board were adamant about one thing. They must not get complacent and curb their ambition. Equally, they acknowledged that much more needed to be done to ensure the long-term sustainability of the game in Ireland. International success was the platform for growth that had underpinned the previous eight years and was deliberately a major focus for the organisation in that period. However, it was essential that the grass roots of the game were not left behind. The investment focus needed to be re-balanced to reflect the importance of a solid foundation for the game.

The new strategic plan reflects that emphasis. The theme of the plan is about cricket becoming a mainstream sport in Ireland. In announcing the new plan Warren Deutrom explained what this means, 'Our goal of playing Test matches by the end of 2020 needs to be broader and more ambitious – it needs to envision Ireland not just being a major force in cricket, but cricket being a major force in Ireland'. At the heart of the plan is a drive to make the game visible, accessible, affordable and inspiring to ensure it takes its place with the other mainstream sports in Ireland, namely Rugby Union, GAA and soccer. The plan reflects the next phase of the transformational journey that cricket and Cricket Ireland have taken in the last decade. Yet again, it represents a bold and ambitious statement of direction. It reflects an organisation that was shaken into action by a group of talented committed players in 2007, and which has responded by matching their ambition and raising the bar significantly ever since.

On the 17 June 2017 a 16-word tweet was issued by cricket's world governing body, the International Cricket Council (ICC). It read as follows *'BREAKING . . . Ireland and Afghanistan confirmed as Full Members of the ICC after a unanimous vote at ICC Full Council meeting.'* A decade-long campaign to achieve full-member status in the international game was achieved. The vision, laid out several years earlier, to become a test nation by 2020 was realised – three years ahead of time. It is not the end of the story; rather the start of a new chapter in the journey of Irish cricket.

Conclusion

Ambition is a powerful driver of performance. Time and time again, the best-performing organisations in the world are ones that understand this concept and act accordingly. They are not afraid to be bold in their ambition. They inspire people within the organisation to achieve things they would not otherwise achieve. They are not afraid to declare their ambition in spite of the scepticism it might attract. They believe that failure is defined by not being willing to try rather than falling short of their target. They are willing to create a positive tension between where they are now and where they want to be in the future. They understand that this creates the platform for fresh thinking and innovation, the dynamic for bringing out the best in people and the spark for organisational energy to allow it to perform at the top of its game.

Cricket Ireland is a case in point. Over the last decade it has leveraged ambition to radically transform itself as an organisation. It has been bold in its intent. It has taken tough decisions that reflect its ambition. It has created a sense of purpose that has driven performance both on and off the field. And it has continually reset its ambition to ensure that driving force is always present.

Ask yourself these questions. What is your organisation's 'unreasonable ambition'? Do you have one? If not, what could it be? What great challenge for the future can you set for your business that will generate a positive tension that will drive people to perform at their very best?

Brian MacNeice
Genesis Director (2004–2010);
Managing Director of Kotinos Partners

CRICKET IRELAND

- **Broke the rules; challenged existing paradigms**

  - They changed the paradigm of thinking within the game in Ireland and more broadly across the international landscape, becoming an agitator for change, progress and performance focus.
  - No longer was cricket the 'Cinderella' sport behind Gaelic games, Rugby Union and football in Ireland.

- **They worked it out themselves – embraced change management**

  - They faced the reality of their position and their performance.
  - They developed a 'vision of success' for the first time in the sport's history.
  - They did not worry that having set the challenge, the path to achieving the goal was not clear. Instead they committed to the journey and trusted that they would navigate through the challenges. They made progress on all aspects of the sport and the business of Cricket Ireland.
  - The professional management, the board and the members were all aligned and committed behind the vision, the goals and the strategy.

- **Planned for a step-change in performance**

  - They set out an 'unreasonable' ambition to become a test nation by 2020 as a driver for change and step-change improvement across the board.
  - They challenged everything in the quest to achieve the ambition goal, safe in the knowledge that, even if the ultimate 'dream' of full-member status was not realised.
  - They celebrated the moment and quickly re-focused on the next challenge of leveraging their new status as a full member to 'make cricket mainstream' in Ireland.

- **Changed organisational performance**

  - Stakeholder management – strong relationships between the CEO, the Chair (after incorporation) and the board, as well as keeping the provincial associations on board.
  - Built strong relationships with the Irish Sports Council and other external stakeholders.

Image 13.1 Cricket Ireland logo. © Cricket Ireland.

Notes

1 For more detail on the research into high-performance organisations please refer to *Powerhouse: Insider Accounts into the World's Top High-Performance Organizations* by James Bowen and Brian MacNeice, published by Kogan Page, October 2016.
2 For more information on the Grameen Bank's 16 Decisions see: www.grameen-info.org/16-decisions.
3 The Grameen Bank and Dr Muhammad Yunus were jointly awarded the Nobel Peace Prize in 1996 in recognition of the contribution they made to addressing poverty in Bangladesh.
4 The Irish Cricket Union was dissolved and reformed as a limited company, Cricket Ireland, at its AGM in February 2008.

14 Sustaining sports in the future

Introduction

'Sport has the power to change the world', Nelson Mandela said.[1]

> It has the power to inspire. It has the power to unite people in a way that little else does. It speaks to youth in a language they understand. Sport can create hope where once there was only despair. It is more powerful than government in breaking down racial barriers.

Sports, their governing bodies and member nations have enjoyed unprecedented media coverage over the last two decades. They have also been the main beneficiaries of record funding from the International Olympic Committee, their national Olympic Committees, national sports councils, national lotteries, broadcasters and commercial sponsors.

Although the 2008 recession, arguably the deepest and lowest in recorded history, led to cutbacks and austerity measures, especially in public sector funding, the revenues from new forms of broadcasting such as streaming content to mobile devices appear almost recession-proof. Many smaller sports have benefited as the cost of broadcasting has fallen, driven by technology. Will these levels of revenue income be sustainable into the future?

More and more sports are now competing for a seat at the Olympic and Paralympic tables at both Summer and Winter Games. Paralympic sports have surged in popularity and now merit status as major games in their own right. How will existing sports stave off the threat coming from the 'new-age' sports and how will the latter present their case to the IOC?

The first part of this chapter addresses the question of how sports should plan to sustain themselves into the future. It is followed in the second part with unique insight from the IOC and leaders of a number of major sports on how they are addressing massive external challenges and, in some cases, changing their game as sporting organisations. Many are pursuing commercially driven strategies that result in their changing the actual game/sport itself, often into a shortened media-friendly format. Sustainability, however, will come from more than creating attractive and entertaining formats of the traditional sport. Without a strong social purpose and attention to the wider environment and issues such as equity and equality, sport will always leave itself open to criticism of its pursuit of greed and self-interest and will not be trusted to lead.

London 2012 – the last of the big spenders?

August 2012. Sebastian Coe, the organiser of the Games, stood up to urge the millions watching to appreciate the unique power of sport. 'There is a truth to sport', he insisted. 'A purity, a drama, an intensity – a spirit that makes it irresistible to take part in, and irresistible to watch'. At the time Coe's words proved instantly prophetic as Britain dived headfirst into a 16-day Olympic bender.

The numbers are extraordinary. Nearly 49 million combined to watch the opening and closing ceremonies. More than 17 million watched Usain Bolt streak away with the men's 100-metres title. Another 12 million watched the British joy of Super Saturday as Greg Rutherford, Jessica Ennis-Hill and Mo Farah won gold over 47 eardrum-shattering minutes. Across London – sullen, manic, heads-down London – everyone appeared to carry a permanent smile on their face, as if serotonin has been pumped into the water supply. Writing in the *Guardian*, Jonathan Freedland even asked whether the Games might 'mark the end of Britain's age of decline'. Coe, it seemed, was right. Sport did have this special capacity to unite, delight and inspire.

Fast-forward four years to August 2016. Rio de Janeiro hosted a glorious festival of sport, despite significant challenges faced in the build up. Since 2012 many nations, adopting austerity strategies, had been forced to reduce, or at least to re-focus, the spending on sport to aid recovery from the worst recession in living memory. The recession that began nearly eight years before was now changing into a sustained period of low slow growth that is now forecast to continue beyond 2020. Low growth, interest and inflation increases at this level provide a degree of stability but do nothing to deliver an environment in which many businesses can thrive.

It is clear that there will be less to go around for sport from traditional sources, especially the public sector, even after the successful performance at the 2016 Olympic Games. The reality is that NGBs (national governing bodies of sport) in most of the leading nations have received record levels of funding over the last decade. How sustainable will this be over the next quadrennial?

Team GB, which finished a record second in the medals table at Rio, received £250m from UK Sport (and the UK government) over the quadrennial from 2012 (less than 0.1% of GDP) to be the envy of many competing nations. Put in context, this represents around £1 per member of the population each year against a GDP of £40k per person. Australia, whose performance dipped below that delivered at Sydney's Olympic Games in 2000, spent $120m Australian each year (around £65m), which represents around £3 per person against a similar GDP per person of £40k.

Post 2016, those who delivered value hoped to retain 80% of their funding levels; those who did not will be forced into survival mode. No one has a divine right to the status quo. However, the playing field is far from level. In their 2017 funding review UK Sport stopped the performance funding of badminton, wheelchair rugby, archery, fencing, goalball and weightlifting. UK Sport stated that none of the six sports had provided 'critically compelling new evidence' that changed the assessment of their medal potential. UK Sport's money has transformed Britain into an Olympic and Paralympic superpower, but its 'no-compromise' approach is under more scrutiny than ever.

With falling ticket sales hitting crucial National Lottery funding, resources are undoubtedly stretched but, for the first time, sports with real podium potential are being excluded from funding, and many are now asking whether the focus on medals has gone too far.

Some sports live in a different world

Even during recession a number of major sports prospered as broadcasting and other commercial rights continued to spiral upwards, fuelled by growth in what broadcasters were prepared to pay for television and other channel rights. The charts in Figures 14.1 and 14.2 track the Olympic Games commercial rights values and the four-year viewing numbers of major events.

While the Summer Olympic Games still head the list, the fastest growth has occurred in football and rugby union. It was FIFA and UEFA that led the way, especially in the sale of commercial rights through the World Cup, European Championships and Champions League properties. The 2014 World Cup generated $4.8 billion in revenue for FIFA compared with $2.2 billion in expenses. Over the four-year cycle, the event turned a $2.6 billion profit, and FIFA made $2.4 billion in TV rights fees, $1.6 billion in sponsorships and $527 million in ticket sales (Figure 14.3).

Much of FIFA's World Cup spending went to participating teams and confederations ($476 million) and TV production costs ($370 million). FIFA

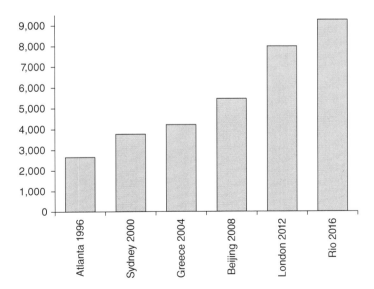

Figure 14.1 Olympic Games: commercial rights values. Chart created by Alistair Gray from World Rugby data.

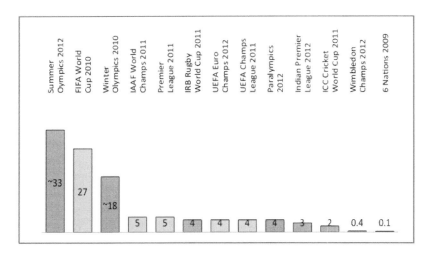

Figure 14.2 Cumulative viewership of select comparators. Chart created by Alistair
Gray from World Rugby data.

contributed $453 million to the local organising committee between 2011 and
2014, and gave Brazil a $100 million 'legacy' payment after the tournament.

However, FIFA did not contribute to the real costs of staging the tournament – stadiums and transportation infrastructure. The tournament cost
an estimated $15 billion, a significant portion of which was public money.
Brazil spent $3.6 billion building and renovating 12 stadiums for the tour-
nament. Less than a year later, some of those were turning into white
elephants. The $300 million Arena Amazonia in Manaus, for example, held
just 11 events in the five months after the tournament.

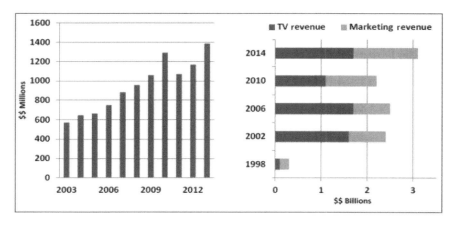

Figure 14.3 FIFA annual revenue/world cup income. © FIFA Annual
Report/*Forbes*.

Rugby Union has joined the party with sales of rights from the Heineken Cup, the IRB World Cup, the English and French Premierships and the Southern Hemisphere Championship. World Rugby enjoyed a growth in financial surplus from the World Cup from £20m in 1995 through to nearly £160m in 2015, enabling it to fund significant growth strategies in many developing nations worldwide.

For most sports organisations, the sale of broadcasting and media rights is now the biggest source of revenue, generating the funds needed to finance major sporting events, refurbish stadiums and contribute to the development of sport at grassroots level. The royalties that broadcasters earn from selling their exclusive footage to other media outlets enable them to invest in the costly organisational and technical infrastructure involved in broadcasting sports events to millions of fans all over the world.

Forward to a sustainable future?

Spool forward to 2018 and the picture is nowhere near as rosy. There have been shocking revelations of state-sponsored cheating in Russia, which, according to the Canadian law professor Richard McLaren, 'corrupted the London Olympics on an unprecedented scale', while the sordid tales of corruption in the corridors of FIFA and the International Association of Athletics Federations (IAAF) would put a banana republic to shame.

Meanwhile, sport no longer appears quite as irresistible to watch. In America, ESPN's subscriber base has gone from 100m in 2011 to 88m according to the latest Nielsen estimates. Sky, which spends £4.2bn a year to show 126 Premier League games, saw average viewing on its live TV channels fall 14% over the past season. Increasingly viewers want shorter, sharper, bite-sized chunks of entertainment, and on mobile devices too. No wonder broadcasters are scrambling to revamp their product to avoid being regarded as dull and outdated. The landscape is changing. So what is sport doing about it?

Given current and forecast future economic conditions, businesses, NGBs and other not-for-profit organisations should still plan for the long run and ensure their strategies are sustainable across a number of potential scenarios. Sustainability is often defined as managing the triple bottom line of risks, obligations and opportunities in financial, social and environmental aspects of sport. These three are sometimes referred to as *profits*, *people* and *planet*.[2]

A more robust definition of sustainability is *resiliency over time* – organisations that can survive shocks are intimately connected to healthy economic, social and environmental systems. These organisations create economic value and contribute to strong communities.

Sustainability in sport must address important issues such as: *economic efficiency* (revenue growth, innovation, productivity), *social equity* (contributing to society and the issues it faces) and *environmental accountability* (resource efficiency).

There are a number of good practices that foster sustainability and help sporting organisations move along the path to long-term success. These practices include:

- **Stakeholder engagement**: organisations can engage with customers, members, employees and their surrounding community, to understand opposition, find common ground and involve stakeholders in joint decision-making.
- **Life-cycle analysis**: those sports wanting to take a large leap forward should systematically analyse the economic, environmental and social impact of their performance as a sport, a business and an employer, continuously scanning the horizon or considering divergent scenarios. They should also assess the product offered to build a sporting calendar that is accessible and relevant to future generations and their lifestyles.
- **Managing the environment**: these systems provide the structures and processes that help embed environmental efficiency into an organisation's culture and mitigate risks.
- **Reporting and disclosure**: measurement and control are at the heart of instituting sustainable practices. Organisations collect and collate information, and can also be entirely transparent with outsiders. The Global Reporting Initiative[3] is one of many examples of well-recognised reporting standards.

Organisations that are sustainable have been shown to attract and retain members and employees more easily and experience less financial and reputation risk. They also tend to be more innovative and adaptive to their environments.

Examples of specific sustainability strategies include:

- Being based on reality, establishing the valuable assets and capabilities that can be deployed.
- Raising revenues and lowering fixed costs simultaneously, using a value-based approach, even sharing resources with others.
- Boards getting closer to stakeholders and addressing what their members, staff, customers and athletes demand (not what the board thinks they should have); looking at leadership and governance from a stakeholder perspective.
- Committing to improve leadership capacity and capability while at the same time complying with governance requirements.
- A commitment to make a difference to people's lives as well as winning medals, e.g., swimming in the UK and Switzerland's approach to improved sustainability.[4] They aimed to achieve new standards of performance in areas of diversity, e.g., women's participation and increased numbers of athletes with a disability.

Unfortunately, short-term thinking is often endemic in sport and confined to the size and shape of their begging bowls to stakeholders – from the IOC, national governments and NOCs to member subscriptions.

To endure in a changing world with greater limits on resources and less credit, organisations must develop and execute a strategy for real sustainability, which takes into account every dimension of the sporting environment: athletic performance, economic, social and cultural, as well as natural. Those that take into account broader social issues will be better able to thrive and to lead. Until the 1980s, leaders used the word sustainability to mean the ability to increase revenues steadily and balance their books. Nowadays sustainability means planning to thrive in the long term and appeal to the millennium generation and those who follow.

Imagined and implemented fully, sustainability drives a top-line strategy to reach new consumers, members and fresh revenue streams combined with a bottom-line strategy to add value and save costs – beyond membership subscriptions, fundraising and grants. It also includes a talent strategy to acquire, keep and develop great creative employees. The strategic framework, with four key components for sustainable sport, is illustrated in Figure 14.4.

- **Economic**: to meet the sport's economic needs for:

  ○ Business – identifying new sources of revenue and raising more from them while optimising costs.
  ○ Replacing grants – reducing public sector dependency.

- **People**: securing value-for-money talent and leading them to the world class – staff and volunteers.
- **Social and cultural**: to understand how sport can benefit society by addressing the big issues – health, crime, violence, poverty – defining a richer purpose than before while protecting and valuing diversity in communities. Leadership and governance play a key role here. Society, of course, benefits too.
- **Environmental**: to protect and restore the natural resources – for example, by controlling the impact they have on climate change, preserving natural resources and preventing waste.

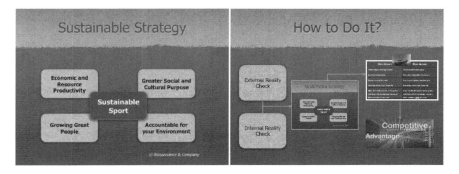

Figure 14.4 Sustainable strategy/How to do it. Model and framework created by Alistair Gray (2013).

New Vision - into the Blue Ocean

Red Ocean Strategy	Blue Ocean Strategy
Compete in Existing Market Place	Create Uncontested Market Place
Beat the Competition	Make the Competition irrelevant
Exploit Existing Demand	Create and Capture New Demand
Make the Value-Cost Trade-Off	Break the Value-Cost Trade-Off
Align the whole system of your activities with your strategic choice of low cost *or* differentiation	Align the whole system of your activities in pursuit of low cost *and* differentiation

Figure 14.5 New vision: into the blue ocean. Table created by Alistair Gray (2016).

Although the challenges to sustainability are acute, there has never been a better time than the present for a sporting organisation to play a critical role in helping to resolve them while achieving lasting success.

The current context creates a *red ocean* of competition between sports as well as other not-for-profit organisations. Any sport aiming to achieve greater sustainability must craft a strategic direction (including strategic goals or outcomes) that embodies finding a *blue ocean* – clear water between competing organisations and of greater value to stakeholders (Figure 14.5).[5]

Such goals should:

- Be consistent with the strengths of the sport – connected to a strong core.
- Differentiate it from the pack.
- Have a connection to its core purpose and activity.
- Elicit the personal contributions and passions of its members.

Finally, the goals ought to be optimistic and aspirational but not impossible – achievable, incrementally, within 5 to 15 years. Leaders in sport must point to a destination and enable their people to figure out what to do to move the organisation forward.

Strategies of sporting organisations are changing

Many sports have modernised their organisation and governance over the last two decades through incorporation, restructuring and appointment of new board members, as well as recruiting key staff from business and sport. Gone are the days when national associations simply held council meetings of volunteers, sent international teams into the world and attended congresses in smoke-filled rooms. Sporting organisations in nations like the UK, Australia, and Netherlands are increasingly run by experienced and well-qualified executives, led by a board chaired by an individual independent from the sport. Increasingly boards and executive teams are gender-balanced and include athletes, independents and specialists in key functions. The big change over recent years has been the impact on sports of major external forces – revenues from broadcasting that previously could only be dreamt about, demands for greater equity and equality, and the impact of drugs. The agenda for sports has changed and governance alone has not been fundamental. It has raised the question of the sport's leadership being trusted to lead and not simply to comply with increased governance.

I have been privileged to raise these questions with a number of the leading executives running international sport. They include Kit McConnell, Head of Sport at the International Olympic Committee, Brett Gosper, CEO of World Rugby, David Richardson, CEO of World Cricket, Antony Scanlon, CEO of World Golf and Kelly Fairweather, the former CEO of World Hockey.

All were clear that the sophistication of the strategies of global sports had increased from the initial versions put together during the first decade after 2000. More and more professional executives with real experience of leading and managing enterprises are now running sports and their boards are more balanced, better qualified and more experienced to lead their organisations effectively. Strategic plans are more wide-ranging and sport's role in society recognised. New metrics to measure performance are being used and communicated widely to stakeholders. The key is to find the balance between the short term (e.g., the four-year Olympic cycle) and the long term.

There is no question that the macro economic environment is affecting governments and their ability to fund sport. The changes in the physical environment – climate change – are also impacting on sport, e.g., skiing and golf. Too much or too little water can adversely affect many sports. In addition, the pace of change fuelled by technology is something all sports now have to address.

IOC – showing the way

The Olympic Charter recognised the need for nations and sports to be responsible for the environment and the topic of sustainability of sport was given real momentum when the IOC embraced the issue in 2014. Its Sustainability and Legacy Commission advises the IOC Session, the IOC Executive Board and the IOC President on sustainability and legacy matters to enable them to make informed and balanced decisions that maximise positive impacts, minimise negative impacts and foster positive change and legacies in the social, economic and environmental spheres. Its recent strategic document, *IOC Agenda 2020*, recognises that we live in a modern, diverse and digital society, and focuses on key themes such as sustainability, credibility and youth.

The Olympic sports are focused on the 'Best of Sports' and presenting 'Sport at its Best', but smaller youth-focused sports, e.g., skateboarding, BMX, surfing and karate, are now threatening the place of the larger, more traditional sports such as field hockey. Keeping people emotionally engaged inside and outside Olympic venues is critical and this engagement must take account of the revolution in the way in which sport is consumed – on a mobile device, anywhere, anytime. All sports and disciplines must be able to present and display their product to appeal to current and future generations.

Kit McConnell (IOC) believes it is essential for sport to have a social purpose and links this to engaging through the IOC's values of excellence, friendship and respect. Sport has a real role to play in bringing society together – be it across religion, gender or countries – hence the importance of social programmes around the Olympic Games, as happened in Brazil in 2016. The Olympic Games at Rio in 2016 delivered many inspiring athletic achievements that were witnessed and shared by a vast global audience through record-breaking media coverage and unprecedented levels of digital engagement. Against a backdrop of economic, political and social challenges, they also set new standards for legacy planning that have left an important heritage. At the heart of the Rio Games was a commitment to help children and young people connect to sport by focusing the world's attention on sport's greatest athletes and giving today's young people more education on sport, better access to sport facilities, competition, coaching and sporting events. The Rio Games had the potential to leave an important social legacy, not just for the people of Rio de Janeiro but further afield in Brazil, South America and internationally. These wider social responsibilities are also recognised by other global sporting organisations (Figure 14.6).

| Social responsibilities of sports | | | | |
IOC	World Rugby	World Cricket	IGF (Golf)	European Hockey
Excellence		Excellence	Excellence	
	Teamwork	Teamwork		
	Discipline	Accountability	Solidarity	Accountable
Friendship		Commitment to the global game and its spirit		Inclusive
Respect	Respect	Respect for diversity	Respect	Dynamic
	Enjoyment			Positive
		Fairness and integrity	Integrity	

Figure 14.6 Social responsibilities of sports. Table created by Alistair Gray from IOC data (2017).

More youthful, more urban

Following a lengthy period of discussion and consultation, which generated a host of suggestions and ideas from around the world, the President of the International Olympic Committee, Thomas Bach, announced that freestyle BMX and three-on-three basketball would be introduced as events in the Tokyo 2020 Olympics, joining karate, surfing, climbing, skateboarding and baseball/softball. The reason was obvious, although Bach did not quite put it in these terms – the Games needed to be funked up for a younger generation.[6]

Bach called it a 'step-change' and insisted the Games in Tokyo 'will be more youthful, more urban and will include more women'. Many inside the Olympic movement wonder what took him so long. Certainly the IOC has been late to the party. Twenty20 cricket started in 2004 and quickly became the game's most popular format. Rugby Sevens has been around since 1883 but, since receiving the IOC's stamp of approval in 2009, it has become more relevant than ever. Others, too, are chasing the millennials – realising that if they do not attract new audiences now, in 10 or 20 years' time they could be increasingly irrelevant.

Team sports – especially those other than football

It would have been tempting in *The Game Changer* to include football, the world's largest participation team sport. The recent publicity around the levels of corruption in succeeding regimes in FIFA, the governing body of the sport, convinced me that this would not be worthwhile. It is not that great work is not being done by many national associations, or indeed by a number of FIFA executives. I have witnessed, at first hand, the work done by the football associations in England, Scotland, Ireland, Wales, Northern Ireland and other European, Middle East and Far East nations, as well as by UEFA and by FIFA itself on a number of development projects.

The FIFA Forward[7] programme provided impressive statistics as to the level of activity in support of member nations (Figure 14.7).

UEFA carry out similar investment, and generally with much better governance than the world governing body of the sport. Also Rugby Union, in particular, as a leading team sport, is adopting many of the good practice 'game changer' principles suggested earlier.

World Rugby has shown a much greater appreciation for a wider social purpose during the last ten years than at any time since the formation of the International Rugby Board (IRB) by Scotland, Wales and Ireland in 1886. Changes and the global development of the sport, from its previously sleepy hollow in Dublin's St Stephen's Green, have been driven by the success of the Rugby World Cup (now in the top four ranked broadcast revenue global sporting events). Rugby Union has been transformed in the last 25 years with the introduction of professional rugby and associated

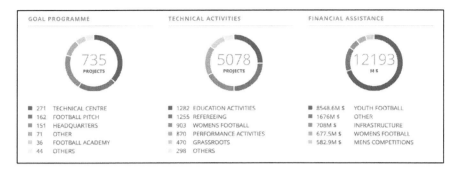

Figure 14.7 FIFA Forward Programme. Source FIFA Annual Report (2017).

league and inter-nation competitions in the northern and southern hemispheres. Rugby is now played in more countries around the world than ever before. There are now 119 countries participating in the sport, supporting an estimated 6.6m players worldwide.

It took until 1985 for the International Rugby Board (now known as World Rugby) to sanction a World Cup, originally splitting the revenues of a few £m from the tournament between the international governing bodies and the host nation. Since then, World Rugby has seized the opportunity to make the game more attractive – competing for participant and consumer attention against other distractions for the consumer/audience and communicating compelling content.

Having a strong social purpose and cross-cultural attraction is important to the game. This has involved significant product (format and event) development, changes and modifications to laws and rules, thus making the sport entertaining and attractive to many more people while retaining the integrity of the sport.

Rugby 7s is often the point of entry for spectators and players. It was the entry ticket for Rugby Union as an Olympic sport at Rio in 2016. It is a nicely limited and therefore understandable form of the game in terms of laws, entertainment and timing (2 x 7-minute halves). In 2016 the total number of registered players increased from 2.82 million to 3.2 million (nearly double the number in 2009), while the total number of non-registered rugby players rose from 4.91 million to 5.3 million. Almost two million children were also introduced to the sport via World Rugby's 'Get Into Rugby' programme, helping to boost female participation so that 25% of players are now female.

Rugby Union's intent to put players first has come under challenge recently. Professional rugby has also seen major change in the physicality of the game and has transformed international players into world-class athletes. Although Rugby Union is still a game for all shapes and sizes, the most recent World Cup highlighted the skills and sheer physicality of the professional players as the demand for faster, fitter and stronger players

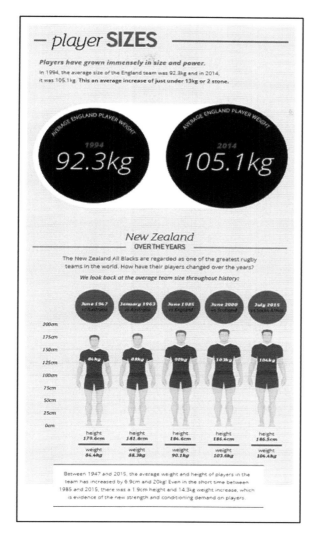

Figure 14.8 Player sizes. Chart created by Alistair Gray from New Zealand Rugby data and the Annual Report (2016).

grows. Size is not everything and being large is no longer enough as rugby has evolved into a sport of hyper-fit men and women who push the boundaries of human ability (Figure 14.8).

The challenge is that the sport is perceived to be less safe for young players, especially those outside the professional ranks who do not go through the new fitness, strength and conditioning regime.

On the back of increasing numbers of head, neck and other impact injuries World Rugby, at long last, introduced a number of education programmes around the topic of concussion and introduced head-injury-assessment (HIA) into matches.

However, mothers of young players are increasingly voicing their concern for the future safety of their sons and daughters, especially in the 15-a-side game. Team sports such as field hockey and basketball have gained numbers from rugby union in recent years and safety is cited as a major reason for making the sport less attractive. In 2017 New Zealand introduced upper weight limits in youth rugby in an attempt to retain young players in the game.

The strong social purpose of rugby

Sport, especially team sport, can build character, teaching young children life skills such as mutual respect and discipline. Rugby unions are now developing the game in lower socio-economic groups and new nations and, while World Rugby provides evidence that good progress has been made at community level, they admit there is still considerable room for progress at the elite level.

As is outlined in Chapter 20, The New Zealand All Blacks (the world's most successful team) have broken the mould in many areas. Their mantra that 'Better people make better All Blacks' sets clear expectations for behaviour with 'The Black Book' (their internal guiding principles) and is at the heart of their philosophy. They set themselves the challenge of delivering the 'perfect game' on the pitch, alongside an unreasonable ambition to unify and inspire the nation.

World Rugby has also introduced online education, a major tool for the development of players and administrators as well as spectators. Through this and other mechanisms they can accredit national associations and provide genuine evidence for the allocation of development funds.

The importance of the Rugby World Cup

The leading nations face the challenge of player salaries racing ahead of the money coming into the game. Broadcasting revenue, rather than sponsorship, is the main source of profit. This means attracting and providing products (media channels and competitions) that attract ever-increasing audiences. The largest driver of revenues is the Rugby World Cup, a low-risk high-return event building on existing organisations and facilities. It is spearheaded by Rugby World Cup Ltd, a subsidiary of World Rugby. Supported by World Rugby and Rugby World Cup Ltd, the 2019 host nation of Japan is learning a great deal and building capability – playing and administrative – that will support its future development. World Rugby have invested significantly in creating new audiences across more cultures and now broadcast in an increasing number of languages.

Since its inception in 1987, the increasing scale and reach of Rugby World Cup Ltd has helped attract a global audience and provided each host nation with significant opportunities to attract international tourism, develop infrastructure, advertise itself to investors from around the world and leave a lasting legacy of growing participation at all levels and across a diverse player spectrum. The Rugby World Cup 2015 in England attracted more international visitors than any previous Rugby World Cup, with up to 466,000 visits across the duration of the tournament. These visitors bring with them significant incremental spending to the host economy, from purchasing tickets to travel costs, accommodation expenses, match-day entertainment and in visiting other local tourist attractions. In total, it is calculated that international visitors contributed up to £869 million in direct expenditure. Investment in infrastructure for the tournament in the UK reached £85 million, bringing lasting benefits to the host cities. The added exposure to a global market provided opportunities to attract future tourists and businesses alike. In total, Rugby World Cup 2015 delivered up to £2.2 billion in output to the UK, translating into an additional £982 million of value added to GDP. Revenue from gate receipts, broadcasting and sponsorship rose from £40m in 1995 to over £500m in 2015, when much of the global economy was still in recession.

Cricket

The long-term vision for World Cricket (International Cricket Council) is to become the 'world's favourite sport', which is possible numerically given its popularity in the Indian sub-continent. Sustainability is one of the stated goals in the most recent strategic plan. The goals are represented by four strategic pillars:

1   **Cricket – providing a world-class environment, making sure men's and women's international cricket is attractive to play and watch.**
2   **Integrity – protecting the integrity of the game – focus on anti-corruption, doping, racism and ethics.**
3   **Major events – delivering successful major events and building their value – from five-day Test cricket through to T20 and one-day Internationals (ODIs).**
4   **Game and market development – improving the quality and reach of international cricket.**

World Cricket sees its role supporting these pillars through the distribution of funds and providing outstanding leadership where it is needed. Genesis supported the ICC with their first major strategic plan and, since then, the sport has invested significantly in the support of the developing nations. The focus over the last eight years has been on 25 nations and those with potential, e.g., Hong Kong, UAE and Nigeria. The USA, Canada and China provide real potential for new markets and nations like Nepal have potential to grow the numbers playing cricket. While cricket has historically been a sport based on Commonwealth nations, the growth potential lies in the major nations outside that historic club.

Where athletics and football focus their integrity on anti-doping and compliance respectively, cricket's focus is on people and areas such as transparency and accountability of organisations leading the development of the game. A few years ago the big three of England, Australia and India drove through an agreement to provide them with the lion's share of revenues from the burgeoning properties of the World Cups (ODI and T20) through to 2019. There has been good progress in recent years to replace this with a genuine global alliance between nations and a strong sense of integrity with more appropriate distribution of funds. In 2017 Ireland and Afghanistan were afforded full membership (Test Status of the ICC). Test status was Ireland's destiny – a long battle, fought on the field and in the boardrooms of world cricket that would be waged until victory was assured. Brian MacNeice and I have worked closely with Irish Cricket since 2008. Brian was a volunteer with the sport and rose to the position of selector. Our first project with Irish Cricket was to prepare and seek funding for a four-year development plan.

The sport really took off after St Patrick's Day (17 March) in 2007 with a famous victory over Pakistan in the World Cup. The notoriety that followed brought in significant financial support from a major insurance company and the Irish Sports Council to modernise the organisation and fund the programmes for growth. Warren Deutrom joined as CEO from the ICC in 2006 and, under his leadership, working closely with a reformed board, the sport went from strength to strength. Their aim was to not only make Ireland a major nation in cricket, but also to make cricket a major mainstream sport in Ireland. Rivalling the big beasts of football, GAA (Gaelic Games) and rugby union in the Irish sporting landscape is a massive task for a sport that rarely features on the back pages, but participation levels quadrupled over the next ten years. However, full membership of the ICC only marks the end of the beginning. Ireland and Afghanistan face a major challenge to secure future sustainability. Cricket is indeed a growth sport but pushing on to the next level will require success in the Test arena to inspire the young to pick up bat and ball.

The majority of World Cricket's nations are now in favour of the T20 format of the game applying for a place at the Summer Olympic Games. This is seen as a major platform for global development of the game. World Rugby has provided a good example of what can be achieved – Rugby 7s was a popular sport at the 2016 Rio Olympic Games. Interestingly, England and India remain two of the doubters of the benefits of cricket's participation.

World Cricket see cricket as being a 'true character building sport' – teaching young people how to win, how to lose and how to be better members of society. There is a wide range of cultures among the cricket-playing nations of the world and this is seen as an opportunity to break down traditional barriers. There is an understanding that it will not all be plain sailing. Extensive community programmes will be necessary, especially to focus on the lives of young people and their communities. Cricket has always felt there is a unique spirit[8] in the game, perhaps typified by the picture of fierce opponents Andrew Flintoff and Brett Lee consoling each other at the end of a closely fought Test in the 2005 Ashes series.

In many ways the meaning of spirit needs to be wider than just sportsmanship. Cricket has been troubled over the years by dealing with anti-corruption in the game, fuelled by spread betting in many cricket-playing nations and elsewhere. The sport has dealt with this threat positively, not only at the top end of the game but also at the grass roots through their education and community development programmes. Their focus on getting the message of the 'Spirit of Cricket' across to young people is perhaps the most important focus for the emerging federation of nations in World Cricket. This is supported by increasing education of young people (men and women) in areas such as nutrition and hygiene. Cricket also promotes itself as a sport for people with a disability. The Lord's Taverners is the UK's leading youth cricket and disability sports charity dedicated to giving disadvantaged and disabled young people a sporting chance.[9]

Golf and other individual sports

Golf is one of the world's oldest sports, traditionally governed by the Royal and Ancient Golf Club of St Andrews and the US Professional Golfers Association, yet it is led by one of the youngest federations – The International Golf Federation (IGF). Formed in 1958, the IGF really only became organised and active in the last ten years, in time for the sport to be included in the 2016 Olympic Games. In 2009 the IOC and IPC (Paralympics) welcomed the IGF into the Olympic and Paralympic Movement for the first time since 1904, enabling men's and women's golf competitions to be part of the 2016 Olympic Games in Rio de Janeiro. This reflected the rapid expansion and globalisation of the game. The headquarters of the IGF is located close to the IOC and IPC by the shores of Lake Geneva in Lausanne, Switzerland.

The IGF consists of two membership categories representing the administration of golf internationally – national federation members and professional members, e.g., clubs and businesses. There are 149 national federation members from 144 countries and 25 professional members (e.g., clubs and other businesses). Governance is a particular issue, especially for those amateur federations that serve tiny numbers of members (as is the case with many national federations in Africa). The IGF is relatively resource light, compared with other sports, and plans to remain so. The main resources are in the main tour in Europe and the US, with smaller versions across the globe. It is the Tours that enter into major negotiations with broadcasters – satellite, cable and terrestrial.

Recently reformed as part of their bid for golf to become an Olympic sport, their mission is to:

- Promote golf as an Olympic and Paralympic sport.
- Encourage the international development of golf.
- Administer golf as the recognised International Federation within the Olympic and Paralympic movement.
- Organise the golf competitions at the Olympic Games, Youth Olympic Games and the World Amateur Team Championships.

The federation is led and managed through a number of committees drawn from the membership. The strategy is based on building six strategic pillars, which are:

1   **Golf for all**
    Enable access and grow participation by reducing the barriers and increasing the opportunities to play golf at all levels.

2   **A great games**
    Deliver a great Olympic event and a memorable experience for the athletes, fans and golfing fraternity cementing golf's place within the Olympic programme.

3   **Pathways**
    Facilitate innovative educational and developmental programmes that provide pathways for athletes, coaches and officials from the grass roots to the elite levels of golf.

4   **Engage and excite**
    Creatively engage and excite the world about golf and its values.

5   **Sustainable and responsible**
    Promote sustainable and environmentally responsible practices within the golfing industry.

6   **Good governance**
    Provide leadership in diversity and good governance practices.

Clearly the focus for the IGF is linked to the development of the game, which it can influence especially through the design of golf courses and promotion of good practice. In my conversation with Antony Scanlon, the recently appointed IGF CEO, he stressed that sustainability was taken very seriously and is at the heart of operations across the sport as exemplified through:

- Day-to-day operations.
- Design of courses.
- Being active in communities.
- Golf Environmental organisation to support clubs.
- Addressing the pressures from modern society.

The Olympic Golf Committee is made up of members of The R&A, PGA European Tour, USGA, PGA of America, PGA Tour, LPGA and Augusta National Golf Club (home of The Masters). Participation in the Olympic Games provided a real impetus for the sport through the broadcasting opportunity, introduction to new media and the provision of statistics and data. The IGF studied the NFL (American football) in particular to better engage their viewing public. There were initial concerns for the credibility of the event with the withdrawal of a number of the leading male competitors, e.g., Jordan Spieth, Rory McIlroy, Jason Day – concerned about the potential impact of the Zika virus. Their concerns were treated seriously and the regulations for future Olympic competition changed. The men's event – won by Justin Rose (GB) – was a great success, as was the women's tournament, the latter fully supported by the leading players and won by Inbee Park (South Korea).

All sports are under pressure to address their sustainability and golf in particular faces big issues such as the ageing of its memberships and institutions (clubs and national federations) and the challenge of adapting the sport, where playing 18 holes frequently takes over four hours, as well as the demands on members' time such as family and work. The traditional golf-club model does not generate the same levels of revenue as in past years, other than through membership subscriptions. Typically, for a golf club with 1,000 members, only 200 will be playing. The sport has come under attack for its strong male gender bias, especially in those nations where gender-focused organisations are most active. In recent years the R&A and USPGA have admitted women members to their organisations and many clubs are being moved to a similar position, especially those hosting major championships for the top professional players.

Golf fights old perceptions to attract a new audience and struggles to reverse recent drops in player numbers in many of the leading and established nations. New models have to be found, e.g., in France, where clubs have gyms and other forms of entertainment for their members, and in Sweden where the emphasis is on family-friendly multi-sport clubs. Attempts have also been made to develop shortened forms of the game. In May 2017 the European Tour hosted its first GolfSixes tournament, featuring 16 two-man teams from 16 countries competing on a specially designed six-hole course at the Centurion Club in St Albans. Each hole had a different theme – the third, for instance, had a long drive competition while the fourth had a 40-second shot clock. Henni Zuel, who covered the tournament for Sky, believes there were encouraging signs.

Of course it isn't going to replace the 18-hole game', she says, And, as with anything like this, there are going to be things that could be better. But it was really noticeable that it seemed to bring in a younger audience. One of the things I kept hearing from families was that you can take your kids along to six holes, because it is not a massive long walk, and it made for a great atmosphere.

For years the leading organisations in golf have made significant charitable contributions to demonstrate real social purpose as a sport, supporting clubs and communities throughout the world. This has been especially strong in disabled sport where those athletes and participants with severe disability, e.g., blindness or loss of limb, have been encouraged at local, national and international level to play the game, often with modified rules. There has also been a special focus on the rehabilitation of armed forces personnel.

Individual sports must learn to change more quickly than they have done in the past. Athletics is another sport that is tentatively trying to recapture its former glories by slicing and dicing events. The most recent attempt to mix things up is Nitro Athletics – a new format involving six teams of 12 male and 12 female athletes competing in a potpourri of new and old events – which was launched in three Australian cities this year. There were mixed relays, javelin throwing for distance and accuracy, and a men's mile where the last-placed runner was eliminated at the end of each of the first three laps of the track.

It attracted a lot of media coverage, largely because Usain Bolt – who was rumoured to have been paid $1m to compete – was there. But not everyone is convinced Nitro Athletics is the way forward. Many observers of Nitro Athletics were left feeling nonplussed. They appreciated the experiments and fresh thinking. The problem with Nitro is that not much was earth-shatteringly innovative and some of it even made supporters cringe. Their views echo those of agents and race meeting organisers. They believe Australians came mainly to see Bolt and tick it off their bucket list, rather than for Nitro Athletics.

Another format that has been tried in the UK, with some success, is street athletics, where fans can get to see the action up close on specially built tracks in city centres. For many reasons athletics is in a bad place, but the CityGames showcases the sport in the right way.

Traditional sports also need to be aware of the growing popularity of e-sports. The mainstream often dismisses them as being played by spotty adolescents who are deprived of vitamin D and a social life. However, many PR and brand experts insist that is a mistake. Many believe sports will suffer because increased audiences are about eyeballs and selling product and increasingly that is what e-sports do. Once upon a time darts and snooker were seen as joke sports played in smoky men's clubs, but now they are respectable. There are a number of big agencies, who represent Hollywood stars, who are paying close attention to e-sports.

A question of trust

Many problems faced by sports are far from new. Exclusion of minority groups and accusations of bullying and child abuse regularly emerge from the shadows with increasing prominence, especially now through social media. Doping and corruption have festered and lingered for decades. But recently it has developed a fresh twist. Taking performance-enhancing drugs is no longer a black and white issue, but one of ever-darkening shades of grey.

Recently this issue has come worryingly close to home in the UK. Bradley Wiggins' (now Sir Bradley) victory in 2012 in the London Olympic time trial added to his Tour de France triumph. At the time of writing, Wiggins is fighting to save his reputation amid questions over what was in the jiffy bag delivered and administered to him on the final day of the Critérium du Dauphiné in June 2011, and whether he might have broken any anti-doping rules at the time. He was also granted therapeutic use exemptions (TUEs) for the powerful corticosteroid triamcinolone, supposedly for his allergies, before the 2011 and 2012 Tour de France and the 2013 Giro d'Italia. The drug is illegal to use without a TUE and potentially has a posi-tive effect on performance. Wiggins has always maintained he used it to combat pollen allergies and has always denied wrongdoing, but a British House of Commons report concluded that its use was unethical, although within the rules. Leading coaches, especially in athletics, have also been exposed and their practices scrutinised as never before.

Increasingly a sceptical public must wonder whether lofty words on anti-doping match the reality. Before London 2012 there had been reports about how science was ahead of the dopers, and that the authorities would have 1,000 staff on call 24/7 during the Games (Figure 14.9).

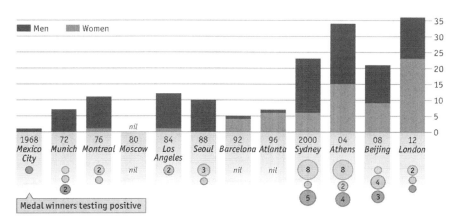

Figure 14.9 Medals of dishonour: athletes tested at Summer Olympics disqualified after testing positive. Sources: International Olympic Committee; World Anti-Doping Agency; *The Economist.*

Yet that clearly was not the case. It has only been in the last few years, after hundreds of blood and urine samples from London 2012 were defrosted and retested using a new technique, that dozens more positives have come to light. As things stand, six of the 13 athletes who competed in the London 2012 women's 1500m final have been suspended for taking illegal substances at some point in their careers.

Anti-doping agencies are underfunded and they find it hard to carry out tests in many areas of the world, e.g., Kenya and Ethiopia. Dopers can expect to be able to stay several steps ahead of the authorities. The World Anti-Doping Agency (WADA) often talks about the need for better intelligence and investigations but it only has a yearly budget of around $26m – less than most Premier League teams – and six investigators on its books.

'The corruption was embedded'

It does not help, either, that too many international federations have been infiltrated by crooks or chancers. During Sepp Blatter's tenure as president of football's world governing body, FIFA became a byword for corruption, with officials brazenly lining their own pockets by taking their own cut of TV deals or other scams. At its worst, this meant the US Department of Justice alleging that the former CONCACAF president Jack Warner had misappropriated funds meant for Haiti earthquake victims.

If anything, the IAAF might have behaved even worse, with many senior figures in the organisation having since been expelled for life for their part in extorting €450,000 (£330,000) from the Russian marathon runner Liliya Shobukhova to cover up her doping violations. The exposure started with the president of the organisation. It also involved the treasurer and the personal counsel of the president, acting on instructions of the president. It involved two of the sons of the president. It also involved the director of the Medical and Anti-Doping department of the IAAF. The corruption was embedded in the organisation.

Perhaps the scale of the problem is highlighted by research by the Danish Institute of Sports Studies, which in 2015 ranked all 35 federations belonging to the Olympic family based on how transparent, democratic and accountable they were. Incredibly the organisation that came second, behind only the International Equestrian Federation, was FIFA. The study also found that only four out of the 35 had a committee that performed integrity and professional checks on those nominated for senior positions, while fewer than eight published externally audited annual financial reports. Lord Coe deserves credit for pushing through a new IAAF constitution last year, which included the establishment of the independent Integrity Unit to oversee the entire anti-doping process from testing, term limits for senior officials, and giving athletes a greater say in running the sport than ever before. However, such measures are still highly unusual for most sporting bodies. And with such low levels of scrutiny across the board, how many more FIFAs and IAAFs are there out there?

What next?

There are several strands in all this, and many of them should sound alarm bells for sport. When NBC reports a staggering 31% decline in ratings for its prime-time Olympics coverage among adults aged 18–34 between London 2012 and Rio 2016, or total Premier League viewing hours fall by 6%, you know something is afoot.

Yes, some of the fall in figures is down to illegal streaming and the high cost of subscriptions. However, much of it is also due to the way we live now: always on the go, always on social media, always trying to do three things at once. No wonder so many sports are tinkering with formats in a bid to be seen and heard.

Meanwhile some of the scandals we have seen in recent years, and especially those involving FIFA and the IAAF, are having consequences, with both organisations struggling to attract big-name sponsors. For the 2014 World Cup, FIFA had 20 corporate partners on board; for Russia 2018 it was half that, with sponsors balking at the high cost and potential risk to their reputation with being involved with FIFA.

Of course, when a match or event is about to start, much appears to be forgotten – sport might horrify us, but it still draws us in even more. Yet it is hard to argue that, for some sports, and especially athletics and cycling, the endless scandals have not damaged their appeal in some way.

There is no doubting Lord Coe's (recently appointed President of the IAAF) conviction to clean up athletics' act, but is there evidence to believe him? The pace of change in society requires sports to match the changes being made. Issues around doping, child abuse and gay rights cannot just be left to one side until after the next Games.

The role of international and national governing bodies of sport has to embrace a much broader agenda than simply planning and delivering championships and leagues. Recognising sport's place in society as a force for good is important. This diversified role for sport is a potentially powerful unifying new force. It requires longer-term strategies that probably cover three or four Olympic cycles, where the pathways to longer-term goals are clearly visible. The changing composition of sports' boards is helping to make this happen. Increasingly they are gender-balanced and include athletes, independents and specialists in key functions, e.g., marketing, people management, branding and communication. The role of non-executive directors will be crucial in bringing independence, experience and knowledge to setting future direction and fostering commitment (more than compliance) to a relevant modernised agenda.

Sustainability will come from more than addressing more attractive and entertaining formats of the traditional sport. That is fundamentally a commercially driven strategic intent. Without a strong social purpose, attention to the wider environment and issues such as equity and equality, sport will always leave itself open to criticism of its pursuit of greed and self-interest.

In our work with The FA (the Football Association of England), outlined elsewhere in this book, one of the strategic goals chosen in 2007 was 'Trusted to Lead'. This stated outcome, with associated objectives and plans, should surely feature in the strategic plans of all national, continental and international sports federations, if they are to be taken seriously, coupled with an openness to report regularly on the progress they are making.

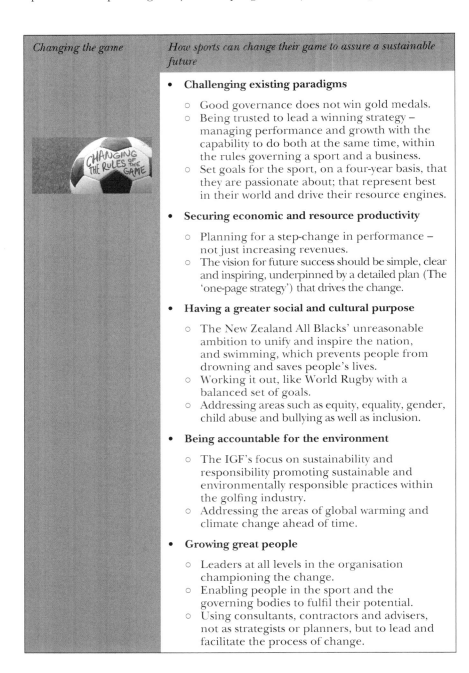

Changing the game	*How sports can change their game to assure a sustainable future*
	Challenging existing paradigms ○ Good governance does not win gold medals. ○ Being trusted to lead a winning strategy – managing performance and growth with the capability to do both at the same time, within the rules governing a sport and a business. ○ Set goals for the sport, on a four-year basis, that they are passionate about; that represent best in their world and drive their resource engines. **Securing economic and resource productivity** ○ Planning for a step-change in performance – not just increasing revenues. ○ The vision for future success should be simple, clear and inspiring, underpinned by a detailed plan (The 'one-page strategy') that drives the change. **Having a greater social and cultural purpose** ○ The New Zealand All Blacks' unreasonable ambition to unify and inspire the nation, and swimming, which prevents people from drowning and saves people's lives. ○ Working it out, like World Rugby with a balanced set of goals. ○ Addressing areas such as equity, equality, gender, child abuse and bullying as well as inclusion. **Being accountable for the environment** ○ The IGF's focus on sustainability and responsibility promoting sustainable and environmentally responsible practices within the golfing industry. ○ Addressing the areas of global warming and climate change ahead of time. **Growing great people** ○ Leaders at all levels in the organisation championing the change. ○ Enabling people in the sport and the governing bodies to fulfil their potential. ○ Using consultants, contractors and advisers, not as strategists or planners, but to lead and facilitate the process of change.

Notes

1 Nelson Mandela, November 2012.
2 *MIT Sloan Management Review*, Fall 2014.
3 Global Reporting Initiative (www.globalreporting.org).
4 Sustainability in Switzerland: www.are.admin.ch/are/en/home/sustainable-development/strategy-and-planning/understanding-of-sustainability-in-switzerland.html.
5 *Blue Ocean Strategy*, W. Chan Kim and Renée Mauborgne, Harvard Business Review Press, 2005.
6 The *Guardian*, 'Sport 2.0: Crumbling Traditions Create a Whole New Ballgame', Sean Ingle, June 2017.
7 FIFA Annual Report 2017.
8 *Spirit of cricket*: preamble to the laws. '**Cricket** is a game that owes much of its unique appeal to the fact that it should be played not only within its Laws but also within the **Spirit** of the Game. Any action which is seen to abuse this **spirit** causes injury to the game itself.' Source: the MCC. The truth of this statement was clearly demonstrated by the ball-tampering actions of leading members of the Australian team in South Africa in 2018 – actions that were not only outwith the rules but also the spirit of the sport – and that undoubtedly did enormous damage to the image of the sport.
9 *Sporting chance*: 'it is the chance to interact, play and train; to compete, win and lose; to learn, have fun and make friends'. Source: The Lord's Taverners.

15 Cathy's pillars and the reform of The Football Association (in England)

Introduction

Who is the most successful women athlete ever? The case could be made for a number from Steffi Graf or Martina Navratilova in tennis through Anneka Sorenstam in golf and Katherine Grainger in rowing. However, head and shoulders above them all is Catherine (Cathy) Freeman, the Australian 400m multi-championship-winning athlete. During ten glorious years from 1994 to 2004, including her home Olympic Games at Sydney in 2000, Freeman won 25 of the 30 major championship races in which she competed.

After her retirement she was persuaded to reflect on her career and the lessons from that – Cathy's four pillars – have real messages for sporting organisations. They are also lessons of real relevance to businesses as they compete in the new global economy as it emerges from this extended period of uncertainty.

One example of where these lessons proved invaluable was in Genesis' work (from 2006 to 2008) with The FA (the Football Association of England) in helping them develop their first-ever 'seriously-strategic' strategy in nearly 150 years. You can surely imagine the temptation for me, as a Scot – working with an Irish colleague – in having the opportunity to ensure that England never wins the FIFA World Cup ever again?

Thankfully, for the sake of my profession and my own integrity, the opportunity provided by Brian Barwick (the CEO of The FA over that time) was for me a privilege. Barwick had assembled an executive team in the wake of several scandals that had hit the sport's governing body as a result of accusations made concerning the behaviour of Sven Goran Erikson, the England Coach, and Mark Palios, the previous Chief Executive. Barwick was keen for the executive to prepare a strategic plan through to 2012 and to take this to the board of The FA.

This was to be the first integrated strategic plan for the development of football in England since its foundation in 1863. Would Cathy's four pillars of body, heart, mind and spirit potentially transform one of the most fixed mind-set governing bodies of sport in the world? That was the challenge facing my colleague Brian MacNeice and myself (an Irishman and a Scotsman) as their guides for a journey.

Catherine the Great – her four pillars

Who can forget Cathy Freeman's performance of a lifetime over 400m on 'Magic Monday' at the 2000 Sydney Olympics? In front of over 70,000 expectant fans she delivered the performance of her life, fulfilling the expectations of millions of Australians all over the world, and especially those of ethnic Aborigines in her homeland. What lay behind her phenomenal success?

Freeman may not excel as a speaker to the level she achieved as a runner, but her description of the four pillars that underpinned her outstanding performances during the nineties cannot help but impress. It provides real insight into how organisations, as well as athletes, can respond to an era of unprecedented competitive intensity in sport, arts, business and public sectors.

As in most sports, track and field athletics has professionalised physical training and conditioning to new and sophisticated levels over the last two decades. Any athlete who aspires to World or Olympic glory has to follow training and conditioning routines that are well known to coaches and scientists throughout the world. It follows, therefore, that the bodies of all elite athletes are honed to a state of near-perfection. So what separates the winners from the losers? For Freeman, the difference between winning and losing was more to do with heart, mind and spirit than with the near perfect conditioning of her body for the 400m event. Freeman explained that the difference for her lay in her:

- **Heart** – her passion to win, which came from a love of running and winning; running, for her, was like flying, without restriction and with freedom.
- **Mind** – an inner strength and mental belief that she would win every race she entered, safe in the knowledge that her training and preparation were so detailed in nature that nothing was left to chance. She knew how fast she and her competitors were running in advance of each race.
- **Spirit** – for Freeman she was at one with the various communities in her life – her family, friends, neighbourhoods, Australia and the whole Aborigine nation. Her purpose was greater than individual personal success.

Individual elite performers, operating in an increasingly competitive and global environment, have much to learn from Freeman's insight and experience as they aspire to future success. But this insight and experience can be just as relevant to teams and other organisations as they seek to improve their performance and emerge as winners in this increasingly competitive world. Good corporate governance is a given, without which they cannot even reach the starting line – but will it be enough to win? 'An athlete without a healthy and positive mental attitude is as about as efficient as a Formula 1 racing car with flat tyres' (Cathy Freeman).

2012 and all that

The 27th of July 2012 saw the start of the XXX Olympiad in London, part of a golden decade of sporting events to be staged in the UK. This gave the UK not only the opportunity to design and realise a world-class event, but also the chance for Britain's sporting organisations – National Governing Bodies (their coaches, administrators and support staff as well as their athletes), Institutes of Sport and Sports Councils – and government departments to deliver the performance of their lives. Indeed, this was literally a 'once in a lifetime' opportunity for these organisations to engage with sport as a whole, raise the overall level of performance and build a legacy for British sport far beyond the three weeks of competition in 2012.

Team GB delivered a record number of medals in Beijing in 2008, and even more in London in 2012. The UK has now established a world-leading performance system for our athletes and their coaches. But have the sporting organisations themselves grasped the opportunity to change and perform in the same way? In many cases the outcome has merely been to tinker with the body of the sport in terms of its physical (facility) infrastructure and organisational structure to create more staff to monitor the athletes on their path to glory.

The 2006 Commonwealth Games in Melbourne, Australia, showed that little progress had been made by many sports, with athletics being the prime example. Despite investment from Lottery funding since 1997, UK Athletics' IAAF ranking had fallen from 4th to 15th (Men) by 2006. The women's equivalent rankings painted a similar picture. Things have improved since then, though mainly due to the individual efforts of Jessica Ennis-Hill, Mo Farah and Greg Rutherford. In 2010 England Athletics was not without company in their performance, not helped by many of their top performers who shunned competition. Despite some excellent performances in, e.g., swimming, cycling, hockey and shooting, England's overall medal count in CG 2010 in Delhi was 15% down from the heady heights of Manchester in 2002. Scotland was rescued by shooting from an otherwise poor performance relative to that achieved in Melbourne.

The main thrust of modernising National Governing Bodies (NGBs) over the last decade has focused on corporate governance, re-structuring and performance/information systems, hardly enough to deal with the increasingly competitive sporting environment. At the same time, major reviews of organisational structure that have been undertaken, such as the Foster Review of athletics, have led to little effective change for the sport as a whole.

Sport is not alone in facing these challenges. The business world faces similar challenges in times of recession/low growth and increased internationalisation. Recommendations on corporate modernisation emerging from the reports such as Higgs, Greenbury and Cadbury on corporate governance provide a hint of what should be adopted by sporting organisations to enable them to cope with the turbulent times that lie ahead.

The tough competitive environment faced by sport is no blip. Competition from the likes of Australia, China, India, South Africa, France, Spain and Ukraine is as strong as that from the US – indeed they are making faster and more significant progress than the super-power. Great Britain often claims to punch above its weight, but how long can they rely on this as a sustained source of competitive advantage? Performance cycles are a thing of the past in an increasingly professional and well-prepared industry of world-class sport. The year 2016, in the wake of the Summer Olympic Games in Rio, had the dark spectre of drug abuse all over it, culminating in the banning of Russian athletes from major world competition and several senior officials, especially in athletics, being removed from their positions to face criminal prosecution.

The longest 'bear' stock market in history, coupled with one of the biggest recessions in history, has reduced corporate spend on everything and made areas such as sponsorship and patronage of sport easy targets for cost reduction. Government Comprehensive Spending Reviews and associated reduced public expenditure/lottery income levels add to these financial challenges. Austerity is a theme promoted by many national governments at a time when real wages have failed to grow beyond inflation.

Tough times demand strong and brave initiatives by passionate fit organisations that plan to win, not just compete.

Good bodies alone do not win World Cups or Gold Medals

Current responses by governing bodies and sports councils seem to focus on improved organisation, better governance and addressing 'body'-related areas including:

- Corporate structure.
- Planning and systems.
- Incorporation.
- Business risk.

Although these are undoubtedly necessary, they will not in themselves deliver the performance of a lifetime – they do not address 'heart, mind and spirit'. To achieve world-class performance, organisations must place greater emphasis on developing a compelling vision of success, competitive strategy and performance plans to create the future, while at the same time facing up to the reality of mediocrity in the recent past. This requires boards to concentrate more on corporate *leadership* rather than corporate *governance*. It means fostering a sense of community, engaging the whole sport and empowering inspirational players – coaches, administrators and athletes – to lead. It means coming up with game-breaking ideas as never before.

Affairs of the *heart* require raising the passion of volunteers and professionals within the sport to achieve new goals to transform the sport.

The *mind* will address raising the bar of performance to new levels and building real knowledge as to how these aspirations will be achieved. This will mean opening up minds to new ideas and planning on a cause-and-effect basis to achieve real milestones rather than continuing to make excuses for past failures and rely on false hopes and dreams. Most sports still rely heavily on volunteers for leadership, if less on the day-to-day management of operations. This is even the case in the big five of football, rugby union, cricket, golf and tennis. Volunteers act as shareholders by investing their time, and a healthy *spirit* ensures they continue to receive dividends as well as seeing their investment yield higher levels of performance and return from their sport.

Support, respect, challenge, motivation, influence and trust are key words that seldom appear in governance statements in annual reports. Healthy heart, mind and spirit, often expressed in an organisation's values – assuming they are implemented – will ensure these features are intact. Boards should check the health of the heart, mind and spirit as well as the body corporate as part of their own annual performance review. Business corporations and public-sector organisations as well as NGBs should also adopt processes like this.

Tough times demand innovative and robust solutions, designed and delivered by brave people. Those who remain stuck in the past in a self-preservation society focused on good governance, tinkering with structures and relying on government support, will surely lose. Those who win will see the potential for their sport to grow and develop. They will thrive on the challenge of change, designing and implementing strategies to deliver great performances for themselves as organisations as well as their athletes. 'Be passionate, live your dreams and always remember to laugh' (Cathy Freeman).

The FA: a world-class organisation with a winning mentality?[1]

The Football Association (The FA) of England is one of the oldest football associations in the world, and is also one of the largest and most complex sporting organisations in the world. In 2006 its size and scale was high-lighted in the following numbers and statistics:

- Number of people playing (over 11 million – with 2.34m women and girls).
- Number of volunteers (over 500,000).
- Number of leagues (1,100).
- Number of clubs (around 20,000).
- Number of qualified coaches (over 370,000).
- Number of qualified referees (over 27,000).
- Turnover in excess of £300m.

Over the decade prior to 2006 The FA had stumbled from crisis to crisis, ranging from delays and cost overruns with the construction of the new Wembley stadium to a number of public personal issues with key senior personnel. Over the years, a number of strategic planning initiatives had taken place, but few had been effectively implemented.

Performance on the field had also been variable. In 2007 England was ranked 12th (men's senior team) in the world, with a playing population in the top five. As a national football team England had not won a major international trophy since 1966 and only two semi-final places had been secured in the previous 40 years at World and European Championships.

In 2007 CEO Brian Barwick decided to develop an integrated strategy for The FA and football in England through to 2012. The strategy was to be developed by the FA's senior management team, and Genesis was chosen to design and facilitate the process. The key objective was to develop a compelling vision and strategy for The FA through to 2012 that would provide the focus, direction and confidence for future initiatives, investment and plans. There was an additional objective to build the senior management group as a team and for them to own the emerging strategy.

What we did together

We designed a process that took into account the special context in which The FA found itself. In particular we considered:

- The recent progress made by the organisation – individually and collectively – including the on-going implications of implementing the recommendations of Lord Burns' review.
- The commissioning of Wembley stadium and the change this would make to The FA's resources.
- The ever-changing dynamics of the professional game in England and indeed the rest of Europe and the World.
- The special impact that the staging of the 2012 Olympiad in London would have on football.
- The changes in the competitive intensity of football internationally at club and national level.

The process represented a great opportunity to build on recent progress in the organisation and produce a way ahead that would deliver even higher levels of performance and satisfaction for the sport and its stakeholders in the future. It also gave the management team the opportunity to develop real collective ownership of their strategies and plans for future engagement with other key stakeholders in the game.

We designed a participative process to evolve a strategy that would be built and owned by the management team. Commitment and cohesion would be vital in the months of consultation and years of implementation that lay ahead towards 2012. Genesis's role was to:

- Be the custodian of the process of developing the strategy – its context and content.
- Guide, facilitate and support the management team through a participative and challenging process that would ensure the best possible conduct for developing strategy.
- Provide practical planning and other resources to draft the emerging strategy.
- Assist the management team to develop their plans into actions that would form the basis of future operating/business plans.

Our approach

We appointed a small steering group to lead the process and present input to the whole management team (first two layers). We also established a working group of six young executives from The FA's key functions to work with us and prepare for each event.

We designed a two-stage process (a 'game of two halves'). The first of the two stages was Stage 1: vision and goals (Figure 15.1).

The FA – England's favourite sport

First half – vision and goals

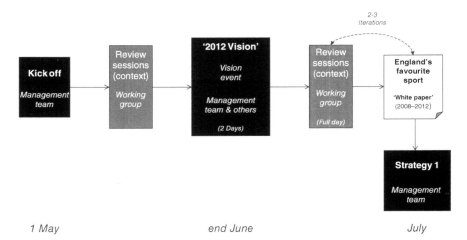

Figure 15.1 The strategy development process (first half): vision and goals. Process designed by Alistair Gray (2007).

Building the leadership capacity

Part of our approach was to use the strategy development process as a tool to increase the leadership capability and capacity of the management team. We gathered information on individuals (members of the management team), their preferred team roles, personalities and learning styles. This facilitated conversations around the performance of the management team as a team, and allowed them to articulate the challenges they faced as a leadership group. This proved an invaluable element and was an essential part of the strategy development process.

The vision event

At the end of the information-gathering stage we planned and held a two-day event with the steering group to develop the vision of success for The FA and football in England. A number of direct reports to the management team also attended the first part of the event. The event addressed the following:

- Understand the competitive environment faced by The FA (beyond 2012, and up to 2020).
- Consider the challenges faced by creating together a number of alternative external scenarios.
- Develop a 'vision for football and The FA' and confirm the goals for the sport – to 2012.
- Confirm the new focus and role for the sport and The FA.
- Agree the big issues and key success factors for the sport and The FA into the future.

We used a number of innovative approaches to engagement during the event. These included:

- Thinking partnerships.
- Presenting the strategies from a number of 'remarkable people' and comparator or stakeholder organisations, e.g., FAI, Cricket Australia, New Zealand All Blacks and Scottish Swimming.
- Limiting assumptions – getting rid of any baggage from the past.

The outcome from the vision event was clarity and a degree of commitment to the following:

- A vision of success.
- Key future success factors.
- The strategic goals and priorities.
- The big issues.
- Integrated strategy emerging.
- Business model for the future.

In addition we confirmed the leadership challenge facing the management team and established how this might be addressed in the near and longer-term future. We also agreed how the results of the vision event would be communicated to other key stakeholder groups.

Stage 2: planning to win

The process for Stage 2 is illustrated in Figure 15.2.

The second two-day event for the management team followed a similar format to the first 'vision' event. The event was highly participative and enjoyable, while at the same time building on the commitment secured at the end of Stage 1.

The event considered the recommendations of the working group and confirmed the priorities for action over the period of the strategy. Together we prepared the new performance measurement scoreboard for The FA, including the key performance indicators (KPIs) that would be used to monitor performance. In addition we considered together the requirements of the functional strategies for The FA, including marketing, people, finance, technical and information.

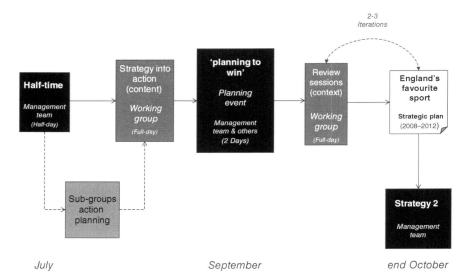

The FA – England's Favourite Sport

Second half – planning to win

Figure 15.2 The strategy development process (second half). Process designed by Alistair Gray (2007).

Over the weeks surrounding the event we were fortunate to attract the support of three leading CEOs from the world of sport and business:

1   Sir Stuart Rose, CEO of Marks & Spencer PLC;
2   Sir Terry Leahy, CEO of Tesco PLC;
3   Steve Tew, CEO of the New Zealand All Blacks.

All three described their experiences leading organisations that were facing considerable challenges, ranging from major turnaround to maintaining peak performance. This proved invaluable, not only to provide pointers for strategy, but also to give the management team confidence to face the final planning and implementation challenge.

Strategic plan

The framework in Figure 15.3 illustrates the final strategy. The framework helped to ensure alignment and guide implementation. It provided a sound basis on which The FA's functions/departments could develop their strategies and plans. The three strategic goals together represented a new beginning for the FA and, when achieved, would deliver a position of superior performance.

The FA's scoreboard

After decades of being hounded by all corners of the media you can understand why the executive of The FA was reluctant to agree to any performance outcomes for the strategy, especially if the strategy was to be publicised.

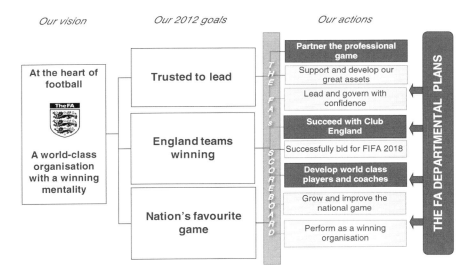

Figure 15.3 The FA: at the heart of football. Strategic framework created by Alistair Gray (2007).

However, having gone through the process together, the team felt confident to set a number of outcomes, linked to the strategic goals and actions against which they wished to be judged. These were:

- England's senior men's and women's teams qualifying for major competitions, and reaching the semi-finals at least, by 2012.
- Successfully bid to host the 2018 FIFA World Cup.
- Partnership in place with the Premier League and the Football League, making clear reported progress on major joint ventures in 2008 and 2009.
- Commercial/broadcast revenues increased by a substantial amount at the next review date in 2011.
- National Football Centre operating by 2010.
- One million 5–11 year olds training through the FA Tesco Skills programme by 2010.
- 125,000 existing teams retained and 20,500 new teams created by 2012.
- 26,000 referees retained and an additional 8,000 referees recruited by 2012.
- RESPECT campaign improving overall disciplinary performance by 35% by 2012.
- Consistently increased distribution of funds to the national game by 2012.
- Development and continued success of women's football.
- Wembley achieving an annual operating profit by 2012.
- The FA's move to Wembley completed and Investors in People accreditation achieved by 2010.
- Approval rating of The FA shown to improve, year-on-year, through the period of the strategy.

The final content and outcome

In February 2008 Lord David Triesman was appointed Executive Chair of the FA. His appointment was a key milestone in the implementation of Lord Burns' review of the FA's constitution and governance (agreed in 2007 by The FA Council). He, along with Brian Barwick, oversaw the final stages of the planning process. The strategic plan and associated business plan for The FA followed the completion of the framework.

Yet, once again, Lord Triesman and others fell on their swords through the seriously flawed bid for the 2018 FIFA World Cup. The reality was that the chances of England winning such a bid were 'zero' before they even started (as the final vote confirmed). Millions were wasted on the bid and the FA's image tarnished by their continued propensity to irritate fellow national associations. Hopefully the current leadership and administration will learn the lessons of the past. 'Football's coming home' is one of the most exasperating and arrogant slogans in world sport.

The end outcomes of the nine-month process were:

- A strategy for The FA through to 2012 that provided a framework to guide implementation of a number of key goals for the sport and the organisation.
- Strengthened personal and collective ownership of the strategy by the management team.
- Clear direction and leadership for the sport and other stakeholders in football in England.

In terms of actual outcomes when viewing the success of the strategic plan, with hindsight the following would never have been achieved for football in England without the new direction and commitment to execution of the strategic plan:

- Regular qualification and improvement in rankings of England teams.
- The growth and position of women's football.
- Increased investment in the national game at its grassroots.
- The development of Wembley Stadium.
- The creation of St George's Park as a world-leading national performance centre for football.

One of Barwick's key personal objectives was to develop The FA as a 'world-leading sporting organisation'. We had to work pretty hard to convince him and his colleagues that they had some way to go.

We stressed the fact that to achieve such status they had to develop strategic capabilities that were quite simply at that time – missing. Figures 15.4 and 15.5 represent how we illustrated to the management team the need for them to plan for and build integrated strategic capabilities, defined as unique combinations of assets, skills and systems/organisation that, taken together, would represent the architecture of The FA in the future. It showed them they were on the starting grid relative to good practice. Strategic architecture is a blueprint for sport leadership and business transformation.

In the beginning the relationships between the people of The FA and their leaders – executive and the board – were very poor. Our proposal to utilise an inclusive facilitated approach rather than a 'study' was challenging. At the end of the process the management team began to own the eventual outcome.[2]

The structure developed with The FA enabled real functional excellence and strategic capabilities to be built, as never before, in what they called their 'house' (Figure 15.6).

The FA's strategic capabilities in winning, growing and having fun

Figure 15.4 The FA's strategic capabilities. Model created by Alistair Gray (2007).

Trusted to lead?

Some progress can be demonstrated towards their goals of being 'the nation's favourite game' and 'England teams winning'. The goal of being 'trusted to lead' still seems far off and progress with governance reforms remains slow.

The failed 2018 FIFA World Cup bid is a good example of where The FA are not readily respected by their fellow national football associations. You can understand the concerns of smaller nations who are overwhelmed by the size and resources of The FA. When the likes of Germany, Spain, Italy and other leading nations in other continental federations fail to support their bid, it should send messages to the top and bottom of the game

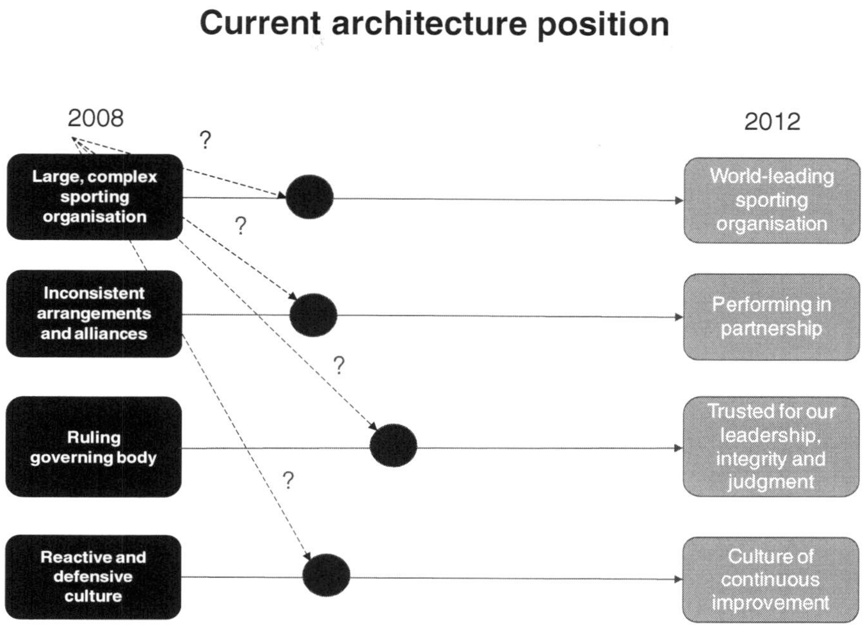

Current architecture position

Figure 15.5 The FA's strategic architecture position. Model created by Alistair Gray (2007).

in England. The FA needs to show greater humility and appreciation in their dealings with other football associations, rather than forever going on about the work they are doing and resources they are spending. The FA does great works with some associations, but it is almost in the fashion of the old Empire and genuine support can come across as patronising to the very nations they are generously supporting.

In 2008 they made a good start to the process of addressing The FA as an organisation (body) but also their heart, passion and spirit (culture of performance and mutual respect). However, their failure to really embrace Lord Burns' reforms has continually haunted them. The FA's Council steadfastly refused to execute a number of the recommendations, in many cases until a crisis has forced them to do so.

Recent events relating to duty of care and the fallout from the allegations made against Mark Sampson, the women's football senior team manager, have dragged the association into further disrepute. In addition, over 200 clubs are involved in allegations of child sex offences. These hang over the sport in England. It is encouraging to see the reaction by the current CEO Martin Glen and Chair Greg Clarke and their apparent commitment to reform. We have heard this before from The FA and Clarke and Glen's

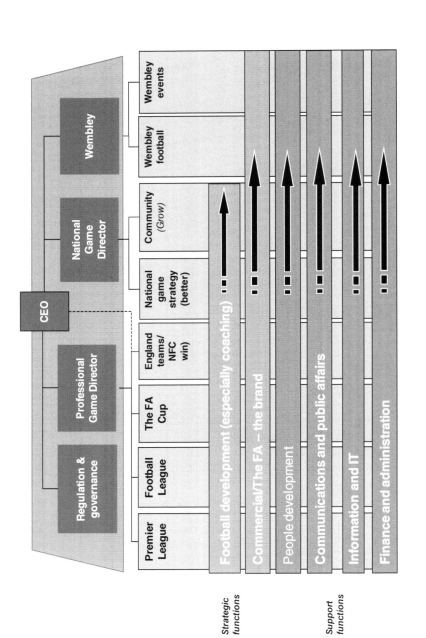

Business units and functions operating in a matrix

Figure 15.6 The house of The FA. Organisation structure created by Alistair Gray (2007).

challenge is to get The FA on the front foot in the forefront of leadership and governance reform, rather than playing catch up in a game they are unlikely to win.

Postscript: why England will never win the World Cup (at football)

In 2016 England suffered a humiliating defeat at the hands (or feet) of Iceland to exit the UEFA Championships at the quarter-final stage. This followed their exit at the group stage of the 2014 FIFA World Cup. Every two years the English media pile on the expectations for success and suggest England can win a major competition. Everything that happens is referenced back to 1966, 1990 or 1996 with the stated aim of removing years of hurt. The opposition are expected to lie down in the face of England's superiority. In fact England has never looked in danger of winning another World Cup at any time since their sole victory (at home) in 1966. England has not played in a major international final since 1966, never mind won a major competition.

There are many reasons why, despite significant investment and revenue spend, the Jules Rimes trophy is safe from English hands.

- The very success of the Premier League in attracting the best players from around the world. Most England international players are not members of the top clubs. The top clubs do not have a goal to produce England international players. The very wealth of the clubs is not necessarily ensuring that their resources are well spent. The power of the Premier League, driven by their burgeoning economic wealth, means that The FA's ability to challenge the League and their clubs (even though they are affiliated to The FA) is very limited (Figure 15.7). In comparison the German Bundesliga agreed media rights of €4.6m for four years to 2022.
- Europe is the hotbed of international competition, especially since the break up of the former Soviet Republic. Sixteen of the top 20 nations in the world are in Europe. Players from other (smaller) nations play regularly in continental European leagues where they learn the language and the other styles of play. Traditionally English players do not and language is a real barrier.
- Many nations – Germany, Spain, Holland and even the likes of Portugal, Czech Republic, Croatia, Switzerland and Belgium – have been developing and executing high-performance strategies and systems longer than England. When UEFA was founded there were 25 member nations. There now are 53. It is a similar position to high-performance sport where Australia and the US had systems in place before 1990 and in the UK this only began after 1998.

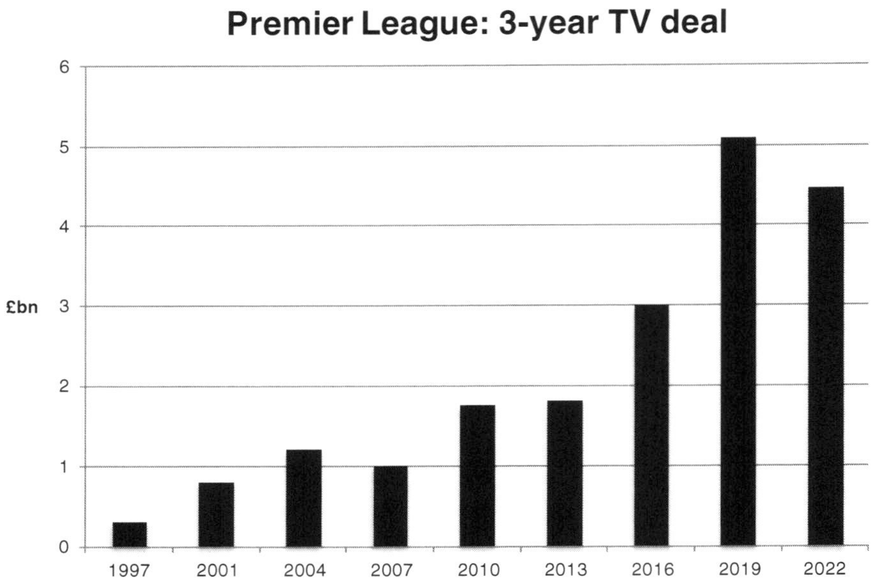

Premier League: 3-year TV deal

Figure 15.7 Football media rights. Chart created by Alistair Gray from Premier League data (2018).

- The very complexity of English sport and English football in particular (over 50 county football associations) make playing 'best vs best' from ages 12–18 very challenging. It is only in the last five years that the English FA has begun to address:
  - Developing technique and skills.
  - Building game intelligence.
  - Systemic skills development at a national level.
  - Reduction in competitive focus (especially at younger ages below 12).
  - Exclusively small-sided games and skills challenges at younger ages.

Coaching systems and content have been stuck in systems like the UK Coaching Certificate and UEFA coaching, with the focus on achieving badges rather than how best to coach young players. Many coaching courses are focused on developing former players into coaches rather than exploiting the excellent base of teaching that exists in England.

Our work with The FA led directly to the £150m investment in St George's Park and the National Game Strategy also pointed the way. New strategies for coaching and football development followed. Strategies, plans and major facility investment are all very well, but the answer to achieving the unthinkable (England winning a World Cup) lies firmly in the leadership in the sport, at all levels, forgetting 1966, slaughtering the sacred cows of the past and accelerating the execution of their good plans to develop and grow their players from ages 12–21 to play more and better football more often. The issue is one of focused execution rather than developing new ideas, complicated systems or imitation of the strategies of others. The appointment of a performance director and the consistent improvement in the performance of under-age teams (men and women) give cause for some optimism.

England exceeded the muted expectations of their media at the 2018 FIFA World Cup. The young squad, ably led by Gareth Southgate and containing players who had performed for the under-age teams in global competition, reached the semi-final. They were the most professionally prepared squad ever assembled by The FA. Here they lost to Croatia (a nation with a population smaller than Scotland, though greater than Iceland). All of the Croatian starting line-up in the World Cup final had played for clubs outside their homeland over the last seven years. Over that time nine Croatian players have all played for top clubs in the top five leagues in Europe – England, Spain, France, Germany and Italy – with two others playing for Dynamo Kiev in Ukraine. Only one of the English squad (Eric Dyer – in Portugal) has played outside England.

Our work with the FA continued with a review of women's football. At the time this was essentially based on part-time amateur teams and international teams run by a committee of FA Council members (made up of all men plus Beryl!). Brian Barwick actively supported our recommendations in 2008 in a paper that sought approval and funding (£5m over four years) for three significant new initiatives for women's football for 2008–2012.

- A new summer Super League launching in March 2010.
- A new performance manager for women's football leading a new performance unit.
- FA central contracts for senior England players.

The league was founded in March 2010 and professionalised in 2016. The participating clubs raised their game and embraced the new era and the opportunities it provided corporately for the clubs and individually for players. England's women finished third in the 2015 FIFA World Cup and in the same position in the 2017 UEFA European Championships, in many ways showing the way for their male counterparts.

In September 2017 The FA announced that the top tier of English women's football would be only for full-time clubs from 2018–2019, with all top-flight clubs being required to run an academy under new criteria. This further demonstrated real progress in working towards those early strategic goals established in 2007, especially the goal relating to England teams winning.

The FA

- **Broke the rules; challenged existing paradigms**

  - They planned to win, across a wider range of initiatives and focused on the strategic goals – for the first time in nearly 150 years.
  - The executive took individual and collective responsibility for performance.
  - They accepted they had to work with the Premier League and that they did not totally own football in England.

- **They worked it out themselves – embraced change management**

  - Faced reality as it was in 2006/2007, i.e., not trusted to lead and not winning.
  - Developed together an exciting vision of success (in the Focus Framework) that was shared by all.
  - Achieved performance improvement through planning to achieve clear short-term goals – by 2012.

- **Planned for a step-change in performance**

  - The vision was simple, clear and inspiring, yet it was underpinned by a detailed plan (The 'one-page strategy') that drove the change.
  - Appointed a Performance Director and made the £150m investment in St George's Park – a decision they had dithered over for more than 20 years.
  - They moved from Soho Square to Wembley.

- **Changed organisational performance**

  - Engaged a critical mass of executives, especially their bright young people, in pursuit of winning – cross-departmental teams worked out what to do.
  - Deployed matrix management – dealing with complexity.
  - Everyone knew how their role would deliver the goals of the strategic plan.

- **Leaders at all levels in the organisation championed the change**

  - Many people fulfilled their potential, not only in The FA but also in other organisations, e.g., UEFA, major media organisations.

Notes

1 The FA's Vision (2008–2012) published in 2007.
2 I would wish to express particular appreciation for the help given by Jonathan Hall, then Legal Director of The FA, in supporting Brian Barwick to get the strategic plan across the line.

16 Good governance does not win gold medals

Introduction

In my career in sport I have been privileged to serve as a volunteer and leader in the sport of hockey for over 30 years at national, continental and international levels. In 2005 I was appointed chair of British Performance Basketball to prepare teams for the London Olympics. In 2008 I was appointed to lead the board of British Swimming up to the 2012 Games. During that time the boards of both sports developed their leadership, governance and succession planning to increase the focus on performance management after a divisive period over the previous eight years. With the advent of National Lottery funding in 1998, most sports, and certainly the leading ones, were encouraged by UK Sport and other paymasters to address the governance of their sports. Few had incorporated and many struggled with the mix of voluntary leaders alongside increasingly professional management. At times the rush to governance and risk management overtook the quest for higher levels of performance.

The case study that follows reflects on the performance of the British swimming team at the Olympic Games in London in 2012 and the role of a board, working together with their executive, to deliver what was ultimately a disappointing performance at the Games. It highlights the respective roles of those involved in performance management and provides lessons for the leadership and governance for boards of national governing bodies of sport and other not-for-profit organisations.

The modernisation of sporting organisations

The darkness lightens

The summer of 2005 provided much needed relief to many in British sport, as well as new hope with the award of the 2012 Olympic Games to London. This, coupled with England's performance in the Ashes and the emergence of new winners like Andy Murray in tennis, offered hope where there was despondency. Sporting bodies like UK Athletics consistently failed on the track and as an organisation, despite a number of high-profile reviews and their own publicity to the contrary. British sport faced greater competition than ever before from an ever-increasing number of sporting nations. It was also encountering probably the greatest competitive intensity in the history of sport from the wider external environment. The environment demanded a degree of modernisation never before encountered in the history of organised sport.

The main thrust of modernising National Governing Bodies (NGBs) post the millennium focused on corporate governance and information systems, hardly enough to deal with this environment. Recent challenges faced by governing bodies in the UK such as Basketball, Hockey, Squash, Rugby League and British Cycling in 2017 bear testimony to this.

The business world faced similar challenges at a time of low growth and increased international competition. Recommendations on modernisation emerging from the Higgs Report[1] on corporate governance provided a hint of what should be adopted by sporting organisations to enable them to cope with the turbulent times that lie ahead.

The tough competitive environment faced by sport is no blip. Competition from the likes of Australia, China, India, South Africa and France is as strong as that from the US and Russia – indeed they are making faster and more significant progress than the superpowers. We in the UK often claim to punch above our weight, but how long can we rely on this as a sustained source of competitive advantage? Performance cycles are a thing of the past in an increasingly professional and prepared industry of world-class sport.

The longest 'bear' stock market in history reduced corporate spend on everything, and made areas such as sponsorship and patronage easy targets for cost reduction. Reductions in public expenditure and lottery income levels added to these financial challenges. This was then exaggerated with the longest and deepest recession in corporate history after 2008. Demographic trends are accelerating against sport at a time when physical activity rates are woefully low and obesity levels have risen to epidemic levels. As recently as 2017 mortality rates have increased after years of decline.

Good governance does not win World Cups or gold medals

Current organisational responses by governing bodies and sports councils seem to focus on improved governance, addressing areas such as structure and organisation; planning and systems; incorporation and business risk.

The positive outcomes from these processes include greater comfort from having prepared (or having prepared for them by lawyers) lengthy Memorandum and Articles of Association and more robustly generated financial accounts. There is improved awareness and management of risk. More full-time professional management should be able to address these external changes better than volunteers, but many have been found wanting and unable to cope with the complexities and traditions of sport. Investment in IT systems without a clear and compelling strategy or redesigned business and sport processes will do little more than enable sports to measure their decline more accurately.

Such approaches achieve the same outcome as digging lovely trenches with an elegant spade while someone else is moving the soil away with earthmoving equipment. The governance-led agenda does not enable the boards of our NGBs and supporting organisations to deal effectively with the environment described above, although it can sometimes give the impression of security from the storm raging outside.

In conversation with Derek Higgs, the author of the report to follow in the footsteps of Cadbury, Greenbury and Hampel, I raised the question of corporate leadership and how boards should change. Higgs' report deals with the tenure and appointment of independent non-executive directors and the content of boards. Like those of his predecessors, this report says little about what boards should do and the processes they should use to lead organisations to future success.

Real modernisation – leading the way to future success

Here is what I believe is the best modernisation agenda. It leads to boards and their executives answering the following questions:

- Facing reality – the recent, relative historical performance and context for the future.
- What is competition doing? What are the competing sports or other sources of demand for investment by the public and/or private sector?
- Scenario thinking – thinking the unthinkable about what is around the corner by considering divergent futures.
- Compelling vision, strategy and goals – what will be the big play that will deliver future success? What capabilities will be required to underpin the vision?
- Engagement of the sport and its people in its future?
- Sustainable economic viability of the sport?
- Improvement in relationships between professional management and voluntary leadership?
- Improved use of information and management of knowledge?
- Raising performance – business, organisation and people?

The award of the Olympics to London in 2012 afforded many sports the opportunity to view their future at three horizons – 2012 itself, followed by:

- 2016 – what was to become the Rio Olympics.
- 2020 – what was to become the Summer Olympics in Japan.

Crafting the desired vision of success for sporting organisations at these horizons should not only cover the performance planning for increased medals. It should also envisage the type of organisation and people leading the sport over the next 15 years, and how this should change to improve overall performance of the sport.

Understanding corporate leadership

This new agenda for modernisation requires the board of a sport to address the following:

- Leading the change:
  - Spending time in the future, rather than arguing over the past.
  - Vision, strategy and a new agenda to grow the sport in a new era of values – to guide the behaviour of the organisation.

- Performing as world class athletes:
  - Execution with velocity.
  - Focus on results and performance – real time and financial.

- The new board – leaders, not managers or controllers:
  - Governance (including the role of independent non-executive directors).
  - Context – understanding the reality of the current and future competitive environment.
  - Content – the new board agenda and processes – how to score.
  - Conduct - the new board behaviour and themes for meetings.

- Building leadership capacity:
  - Developing influencing capability and awareness – externally and internally.
  - Developing enthusiastic, passionate and performing people.
  - Adopting leading practices for the development and welfare of their people.

- Communication and consultation:
  - With the sport and other stakeholders.

Support, respect, challenge, motivation, influence and trust are key words that have never appeared in any 'mem and arts'. Boards should review their own performance at least annually, a process that should be independently facilitated. This is a vital and often missing ingredient of the assessment processes adopted by large corporations, far less NGBs.

Tough times demand innovative and robust solutions, designed and delivered by brave people. Unfortunately, too many sports and their boards have taken on the challenge, often in adversity and too late. Those who win see the potential for their sport to grow and develop. They take on the challenge of change. Those who remain stuck in the past in a self-preservation society will surely lose. Fortunately the hostile environment ahead leaves little choice.

Our deepest fear is not that we are inadequate. Our deepest fear is that we are powerful beyond measure. It is our light, not our darkness, that most frightens us.

Nelson Mandela, inaugural speech,
Cape Town, 1994

British Swimming at the London Olympic Games in 2012

Despite there being a challenging board, supported by UK Sport and spending more time than ever receiving and reviewing reports on the state of the nation's swimmers and coaches, the ultimate objective (to deliver GB's best ever Olympic performance) was missed, just. The best governance and risk management in sport failed to address the biggest organisational, technical and commercial risk in the history of the sport – underperformance at a home Olympic Games. How did this happen?

Increasingly challenging context for sport

Over the last decade the competitive environment faced by leading sports has intensified, driven by the explosion in performance programmes, broadcasting, media rights and sponsorship that almost ignored the worst recession in living memory.

This led to new governance challenges for the leaders of sport and their board. Over the last decade I have had the privilege of chairing the management boards of a number of British sports and have witnessed these challenges at first hand. I felt I should share experiences I hope will be of value to others, including the special experience leading British Swimming during the four years up to and including the London Olympic Games in 2012. This case study especially focuses on the sport and the preparation and performance of their board, executives, athletes and coaches up to and including London 2012.

The best team GB ever prepared

Team GB, as a whole, enjoyed glittering success at London 2012 in sports such as cycling (12 gold), rowing (9 gold) and equestrian (3 gold). But in these sports fewer than four nations won gold medals, from an average of 30 competing nations, averaged across the three sports. This compared with the likes of swimming and athletics where over 30–40 nations respectively won medals (120/132 nations competed). Six athletes in swimming and athletics delivered medals and we were in awe of the gold-medal-winning performances of Mo Farah, Jessica Ennis and Greg Rutherford. Those three apart, both athletics and swimming performed poorly in London, yet both have probably done more than most to improve their governance.

British Swimming is (still) highly regarded by UK Sport and FINA as one of the best-governed national associations in their sport. This regard came from improved performance from 2000 through to 2008, the structure and balance of the management board, e.g., the number and quality of independent directors on the board, their management of risk and governance, and the integrity of people, processes and systems.

At the beginning of 2012 the board and executive were confident the 2012 Olympic Games target would be achieved. The National Performance Director described the team, the week before the Games and on leaving the holding camp in Edinburgh, as 'the best prepared ever to compete in an Olympic Games for Team GB'.[2]

It was therefore a great shock to everyone that the athletes delivered only one silver and two bronze medals (against a target of five) from twelve apparently genuine medal prospects at the beginning of the year. The team and the executives responsible for the planned performance delivered the highest number of finalists in recent history, with GB teams in every relay final, yet the lowest medal return in major championships in ten years. British swimmers froze in the Aquatics Centre at Olympic Park. Over £40m of investment over four years into the high performance end of the sport delivered a disappointing return.

The warning signs were there in Shanghai in 2011. With improved data analytics it was obvious that the times for starts, turns and finishes were off the pace of other leading nations and their swimmers. Despite resistance from many of the executives, the board commissioned a project to focus on these three important parameters of performance. The board, at its meeting in January 2012, sought assurance as to the progress being made with the medal prospects for the Games. The executive gave that assurance, yet by June it was clear that the basis of this assurance was flawed, with the apparent 'decision' to avoid head-on competition (against real opposition) at the European Championships during the months leading up to the Olympics. The Director of Operations, when questioned about the progress and impact of the starts, turns and finishes project, reported that 'it was not dead'.

The subsequent independent review carried out after the London Olympic Games concluded:

> Overall, the consensus arising from the consultation completed is that the (British Swimming) World Class Programme is broadly delivering its objectives and has the right programme elements, initiatives and systems in place. Put simply, it is not broken, in need of a major overhaul or requiring a radical change of direction.
>
> However, the process highlighted a number of areas where there were shortcomings in leadership and delivery, or where systems and processes did not function as well as they should have, particularly over the final period of the quadrennial cycle:
>
> - The overall planning of the programme remained a strength.
> - The principal weaknesses relate to coaching and technical leadership. Under pressure they, and their athletes, failed to deliver.
> - Too much flexibility was afforded and some deviation from tried and tested training and preparation plans resulted from this.

Despite investment in a performance system – the envy of the rest of the aquatic world – the fundamental performance of managers, coaches and their swimmers did not deliver athletes who were competition-ready for London 2012, a home Olympic Games where host nations usually exceed previous performance standards. The harsh reality is that British swimmers peaked in Rome (2008) and failed to compete often enough at the highest level in the world over the three remaining years leading to London. Instead they 'hid', competing against their British peers, convincing themselves in the training pool that they were capable of delivering medal-winning performances in the world class.

Despite a challenging board, supported by UK Sport and spending more time than ever challenging and supporting executives through receiving and reviewing reports on the state of the nation's leading swimmers and coaches, the ultimate objective (to deliver GB's best-ever Olympic performance) was missed.

The best governance and risk management in sport failed to address the biggest organisational, technical and commercial risk in the history of the sport – under-performance at a home Olympic Games. The £0.5m of annual salaries paid to executive and performance management, regarded by their peers as world class, delivered their poorest performance for a decade. How was this possible?

Complacency at a time of the greatest competitive intensity

At the top end of elite sport the margins between success and failure are small. In four final swims a total improved performance of two seconds would have delivered an additional four medals, and Team GB's swimmers their planned performance. British Swimming was embarrassed by the 'gold rush' elsewhere, arguably in sports where there is less competitive intensity than in athletics and swimming. UK Sport, having held British Swimming up as a model of excellent performance systems and governance, were quick to demand sackings of the technical leads. Others who had built the very system – found wanting in the nation's hour of need – should have followed.

British Swimming set up a panel of experts to review the performance at the London Olympics. Amazingly athletes did not form a part of this review (or the review by the sport's performance management) until too late in the process, despite earlier suggestions being made. The review panel made clear recommendations that were logical and capable of implementation. However, returning to the podium with greater frequency required much greater focus:

- Making a good system great, embracing innovation at all levels, rather than relying on science and resisting real innovation.
- Getting all athletes and coaches inside the system. No longer can people sit outside the system and be supported. The best must train and compete with the best, day in, day out.
- Race a lot more. Too many swimmers were mental lightweights who could not cope with under-performance, never mind trying to beat the person in the lane next to them.

It is staggering to think the sport had not realised these fundamentals after four quadrennials (16 years) of intensive management, reports and reviews. Executives and coaches were encouraged to do everything necessary to assure the best performance outcome and were held to account. What more can boards do to ensure the best infrastructure and culture is in place to develop and deliver winning athletes and coaches, time after time, again and again?

Despite the system and all the investment, the board failed to demand real-time and relevant information on 12 athletes as they prepared for the races of their lives. Despite the best training and science-focused system in the world, the coaches and their system failed to ensure that our athletes were at a competitive peak going into the ultimate test. The very strength of governance created world-class inertia and complacency in a system that failed to test itself in the true competitive environment of the swimming world. We were world class in our own little world.

Leading the way to future success

What are the lessons for leadership and governance? There is only so much a board can do to ensure success. The answer must always lie with senior executives, coaches and athletes to secure and deliver performance, especially when empowered with world-leading levels of resources. The more technical performance sport becomes, the greater the challenge for traditional boards.

Twenty-first-century sporting organisations need to learn from other high-performing organisations elsewhere to win in an increasingly competitive environment, as well as building on the lessons learned from recent history. This means sporting organisations must display the following features:

- 'Built to change', rather than 'built to last' – British Swimming had too many people in self-preservation mode on the board and in an executive who hid from the reality of performance.
- Greater focus on vision, competitive strategy and performance to create the future.
- Building corporate and individual leadership as well as corporate governance.
- A sense of community with inspirational athletes, coaches, support staff and administrators.
- Game-breaking ideas in an integrated coaching system, supported by leading sports science, medicine and technology.

One of the successes in the sport over the four years leading up to the London Olympics was to establish an agenda to improve the performance of people in the organisation. You do not change an old organisation overnight and a new generation of leaders will be required by the sport to deliver future success.

Boards should review their own performance at least annually. This was done at British Swimming, to the discomfort of too many members. It is a vital and often missing ingredient of the assessment processes adopted by large corporations, far less NGBs.

Everyone in British Swimming learned from the harsh lessons of 2012. Newly appointed performance leadership and management were empowered to execute fundamental change to deliver new horizons of performance in Rio in 2016. This was achieved, endorsing the view of the review panel in 2012 that the system was not broken.

2016 Olympics – the system delivers

After the letdown of London 2012, Britain secured its biggest Olympic medal haul in the pool since 1984 (three of the swimming medals at the 2008 Olympics came in the open water event). That follows on from record performances at the 2015 World Championships and 2014 European Championships. There were a number of reasons for this:

Coaching

Following the tenures of American Dennis Pursley and Australian Bill Sweetenham that stretched back to 2000, British Swimming turned

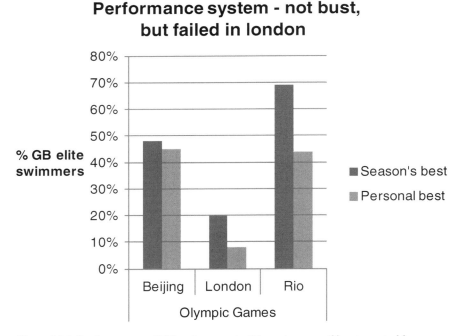

Figure 16.1 Performance of GB swimmers in Olympic years. Chart created by Alistair Gray from British Swimming data (2018).

in-house to Bill Furniss, who was appointed as head coach alongside Chris Spice, a former performance director for British Basketball and the Rugby Football Union, in the aftermath of London 2012. Spice had been a gold-medal-winning coach in hockey at the Sydney Olympics and had worked with me at British Basketball with great success. He had also operated as Performance Director of English Rugby (The RFU) alongside Sir Clive Woodward at the time when England won the Rugby World Cup in Australia in 2004.

Furniss, who coached Rebecca Adlington to two gold medals at the 2008 Beijing Olympics, straight away made three things clear:

1   Mediocrity was unacceptable.
2   We will be doing things the 'British way'.
3   We will race much, much more.

That meant setting standards rather than copying them. It has also involved the administration in some tough love. Britain's qualifying standards at the Olympic trials were the toughest in the world. Chad le Clos, then 200m-butterfly Olympic champion, would not have gained an automatic berth, which was only achieved by eight British swimmers – although a further 18 were selected for Rio having fallen within 2% of that time at the trials. That meant no place for the likes of Ross Murdoch, the 200m-breaststroke Commonwealth champion and holder of the fifth fastest time in history.

'You put five Olympic rings up there and it brings a whole tension with it', Furniss said. 'In some respects, it sorts out the wheat from the chaff. It gets the people on the plane who you want on the plane'.

Pressure

Whereas the home support of London 2012 inspired British athletes to run faster and jump farther in track and field, it had the opposite effect at the Aquatics Centre. Not only was the return of one silver and two bronze medals below expectations, but only a minority of the British squad were able to set personal bests – Michael Jamieson, the silver medal winner in the 200m breaststroke, stood out as the only athlete to deliver successive personal best performances. Many did not even produce season bests.

Breeding mental resilience quickly became a priority for the new coaching leadership. Setting the bar very high at the trials was part of that, yet they have also been careful not to confer extra pressure by setting medal targets, preaching the sports psychology's fundamental tenet of prioritising performance over result.

Preparation

No stone, from the biggest rock to the smallest pebble, was left unturned by British Swimming in their preparation for Rio. Team GB's training base at

Belo Horizonte featured the only 50m indoor swimming pool outside Rio de Janeiro, while training was tailored on the basis of two years' worth of research to ensure the squad's body clocks would be attuned to the late timings of the swimming finals. While most major championships start at around 7.30pm, in Rio the finals did not get under way until 10pm for the benefit of American television audiences and swimmers often did not get to bed until 3am or later. 'It is pointless being upset by the times like some countries have been', Furniss said. 'It is what it is, you just have to deal with it.'

To ensure the swimmers got a good night's sleep, they were booked on the top floors of their accommodation block while specially moulded earplugs, blackout blinds and mattress toppers were installed. Speaking after her silver medal in the 200m individual medley in the early hours of Wednesday morning, Siobhan-Marie O'Connor said: 'The conditions we had for the holding camp were brilliant. To get the only 50m pool in Brazil to train in was perfect. We had a tough trials but it meant we came here the best prepared team'.

Furthermore, Nigel Redman, the head of elite coach development, and Spice are already studying this cycle and planning for Tokyo in 2020.

Talent

All the earplugs and exhortations in the world would be fairly redundant if British Swimming did not have the raw talent with which to work. In that respect, Furniss and Spice had luck on their side to be Head Coach and Performance Director at a time when a once-in-a-generation talent such as Adam Peaty burst on to the scene with his three World Championships and records. O'Connor was a little girl lost at London 2012 and still had her peak ahead of her at 20. So, too, James Guy, who made up for his personal disappointment in the 200 and 400m freestyle by anchoring Britain's 200m freestyle relay to silver. Overall two thirds of this squad did not compete at London 2012. Those that did, such as Fran Halsall, have spoken in detail about how they have put it behind them. As Guy put it, 'London wasn't great but there were three medals and fair play to Becky and Michael – but this is a new era now. London is done and we are turning it around'.

From a pool of despair and disappointment, British Swimming is now leading the way. Returning to the role of leading executives, the main difference was that in 2012 performance was left in the hands of Michael Scott, the then Performance Director, and his team of specialists in many aspects of sports science and medicine. In many ways senior management left him to his own devices and indeed he showed little energy to share the 'state of the swimmers' with colleagues and the board. In Spice and Furniss there are two leaders who have been empowered to deliver success from the system. The key difference is that they have taken responsibility for that performance and, through their relationships with the swimmers and their colleagues, they are happy and confident to share the progress they and their charges are making towards the podium in Tokyo in 2020.

- **Broke the rules; challenged existing paradigms**

  - Became an exemplar for an athlete-centred coach-led approach to performance management.
  - Removed the remote science-based leadership of performance, with individual coaches operating in their own centres, and returned to a more coach-led and more collegiate team of high performance coaches, supported by appropriate science, medicine and technology.
  - Changed the expectations for athletes.

- **They worked it out themselves – embraced change management**

  - Faced up to the reality of the performance at the 2012 Olympics, recognising that the talent development system was not broken.
  - Shared a vision of success for the future that coaches, athletes and administrators bought into.

- **Planned for a step-change in performance**

  - The vision was simple, clear and inspiring, yet it was underpinned by a detailed plan for each athlete and their coaches that drove the change.
  - Planned competition opportunities to ensure the athletes were at their peak for major events, e.g., the World Championships.

- **Changing organisational performance**

  - CEO focus was totally on British Swimming (separate from the Amateur Swimming Association – the governing body of Swimming in England).
  - Reduced the scope of activity for the World Class Operations Director, removing diving, water polo and synchronised swimming from the swimming programme.
  - Developed a world-class coaching community.

- **Developing leaders at all levels in the organisation**

  - The appointment of Bill Furniss and Chris Spice was timely and due, reducing the emphasis on science and getting back to the basics of performance and coaching.
  - Many people fulfilled their potential – not just the swimmers.
  - Continued investment in training and development of people, especially in innovation.

Notes

1 In April 2002 Derek Higgs was appointed to lead an independent review of the role and effectiveness of non-executive directors. Derek Higgs published his report on 20 January 2003.
2 Michael Scott, Performance Director: British Swimming 2008–2012.

17 Performance strategies for national football associations

Introduction

Despite football being the world's largest participation sport and having staged World Cups every four years since the inaugural tournament in 1930 (except during the Second World War), few football nations have a structured approach to developing talent through to the development of future international players. Most nations depend on relatively loose unstructured methods of development, relying more on their clubs and national coaches to assemble squads for qualifying campaigns and participation in finals. Most national associations also employ a technical director who oversees all matters football. Changes in the sport, especially over the last 25 years with the introduction of technology and investment of considerable sums of money, have meant that the scope and spread of such a position has become increasingly wide and complex.

Success and sustainability in sport are achieved through a twin focus on growing the game and winning. The specialist nature of both functions is now at a level never seen before in the game. As a result, national football associations require to develop and acquire real expertise in both functional areas of leading and managing the game.

The current world champions are France who won their second title at the 2018 FIFA World Cup. Their first title was won on home soil in 1998. They have had an established performance system for more than 20 years based on their national performance centre at Fontainebleu. The previous world champions were Germany, who won their fourth title at the 2014 tournament in Brazil. In 2000 Germany failed to qualify for the final stages of the UEFA World Championships. Such was their embarrassment that it led to a wholesale change in the way they organised the game. Over the last two decades they have developed a carefully prepared national performance strategy that secured the buy-in of all clubs in the top two divisions of the Bundesliga.

During the last decade Genesis consultants have worked with a number of national associations in a variety of team sports to develop their performance strategies. I have been privileged to work in football over the last 15 years – ironically since Roy Keane

*returned early from the 2002 FIFA World Cup. I have been deeply involved in perfor-
mance sport since 1995, and especially after 1998 as a chair of the Scottish Institute
of Sport and through my involvement in the development of Mission 2012, the UK's
successful high performance system. The question was how might such a performance
philosophy be applied to football and, indeed, would it be accepted?*

*In this chapter I outline the approach taken to develop performance manage-
ment systems in the football associations of England, Ireland, Northern Ireland
and Scotland, as well as in other team sports (rugby union, rugby league, cricket
and hockey). A detailed case study of how this is being applied in Scotland follows.*

Building on Mission 2012

Following my service as a volunteer – as Chair and President of Scottish
Hockey – coupled with my experience in strategic management consulting
in business and latterly sport, I was in a good position to provide UK Sport
with monitoring and evaluation of the performance plans designed and executed by sports following the introduction of the National Lottery in 1998.
As Chair of the Scottish Institute of Sport, I was also on the board of the UK
Sports Institute and involved in the development of Mission 2012, the performance system designed in 2004 to support the investment in sports up
to and including the Olympic Games in Beijing and London. Subsequently,
as Chair of British Basketball and British Swimming, I was able to experience the UK performance system from both sides – government agency
and Olympic sports.

In order to create an environment to succeed, UK Sport developed the
pioneering Mission 2012 review process that tracks, checks and challenges
each funded sport on their Olympic and Paralympic journey. Mission 2012,
which was originally developed for London 2012, is a tool to ensure continuous performance improvement and has developed greater capability
to identify issues and find solutions before they have a negative impact on
athletes' performances.

UK Sport worked with each sport's performance team to assess and
reflect on areas of strength and weakness. Sports analyse elements of their
athlete development and support programmes in three key areas:

1   Athletes – performances, development profiles, well-being, health and
    commitment.
2   System – the staff, structures, facilities, processes, knowledge and
    expertise.
3   Climate – the culture, feel and day-to-day function experienced by ath-
    letes and staff.

Once a year each sport undertakes an extensive review during which progress is measured using a traffic light system and action plans are developed on a plan-do-review basis. This is supplemented by a six-month check-in and a fuller debrief after major events and championships. It is interesting to note that debriefing as a tool is used little after major championships in football, other than in a crisis such as disappointing performances or early elimination.

UK Sport also work with each sport to improve, share knowledge and identify areas where external expert support from another sport, the home nation sports institutes, or even from another 'performance' industry – such as the arts or the business sector – is needed.

The performance model in football

There are five key ingredients in developing any high performance programme:

1   Clarity of focus.
2   High standards.
3   Responsibility.
4   Feedback drives learning.
5   Teamwork.

> **Performance**
> *Doing the simple things extraordinarily well, time after time, after time. You need stability in which to implement real change. Instant success takes time.*

The model outlined in Figure 17.1 represents our approach to planning for high performance in team sports. Performance planning for team sports

Figure 17.1 High performance model in team sports. Created by Alistair Gray (2010).

adds a number of additional complexities to planning for individual performance improvement, but the principles are broadly the same. It is based on 32 question areas (in five boxes) that determine the extent to which a high performance environment exists in a sport, and reflects principles applied in leading Olympic team sports, e.g., hockey and basketball, and world-leading non-Olympic teams sports, e.g., rugby union, rugby league and cricket.

Players and coaches

The key starting point is one of critical mass. Ask the question 'do we have sufficient players and coaches playing at a competitive intensity at or near that of international football?', i.e., the number of players and coaches actually on the field, not just watching or warming a bench. Most academies will have two–three players covering each position with the flexibility to play other tactical formations, positions or roles, as well as their core or preferred position.

The focus is on producing more and better players playing better football more often. These are no ordinary players – they should aspire to be international quality. Consequently data should be gathered, analysed and debriefed to show the player is on the way to that standard. Measures used in team sports include, for example, percentage pass completion, total passes made (football) and circle penetration (hockey). Some form of central charter, with club commitment, should be developed for international players, especially as they work through the age-group teams.

National federations need to grow a cadre of coaches at all age levels, working to an agreed style, in a positive learning environment, if they are to develop the next generation of international players. The development of coaches can be compared with a supply chain where raw ingredients are acquired, assembled, trained and nurtured to produce the finished article. Most national football associations do not do this in a planned or effective way. They do deliver coaching courses to continental federation standards, but few plan for a successful coaching workforce and consequently fail to address issues such as capacity building, succession or career development. UEFA recently set a derisory standard of continuous professional development (in order to sustain a qualification badge) of 15 hours over three years. Other professions such as accountants, lawyers or even management consultants set the standard of five days each year. Coaches form communities naturally and national associations can derive great benefit by bringing the community together a few times each year to share good practice and stimulate learning.

The supply chain of players and coaches has to be developed and therefore led and managed. Developing leaders is typically not well practised in sporting organisations, though it is much better than it was 20 years ago. Leadership at all levels, and among both volunteers and professionals, needs to be stimulated and practised in players and their coaches. Empowering leaders and enabling them to flourish and grow are two of the main ingredients in the development of a performance culture.

High performance system

Having established a critical mass of players and coaches, the next step is to design a systematic way of developing talent towards the top end of the pathway. In Germany this was carried out in partnership between the DFB (national association) and the Bundesliga (the clubs in their league). In England The FA sought to define to the Premier League clubs how they should develop their players and run their academies. This was mission impossible, given the wealth and power of the Premier League, and, in any case, they were employing coaches and academy directors with greater capability and experience than those residents of Soho Square (before their move to Wembley).

Learning from Mission 2012, the first step for any system is to 'face reality as it is, not as it was or you would wish it to be'.[1] Where are you in the World rankings? – they do not lie. In Europe UEFA also publish a coefficient that ranks nations and clubs relative to their performance in domestic and European competition.

Football has been slow to embrace principles of sports science and medicine, far less performance lifestyle management. (Modern professional footballers may be earning £100k each week with no appreciation of the impact this might have on their lifestyle or them personally as a top earner in today's society.) In addition, advances in technology and analytics now play a major part in securing the critical edge required for top performance, and many systematic models and software are available to today's laptop coach. The association's challenge is to devise a system that not only appeals to the technologically gifted but also the 'retiring professional footballer' as they enter the coaching pathway.

Performance management is a new concept for players, coaches, managers and club administrators and directors. The systems are now there for clubs to understand exactly the state of their squads and players, as well as managing their balance sheets. Such systems should also provide data to the national association to understand the state of potential future international players. Consequently it is imperative to secure the engagement of clubs in the development and deployment of any performance system, just as UK Sport engaged with sports in the design and implementation of Mission 2012. Given the increasingly specialist nature of performance management, it is advisable for national associations to appoint an international performance director to lead the performance function and the implementation of the performance system. Given the specialist nature of growing the game and winning as two themes to improve performance management, the idea of this being within the scope of a single technical director with limited knowledge and experience in both areas is no longer tenable.

Jim Collins, the leading Stanford University business guru and author of *Good to Great*,[2] which charts the practices of companies that have grown and sustained their performance for decades, proposes that any performance strategy must set performance goals that are 'big, hairy and audacious' and in areas:

- That you are passionate about.
- That you are best in your world at.
- That drive your economic engine.

Taken together the goals represent a vision of success – a higher ranking in world football. They also provide the basis for performance planning as will be described for the Scottish FA in the case study that follows. This vision of success brought stakeholders together and provided a view that would be worth the effort of the climb to get there.

Performance infrastructure

National associations cannot control clubs and their development of talented young players to represent their country. In most of the leading professional football leagues fewer than 35% of registered players are eligible to play for the country in which the league is operating. The governing body can only provide the infrastructure in which leading performance management is encouraged and rewarded. Two fundamental principles of performance management are engagement and alignment of activities towards the strategic goals. This requires the association to engage effectively with clubs and ensure that, through the quality of their engagement, the club activities are aligned, as far as is practical, to the strategic goals of the association's performance strategy. The key features of the infrastructure for performance must include:

- A system for the development of talent – in the main age categories of 5–11, 12–16, 17–senior.
- A performance pathway from 12–21 – assuring the concept of 10,000 hours of purposeful practice and meaningful competitive football for their elite athletes. In many associations the performance pathway is fractured at 18 as players move on to professional contracts. Many rising stars spend fruitless years warming the benches of the parent club,

rather than being loaned out to another club to gain valuable match experience in its first team. The key role for the performance director is to lead and manage the health and productivity of the performance pathway.

- Great people – few national associations have a developed human resource strategy. Young football professionals should be regarded in the same way as apprentices in accounting and law, especially in the light of their potential earning capacity. Players as well as coaches should commit to continuous professional development. Schemes such as Investors in Young People, Modern Apprenticeships and a number of charitable foundations will fund a more holistic development of the young people that are today's young footballers. Such development strategies should embrace players, coaches and their support staff as well as the clubs' owners and senior management. A number of national associations, for example in hockey, have trained their leading players in the 16–21 age group to become umpires, with an associated improvement in discipline as one of the best results.

- Monitoring and evaluation of players and coaches – the performance system can also incorporate an overview of the development of coaches. A workforce strategy and plan for the development of performance coaches should be a start, with 360° feedback on coaches from players built into the system. A number of nations are now launching a 'top coach' programme where a small number of young coaches can be seconded to other associations or sports, and the future succession of national team managers can be assured. Debriefing after major tournaments is a simple skill and process developed by performance functions in business and other sports. By treating coach development as a business would its critical supply chain, governing bodies can ensure stability and consistency of performance.

- Facilities are at the heart of any investment in infrastructure. The quality of pitches, both artificial, synthetic and mixed, has improved out of all recognition over the last ten years. Many nations have also designed and built national performance centres to be the focus of their commitment to improved performance. Success at the elite end of any global sport, and especially team sport, is to regard any progress as generational (a ten+-year programme). The art of the long view does not prevent associations from measuring progress in the short term and giving appropriate reward and recognition where it is due. Perhaps the largest and most discussed example is The FA's decision to build their national performance centre at St George's in the Midlands of England. This £150m investment was the subject of debate over a period equivalent to the lapsed time since England last won a FIFA World Cup

(1966). In most nations there is a recognised regional structure often replicated by other public services such as the health service, enterprise companies and tourist boards. Leading clubs must form effective relationships with local authorities and other semi-professional and youth clubs, thereby creating their own infrastructure to develop performance in line with the national strategy.

Culture of performance

England won the FIFA World Cup in 1966 and since then there has been the expectation that they will win every major championship for which they qualify. For months before and during the tournament itself expectations are raised. Although the reality has been one semi-final place since 1966, the expectations continue unabated.

Nevertheless, the home nations often achieve more than they should, the exception being Scotland which, since 1998, have not qualified for the World Cup finals, and in 2016 even failed to qualify for an expanded UEFA Championships. To the credit of Scotland's 'Tartan Army' and media, expectations have been lowered and replaced by a real commitment to improve through an unprecedented new performance strategy linked into the first corporate strategy for the Scottish Football Association. The culture – the expectation, attitudes and behaviour of stakeholders – is critical in determining future success. Prior to 1996 the performance of British Olympic teams, and their counterparts in the Commonwealth Games of the constituent nations, was down to the ambition, attitude and self-belief of individual athletes and their coaches. Since then, systematic performance planning and investment have delivered improved performances from more athletes in more sports.

A key element of any performance improvement is to build a performance culture in athletes, coaches, the public, government and media. This has to start with publishing and committing to achieve a 'goal to win' – not necessarily the trophy itself but certainly to make a step-change in performance, and to manage expectations accordingly.

Leadership plays a major part in this quest, not only in the national association but also in other key stakeholders, e.g., government and media. Bringing stakeholders together and setting an agreed goal is a critical first step, as well as really understanding the 'reality of now'. Poor performances in major championships are often associated with damaging reviews of what went wrong, with key people ducking and diving to avoid being saddled with the blame for defeat and disappointment. Leaders at all levels have to face up to the new goal and play their part, individually and collectively, in achieving the performance improvement. Empowerment of players, coaches and managers plays a major part, along with their taking responsibility for their performance.

Most nations will take pride in success and there is clear evidence that the whole productivity of a nation can be positively influenced by success at world or continental championships, e.g., New Zealand winning the Rugby World Cup in 2011 and 2015, as well as the America's Cup in yachting in 1995 and 2000. Simply sharing the success publicly in the media is not enough. Turning again to the nation of the Silver Fern, New Zealand Rugby invest 50% of their revenue in their provinces and clubs year on year, a strategy followed by British Cycling. The latter invest in similar proportions between growing participation in the sport and their world-renowned performance system.

Changing culture in any organisation requires three key elements:

1   Achieving dissatisfaction with the status quo or current and historic performance.
2   Building a realistic yet inspiring vision of success.
3   Planning to win – to make the changes that will build confidence that future goals are achievable and communicating that progress, as well as celebrating and sharing early successes.

The national teams

Our research found that the more the national teams (senior and under-age) replicated the environment in a leading club, the more successful they became. The senior coach has a special role to play, leading the group of under-age team coaches in building a style of play backed up with a simple and inspiring philosophy such as that displayed over decades by Sir Alex Ferguson at Manchester United.[3] The senior coach also needs to have a number of full-time coaches and support staff in his team. Previous regimes often assembled part-time coaches who had full-time jobs with clubs to support major championships, which resulted in learning leaving with the staff when they left the bus after the tournament. The role of the manager, the international performance director and the CEO of the national association is to replicate the performance environment of leading clubs.

As late as 2010 in some nations, squads of players were traditionally selected by the international committee of the association. Thankfully these days are gone. Players and coaches expect to find the same environment when they move from a Premier League or Bundesliga environment to that provided by their national association. The traditional roles of manager/coach and international committee need to be replaced by an international performance group led by the CEO and made up of the international performance director, who designs, leads and manages the performance system, and the senior national coach, along with other key executives. Such a group also brings the opportunity to engage the professional leagues and secure their commitment to building successful national teams.

In conclusion

The recent changes in performance management in sport are gradually reaching football. Attitudes towards the development of young players are changing along with the need to embrace and apply sports science and medicine, performance lifestyle and the creation of sustainable infrastructure in support of performance. At first, football in many of the leading nations simply threw money at the problem, e.g., England created over 90 academies and Scotland 36. Evaluation has brought a sense of value to the previous profligacy and subsequent reviews are now producing positive results and real change. In performance sport nothing can be left to chance. No longer will the expectations of a nation drag the national teams across the line. Clear plans to win, leaving nothing to chance and professionally executed to an agreed model, will increase the chances of success in today's world of football.

First performance strategy for Scottish football after 138 years

Background

Most nations perform to their population size. Fewer than 20% of European countries rank five places higher than their European population ranking. Croatia, Ireland, Uruguay and Slovenia are among the few countries with a population lower than that of Scotland to have qualified for any of the last six World Cups. However, historically Scotland has often performed internationally several classes above its weight. Scotland is ranked 27th in European populations, so to reach the top 20 in football rankings in Europe Scotland would need to have the second-highest out-performance rate relative to its population. National expectations, however, seldom follow logic and remain optimistic.

In 2011 Scotland was ranked 54th in the FIFA world rankings. In performance terms the UEFA coefficient of the Scotland national team was declining. The senior men's team had not qualified for a major final since France in 1998.

Our approach

The model in Figure 17.1 (see p. 291) represents our approach to planning for high performance in team sports as described earlier in this chapter.

Our early investigations focused on the effectiveness of structures, systems and processes deployed in the game in Scotland. Of particular importance was the quality of competition in the Scottish Premier League (SPL), Scottish Football League (SFL), and the impact of the Youth Initiative, especially the extent to which together they provided an environment in which talent might flourish in Scotland.

Conclusions from the review

Scotland, on the basis of the size of the nation's population and the relatively low number of Scottish players playing for top clubs in top leagues, has no right to expect to qualify for future World Cups or to be ranked better than Top 50 in the world. In addition, the competitiveness of European/international football and the relative ease for players to move between European nations had increased, in marked contrast to that in the Scottish Premier League (SPL) and other Scottish leagues. There had also been significant changes in the game in the UK with the recruitment of non-UK qualified players, which left few places for Scottish players in top league football. In addition there was a lack of any systematic performance system and infrastructure in Scottish football alongside a static pace of change and investment in development.

In considering all of the above, Scottish football needed to over-invest relative to other comparable national associations and, more importantly, in a way that was smarter and very different from the strategies and plans deployed in the past. The level of investment and associated structure, processes and systems in 2010 would not deliver the success desired by the Scottish FA and its stakeholders.

The planning group's[4] key conclusions were as follows:

- Scottish football needs to change significantly – tinkering with existing structures, responsibilities and processes will not suffice. There is the need for a new landscape.
- Any technical or structural change needs to be supported by a new economic model, linked to the development of more and better Scottish international players.
- Against any benchmark, the current performance system in Scottish football does well to score 2/10.
- Coaching is a vital and key element in the pathway – the challenge is to remove complacency and move from 'good to great', with a special emphasis on improving capability, attitude and behaviour of existing coaches in the system.
- The current Youth Initiative (ages 11–16/17 years) and the SPL/ SFL development leagues have improved the performance of average players. But there are too many players in the Youth Initiative squads (around 3,000) and the Initiative has done little to produce more and better potentially elite players.

- To optimise football's resources, there is a critical need for more and fitter young people with higher skill levels playing football more often, as well as taking part in other physical activity. This is not a quick fix, yet making an impact on those aged 5–12 is an imperative, not just for Scottish football but for the nation.
- Current long-term player-development/pathway proposals and associated investment will not improve the position significantly. The current regional structure provides the basis for development and performance. Football development work is innovative, creative and entrepreneurial – yet generally unsupported and not integrated into an agreed pathway.
- International squads are not integrated or managed as a whole. There is no 'Scottish' style and limited leadership or performance management of Scotland's national teams.
- Scottish FA activity must add value – through their effective administration and coaching in partnership with the clubs, especially the elite clubs.
- Scottish FA and its partners need to foster and build a performance culture – moving away from being 'governing bodies' to 'enabling partners'.

The power of 2

It will be clear from the above that simply maintaining the status quo in terms of activity, and tinkering with existing structures and processes, would not achieve the change desired or the transformation required. Having considered the key success factors outlined above, the planning group discussed and generally agreed with the challenge presented by Renaissance that outlined the key change areas and the scope of change required. The key elements of the challenge were as follows:

- The performance strategy must be for football in Scotland, not just the Scottish FA.
- The Scottish FA and the leading clubs do a lot of good work with limited impact – setting big and shared goals was a key future success factor.
- The factor of 2 should prevail in the Youth Initiative and football development generally:
    - Two times the investment in half the number of initiatives in football development.
    - Half the number of top (elite) club academies (36 in 2010).
    - Significantly reduce the number of players in the Youth Initiative (3,000 in 2010).
    - Double the age-band range at selected levels with a two-year commitment at each age band.

○ Half of any grant to be outcome-related – producing fitter, faster, better players for Scotland's international squads.

- The Scottish FA provides a good coaching framework. It has the potential to be transformed to become great – with even greater focus on how to coach young people and coaching for performance:

  ○ Two times the investment in coaching, especially youth and elite performance.

- Scottish football should monitor its elite players or coaching workforce to ensure these scarce resources are optimised.
- The Scottish FA's international squads should be integrated in terms of style, performance and shape.

Scottish football's strategic framework – for performance

Having considered the action areas, a strategic framework was developed to guide the implementation of the performance strategy for Scottish football, as well as for improving that performance in the near term. This Focus Framework is illustrated in Figure 17.2.

The five strategic goals represent together the high ground in the battle against the forces dragging down the performance of Scottish football and their international teams.

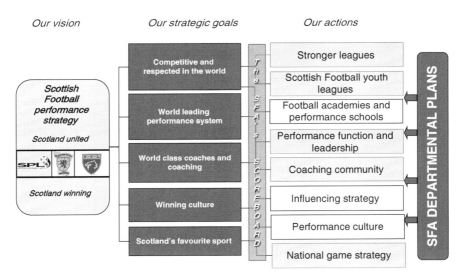

Figure 17.2 Scottish FA's performance strategy. Framework created by Alistair Gray (2011).

There are four fundamental principles driving the performance strategy – entitled 'Scotland United' – as proposed:

1   Assure the possibility of 10,000 hours – to deliver a step change in the development of young talent.
2   Optimise opportunities for best vs best – to provide a new standard of competition.
3   Take our coaching from good to great – to ensure a critical mass of coaches are performing and to build a best-in-the-world coaching community.
4   The new Scotland way – to build a culture of performance across all organisations associated with the development of football talent in Scotland and ensure that all organisations are engaged and aligned behind a new Scottish way of developing elite players, towards the goal of Scotland winning consistently.

The integrated nature of the themes is illustrated in Figure 17.3.

Planning to win

The strategic goals were to be achieved by focused execution of a number of action plans. The Framework above contained eight strategic action plans to be implemented over the following five years, supported by a increased investment over that period.

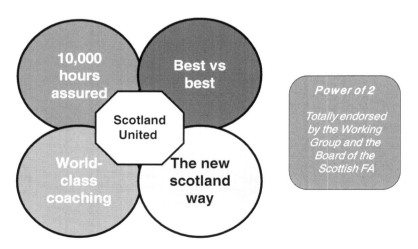

Figure 17.3 Scottish football performance themes. Model created by Alistair Gray (2011).

The additional investment planned for the action plans was as follows:

- New performance-based remuneration system for the Scottish Professional Football Development Leagues.
- The investment in a performance director and performance system.
- Recruitment of coaches for the under-age national teams.
- Doubling the investment in coaching and coach/referee development.
- Establishing the regional/national performance centres and a number of performance schools.
- Scholarships for a number of players each year as potential international players.
- Rewards to clubs for developing international players at U17, U19 and U21 level.
- A fund for innovation to provide seed-corn for new ideas.

Securing the return

What price success? At a time where the average 'price' of an Olympic Gold medal is around £4m over four years,[5] the Scottish FA needed to believe the 'view has to be worth the climb'.

That they did and in 2011 the Scottish FA embarked on a journey never before contemplated or conceived. The first Performance Director appointed was Mark Wotte from the Netherlands, to be succeeded in 2015 by Brian McClair, Manchester United's Head of Academy. Initially relations between the Performance and Development departments were frosty at best, but over the years relationships improved and a number of joint projects have been implemented. Within three years the following outcomes had been achieved:

- The National Performance Centre had been commissioned, built and opened at Oriam, Heriot Watt University, Edinburgh.
- Scottish FA's corporate strategy set clear goals, including performance, and monitored progress through its scoreboard.
- Performance function was established.
- Club Academy Scotland criteria had been revised and executed. Measurable Performance Outcomes (MPOs) had been established; 15% of payments were performance outcome related.
- The women's senior team qualified for the finals of the 2017 European Championship.
- The U17 and U19 men's and women's teams had qualified regularly for the final stages of UEFA competition.
- Record levels of CPD was being offered to coaches – the workforce of 250 coaches (75% part-time) in performance-related activity.

- Development of regional and joint club academies, e.g., Fife, Forth Valley.
- Positive development of young players in their early years:

  - 50,000 young players, their parents and coaches trained in principles of Positive Coaching Scotland.
  - 30 clubs engaged with the Scottish FA and the Winning Scotland Foundation.
  - Small-sided games now standard.

- Seven performance schools established (now in their third year).
- The U20 Development League established.

However, in reality, the 'Power of 2' had not been fully implemented and the Scottish FA accepted that the full benefits of the performance strategy had not been achieved. They recognised that the clubs had to take greater ownership of any future strategy.

Project Brave

In 2016, following a review of performance, more disappointing senior international team results (Figure 17.4) and the departure of Brian McClair, the board of the Scottish FA invited me to chair a group of club representatives.[6] These included chairs, directors of football, academy directors and heads of youth, as well as senior Scottish FA staff.

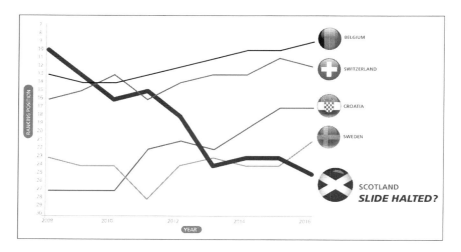

Figure 17.4 The reality of now. Chart created by Alistair Gray (2017).

We found that the big issue was 'bridging the gap' between 18 and senior football. The performance pathway was fractured and, despite performance-related 'pay' having been offered by the Scottish FA for playing under-21 players in first teams, the take up had been poor. As mentioned earlier, the 'Power of 2', a key feature of the 2011 strategy, had not been fully implemented, i.e., half the players, twice the investment. A workforce of around 250 coaches was deployed across the club academies and the performance schools. This group was not functionally led or managed either at club or national level. There was too much focus on coach education rather than coach development. The MPOs (Measurable Performance Outcomes) that had been introduced two years previously by the Scottish FA were having a positive impact, but with varied and limited results (Figure 17.5).

Following a positive discussion, a vision of success was agreed for 2020. It had the following features:

- More and better Scottish international players, playing better football more often:

  o   Competition-ready international players.
  o   More effective loans for 'game time'.

- The Scottish U21 team qualifying for UEFA Finals in 2020 and sustained performance at U17 and U19.

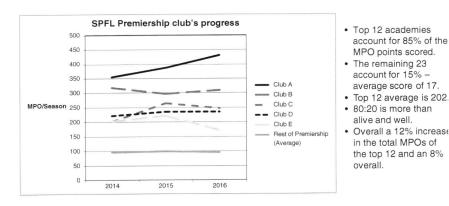

Figure 17.5 Measuring club progress. Chart created by Alistair Gray using Scottish FA data (2017).

Figure 17.6a, b, c and d Examples of Project Brave outputs. Charts created by Alistair Gray using Scottish FA data (2017).

- Targeted investment in performance academies – following a bidding process.
- A new programme for those clubs not in the performance academy programme:

  ○ Sustainable talent development (1,200 players).
  ○ Advanced talent and community development.

- Performance coaching workforce – growing more and better coaches.
- Clubs engaged in leadership of performance academies.

The original strategy was positively endorsed and the revised vision was underpinned with seven strategic action plans:

1   Increased focus of investment – on 16 rather than 29 academies, with the performance schools integrated into the top club academies in the key cities.
2   New concept and system for club-based performance academies.
3   Innovative development programme for clubs with no performance academy.
4   New games programme for performance academies – including a top group of eight clubs and a second tier of eight, and a new games programme through to U18 and a new reserve league and cup competition.
5   Dynamic and more flexible loans – rewarded for lending players out and bringing players in.
6   Performance coaching strategy and workforce plan – with double the number of full-time coaches.
7   Leadership of performance – the clubs engaged in the overall leadership of the programmes.

Each club would be invited to bid, through the presentation of a technical/business plan, to secure performance academy status. This would require them to address issues around leadership and governance, including the formation of a technical board for each performance academy and a significantly increased investment in full-time staff. They had to demonstrate a clear unbroken pathway to full-time professional football. There needed to be greater commitment to the employment and development of full-time coaches and other specialist staff, e.g., strength and conditioning, sports medicine, analysis, with access to first-class facilities (outdoor, indoor, conditioning). Examples of some of the outputs from Project Brave are shown on p. 306 (Figure 17.6a, b, c and d).

Extensive consultation followed to ensure that every club had the opportunity to revisit their ambition and present their best bid. The total investment by the Scottish FA was slightly higher than they had made previously across 29 club academies, and it was now much more focused. The new Advanced Coaching and Talent Development programme partially compensated those clubs that did not wish to be in the top games programme. The innovative loan scheme had been successful and, with the adjustments, was a key feature of the new way.

The programme and associated action plans were approved by the Scottish FA board at the end of 2016. Malky Mackay joined the Scottish FA as Performance Director. Having come through the system himself to be a full internationalist and a successful manager in the English Premier League, he gave the revised strategy fresh enthusiasm and developed a positive relationship with the clubs, something his two predecessors had struggled to do.

Scotland will always struggle to punch above its weight in international football – size matters at the performance end of football and Scotland is small. However, five years into their performance journey there are real signs of progress. The under-age teams (men and women) have qualified regularly for the final stages of European championships over recent years and in September 2018 Scotland's senior women qualified, for the first time ever, for the 2019 FIFA World Cup to be held in France. Key stakeholders in Scottish football are beginning to recognise that 'instant success takes time' and that comparable initiatives in other sports and nations have taken four 'Games' cycles (16 years) before sustained success could be consistently achieved. There are real signs that Project Brave has at least captured the imagination of clubs and, given early success, it is likely to provide a template for sustained investment into the future with associated improved performances and results.

Scottish FA

- **Broke the rules; challenged existing paradigms**

  - Focused on producing more and better international players, playing more and better football more often.
  - Rewarded more and rewarded clubs for performance of their academies.
  - Clubs rewarded for better performance of their academies.
  - Changed the role of the all-embracing Football Development department, to coach development over running coaching courses.
  - Invested in performance management with a clear strategy and goals, behind an inspiring vision of success.

- **They worked it out themselves – embraced change management**

  - Faced reality as it was in 2010 with consistent under-performance at international level since 1998.
  - Developed together an exciting vision of success (in the Focus Framework) that was shared by all.
  - Regularly debriefed their performance and corporate strategies for the first time in 140 years.
  - Engaged effectively with the clubs and secured support for the recommendations from Project Brave's proposals.

- **Planned for a step-change in performance**

  - Reinforced the principles of high-performance strategies for team sports – everyone planning to be the best they can be.
  - Secured investment of £30m for Oriam, the new centre for high-performance sport.
  - The Scottish FA and clubs were fully engaged in the process of change.

- **Changing organisational performance**

  - Stewart Regan, the CEO from 2010, transformed the executive organisation of The Scottish FA and introduced a performance culture.
  - Took on the challenge of external scrutiny from Henry McLeish, the former First Minister of Scotland, implementing 100% of his recommendations within two years of the unanimous acceptance at an annual meeting of clubs.
  - Keeping it simple – in the early years relentlessly focusing on improving quality and keeping close to their key stakeholders, e.g., clubs and their players.

- **Leaders at all levels in the organisation championed the change**

  - It has taken over five years but there is now general acceptance of the need for a performance strategy and function if on-field performance is to be improved.

Notes

1 Jack Welch, when GE's CEO, on reviewing the performance of his companies, their position relative to competition and their place in the market and their industry.
2 *Good to Great*, Jim Collins, Collins Business, 2001.
3 *Leading*, Sir Alex Ferguson, Hodder and Stoughton, 2015.
4 The planning group was made up of representatives of key organisations in Scottish football and lead executives in the Scottish FA, facilitated by Renaissance & Company.
5 Source: UK Sport (2016).
6 Iain Blair – SPFL, Jim Chapman - Annan Athletic, George Craig – Hibs, Les Gray – Hamilton, Steven Gunn – Aberdeen, Craig Levein – Hearts, Roy Macgregor – Ross County, Chris McCart – Celtic, Craig Mulholland – Rangers, Creag Robertson – Falkirk, Derek Hunter and Campbell Money – Scottish FA.

18 Performance sport
The winning formula

Introduction

Over the last two decades I have been privileged to work at the heart of the development of the UK's high performance system in sport. From the early days of the 'Institute of Sproat' (named after the Minister of Sport[1] in the UK government at that time) it was my privilege to be appointed the founding chair of the Scottish Institute of Sport for its first seven years. I was involved in the development of Mission 2012, the UK's highly successful systematic approach to delivering the record medal-winning performance at the 2012 Olympic Games in London. I also chaired the boards of British Basketball and British Swimming between 2005–2013 (See Chapter 19). As a result, I gained a unique insight into high performance systems in sport. Interestingly for businesses, the principles described here can also be closely related to the performance of their organisations.

In the case study that follows I provide my own perspective on Team GB's performance at major Olympic Games (Summer) from the nadir of Atlanta in 1996 through to the triumphant performance at the Games in London in 2012 and Rio de Janeiro four years later.

I also reflect on the creation and progress made in building the Scottish Institute of Sport into one of the leading sports institutes in the world, and the impact the Institute has had on Scotland's performance at the Commonwealth Games, from their own nadir at Kuala Lumpur in 1998 through to the 'best ever games' in Glasgow in 2014. The Glasgow Games provided a welcome follow-through from the Olympics in London and arguably saved the Commonwealth Games from obscurity after the miserable events at Delhi in 2010.

Performance sport – the winning formula

Winning in sport is easy – to understand!

Research and current expert opinion would suggest that it is relatively easy to understand winning in sport and thus prepare a strategy for future success – both at the participation and high performance ends of sport. The key is in the focused disciplined execution of strategy that is developed *with* the sport and its stakeholders rather than *done to* the sport.

Instant success takes time, especially in a long-distance race. The key success factors for nations, their National Olympic Committees (NOCs), federations and institutes are relatively simple to articulate:

- Build a shared vision of success to which every stakeholder is committed.
- Separate the leadership and management of participation (growing sport) and winning (high performance sport) and build world-class capacity and capability in both.
- Build competent focused plans for the sports that will deliver the best chance of medal success and plan to continuously improve these performances, year on year.
- Ensure the 'business' performance of all sporting stakeholders, focussing on performance and adding value, rather than spending money and building resources for their own sake.
- Plan to win. Develop plans for each cycle that will 'grow and win' at the same time. This involves setting targets (clear outcomes and process goals), developing and executing performance plans and building debriefing and other strategic capabilities.
- Pick winners and over-invest in them.

Selecting priority sports

The focus sports that will form the vanguard of high performance should be clear. Within the existing sports they will be those that continually improve their performance on the field of play and in their leadership/governance as an organisation.

The first step for any nation considering its approach to improving performance at the elite end of sport is to face reality as it is, not as it was or as it was hoped to be. This involves taking into account:

- Actual recent performance at major games.
- Potential realistic objectives for the future.
- Recognition that to make a step change in performance is often generational, not only for the athletes and coaches but for the sporting organisations.
- Sporting organisations must build capacity and capability, just as they require of their athletes, coaches and administrators.
- There needs to be a clear plan to win – the doers have to be the planners. The role of consultants and planners is to facilitate and integrate the work of those at the heart of the sport.

In reality it means, for any nation, choosing sports with the ambition and desire not only to win but also to change, to be in the vanguard of performance improvement. These vital few will be chosen through a clear and objective view of global competitiveness and the realistic chances of medal-winning potential in the long term.

Initially the choice should be made on external factors such as:

- Number of competitors.
- Number of medals.
- Number of nations winning medals.

Team GB's gold rush in 2012 was based mainly on success in rowing, cycling and equestrian events. Those sports provided better opportunities than, for example, swimming or athletics, determined by the competitive intensity and numbers of athletes in the world class. Between them they won 24 of 29 gold medals and nearly 50% of total medals won. This is not intended to be critical of an outstanding performance across the board but bring a sense of reality to the success.

Most athletes and their coaches tend to perform well despite their federations. However, in recent years a number of federations have themselves delivered world-leading performance, radically addressing their own capacity and capability to perform at the highest level and setting themselves apart from the pack.

For sports to be sustainable they will require to address, as part of their leadership and governance:

- Setting and delivering strategic goals.
- Economic and resource productivity.
- Greater social and cultural purpose.
- Accountability for the environment.
- The growth of great people – athletes, coaches and administrators.

Setting goals in sport is critical, not just for athletes and coaches, but also for nations and their federations. Goals need to be fashioned along the lines of:

- What are the sports passionate about?
- What they can be best at in their world?
- What drives their economic and athletic performance?[2]

Creating high performance culture and systems

High performance strategies work, if properly executed, as Figure 18.1 demonstrates:

Australia began the movement in 1986, after their poor performance at the Montreal Olympics, with the establishment of the Australian Institute of Sport, and many other nations have tried to replicate the Australian high performance system. Few have succeeded simply by copying Australian practices

Olympic Medal Productivity

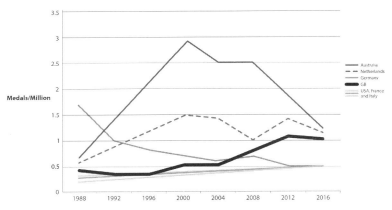

Figure 18.1 Olympic medal productivity. Chart created by Alistair Gray (IOC Data 2016).

and programmes or by recruiting Australian staff. Success is not that simple to buy. But the Netherlands is an excellent example of where sustained investment has been made in 20 priority sports over a long period of time.

The UK initiated the UK Sports Institute Network and National Lottery programmes in the late 1990s through the introduction of performance planning. The 'Mission 2012' approach, introduced after the award of the 2012 Olympic Games to London, delivered particular success and is now the envy of many. Just replicating the features of this, however, will not guarantee any nation the equivalent success.

Winning is not the sole prerogative of large nations. Clearly size matters but many smaller nations and others starting late have demonstrated that smart nations can also win, and out-perform what their relative size might suggest is possible.

Planning to win

Planning to win in sport is no different from the approach taken to plan to win in business or any other industry – see the model outlined in Figure 18.2. The NOC or federation will develop their vision of success including a set of goals for their high performance strategy. The strategic goals underpin the journey towards the vision and, each quadrennial and indeed each year, strategic themes and breakthrough initiatives should be established to drive the effective execution of the performance strategy. For example, Team GB's success was supported by commitment to Mission 2012, the umbrella philosophy and approach to securing performance at a home Olympic Games for an already mature and leading sporting nation.

It would be entirely wrong for a new and emerging nation to copy the features and plans for any leading nation, given their early-stage evolution as a sporting nation. It does not mean that the overall approach and philosophy underpinning planning cannot be adopted, it should just be tailored to meet the reality of the current and future position. As an example, a number of nations have started their journey from a lowly position and focused on no more than six to eight sports over the first Olympic cycle.

Planning towards three horizons

One of the most effective ways of securing step changes in performance is to plan towards a number of future horizons that will ultimately lead to the vision of success. At each successive horizon the vision of success becomes clearer. Aiming too high too soon will inevitably lead to failure, disappointment and disillusionment. The model illustrated in Figure 18.2 shows the approach that might be taken by any sport or NOC to secure greater success at the future Olympic Games. It suggests planning is a three-horizon approach.

The first steps are to:

- Execute a programme with the greatest discipline and diligence to secure a better performance at the next major Games or Championships.
- Establish the strategic plans for the next continental Games and each sport's World Championships, as well as developing initial thoughts for the next Olympiad and future Olympic Games. Continental Games and small nations' tournaments represent ideal preparation events for the major global Games.

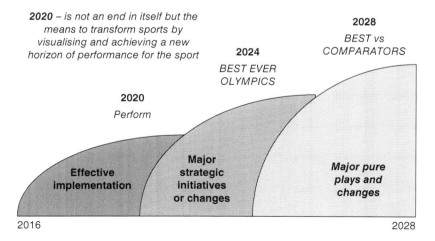

Figure 18.2 2020: part of the journey. Chart created by Alistair Gray (2012).

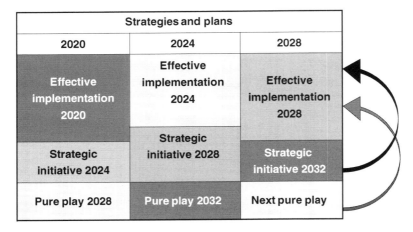

Figure 18.3 Planning back from the future. Model created by Alistair Gray (2012).

The second step is to establish ambitious longer-term objectives for the next Olympic cycles. Planning can then take place for each of the three horizons, recognising that short, medium and longer-term planning needs to take place each year, as is illustrated in Figure 18.3.

Having established the objectives, the next step is to develop a Focus Framework to convert the strategic vision and goals into objectives, action areas and eventually plans to win, along the lines illustrated in Figure 18.4.

The 5-Box model

Most performance strategies are based on a small number of key principles:

- Focus on priority sports.
- Planning down to the level of athletes and coaches, even in team sports.
- Building a world-class system and infrastructure.
- Addressing aspects of culture.
- Adding value to the athletes and coaches by performing as a team at major Games.

The 5-Box model illustrated in Figure 18.5 was developed as a result of working with over 30 sports, developing, monitoring and evaluating their performance at major championships. The model can be used to both audit the reality of a nation or sport's performance plans, culture and systems, as well as to develop the vision of success and focus for the new performance strategy.

Consider the success principles in each element of the model in turn.

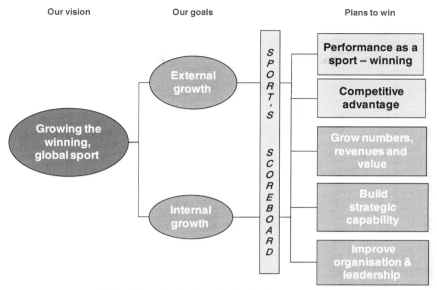

Figure 18.4 Strategic framework for sports. Model created by Alistair Gray (2008).

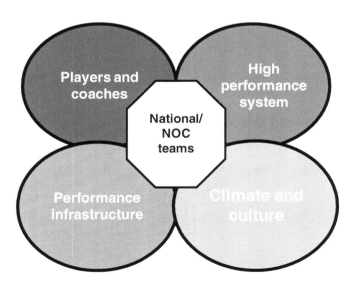

Figure 18.5 The 5-Box model for nations. Chart created by Alistair Gray (2006).

Athletes and coaches

Building performance requires a tailored approach to the development and monitoring of a pool of talented and focussed athletes and their coaches supporting their progress.

Numbers playing, not watching

A critical mass of athletes and coaches need to be competing regularly at a level near the world class. This means, for many nations, developing plans to take their athletes to where the highest level of competition is organised, e.g., badminton to the Far East, curling to Canada, athletics to the USA. Equally, domestic competition needs to continually develop to provide effective competition programmes and pathways to develop the performance of athletes and coaches.

Achieving and continuously improving key metrics

In any sport there are key metrics of performance, e.g., first serve % in tennis, personal or season's best in athletics and swimming, pass completion in football, circle penetrations in hockey. Sports need to monitor and plan to improve these metrics continuously, as well as levels of fitness and rate of recovery from injury. The use of such data and analytics is becoming commonplace in most sports and nations.

Commitment to improved performance

Some form of central charter needs to be developed and agreed with commitment from athletes, coaches and clubs in return for the investment made in them. Some form of performance-related reward may also be considered. The commitment relates to availability for key events and the associated training programmes.

Coaching workforce

Each sport must regard the development of coaching in the same way as a business plans the development of its supply chain and associated capabilities. Cadres of coaches for athletes at all age levels, working to an agreed style, need to be developed. Much can be done through the development of academies and institutes. It is important to develop coaches domestically as well as attracting 'mercenaries' from abroad, although the latter are very useful to encourage the step change that is often required. Leadership at all levels needs to be practised by coaches, athletes and administrators.

High performance system

The performance system for any NOC or federation will include development, implementation, evaluation and quality assurance, incorporating objective setting, talent ID, sports science and medicine/wider athlete lifestyle support and development services as well as funding support.

Performance director leadership

Most advanced nations, including many smaller nations, appoint a performance director to oversee the development and implementation of the performance system, as well as contributing to the infrastructure development. The director will recruit a small team of specialists, usually covering areas such as sports science and medicine, performance lifestyle services and analytics, as well as recruiting specialist coaches who challenge and support athletes and squads. In early-stage-development nations it may be advisable to appoint a high performance coach for the priority sports who is part of the performance director's team, deploying services in association with the priority sports. This relationship can be changed as federations professionalise, modernise and build capability and capacity.

Performance management

There are many proprietary systems available through which data on athlete performance can be gathered and published. These can be easily customised for different sports. Reviews should be carried out of each athlete or performance group on a regular basis (every six to eight weeks) and with increasing frequency as major Games approach.

System for talent identification and development

It is critical to have a talent identification and development system that is worked out for each sport. The participation strategy should focus on the growth and retention of numbers of participants, as well as coaching the basics of physical activity and the sport itself. There is considerable evidence that, over a ten-year period, talented athletes need to spend around 10,000 hours (20 each week) in purposeful practice, often in the company of a coach. Different age groups require tailored approaches, including specialist coaches, and domestic competition calendars also need to be tailored to foster the development of young athletes.

Sports science, sports medicine and performance lifestyle services

These services are an essential and critical part of any performance system. They have to be demand-led by athletes and coaches as well as reflecting good practice, and they should be integrated with the performance plans for individual athletes and teams. Their delivery should be led by the performance directorate working closely with sports and especially the priority sports. Coaches should be integrated with scientists and other service providers. Regional institutes and specialist centres may be developed as part of the system. The impact of science and medicine should be clearly linked to athlete performance through the performance system.

Funding

Key to successful sports is commitment by governments and their agencies to funding the performance system and federations for an Olympic cycle or equivalent quadrennial and linking this to targeted outcomes. Performance and related return on investment should be monitored and evaluated on a regular basis. Quarterly reviews should be held with priority sports and those with potential medallists. Others might be reviewed on an annual basis. Funding should be awarded on the achievement of outcomes at major Games and the achievement of process milestones. Funding should not be awarded solely on the basis of medals won, but should also consider overall performance improvement, numbers of finalists, world ranking, etc.

Focus on excellence

The key for any performance system is not to accept second best. Excellence can be defined as well above average performance in the long term. Creating excellence comes from focus, emphasis on sustained quality underpinned by real innovation and a passion for continuous performance improvement.

World class performance infrastructure

A robust framework is needed to support the development and delivery of high performance systems, with strong federations, world-class facilities, a robust coach/ club/athlete development model and high-quality/accessible infrastructure for the delivery of sports science and medicine.

Strong sports federations

The sports federations have a key role in the development of high performance. They themselves have to become performing organisations with the priority sports being staffed by experienced professionals. They have to have the capacity to grow their sports as well as leading performance at the elite end. They must have excellent leadership and governance, as well as performing as any business would do in pursuit of its goals.

Facilities

World-class facilities are another key element of infrastructure. Domestic facilities need to be of a level capable of supporting competition and the training of athletes and coaches. In addition, smaller nations can access competition and facilities in other 'partner' nations, e.g., Australia's rowers in Italy, Britain's curlers in Canada. It is too simplistic to recommend that each priority sport should have a centralised programme with world class and potential athletes resident during the execution of a programme. Each sport should produce a plan to access the optimum facilities and services, be they domestic or international.

National performance centre

There are many reasons to recommend the establishment of a national performance centre for sport that can be a symbolic facility reflecting the commitment and investment to high performance sport. However, this is often dependent on the priority sports and their specific requirements. The creation of an 'institute-type' structure is often based on facilities to optimise the delivery of services to athletes at these centres, as well as performing an important role as the 'brain' for innovation and performance improvement.

Regional approach with club academies

There should certainly be regional facilities and institute outposts in the major cities of any nation to nurture the next generation of champions. Individual sports should have a clear strategy for the development of potential performing athletes and establish a strong regional presence, competition and support facilities. Leading professional clubs should have academies, frequently in partnership with schools or universities, where young elite athletes can continue their studies towards a professional or vocational qualification while training for their sport and the annual competition schedule. They can become multi-sport clubs, e.g., in Germany where tennis and hockey frequently combine.

Partnership

Effective partnerships are critical to any performance infrastructure. Few sports can secure sustained success on their own, or simply through receipt of government funding. Alliances with specialist medical centres, overseas training facilities, external institutes, local authorities, cities and universities are of great importance. This approach can also be applied to clubs, coaches and players as well as their federations.

Performance development pathway

The performance pathway for each sport should be clearly defined and committed to by each sport's federation and other key stakeholders. Of particular importance from a performance perspective is the pathway for athletes aged 12–16. The leading nations also deploy a 'scouting' system where young potential elite athletes are spotted and introduced to the best possible environment for their future development.

Sports science, sports medicine

The infrastructural element of any sports science and medicine provision is to ensure that adequate provision is available close to the athlete, be they at home or abroad. The quality of facility available has also to be world class and capable of delivering the support to performance improvement. Just as with athletes and coaches, so the performance of delivery of science and medicine should be monitored and evaluated to ensure that it is satisfying athlete and coach demands.

Great people

No performance infrastructure can succeed on the basis of world-class facilities, institutions and systems alone. People design and execute strategies and deliver the performance on the field of play, the track or arena. To secure success, the leadership and performance of people need to be at the highest level. A key element of any infrastructure is a people development philosophy, system and approach that ensures effective leadership and optimum performance of all people associated with performance – athletes, coaches, officials, support staff and other stakeholders.

Climate and culture

A national performance culture that celebrates sporting excellence and supports talent development, and in which government, education providers, the media and families all play an important role alongside sports organisations.

Published goal to win

There is no hiding place in a high performance environment. The NOC should publish the goals of the high performance strategy. These should not be developed and applied in a 'top-down' way but developed in conjunction with the federations and other key stakeholders. Media briefings should be held to explain the rationale behind the goals and to secure their buy-in to supporting the plan. A scoreboard should be prepared that enables progress to be charted. This should be published as part of the annual reporting process for the NOC.

Manage expectations

Expectations should be carefully managed and, in particular, it should be stressed that there are no quick fixes in the journey to world-class performance. There can be early wins, however, and these should be promoted and celebrated. Creating a balanced view is vital. Managing expectations should not assume that these are always expressed downwards. The positive ambition, attitude and self-belief of all stakeholders are vital in a high performance environment.

Leadership

This should be developed in all stakeholder organisations, coaches and athletes alike. This is not a 'sheep-dip' training process but is achieved by engaging and encouraging individuals and their organisations to continually raise their bars in alignment with the vision of success and strategic goals.

Empowerment of coaches and managers

Once a performance plan is agreed, the athletes, coaches and managers should be empowered to deliver the programme without excessive monitoring and evaluation. In return they have to commit themselves to delivering performance and take responsibility for their own and their organisation's performance. Debriefing is an art, and most successful nations perform this process soon after major competition and commit to making necessary changes.

Pride in success

Sport has the power to change nations and especially to inspire people to get behind their nation and the performance of the nation's athletes. Marketing programmes are frequently run by NOCs to stimulate pride in a nation's sporting success. The Netherlands represents a world-leading example of this aspect of culture building.

Share in success

Sports should be encouraged to share in their success, ensuring that reward and recognition is freely distributed amongst the grass roots of the sports. British Cycling and the New Zealand All Blacks are two good examples of successful organisations that ensure a regular distribution of resources (50:50) between elite sport and grass-roots development. Athlete reward systems have limited success, especially if specifically associated with money. The use of foundations especially focused on youth or retired athletes tend to have greater impact.

The special role of major sports

Although in most nations in the world football is the biggest and most popular sport, in many nations it does not embrace the principles of high performance sport and indeed often flies in the face of much good practice employed by other leading sports. But there are signs of change – FIFA ('For the Good of the Game') is especially active with early-stage nation development and many emerging nations have received a number of FIFA coaching interventions. Even if football is not a priority sport it has a role to play, especially in changing the culture of the nation and developing a culture of performance in sport. The same can also be said about basketball, a major sport with real global reach.

A winning team

Any nation competing in major games needs to focus on assembling a successful team of talented athletes and coaches, with the best possible support, all working together towards common performance goals with a unified ethos.

One of the key roles for any NOC is to manage the preparation and planning for their national team to deliver performance at major Games. The key activities should centre on an operating plan to continually learn from campaigns and deliver the best possible programme, athletes' village, transport and medical facilities as well as other key locations. The NOC team on the ground must include medical and sports science support as well as promotional and press relations personnel. Accreditation of officials and coaches is always one of the most sensitive areas.

Today's leading NOC national teams should be staffed with full-time staff behind the national coach/chef de mission. Ambitious nations should continually improve their influence with international sports federations as well as the likes of the IOC and continental OCs. Many have appointed an international director to lead and manage influence alongside the president or chair of the NOC. Key appointments need to be made at the beginning of the quadrennial. The NOC/federation will need to lead, design, build and run the performance system as well as carrying out the appropriate monitoring and evaluation of performance and their investment in sport. Finally, the NOC should plan to attract events to encourage public interest in their teams as they compete in major championships.

Good practice also suggests a performance group be established by the NOC/federation. This should bring together representatives of key stakeholders and experts in performance sport to work alongside the key executives of the NOC/federation to guide the overall execution of the performance strategy.

Any high performance strategy needs to have a number of key success factors for nations to make a step change in the sporting performance.

Any early-life-cycle performance strategy needs to focus on:

- Continuous improvement in the nation's sporting performance.
- Priority super-effective sports.
- Effective pathways for athletes.
- Leading service expertise.
- Real quality infrastructure for athletes.
- Recognition of the benefits of high performance sport for the nation.

Recent commentaries on performance sport describe examples of where a focus on marginal gains or attention to detail has delivered sustained medal success, e.g., in British cycling and New Zealand rugby. Sporting organisations need to apply the same principles to the leadership, management and development of themselves. In so doing they can plan for and deliver their own gold medals.

From zeros to heroes

Team GB – plummeting to new depths

At the Atlanta Olympic Games in 1996 Team GB, including Jonathan Edwards, Denise Lewis, Chris Boardman and Ben Ainslie, conspired to win just 15 medals and one solitary gold, finishing 36th in the medal table. Ahead of them were sporting giants Algeria and Ethiopia. Belarus was beaten only by virtue of having won fewer silver medals. Atlanta was a miserable chapter in the story of the modern Olympics, soured by poor organisation, rampant commercialism and a lone bomber.

It would have been worse but for the defence of the coxless pair's title by Steve Redgrave and Matthew Pinsent. In every sense they were rowing their own boat in a team that fell consistently short of expectations.

Atlanta was a massive low point. A sense of despair began to settle over the team. With just one gold medal, the lowest place in the medal table since the early 1900s, it was a really significant underperformance by the British team. It was clear that the GB team was in a downward spiral and it would require something special to get out of it.

Yet that is precisely what British Olympic sport has done. Atlanta was a turning point and in 2012 – four Olympiads later – Team GB finished third in the medal table with 65 medals of which 29 were gold.

In 1996, the elite sporting system in the UK was politically divided and lacked a long-term vision. Decision-making was based on short-term expedient factors and the needs of athletes were far from the first things considered. It was hardly surprising that the results at the Atlanta Olympics were so poor, and Team GB athletes rightly felt that they were not being given a fair chance to compete with athletes who were being supported by the supremely 'professional' high performance systems in other countries.

Dissatisfaction with the status quo – the first ingredient in creating lasting change

The acute disappointment was so great that it accelerated a wholesale reform of the way sports were funded, organised and supported in the UK. The National Lottery (launched in 1994) was already on stream and a new agency, UK Sport, was established on 1 January 1997 to distribute funds to elite athletes. The British Olympic Association (BOA) was spurred into reform as well, determined to jettison its 'luxury travel agent' tag and foster a British team, rather than a group of disparate athletes who happened to be British.

Funding began comparatively modestly. UK Sport and Sport England distributed £74 million in the four-year cycle to Sydney, with the focus on the sports most likely to deliver. Sailing, cycling and rowing received the most money, along with the two sports with most medals on offer, athletics and swimming. The injection of funding created the conditions for recovery and the dividend was immediate. Great Britain climbed the medal table. Sydney yielded 28 medals, 11 of them gold (three of which came from Edwards, Boardman and Lewis, turning disappointment into victory).

It propelled the team to tenth in the medal table and unlocked more funding. Athens in 2004 continued the improvement, with £102.5 million delivering 31 medals. Although just nine were gold, tenth place was maintained.

Expectations shifted radically the following year when London was awarded the 2012 Games. Having promised to build great arenas, great athletes were required to use them, and the government came under pressure to unlock more money. After concerted lobbying, the then chancellor Gordon Brown agreed in 2006 that elite sport would receive £100 million a year. The Beijing team benefited from close to £260 million and rewrote the records with 47 medals, 19 of them gold, to rise to fourth in the table. The target for London had been met four years early.

In the four years after 2008 £264 million flowed into the Olympic disciplines, with the target of winning more medals from more sports and remaining fourth. Britain's rise is a story of unprecedented financial investment – more than £740 million over 15 years – clear thinking, the professionalisation of the Olympic pioneer spirit, the serious pursuit of excellence, and a little luck. It is a world away from the disparate group of highly talented poorly integrated athletes who walked into the main stadium in Atlanta behind the British flag in 1996.

Leading the charge

Baroness Sue Campbell is rightly praised for her leadership of UK Sport (Chair from 2004–2015). In a recent article[3] she stresses that significantly increased funding was not the main reason behind the step change in

performance. It was vital to secure agreement from politicians, administrators, coaches and athletes around the vision for British sport, in which
athletes should be at the heart of the system and their needs paramount.

As an example, the rowing squad used the challenge 'does it make the
boat go faster?' about every decision they took in order to ensure that
there was no variation in preparation or performance. The challenge was
whether this approach could be mirrored across all Olympic sports (the
equivalent to all departments or locations in a company). What was the
moral purpose of the whole team? Was it simply to win more medals or was
it to ensure that every athlete who had the potential and desire to be the
best in the world was given every opportunity to fulfil that potential? Of
course the two are linked but it was the second that steered every decision
that was made. This led to the adoption of an athlete-centred 'no compromise' approach to the task.

Mission 2012 – transparency and openness around performance

A vital factor in achieving success at the 2012 Games was to reduce the
variation in performance between different sports. What could the less-
successful teams learn from the more successful, and what could the more
successful learn to make them even more effective? Every sport was asked
to rank itself from red to green every six months on three key components:

1   State of the athletes.
2   State of the system or support around the athletes.
3   The climate or culture around the team as a whole.

Results were published and were thus transparent. Sports were positively
encouraged to report concerns honestly – a red rating led not to criticism
but to a system-wide effort to support improvement. This was in marked
contrast to previous systems that encouraged issues and problems to be
swept under the carpet as the begging bowls were submitted for increased
funding behind falling performances.

Sports with a strong rating for a particular area were partnered with
weaker ones to share learning and reduce variation between sports. It
soon became apparent that every team had things they could offer, and
every team had things they could improve. There was a step change in the
approach to the development of 'athletes' – not just those on the field of
play but others in support roles, in coaching functions and even on the
board of directors of increasingly modernised sports.

One of the principal architects of Mission 2012 was Peter Keen, who
experienced, personally, the disappointment of Atlanta. He was a volunteer coach in 1996, a member of 'Team Boardman', whose 'biker' Chris
returned with a bronze. After the Games Keen became performance director

of British Cycling, which, until recently, was the epitome of Olympic professionalism. After the Athens Games he became performance director of UK Sport, effectively setting the tone and policy for a 'no compromise' approach that, fuelled by lavish investment, accelerated rapid improvement. Normally change of the type envisaged is generational. To the eternal credit of UK Sport, their leading sports and the BOA, spectacular success was achieved in half that time.

'No compromise' is shorthand for only funding athletes and sports with the potential to compete for medals. Most profitably, and to secure early wins (something that is essential in any successful process of change), Mission 2012 targeted the 'sitting-down sports' – cycling, rowing and sailing. In all three, Britain can now claim to be the best in the world. The cyclists famously cleaned up in Beijing, their obsessive pursuit of marginal gains and an alignment of the stars delivering 14 medals, eight of them gold. The contrast with Atlanta could not have been more marked.

Driven by a vision of success

> What we tried to do once the investment came on stream, first in cycling and then at UK Sport, was use the money to look the monster in the eye and say, 'OK, if we are serious about winning, how are we going to do it?' Then you work backwards from there.
>
> Peter Keen

Here Keen reflects on his approach. The view had to be worth the climb. Working hard, as never before, created stresses and strains in all aspects of the sports' organisation.

Results were patchy at first. Funding bred complacency in some athletes, who thought they had arrived because they no longer had to combine training with paid employment and were getting paid for what they were doing already. Horizons and expectations had to be recalibrated. The sports themselves had to professionalise and UK Sport re-wrote the rulebook.

'Sport was the wild west then. People said, "I like you, I don't like you, you are on the team, you are not". That had to change.' Keen reflected on the early years. The revolution began in Sydney, where a universally praised BOA preparation camp on the Gold Coast laid the foundations for recovery. The improvement continued in Athens, though the margins were narrow. Kelly Holmes' two gold medals and the surprise sprint relay defeat of the Americans salvaged the Games on the track. Three gold medals were won by less than half a second, the difference between 10th and 15th in the medal table.

Capturing those tiny margins became the mantra of both the BOA and UK Sport in the run-up to Beijing, but it was the victory of London's 2012 bid in July 2005 that set new horizons. Suddenly Britain was an Olympic host and sport was presented with a once-in-a-lifetime opportunity.

The pursuit of that funding was not straightforward. UK Sport's negotiations with government were fraught as they presented a programme that would require a doubling of investment. They were successful, and Beijing provided an emphatic endorsement of the system. For experienced British Olympic followers, their trip to Communist China saw their team dominate like an Iron Curtain power in the Cold War. Next step London and the history-making performance at the home Olympic Games.

The best small institute of sport in the world

My own journey in the transformation of UK Sport began in 1989 when the men and women of Scottish Hockey agreed to merge after a century apart to form the Scottish Hockey Union, a single governing body for the sport in Scotland. Scotland was the first of the home nations to achieve this status and, as the first Chair of the board of the Union, I suddenly found myself and colleagues in demand as leaders of the sporting reformation.

Setting up Genesis in 1992, I decided that the focus for the business would be strategic management in business. Opportunities in sport were discarded in favour of the corporate world. However, in 1994, two directors of the Scottish Sports Council (before it became **sport**scotland in 1998), Brian Porteous (who was to join Genesis as a director in 2000) and Brian Samson, approached me to lead and facilitate a development planning process with Scottish Swimming, which was losing money as well as failing to deliver satisfactory medal-winning performances at recent Commonwealth Games (a total of one bronze medal in the 1990 and 1994 Commonwealth Games).

The process used was a basic strategy development process employed in business:

- **Foundation** – facing up to reality – world class in the real world, not your own wee world.
- **Vision of success** – a view that is worth the climb.
- **Strategy** – how to get to the top of the hill.
- **Execution** – winning together.

This was the first time the executive board of a sport had gone through a participative process of strategy development and, through the inspired leadership of Ian Mason, the Chair in 1995, and Paul Bush, recruited as CEO from the Amateur Swimming Association, the sport began to deliver improved performances in and out of the pool.

The Scottish Swimming project not only set the template for future sport plans, some of which are included in this book, it set me on a personal journey that led to the formation and successful performance of the Scottish Institute of Sport (now the **sport**scotland Institute of Sport).

Scottish sport world class – aye right!

In 1996 the UK Sports Institute was established. Each home country had their own Minister of Sport and overall responsibility was held in the UK Government's Department for Culture, Media and Sport. Following sport's nadir in Atlanta, the then government went out to consultation on setting up an institute network in the home countries. The continuation of the UK Institute of Sport was seen as the 'official future' but feedback from consultation was to set up individual institutes in England, Scotland, Wales and Northern Ireland, which would then form a new network of institutes delivering services to athletes throughout the UK. Scotland was not performing well as a sporting nation in the Commonwealth Games and had fallen from its peak at the 1986 'Maxwell' Games in Edinburgh to what was to become its nadir at Kuala Lumpur in 1998, when only 12 medals (three gold) were secured.

I was invited to lead and chair a working party to consult and make recommendations as to how the Scottish Sports Council's strategy 'Achieving Excellence; Co-ordinate Action' might be executed. An excellent group was assembled that included Jim Telfer and Craig Brown, leading coaches and directors of rugby and football respectively. Professor Myra Nimmo, one of the UK's leading sports science practitioners, and the likes of Ian Mason, the aforementioned Chair of a revitalised Scottish Swimming, joined them.

The Scottish Institute of Sport emerged from the deliberations in 1998 and I was invited (instructed!) by Sam Galbraith, the then Minister of Sport, to form the new board of the Institute and to 'get on with it' to execute the strategy that emerged from the working group that had been christened 'Scottish Sport; World Class'. Our view had to be worth the climb.

This appointment was arguably the best and most important appointment in my career, providing the opportunity to do something special with a relatively blank sheet of paper, in an area where a real difference could be made. In addition, it provided the chance to work with an outstanding board of directors, all of whom agreed to serve within 20 seconds of my making the call. To be honest it represented a great personal challenge. I realised all I could do was to provide the environment in which this excellent and charismatic board could play and prosper. I will always be grateful for the support they gave me as Chair, along with Anne Marie Harrison, the CEO, and her staff. In addition, I was given great encouragement by the likes of Baroness Sue Campbell and Liz Nicholl at UK Sport and Sir Craig Reedie, then a vice president of the International Olympic Committee.

Empowered to deliver

Reflecting on these early years, it would be only right to appreciate the level of empowerment afforded the Institute and its board by **sport**scotland. Given the make up of the board and its collective expertise,[4] the agency

Image 18.1 The entrance to the Australian Institute of Sport. © Alistair Gray (2001).

agreed our business plan and set us off on our journey, with us reporting back quarterly. We were also fortunate to secure the support of the Victorian Institute of Sport (ViS) in Australia (one of Australia's leading state institutes – Victoria at 5m population is similar in size to Scotland). Innovation is fine but imitating the ViS programmes got us off our blocks quickly and into our delivery stride. Their example inspired us to be truly innovative and different in our approach to changing the culture and attitudes in Scottish sport. A photograph I took on my first visit to the Australian Institute of Sport (AIS) in Canberra perhaps sums it up. The image is of a pole-vaulter approaching the bar at the top of his jump – except the bar is missing. What an image for those young athletes and their coaches. 'You set the bar' is the clear message. The role of the Institute is to challenge you to set and achieve your goals, supporting you along the way.

Another important feature was the quarterly meetings. These meetings were informal but nonetheless important and included the chairs of the Institute and **sport**scotland and their respective CEOs (Anne Marie Harrison and Ian Robson – both Australians with a great passion for Scotland succeeding in the world class).

It is only right and proper to pause at this point and reflect on the contribution made by Anne Marie. Herself a feisty Victorian with a background in sports administration, she brought a passion for Scottish success that at times exceeded that of the Scots. She skilfully built an executive team that performed right from the start and provided the challenge and support necessary to change the lives and attitudes of Scottish athletes and their coaches. In her seven years at the helm she not only forged an excellent relationship with me as Chair, she led her team well and brought her own brand of professionalism to this new venture. Without her drive and enthusiasm the Scottish Institute of Sport would not have got off the starting blocks, far less reach the level of success enjoyed.

It will not surprise readers that key principles of strategic management were applied at the beginning. Stakeholders were engaged and the board and executives set about the task of developing the strategy for the Institute. Annual Lottery funding of £4 million helped and the Institute was set up, initially focused on seven sports. We had this great opportunity to change the game and did not disappoint.

Twice-yearly sessions were held with the Institute's sports – their chairs/presidents, CEOs and performance directors. These sessions were especially important to keep them on side, as well as to give the Institute the chance to communicate key ideas.

Our Focus Framework

The Focus Framework in Figure 18.6 displays all the elements of 'Good to Great' – goals we were passionate about; where we could be best in the world of institutes of sport and that would drive our economic and resource engines. Sharing this with athletes and coaches at induction weekends changed their perspectives of what was required to be a member of the Institute. In the first year 30% of those athletes inducted indicated that their ambition was to be champion of Scotland. Two years later that figure had dropped to *zero* – their sights were raised much higher.

Forging global alliances and networks

Our aspiration was to be the best small Institute of Sport in the world and the Victorian Institute had set us the challenge and the standard. We began with a strategic alliance with the ViS and quickly added Stanford University to our network. Chris Martin, our American swimming coach, when asked which NCAA college we should partner, suggested Stanford, which was the leading NCAA college in most sports. 'But you have no chance, Alistair' was his limiting assumption, which might have cost him his job had he not been such an excellent coach. A meeting was secured with Ted Lealand, the Director of Stanford's Athletic Programme in Palo Alto. An alliance was duly formed on the back of our charm offensive and Lealand's passion for golf, which was fuelled by his admiration for Mhairi Mackay, a Scottish student and golfer who had starred in the College's NCAA team. For a number of years eight athletes from Stanford came to Scotland to play in open competitions on our great links courses and eight of our Institute golfers went to California to play in the inter-college tournament between Berkeley, OCLA and Stanford. Coaches, science and medical professionals ran workshops alongside the golfers. The idea of a tripartite conference with the ViS was also developed between the partners, with the whole relationship underpinned by a network of knowledge. Figure 18.7 illustrates the thinking that enabled us to genuinely be in the world class of leading sports institutes.

Our strategic framework

Sense of mission **Strategic goals** **Actions**

To create winners

To assist the right talented athletes of Scotland achieve and sustain world-class sporting performance ... while also providing the right services, in the right place at the right time

Our values

We aspire to win ...
- Performance with integrity
- Individual and collective responsibility
- Openness and mutual respect
- Innovation
- Leading through quality
- An asset to our nation

Great Scots
Leading performance, earning respect

Quality, athlete-centred services
Challenge and support

Effective partnerships
Winning through partnerships

Great Scottish spirit
Releasing the Scottish spirit

Key performance outcomes

1. Sports programmes
2. New approach to coaching
3. High performance coach education

4. New individual athlete programmes
5. Direct delivery of sports science
6. Direct delivery of sports medicine
7. Evolving Scottish ACE Model
8. Integrated athlete services
9. Enhanced strength & conditioning
10. Responsibility for performance

11. Athlete programme funding
12. Education forum
13. sportscotland initiatives
14. Getting on the edge
15. Area institute coordination
16. Elite sports analysis
17. Commercial sponsorship

18. Communications & marketing
19. Network of knowledge
20. Elite sports index

Figure 18.6 Scottish Institute of Sport strategic framework. Chart created by Alistair Gray (2001).

Global athletes in global locations	The campus – great people	Area institutes
International winning performance		National and governing body centres
	Home	Victorian institute of sport (Aus)
Network of knowledge	Meeting place	Stanford Univ for Ideas
Technology		

- National pride – global focus
- Brilliant athletes in great new programmes
- The best sports science and sports medicine
- Innovative, fresh approach – focused on success

Figure 18.7 The developing institute. Chart created by Alistair Gray (2002).

Driven by vision, values and the 'bravepill'

The Focus Framework gave the Institute and its stakeholders an inspiring vision of success to lift performance to new levels. The vision gave us the grand purpose for our existence, but we needed values to guide our behaviour. Where better to start than with our athletes?

Image 18.2 Scottish Institute of Sport: our values. Permission granted by **sport**scotland.

Sir Ian McGeechan, the leading coach of Scotland and the British Lions, led the initial meetings of an athletes group that delivered a set of values, which in turn, after a number of iterations with the board and staff, were published (illustrated in Image 18.2). The values proved to be an integral part of athlete induction and the performance assessment of staff.

You can imagine that board members were not backward in coming forward with their ideas either. Former Olympic and international athletes in Alison Ramsay (hockey), Shirley Robertson (sailing), Belinda Robertson (swimming) and Peter Haining (rowing) kept us focused on our 'athlete centred: coach led' approach to make sure we were being the best we could be for our athletes and coaches. Frank Dick, Sir Ian McGeechan and Sir Bill Gammell, all eminently successful in their own fields of coaching and entrepreneurship, provided invaluable coaching for the Chair. Rae Macfarlane and Craig Brown kept our feet firmly on the ground while sharing the unreasonable ambition.

Sir Bill was one of the foremost to challenge the sports to aim high. In his words this meant taking the 'bravepill'[5] if proposing a programme or project with little ambition. He brought his entrepreneurial flair to the Institute staff and sports as well as to the board, along with his philosophy on leadership and personal development, so successfully deployed in his main business Cairn Energy PLC. Image 18.3 provides a summary of the 'pills' to be taken.

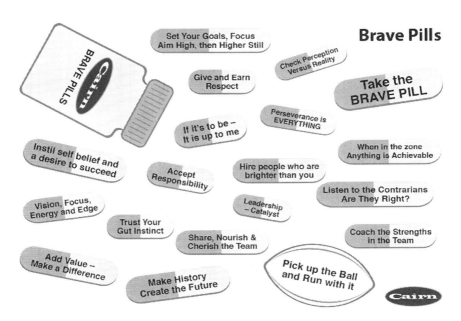

Image 18.3 Brave Pills. © Sir Bill Gammell, permission granted by the Winning Scotland Foundation.

Delivering early wins

Early success is essential in any process of development and change for an athlete and an Institute is no different. Early wins give confidence and self-belief that the mission is possible. Andy Murray was one of the first athletes to be influenced by the Scottish Institute of Sport. In 2004 he was in danger of surgery on an injured knee that would potentially have been an unhelpful procedure for a young growing athlete, requiring a lengthy period of rehabilitation and recovery. Under guidance from the Institute's doctor Brian Walker and Malcolm Fairweather, now Head of Science and Innovation, he was given a programme of strength and conditioning that enabled him to avoid the 'knife'. Thus he was able to compete and win the US Junior Open, beating the likes of Juan Angel del Potro and Sam Querry en route. From there he was able to pursue his professional career in tennis, winning three Grand Slams and Olympic Gold medals in 2012 and 2016, culminating in securing the Number One ranking in 2016.

You can imagine the delight when the GB women's curling team delivered Gold at the 2002 Winter Olympics in Salt Lake City. Rhona Martin and her team had been the subject of one of the first formal Institute programmes from 1998 under the guidance of Mike Hay, their coach and himself an Olympic curler. The programme was stacked full of innovation with three previously untested features:

1   The science of sweeping – measuring the effectiveness of the brush.
2   Stone path tracking – to ensure optimum delivery of the stone 'into the house'.
3   Abstinence from alcoholic beverages for an extended period!

Games	Gold	Silver	Bronze	Total	Gold %
1998 Kuala Lumpur	3	2	7	12	25
2002 Manchester	6	8	16	30	20
2002 Manchester (excl. Judo)	5	5	10	20	25
2006 Melbourne	11	7	11	29	38
2010 Delhi	9	10	7	26	35
2014 Glasgow	16	12	18	46	35
2014 Glasgow (excl. Judo)	10	10	13	33	30
Growth (1998–2014)	7/12	8/10	7/11	22/33	

Figure 18.8 The growth in gold standard. Table created by Alistair Gray from Commonwealth Games Federation data (2014).

Medals	Scotland		Australia		England		Wales		New Zealand	
	Total	% Gold	Total	% Gold	Total	% Gold	Total	% Gold	Total	% Gold
1998 KL	12	25	200	41	138	26	15	20	34	24
2002 Manchester (Excl. Judo)	30	20	206	40	165	30	33	18	45	24
2006 Melbourne	29	38	221	38	110	33	19	16	31	19
2010 Delhi	26	35	177	42	142	26	19	11	36	30
2014 Glasgow	43	35	123	38	170	35	33	15	44	29

Figure 18.9 Scotland: in comparison with others. Table created by Alistair Gray from Commonwealth Games Federation data (2014).

More success followed in 2002 at the Commonwealth Games in Manchester with gold medals from emerging athletes like Chris Hoy and Craig Maclean in cycling and Alison Sheppard and Graeme Smith in the pool.

By 2004 and the Athens Olympic Games we knew we were on a roll. Scots formed one of the largest representations in Team GB and delivered four medals, the highest ever haul to date. All the athletes had been early members of the Scottish Institute of Sport and also on their sport's GB programmes when they were established a few years later. The local heroes were Katherine Grainger (rowing), Shirley Robertson (sailing), Chris Hoy (track cycling) and Campbell Walsh (kayak).

Through to Glasgow via London – Scots in the top 12 nations

In 2012 Scottish athletes won 13 of Team GB's 65 medals, seven of which were gold. If you think that's a fair way to look at it, it means Scotland would be in a respectable 12th place in the world medal rankings, right beside Yorkshire as the two largest contributing regions to Team GB's medal haul and way above the likes of Ireland, Wales, New Zealand or Canada. And if you allow for population size, it's even more of an achievement. With a population of just 5.2 million, Scotland would be in the top five nations of the per-capita medal tables (see Figures 18.8 and 18.9).

Scotland enjoyed its most successful Commonwealth Games performance on the field of play in 2014. Medals/million (population) represents a good measure of national sporting performance. On the basis of this, Scotland now heads Canada, England, South Africa, New Zealand and, for the first time, the mighty Australia, at a Commonwealth Games. Figures 18.10 and 18.11 illustrate the impact of the new high performance system.

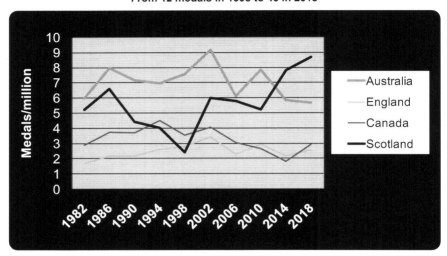

Note: *Medals exclude Judo and include Para Sport*

Figure 18.10 Commonwealth Games (medals/million). Charts created by Alistair Gray from Commonwealth Games Federation data (2014).

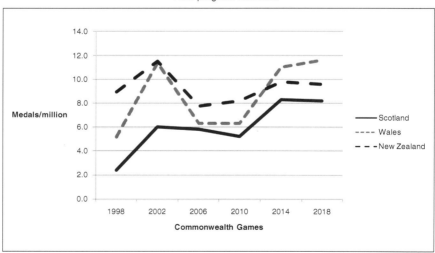

Figure 18.11 The big 3 small nations. Chart created by Alistair Gray from Commonwealth Games Federation data (2014).

In 2014 Australia delivered half the number of total medals and gold medals compared with their home Games in 2006 and England was 25% below their 2002 peak. The big two accounted for 30% of medals won compared with 50% in 1998. With a record number of medals – albeit supplemented by creatively assembled para-sport events and the return of judo after a 12-year absence – 53 Scots stood on a podium at the Glasgow Games and returned to their communities with their medals to inspire future generations: 'pure, dead brilliant'.

Of additional interest is the performance of Scotland, New Zealand and Wales, three nations with a strong and passionate sporting heritage. As Figure 18.11 indicates, these nations regularly punch above their weight and Scotland's athletes, coaches and high performance system (including those who are supported through UK Sport on GB programmes) have enabled it to join this elite club. The progress was continued at the 'away' Games in 2018 on the Gold Coast in Australia.

2014 – Commonwealth Games – the tipping point

The Commonwealth Games has become increasingly fragile as a global sporting event, albeit at a tier below the Olympic Games and World Championships. Delhi in 2010 nearly destroyed the Games. I wrote an article after the 2010 Games that challenged the Commonwealth Games Federation (CGF) to face reality and change the fundamental athletic and business model of the Games. This caused denial to emerge from the CEO and President of the CGF and the CEO of Glasgow 2014 (the latter resigned soon afterwards). My challenge was based on the facts that:

- The Games has been on a commercial knife-edge for years with few cities or states interested in bidding and limited sponsorship support from non-state companies. The Commonwealth Games cannot expect the same level of media coverage and profile as a Summer Olympic Games.
- The economic prize from media rights and commercial partnership will always be much lower.
- The global recession has seen radical cutbacks in government investment in sport at national and local levels in both capital and revenue. This will continue into the future.
- Almost all the major nations in the Commonwealth are unable to provide the level of facilities required for the Games and such additional investment will surely rank way below priorities for the health, education, economic development and well-being of their populations.
- The emergence of a summer European Games and the closer alignment of Oceania nations with Asia present competing events in the key growth economies.
- Without the enthusiastic participation and host commitment of Australia, England, Canada, South Africa and India the Games were in real danger of falling over after 2010.

Glasgow pointed the way to the future

The Commonwealth Games 2014 in Glasgow demonstrated there is a real role for a new-age Commonwealth Games at a time of geo-political turmoil and uncertainty across the world. I argued in 2011 that the Games 'should be about uniting the nations of the Commonwealth behind some rich common purpose'. Perhaps the days of a sporting-only Commonwealth Games are in the past, and inter-national competition of this nature might include other sectors of society. The focus on social equality, equity and culture, combined with the inclusion of more para-sport events than ever before gave real pointers to the future. The alliance with UNICEF was brave and innovative and provided these games with a social purpose far richer than any previous athletic event.

We Scots should be justly proud of our merchant city, our athletes, their coaches and sports, ably supported by **sport**scotland, Glasgow Life, the Institute of Sport, Commonwealth Games Scotland, UK Sport and others working together with Glasgow City Council and the Scottish Government through the CG2014 Organising Committee. Together they conceived and delivered a great Commonwealth Games, as well as providing a vision of a sustainable and successful future for the Commonwealth movement and a real legacy from these wonderful Games.

The Institute was rebranded to become the **sport**scotland Institute of Sport around 2008 and since then has taken a much stronger role in service delivery to a wider range of sports. This was a major contributing factor to the support given to athletes in the period leading up to the 2014 Commonwealth Games in Glasgow. Around 80 people are now employed by the Institute and its network and in Scotland there is now a real industry around the provision of services to high performance sport. Young sports scientists, sports medicine practitioners, analysts and performance lifestyle advisors have career opportunities that were non-existent before 1998. In 1996 there was one full-time coach in Scotland's Commonwealth Games sports. Now the profession has opportunities to build careers like never before.

In summary

I count myself privileged to have had the opportunity over the last 20 years to be involved in many areas of the UK's progress towards the top of high performance sport in the world. What an opportunity it was to operate as a voluntary leader and consultant across a number of sports and to hold positions at British Performance Basketball, British Swimming and the Scottish Institute of Sport, as well as serving on the board of the UK Sports Institute in its formative years. Playing a part in the development of Mission 2012, the high performance system and experiencing directly the benefits of its focus has been an unforgettable experience.

In Genesis we are also justly proud of the work we have done with sport in Ireland, with the Irish Sports Council, the Olympic Council of Ireland

and leading sports including Irish Rugby, the Football Association of Ireland, Cricket Ireland, Irish Boxing and Swimming as well as leading the development of the Federation of Irish Sports. In 1992 we supported the Irish Sports Council with their high performance strategy that led to the development of the Irish Institute of Sport. We followed this by working with the Irish Rugby Union on their first holistic development plan, establishing the provincial-based organisation around the professional game. We also supported the IRFU in debriefing their performance at two successive Rugby World Cups. We carried out a number of debriefing reviews for the Sports Council and the Olympic Council of Ireland after major Olympic and World Championships (Figure 18.12). Our work for the Football Association of Ireland is covered fully in Chapter 20. It is pleasing to note major improvement in the performance of Irish rugby teams since the early development planning we carried out in 1992 and Cricket Ireland's elevation to full Test status in 2017 (see Chapter 13) after a decade of significant performance improvement.

Smaller nations can win in the highly competitive world of performance sport. They just have to be smarter and more passionate to succeed, as well as having the discipline to plan, plan and better plan, and to pay real attention to the detail that matters. The factors that lead to sporting success at the top of sport are now well known. As in everything, the real answer lies in the people, be they athletes, coaches, scientists, medical professionals, lifestyle advisors or administrators. The one common factor is that they are all leaders and continuing to build the capacity and capability of leaders in sport, which is probably the most important factor of all.

📈 High Performance

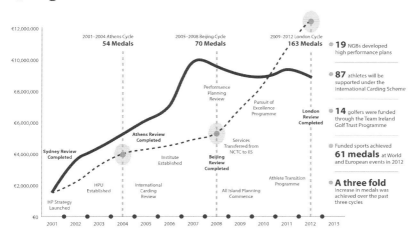

Figure 18.12 Ireland's Olympic performance. Chart created by Alistair Gray, adapted from Irish Sports Council data (2013).

Changing the game	How the Scottish Institute of Sport changed the game

- **Broke the rules; challenged existing paradigms**
    - Operated as a business unit in effective subsidiarity to **sport**scotland.
    - Recruited and retained a first class board – from business and sport and an experienced CEO, programme and athlete service management.
    - Appointed performance coaches, employed by the Institute rather than the sports.
    - The Institute was effectively a mini-campus at the centre of a network.
- **They worked it out themselves – embraced strategic management**
    - Engaged athletes, coaches, staff, the board and other key stakeholders in the development of the vision, the strategy and values.
    - Worked collaboratively with stakeholders on a number of strategic projects.
    - Held regular forums with stakeholders to report on progress and gain feedback.
- **Planned for a step-change in performance**
    - Set clear goals for each programme with the sports.
    - Planned to win with a clear link between the outcome and the plans – at three horizons into the future.
    - Worked with the sports to improve performance through the programmes.
    - Institute staff were encouraged to make a step change in their personal performance.
- **Changed organisational performance**
    - Flat structure with lots of cross-departmental projects.
    - Staff empowered in their own role and on joint working groups.
    - Developed leaders at all levels in the organisation.
    - Personal development planning and appraisal at the centre of people development.
    - Several staff forums each year.

Image 18.4 Original logo of The Scottish Institute of Sport.

Notes

1 Iain MacDonald Sproat (8 November 1938–29 September 2011) was a British Conservative Member of Parliament (MP). He was educated at Winchester College and Magdalen College, Oxford. He worked as a publisher and journalist.
2 *Good to Great and the Social Sectors*, Jim Collins, HarperCollins, 2005.
3 'From Good to Great', Baroness Sue Campbell: www.teachingleaders.org.uk/wp-content/uploads/2014/11/TL_Quarterly_Autumn2014-6.pdf.
4 The Institute's founding board: Alistair Gray (Chair), Frank Dick OBE, Sir Bill Gammell, Peter Haining, Anne Marie Harrison (CEO), Ray Macfarlane, Sir Ian McGeechan, Alison Ramsay MBE, Belinda Robertson OBE, Shirley Robertson OBE.
5 Potentially challenging in a world increasingly concerned about athletes under the influence of drugs and other stimulants. The messages of the 'Bravepill' became part of our language at the Institute and in the Winning Scotland Foundation that was founded in 2006.

19 Good to great
Inside the black box

Introduction

I was particularly impressed by recent works by Jim Collins, who leapt to fame in his joint work with Jerry Porras, Built to Last[1] *in the late 1990s. Collins' next major research was published as* Good to Great *in 2001. He researched companies that had exhibited average performance and, following a point of transition, had then outperformed their comparators by a factor of three over a sustained period. In addition, they demonstrated good-to-great performance independent of their industry. Collins produced a booklet on the application of* Good to Great *principles in the social sectors, e.g., sport and other not-for-profit organisations. Many of these principles matched those I applied in my consulting work and were reflected in my experience as a voluntary leader in sport.*

Funding from the National Lottery was introduced into British Sport (and many other worthwhile causes) in 1998. Few envisaged the positive difference this would have on governing bodies of sport along with the challenges it would bring. Prior to this, sports presented their annual 'grant aid submissions' to their respective agencies in the manner of Oliver[2] with an ever-increasing size of begging bowl. In our work with sports and other not-for-profit organisations we used many of the principles and found they resonated with the leadership of these organisations.

One of the principal objectives was to give the sports the opportunity to modernise their structures, governance and processes in the same way that many UK businesses had done over the preceding decade. Sports responded to the opportunity in different ways – some started to present longer-term (four-year) development plans, while others failed to take advantage of the opportunity. In this case study we outline how two sports, England Netball and British Basketball, responded to the challenge and, in so doing, exhibited the features of a 'Good to Great' organisation.

The journey from 'Good to Great'

Good to Great[3] highlighted organisations such as Abbott, Gillette, Kimberley Clark, Philip Morris, Walgreens and Wells Fargo, which emerged as the front-runners. Unlike many comparison works, this book is well-researched, uses excellent comparators and I believe upholds many of the principles we used in Genesis while working with our clients over 20 years. A number of sporting organisations have transformed themselves using many of the principles and their case studies follow this introductory section. Collins occupies a special position across business and sport, having been a faculty member of Stanford Business School and a member of the board of the Athletic Faculty at Stanford University, arguably the most successful NCAA College in US sport.

So let us look inside the 'black box'. These key features of the *Good to Great* are the factors that systematically distinguished the winners from those who have never won such recognition.

The flywheel in Figure 19.1 represents the basic stages of the journey from good to great.

1. Disciplined people

Level 5 leadership

The researchers were surprised, even shocked, to discover the type of leadership required for turning a good company into a great one.

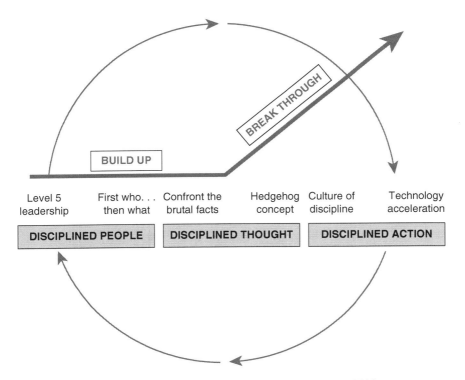

Figure 19.1 Source: *Good to Great* by Jim Collins, Random House 2001.

Compared with high-profile leaders with big personalities who make headlines and become celebrities, the good-to-great leaders seem to have come from Mars. Self-effacing, quiet, reserved, even shy – these leaders are a paradoxical blend of personal humility and professional will. They are ambitious first and foremost for the cause, the organisation, the work – not themselves – and they have the fierce resolve to do whatever it takes to make good on that ambition. They display a paradoxical blend of personal humility and professional will. They are more like Lincoln and Socrates than Patton or Caesar.

In my experience the biggest thing that gets in the way of corporate success is frequently ego, itself often world class.

First who . . . then what

It is also expected that good-to-great leaders begin by setting a new vision and strategy. Instead they *first* get the right people on the bus, and the wrong people off the bus. Next they get the right people in the key seats *before* they figure out where to drive it. They think *first* about 'who', *then* about what. The old adage 'People are your most important asset' turns out to be wrong – people are not your most important asset. The *right* people are.

In any good team there needs to be an excellent core of professionals, equipped for the higher leagues. This frequently relates to the off-field teams as well as those on the field.

2. Disciplined thought

Confront the brutal facts (yet never lose faith)

The *Good to Great* writers learned that a former prisoner of war had more to teach them about what it takes to find a path to greatness than most books on corporate strategy. Every good-to-great company embraced what can be called the Stockdale Paradox. You must maintain unwavering faith that you can and will prevail in the end, regardless of the difficulties and, at the same time, have the discipline to confront the most brutal facts of your current reality, whatever it might be.

Face reality as it is, not as it was, or how you would wish it to be.

The Hedgehog Concept

Greatness comes about by a series of good decisions consistent with a simple coherent concept – a Hedgehog Concept. The Hedgehog Concept is an operating model that reflects understanding of three intersecting circles (strategic goals); what can you be best in your world at? What are you deeply passionate about? What drives your economic and resource engine?

3. Disciplined action

Culture of discipline

All companies have a culture, some companies have discipline, but few companies have a culture of discipline. When you have disciplined people, you do not need hierarchy. When you have disciplined thought, you do not need bureaucracy. When you have disciplined action, you do not need excessive controls. Operating within a framework of responsibilities is the cornerstone of a culture that creates greatness. When you combine a culture of discipline with an ethic of entrepreneurship you get the magical alchemy of great performance. Who said 'Success is 10% inspiration, 90% perspiration'?[4]

The flywheel

In building greatness there is not one single defining action, no grand programme, no one killer technology or innovation, no solitary lucky break, no miracle moment. Rather, the process resembled relentlessly pushing a giant heavy flywheel in one direction, turn upon turn, building momentum to a point of breakthrough, and beyond.

In other words, instant success takes time. You need stability and consistency in which to implement real change.

4. Building greatness to last

Clock building, not time telling

Truly great organisations prosper through multiple generations of leaders, the polar opposite of being built around a single great leader, great idea or specific programme. Leaders in great organisations build catalytic mechanisms to stimulate progress and do not depend upon having a charismatic personality to get things done; indeed many leaders had a 'charisma bypass'.

In a world increasingly driven by metrics, KPIs and analytics there is often a preoccupation with telling the time. A strong vision of success and a culture of continuous improvement striving towards big strategic goals is key.

Preserve the core and stimulate progress

Enduring organisations are characterised by a fundamental duality:

- They have a set of timeless core values and a core reason for being that remain constant over long periods of time.
- They have a relentless drive for change and progress – a creative compulsion that manifests itself in striving towards audacious goals.

Great organisations are clear about the difference between their core values (which never change) and operating strategies and cultural practices (that endlessly adapt to a changing world). Core stability is a key feature of high-performing athletes, combined with powerful attention to detail enabling you to perform in the 'event' in which you are competing.

We have had the privilege of applying the principles of *Good to Great* with our clients in business and sport. Setting ambitious strategic goals (conceiving their Hedgehog) and applying the other principles in execution of their strategies have enabled many to raise their performance as individuals and as an organisation, in both business, sport and not-for-profit sectors.

Good to Great – transforming England Netball and British Basketball

The challenge for the All England Netball Association

In 2002 netball in England was failing as a sport, despite being one of the top four highest-funded sports by Sport England. Genesis was asked by Sport England to evaluate netball's performance as a sport and as a business, and to make recommendations as to how their performance might be improved. Of particular concern was the sport's capability to deliver what was an ambitious programme, targeting every single initiative area contained in Sport England's strategy.

England Netball themselves felt they were performing well. But were they in danger of becoming 'hot'? By this we meant was there real strategy innovation taking place? Were there vibrant confident 'teams' with plans to win across athletes, coaches, staff and volunteers? Was the rest of the sport engaged and enthusiastic about the future? Were exciting initiatives emerging with associated plans for implementation, not just actions or schedules of events/fixtures and training? To what extent did senior management (professional/volunteer) support the development plan and other strategies? Were people hungry to learn new skills and change?

The answer was simple – No! Their very desire to reflect and comply with Sport England's complex approach to leading and managing sport had translated itself into the relentless pursuit of public-sector funding, requiring an organisation that was far from lean and overly complex for the basic tasks of winning at international level and growing what was once a great game.

They were pursuing the wrong goals in an overly ambitious and complex development plan (three central strands, six supporting strands, each with four levels and six underpinning programmes). They were at risk of diluting their undoubted strengths (in their volunteers, members and as a team sport for girls at school), and struggling as their weaknesses were exposed, especially in their clubs and competitions, which meant they were losing out to other sports, particularly in light of significant growth in the popularity of women's football.

The year 2000 had been their *annus horribilis*, with falling membership, reduced funding from fewer sources of income and mediocre performance from their teams on the international courts.

Our approach

I led the assignment with Sheila Gray, my wife, and herself a World Class Adviser to UK Sport. We also worked closely with Pauline Harrison, the excellent Chief Executive of England Netball. We chose to consult widely to carry out the review and met with many of the sport's membership at a number of key events. Over 50 interviews with key individuals inside and outside the sport were carried out, as well as extensive desk research. We chose the framework in Figure 19.2 to develop a comprehensive view of the sport.

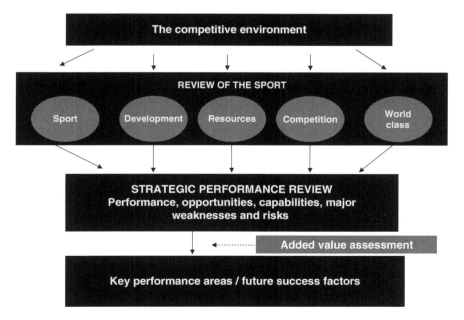

Figure 19.2 The framework for the review. Process created by Alistair Gray (2002).

We concluded that:

- Netball was well administered technically as a sport, with good basic administrative management. Technical management and basic operations of the sport were well managed and there were a number of areas of good practice.
- Netball was not addressing the major strategic issues, e.g., demographic trends – women, participation levels, and ethnicity. Competition from other sports and pastimes was increasing, e.g., women's football, rugby, lifestyle sports and pastimes.
- Positioning and marketing the sport did not make netball an attractive proposition for participants, sponsors and event organisers.
- Netball was not addressing the business issues of a £2.5m business – raising revenue from a wide variety of sources. It was highly dependent on Sport England and other exchequer-based funding streams. It was questionable if netball was delivering value to shareholders/stakeholders.
- More of the same was unlikely to achieve higher levels of performance or greater value for money. A 'game-changing' approach was required.

We endeavoured to summarise this succinctly in six 'good to great' statements:

1   The game was being played *outdoors* and should be played *indoors.*
2   The game was being played in *counties* and should be played in *cities.*
3   Matches were played *when it suited the players* rather than as part of an attractive *commercially viable calendar for the sport with exciting competitions.*
4   Events were arranged for the benefit of *members* rather than attracting wider playing and paying *audiences.*
5   Players were playing in *heavy gymslips* rather than in *Lycra*™. Umpires too needed to address their appearance. Little had changed in decades.
6   The sport pursued *every single source of grant aid* from Sport England and others, rather than developing the sponsorship and broadcasting revenues potentially available to a *vibrant team sport.*

Netball in England faced a choice – one of two possible routes to the future. They could either reduce the scope of activity and resources to secure real performance with a lower and more focused level of resources. Alternatively, they could create a new beginning through which the sport could achieve a real step-change in position and performance, making it attractive to future stakeholders – from players to sponsors – as well as Sport England.

The final outcome

An attractive and exciting future was open to netball in England. The sport needed to develop – all together – a new and compelling vision with associated competitive strategies for the sport. They needed to build plans for the next five years that would address the external and internal issues, and especially the needs of future stakeholders, learning from good practice elsewhere in netball and other sports. Figure 19.3 shows the outline of the Focus Framework as it evolved.

The historic county structure was to be integrated into five or six new regions working in a clearer and more dynamic structure of development and competition. The new regional structure for the sport would enable volunteers and professionals to work together with strong integrated clubs delivering focused development activity, e.g., active sports, volunteers, club mark and a new programme of competitions.

The refocused development plan would de-emphasise the role of schools and increase the focus on the development of youth wherever they play. The pathway to performance would be brought to life through a new competition for top clubs that would be attractive to broadcast and attract new media – the source of future revenue. SuperLeague (as the new competition was titled) secured an exclusive broadcasting agreement with Sky that has transformed the once sleepy sport into a genuine product for television audiences.

Building on existing good practice, there would be increased development and training of coaches, umpires and new professional staff in key areas such as PR, marketing and communications.

To their eternal credit the board of England Netball embraced the findings of the review and commissioned Genesis to work with them to reform their strategy and development plan to change the game for the future. Our recommendations were summarised as follows, and implemented with the passion and enthusiasm that had previously been latent in the sport:

- The new Development Plan for Netball needs to have fewer, clearer priorities and goals with clear measurable outcomes.
- Functional strategies need to be developed for key areas in the sport, e.g., facilities, coaching, umpiring, development and a new commercial function with increased training and development in these key areas.
- A new model is needed for the sport, including proposals to radically change the role of clubs, their competitions and the positioning of netball as a competitive team sport. New forms of the sport should be developed to encourage recreational play.
- Increase revenue from affiliation and other sources and especially consider opportunities to broadcast international matches and new league formats.
- Focus development on the 30–40 top clubs, while at the same time supporting the development of multi-sport/community-based clubs.

Our vision

Our strategic goals

Quality systems and network

- Meeting members' needs.
- Supportive structures.
- Exploiting external opportunities.
- Sustained growth.
- Total quality management.

England – leading the world

- No 1 in 2007.
- Growth in talented athletes, coaches, umpires; living pathways.
- Quality programmes, training and competition.
- Easy access to quality facilities.
- Great support.

Dynamic, integrated competitions

- Dynamic, integrated, clear, progressive structure.
- Higher profile competition – athletes fulfilling their potential.
- Improved access to more indoor facilities.
- Support, training and advice.

Performing as an organisation

- Clear policy of corporate governance.
- Minimise business risk.
- Operationally self-sufficient and sustainable.
- Right People; Right Jobs; Right Way; Right Time.
- IT architecture supporting our needs as a sport and business.

Our Vision for 2007

*England Netball is recognised as the **leading women's team sport** through our success as a great game and our team's performance on the court*

*Our game is thriving in a **network of local communities** providing enjoyment and easy access to lifelong netball opportunities*

*We are successful through our development of **strategic partnerships** and the **quality services** we deliver*

*Our game is growing and sustainable, and **self-sufficient** in acquisition of our resources*

*Our volunteers and professionals are successful by **working together** to fulfil our ambitions*

Our values

Figure 19.3 England Netball: our great game. Framework created by Alistair Gray (2003).

A decade later netball in England is transformed as a sport and as a business, far less dependent on the public-sector support of Sport England. The transformation was achieved with the gold-medal-winning performance at the 2018 Commonwealth Games at Gold Coast, Australia, where England defeated the host nation and undefeated champions 52–51 with the last shot of the match.

Transforming British Basketball

The Olympic Games were awarded to the UK in 2005. Up to this point the British basketball teams were languishing in the third division of European competition with little commitment and resources from the home associations (England, Scotland and Wales) for performance improvement. The sport was loosely coordinated by the British Basketball Federation (BBF), a requirement for potential Olympic Games participation. Each home nation, though competing separately in European competition, had few opportunities to develop, especially as basketball did not feature regularly in the Commonwealth Games. Basketball in England, the largest association, had undergone a number of 'fundamental' reviews that had been largely ignored with little resulting change. Any activity at a British level was regarded with little enthusiasm. Basketball as a sport and its teams were, to summarise, completely dysfunctional in performance terms and in growth in participation. Despite being one of the big five global sports, basketball in the UK represented nothing more than a backwater.

At the same time, the prospect of British teams grasping the opportunity afforded to a host nation and securing places for a men's and women's team at the 2012 Olympic Games in London, though remote, was too good to miss. The challenge was to become competitive enough by 2011 to be granted qualification in their own right. The international federation, FIBA, confirmed that achieving and sustaining a top league EuroBasket status would be the benchmark for qualification for the 2012 Olympic Games.

Recognising this, UK Sport agreed with the BBF that a stand-alone company – British Performance Basketball (BPB) – would be formed in 2006 with the sole aim of building teams capable of securing qualification and delivering a credible performance at the 2012 Games.

I was given the opportunity to chair the board of the new company with Chris Spice, former Performance Director of England Rugby (RFU) and gold-medal-winning Olympic Hockey Coach with Australia,[5] Simon Tuckey, a leading company executive and former director of London Athletics, along with Bill McInnes,[6] the chair of Scottish Basketball. We added representatives from the other home nations and together set off on our journey to achieve what many felt was 'mission impossible'.

In the beginning

The GB basketball performance programme commenced under the guidance of the BBF in 2006 and, within the first two years, promotion was gained by both the men's and women's senior teams from EuroBasket B to the A Division. There was hope!

The two Under-20 teams failed to emulate their senior colleagues in 2007. During that time, through a series of forums, debriefs and workshops, a new strategy, 'Game On', was developed to take the British teams through to 2012. The key was to successfully engage with key stakeholders in the sport in the UK, especially with athletes, coaches and support service providers, as well as the national associations. A number of external expert advisers also contributed to the development of 'Game On'. In parallel, new coaches were appointed and an Operations Manager, Ron Wuotila, was given the task of managing the performance function.

The result of the strategy development process was a vision for the future of performance basketball in the UK over the five years to 2013 and beyond. Its ambitions were lofty, yet realistic – to project GB to a level of on-court performance that stimulated hitherto unforeseen levels of popular, media and commercial support, and to drive the development of the game in all age groups and sectors of the sport. 'Game On' also sought to anticipate and estimate the impact that fulfilment of the vision might have on the rest of the sport, especially in terms of marketing and commercial activity. In summary, 'Game On' saw British basketball as:

- A much bigger and more ambitious sport.
- A sport with diverse funding streams.
- A professionally managed and financially sustainable sport.

Securing the agreement of all key stakeholders to this vision was the first and critical outcome. The barriers to success were significant, largely as a result of the sport's dysfunctionality, complacency and apathy at British and national level. This included the need to capture the hearts and minds of the entire British basketball community that, with few exceptions, was poorly led, not well-governed, fragile and resistant to change. The current squad was not ready for the world class and the examination it would be given. There were few world-class players and no strength in depth of players and coaches. There was huge reliance on a single player – Loul Deng, then playing for the Chicago Bulls in the NBA – for awareness and publicity for the GB men's team, and low-level awareness in general of the GB women's team. There were no structured systems for talent identification and development, and an effective curriculum for development and the state of coaching in general was poor, especially at elite coach level, matched only by the state of the leagues and clubs – unsustainable in 2005. British Basketball as a business was heavily reliant on funding from the public sector, especially from UK Sport, with regard to the GB team programme. Potential commercial properties were limited in terms of packages for sale and the values associated with the British Basketball brand.

The first milestone on the journey towards our destination was to achieve, by 2013:

- GB men's and women's teams qualifying and performing credibly at the Olympic Games in 2012 (in the top half of their pools) and being well placed to secure qualification for 2016. Also, GB teams based on robust communities of players, coaches and support staff who are committed to placing British basketball in the Top 10 of FIBA world rankings.
- Clear structure of leadership and governance for the GB basketball programme that is owned by all stakeholders with commitment to the philosophies and processes that have been adopted and implemented.
- Fully integrated British Basketball performance workforce (staff and volunteers) that is structured and empowered to challenge and support the teams continually to the next level of performance.
- Clear and agreed pathways for the development of elite players from the early identification of talent through to fulfilment at international level and in professional leagues at home and abroad. Elite coach and referee education pathways that span the game from home nation to senior international levels.
- Healthy domestic leagues that serve as the production line for future talented players, coaches and referees with the sport of basketball and its events established as significant entertainment in the UK, not only on television but across all media.
- Shared marketing themes that link the GB teams with the NBA, FIBA and FIBA Europe, the British Basketball League (BBL) and the home associations.
- Diverse income streams that arise from increased leverage exercised against both public and private sources of funding with reduced dependency on UK Sport performance funding.

The overall strategic direction for the sport was laid out in the form of a virtuous circle where improved on-field success drove performance improvement in other key areas (off the court) and they themselves contributed to further, higher levels of success on the court. This is illustrated in Figure 19.4.

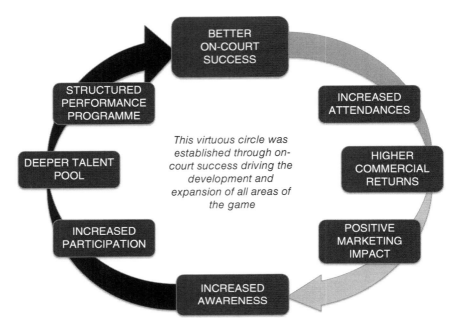

Figure 19.4 The virtuous circle for basketball in Britain. Model created by Chris Spice and Alistair Gray (2007).

Delivering on-field success

There were a number of factors that delivered on-court results relatively quickly, especially around the selection and leadership of newly appointed coaches to the national teams, breaking the mould of past under-performance.

However, the whole improvement of performance was underpinned by the performance beam for British Basketball (illustrated in Figure 19.5). This represented the elite player performance development pathway and encompassed all the processes and activities through which British players should participate. The beam puts elite basketball players and coaches at the centre of everything that we did. There were two main supporting structures:

1   Individual development.
2   Competitive development.

Each was underpinned by resources for long-term sustainability. The individual development structure had a clear focus on individual coaching and technical development away from the competitive environment. The coaches selected to work on this side of the beam had to understand their

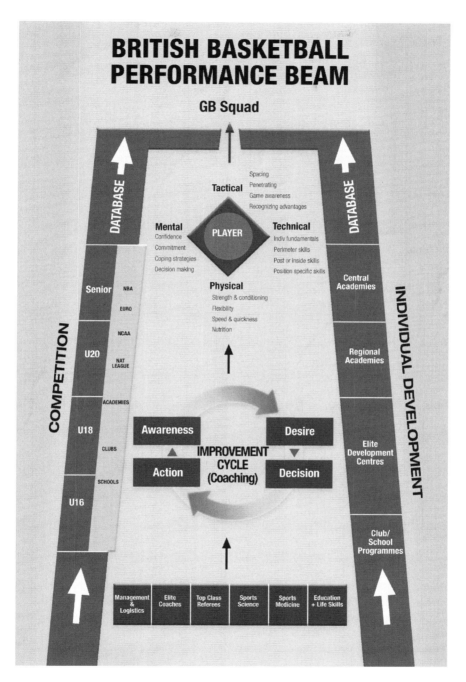

Figure 19.5 British Basketball performance beam. Framework created by Chris Spice, Performance Director of British Performance Basketball (2005).

roles – this required a paradigm shift for most as this mostly related to running teams for competition.

Equally, it was critical that the individual needs of elite players were kept at the forefront of decision making. There were times when it was appropriate for players to compete at a level above their current age group in order for them to be challenged and to accelerate their development.

Each home nation bought into the process and system for the identification of players from a young age. The process used common profiles and protocols, observed a common curriculum of development and operated within a common culture. Each home nation's programme worked towards a common goal – the selection standard applied for access to the GB programme.

This new approach was integrated alongside the move to create a higher quality environment supporting the training and development of teams, given the need for relatively short-term success.

Regional academy/institute structures were quickly established, based on BBL teams. In parallel, players competing in European leagues and the NBA were embraced and taken through the new approach to performance improvement. Players and coaches alike welcomed all this. We recognised that, given the nature of basketball globally, any young player emerging from the talent pathway would seek their future as part of a scholarship at a US college competing in the NCAA or at a major European professional club.

An interesting anecdote

The leading British player was Luol Deng, who was playing for the Chicago Bulls in the NBA. In 2008 he signed a four-year contract worth in excess of $60m. At almost zero notice BPB was informed by the NBA that we would be required to pay $800k to secure his release to play five games for GB in the forthcoming EuroBasket competition, in a year that would be critical for GB's qualification for London 2012. The claim was based on covering the insurance costs estimated as a result of apparent residual injuries being carried by the player. Our evidence gave a different perspective but our appeal was rejected by the NBA's commissioners.

Seeking legal opinion was necessary before embarking on any appeal. Our council, Mark Gay at DL Piper, said 'Number 1, Alistair, you do not sue the NBA. However we can write them some jolly good letters'. This we duly did and secured a reduction in the insurance premium that enabled UK Sport to advance British Performance Basketball the cost of the revised premium from the next year's grant, allowing Deng to play and the team to secure its position in Europe's top league and, through that, to achieve qualification status for the 2012 Olympic Games.

The summary goals and objectives set by British Performance Basketball are outlined in Figure 19.6.

Our goals	2008	2012 (Target)	2016 (Vision)
Performance at Olympic Games	Not there!	Quarter finals and in Top 6	In the mix for medals – top 4 and win one medal
Performance at other major Championships	Both Men's and Women's team promoted to Eurobasket 'A' GB senior teams qualify for World Championship and qualify for finals of Eurobasket A U20 teams promoted to Eurobasket A	Robust communities of players and coaches and winning performance system GB senior teams in top 4 of Eurobasket A – win first medal U20 teams in top 8 in Eurobasket A	Top (1 team in top 4) at 2014 World and 2013 (Top 4)/2015 (Medal) European 'A' Division championships U20 teams in top 6 in Europe
British Leagues	BBL – part-time, fragile league Amateur Women's League No major sponsor On Setanta	Full-time pro league for men with secure income streams >10% of men's squad playing in British League Significant sponsor On Sky	Full-time leagues for men and women with secure income streams 20% of men's squad playing in British League Significant sponsor On Sky and terrestrial television
Income streams	£1.5m income 100% grants Modest grants	£5m income 50% grants Grants for growth	£20m income 25% grants Support as major Olympic sport
Marketing	Themes mixed and fragmented Major sponsor announced for GB teams All GB senior games televised live	United and performing basketball community Major extensions to sponsorship income Long-term TV deal in place	1m volunteers in the British Basketball Army Additional extensions to sponsorship income TV deal on international matches a significant part of income
Leadership and governance	3 National Governing Bodies BBF formed, replacing GBB and recognised by BOA/ FIBA, etc. BPB formed as SPV British Basketball formed integrating BPB and BBF 'Game on' strategy approved	British Basketball provides lead to 3 vibrant and integrated NBAs New strategy for basketball in Britain	British Basketball recognised as leading modern federation by UK sports agencies and FIBA
Culture, climate and social inclusion	Fragile culture Limited presence; no strategy Regional Institutes of Basketball initiated	Culture of winning emerging in London and major part of Olympic Legacy Regional Institutes of Basketball (Phase 2) initiated	'Game on' culture Major presence in major cities in UK Regional Institutes producing increasing numbers of ProTeam ready players.

Figure 19.6 British Performance Basketball goals and objectives. Table created by Alistair Gray from British Basketball's Performance Plan (2008).

Forward to a better future

As a result of improved on-court success in the first two years since British Performance Basketball was established, the sport in Britain was able to get behind a strategy moving forward to 2016.

Great Britain's two senior teams duly qualified for the 2012 Olympic Games and delivered credible performances on the court, without reaching the quarter-final stages. But, despite forming the revised British Basketball Federation, the home nations did not pick up on the potential legacy from the teams' participation in the high profile event in London. Both England and Wales continued to operate dysfunctionally for a number of years, to the great displeasure of FIBA and the NBA who had backed the sport in face of continued hostility from Sport England in particular.

Following 2012, UK Sport also tightened its 'no compromise' policy for funding towards Rio 2016. There was no way the senior British teams would achieve a medal at Rio in 2016 and, as a result, funding for the next Olympiad was cut. However, the sport was to receive support at a reduced level from Sport England on the basis of its important role in increasing participation in sport.

By grasping the chance to modernise through the opportunity afforded by the 2012 Olympic Games in London, basketball in Britain gave itself the opportunity to modernise and reform. Consistent progress since the early reformation in 2005, underpinned by the 'Game On' strategy, has given the sport the structure and framework through which to develop future talent and teams.

England Netball

British Basketball

- **Break the rules; challenge existing paradigms**

  - Aim high for winning – in European, World and Olympic competition.
  - Aim higher for growth of resources – members, participants and of course financial and people resources.
  - Build capacity and capability – both at the same time.

- **Work it out – embrace 'Good to Great'**

  - Face reality as it is, not as it was or you would wish it to be.
  - Develop together an exciting vision of success (using the Focus Framework including 'big, hairy and audacious goals') that can be shared with everyone.
  - People in sport are passionate about achieving goals, they should reflect good practice and address the economic engine of the sport.
  - Instant success takes time – both sports achieved 'breakout' performance through planning to achieve clear short-term goals (early wins) that build confidence in their people that success was possible.

- **Plan for a step-change in performance**

  - The view has to be worth the climb. Create a vision of success that is simple, clear and inspiring.
  - Prepare strategic plans – few in number, big in impact and not lists of actions. Publish the intent (The 'one-page strategy') that leads the change. Develop a strategic planning calendar, with quarterly reviews built in (the plan:do:check:act) and debrief each year's actual performance against what was planned, to accelerate performance improvement.
  - Publish and share the performance – the good, bad and ugly. Go back, plan again and implement again.

- **Change organisational performance**

  - Get the right people on the bus – like Pauline, Sally, Cheryl and Heather in netball; Chris, Simon, Bill, great coaches and players, administrators and agencies, e.g., FastTrack in basketball, and many others.
  - Engage a critical mass of people (staff and volunteers) in pursuit of progress, working in teams as never before.
  - Celebrate success as milestones are achieved and barriers broken down.
  - Keep it simple – in the early years relentlessly focusing on achieving short-term goals, aligned to the strategic goals.

- **Leaders at all levels in the organisation champion the change**

  - Resilience in the face of 'enemy' fire must be exemplary, e.g., British Performance Basketball ensured people at all levels had the opportunity to fulfil their potential – athletes, coaches, administrators, volunteers.
  - Use consultants, contractors and advisers, not as strategists or planners, but to lead and facilitate the process of change.

Notes

1 *Built To Last: Successful Habits of Visionary Companies*, James Collins and Jerry Porras, Random House, 1994.
2 *Oliver Twist*, or *The Parish Boy's Progress*, is the second novel by English author Charles Dickens and was first published as a serial between 1837 and 1839. The story is of the orphan Oliver Twist, who is born in a workhouse and then sold into apprenticeship with an undertaker. He escapes from there and travels to London, where he meets the Artful Dodger, a member of a gang of juvenile pickpockets led by the elderly criminal Fagin. He is known for 'asking for more gruel' at breakfast.
3 *Good to Great*, James Collins, Random House, 2001.
4 Thomas Alva Edison, statement in a press conference (1929), as quoted in *Uncommon Friends: Life with Thomas Edison, Henry Ford, Harvey Firestone, Alexis Carrel & Charles Lindbergh*, James D. Newton, Harcourt, Inc., 1987, p. 24.
5 Chris Spice took up the position of Performance Director of British Swimming in 2013.
6 Bill McInnes sadly died in March 2017 after a short illness. He was a giant of the game and our guiding light over the initial years of British Performance Basketball.

20 The New Zealand All Blacks

The ultimate high performing sporting organisation

John Bull

Introduction

Thomas J. Watson Jr[1] succeeded his father as President of IBM in 1952. Over the following two decades he is credited with leading IBM during its period of greatest growth to dominance in the then emerging computer industry. He became the source of much early wisdom in post-war industrial management and is credited with many quotations including:

> *I believe the real difference between success and failure for any organisation can be traced to how well it brings out the great energies and talents of its people. The most important role for a leader is to create an environment which challenges and allows people to fulfil their potential in the pursuit of a worthwhile objective.[2]*

The purpose of this chapter is to provide insight into the leadership behind the highest-performing teams and organisations in the world. It includes a case study of the New Zealand All Blacks, the world's most successful sports team, on how to create a high performance culture.

Little town of champions

If you drive 130 miles south east of the capital of Ethiopia, Addis Ababa, completing the last 30 miles by dirt road, you will eventually come across a hand-painted sign boldly announcing 'WELCOME TO THE VILLAGE OF ATHLETES'.

Ethiopia is well recognised as a nation that produces world-class middle- and long-distance runners. Since Abebe Bikila ran and won the marathon barefooted in 1960 at the Rome Olympics, they have amassed 21 gold medals in track and field athletics. What is less well known is that ten of their most recent 16 gold medals (and seven of their last nine) have all come from one small highland town called Bekoji.

With a population of 17,000, this quiet rural town has become the world's leading producer of middle-distance runners, taking all four of Ethiopia's gold medals in Beijing and a further two in London in 2012. The runners from this tiny town have hauled in more gold medals than India has won in *all* Summer Olympic categories put together.

When people watch Ethiopian athletes run, they often marvel at what they assume is the natural talent of these athletes. But a closer examination of Bekoji forces us to look deeper. What is it about this particular town that differentiates it from the one down the road at the same altitude, where people have the same genetic make up and the same need to run every-where? Why does the capital Addis Ababa – with 100 times the population and the National Athletics Centre – fail to produce equivalent world-class athletes? The secret behind Bekoji's phenomenal success is that all these athletes have been coached and nurtured by the same PE teacher of the local school – Sentayehu Eshutu.

Every day, upwards of 150 boys and girls, many in bare feet and some as young as six, congregate at the crack of dawn on a grassy plateau just out of town to endure a gruelling 90-minute training session in pur-suit of their dreams. From a young age, coach Eshutu fills his athletes with a belief they can be the best in the world, and a hunger to pursue that dream with all their waking energy. 'I have no doubt', he told Nick

Image 20.1 Little town of champions. Source: © Drew Gamble, Ethiopicrunning.com.

Ashdown[3] in a recent interview, 'that a number of these kids will become a world champion'. Anywhere else, with any other school coach, that comment might be an idle boast. In Bekoji, with Eshutu, it seems virtually a guarantee of future success.

Are Eshutu's athletes especially talented? Yes, of course they are. To ask this question misses the point. Are they *more* talented than any other group of Ethiopians living at altitude? Clearly the answer is no. The difference is in the *environment* Eshutu creates to get the best out of the talent he works with.

This story of Bekoji and Eshutu's coaching highlights the role of the two key ingredients we introduced at the outset of this chapter, and which we find at the heart of every high-performing organisation or team we have studied over the last 20 years – talent and environment.

- **Talent**: high-performing organisations see recruitment as the single most important factor in the success of the organisation. They look for both cultural fit and for people who have both the hunger and potential to be outstanding in their role. They also never compromise. This is critical because, while the vast majority of leaders recognise the importance of talent, they are also often too quick to compromise their standards in order to fill a position.
- **Environment**: the second and arguably even more important ingredient, because so few leaders understand it, is the environment the leaders create around their talent. To borrow an analogy from the 'nature vs nurture' debate of human development, getting the right talent is the equivalent of loading the bullet in the gun, while creating an effective environment or culture around that talent is what fires the gun. Talent *not* used or developed is the same as having no talent at all. The single most striking feature of the leadership behind high-performing organisations is their understanding of the importance of the environment they create, and the amount of energy they put into it. If most leadership teams paid as much attention to the environment and culture they are creating as they do to strategy, they would begin to see a level of performance of which they currently can only dream.

These two ingredients and the relationship between them can be summed up in the following simple equation:

Performance = Talent x Environment [P = T x E]

Notice that talent and environment are multiplied in this algorithm, not summed. This is to convey the dynamic relationship between the two factors. A change in either one has a very powerful and disproportionate impact on the other. Changing the quality of talent you have automatically affects the environment; and changing the environment we create around people as leaders changes how much of their talent we tap into and how successfully we develop it.

Focusing in on the environment side of this equation, our research has highlighted three distinguishing principles that set the best organisations and teams apart from their competitors:

1   The level of ambition in the culture.
2   The level of autonomy they give people, within a framework of very clear goals.
3   A disciplined approach to using feedback and reviews to drive constant improvement.

The rest of the chapter will explore each of these in more detail.

Principle 1. Engage people behind a meaningful goal to motivate and challenge

* **Key insight**: people are at their best when they are in pursuit of a great goal or challenge. This is why most teams and organisations recognise that their greatest moments are often at a time of crisis. It is the crisis, more than the leadership, which creates an environment conducive to high performance. Unfortunately, all too often, as soon as the crisis passes, the environment and the team's performance fall back to the old norm.

The first step in creating a high-performance culture is to switch people on by engaging them behind a great purpose, goal or challenge – one that excites them, gives their work meaning and challenges them to raise their game. Here are two examples.

In 2003 Greg Dyke, Director General of the BBC at the time, planted the seed of an idea in the minds of the digital team, which four years later grew into the corporation's greatest innovation of the last 30 years – the BBC iPlayer. Two years before anyone had even begun to entertain the idea of streaming video over the internet, he set them an audacious challenge to lead the fight back against multi-channel providers like Sky by figuring out a way to make the whole of the BBC's archive available on demand – anytime, anywhere. That single goal became the catalyst for the resurgence of a creative and confident culture across the whole organisation, and its impact can still be felt more than a decade after Dyke left.

Steve Jobs was a genius at using high standards to drive innovation. He challenged the original Mac team with the standard that any computer should be able to start up in less than ten seconds. To this day, every Mac still does and no PC does. To return to the central point of this chapter, this is not because Apple engineers are more talented than their counterparts in other organisations. They simply figure out a way because the environment demands it of them.

These goals and standards are a million miles from the clichéd mission statements and uninspiring goals set by many organisations and their teams. It is not the words, but the intent that matters. Setting out a goal to 'be the best in your sector' will not have the desired impact if it is not matched by great leadership behaviour. If every action is benchmarked against that standard, people soon get the message that you mean business, *and the goal starts to have meaning.*

Jean Krantz, who was flight controller for NASA during the Apollo Missions, talks about how Kennedy's great challenge to land a man on the moon by the end of the decade only started to take hold in the culture when the President asked for an update on their progress towards that goal six months later.

So what are the defining features of a meaningful goal?

- First, it has to be clear, specific and challenging enough to create a positive tension between the ambition (the vision of success) and the current position. People need to believe a goal is possible in order to engage behind it, but that does not mean they need to know how to achieve it from the outset. Great goals stimulate progress by challenging people to think in new ways, to innovate and to reach inside themselves and bring their full talents to the pursuit.
- Second, the goal has to excite people; it has to tap into something they are passionate about. Just thinking about the goal should create positive energy. Everyone in the team needs to be able to see how their role relates to the goal, how they can contribute to it and make a difference.

One of our most successful projects in supporting a client to build a performance culture around clearer and more challenging goals has been with Sport Wales – the national agency in charge of both growing participation in sport and maximising performance on the world stage. They conceived two overarching goals:

1   A sport participation target to get '*Every child hooked on sport for life*'.
2   An elite performance target to achieve the 'Best per capita medal performance of any nation competing at the Commonwealth Games'.

Returning to the above criteria around what makes for an effective goal, it was essential to translate the first of these into a set of performance measures against which they could benchmark and track their performance – measures such as the percentage of people who maintained an active engagement in sport after leaving school. If they had not done this, it would have rapidly become a hollow mission statement. As it stands, both these goals have not only had a huge impact on their own culture and performance, they have also started to have a transformational impact on the culture of their partners, such as national governing bodies of sports and local authorities. They are transforming the performance culture of the sport industry in Wales and the results are becoming a source of real pride for the entire nation.

Principle 2. Create leadership at all levels of the organisation – give people freedom to use and develop their talents

- **Key insight**: while freedom and autonomy *without* the focus of a clear goal can create a laissez-faire culture, when combined *with* the focus of a clear goal people care about, autonomy becomes an engine for innovation and a huge source of motivation. Too many leaders have no idea how much unused potential they are sitting on by being overly directive and controlling.

Distributed leadership is not a new idea; it was Nelson's greatest advantage. Between 1798 and 1805 Nelson defeated the superior fleet of Napoleon on four occasions, not through a better strategy but through a very different approach to leadership. While Napoleon believed in controlling every move of his ships in the battles, Nelson pioneered a new approach. He invested time in advance with his captains to share his thinking and agree the broad principles of their approach, before setting them free to act on their initiative in the moment. This level of responsibility enthralled them, they grew as leaders, and their secret weapon became the speed with which they could change their plan to exploit an opportunity, even in the heat of battle.

This approach to leadership requires us fundamentally to rethink our role as managers – from one of controlling performance and dictating the approach, to inspiring people behind a compelling outcome and coaching them to perform to the best of their ability in its pursuit. Google, for example, gives every engineer 20% of their time to work on their own projects for new products. This policy is responsible for the vast majority of their new ventures, including Google Maps, Google News and Android.

This freedom should not be mistaken for a lack of direction. Empowerment without clear goals and accountability achieves little. Every member of the Google team knows their mission and has quarterly reviews to reflect and review their contribution to these goals. Once provided with the right conditions – a clear engaging challenge within broad principles of strategy – it is critical to let go and give people the freedom to show their talent, to grow and to learn.

Nor does it mean that, as a manager, you should not have ideas of your own or provide clear direction – you should instead view yourself as one leader among many, and actively seek to awaken and give space to this leadership in others around you.

So, how can we create this level of responsibility? Here are three pointers:

1   Lead with questions.
2   Grow your people by giving them clear responsibility.
3   Free people to innovate.

Lead with questions

Share the big challenges and questions you face as a leader with your team. Seek out their views, challenge them to think, and ensure you listen.

On his return to Apple after 11 years in exile from the firm he founded, Steve Jobs knew he had less than a year before the business faced bankruptcy. He challenged his engineers with the question of 'what other areas of consumer electronics might we be able to transform?' One of the Apple team came up with iPod and the concept of '1,000 songs in your pocket'. The rest is history.

Grow people by giving them responsibility

The quickest way to bring out people's natural leadership qualities is to give them responsibility in a spirit of trust and belief in their ability to deliver.

Peter Blake, one of the world's most successful skippers in open-water sailing, saw the development of leadership in others as his most important role on the team. On one voyage he was awakened out of a sleep by a rookie he was taking through the Southern Ocean for the first time, who wanted to alert him that a massive storm was brewing. Peter came up on deck and replied 'so there is' before going back to bed and leaving the young sailor to get on with it. That young sailor was Russell Coutes, who later went on to become the skipper of four successful America's Cup campaigns. The point is not that Peter refused to help; he was simply making a judgment call that Russell was ready to take on more responsibility. Coutes later identified that journey as a big turning point in his confidence and level of skill.

Free people to innovate

Once people understand and 'get' what we, as leaders, are trying to achieve, it is critical that we free their creative spirit by encouraging and allowing them to try new things.

In perhaps the least likely appointment in corporate history, Barry Gibbons had been parachuted into Miami from the Hercules transporter of a British brewing conglomerate to take command of an all-American chain. In *Pushing Doors Marked Pull*, a curious new book about his life and career, he remembers his following five years in charge of Burger King, during which he unleashed the Whopper on Britain. In his first week as CEO of Burger King, Gibbons sought out and visited a franchisee who had been highlighted as a 'trouble maker', but who was also running a very profitable branch. What he found was a shining example of the culture he wanted to create across the organisation. On approaching the restaurant, he noticed they had a queue out of the door at breakfast time and that was unusual as breakfast was an offering other franchises were really struggling to sell. The reason why? They had set up a mini basketball hoop behind the counter and were giving customers an opportunity to shoot for a free coffee. Barry, who has always viewed his role as a leader as being to 'shake organisations awake', used the example of this franchise to articulate the shift in culture he wanted to achieve across the organisation. The transformation in Burger King's profits under Barry's leadership earned him a 'Turnaround Champion' citation from *Forbes Magazine* as the leader in a new generation of 'turn around' masters.

Principle 3. Use feedback and reviews to create a dynamic learning culture

- **Key insight**: the best predictor of long-term success is not how good you are now. It is how quickly you are learning. Effective feedback and review processes have three important impacts on the performance environment:
  - ○ First, they create positive performance pressure through shared responsibility and accountability.
  - ○ Second, feedback and reviews drive learning.
  - ○ And finally, positive feedback on the progress we are making builds confidence and is one of the most important drivers of individual motivation in a work context.

Creating positive performance pressure through shared responsibility and accountability

Setting ambitious goals and standards is powerful, but the effect will be short-lived if there is no accountability. The goals will soon be forgotten or dismissed as meaningless wishful thinking. Reviewing our progress against our goals reconnects us with them, it brings them to life and it forces us to face up to where we are against them. The earlier example of Sport Wales illustrated how they translated their vision of 'every child hooked on sport for life' into measures through which they and their partners could review progress. Many worthwhile goals fail to have any sustained impact on the performance culture because of a failure by leaders to create accountability through frequent review mechanisms.

Using feedback and reviews to drive the speed of learning

Matthew Syed,[4] the former table-tennis champion turned journalist, in his groundbreaking book on this area, uses the aviation industry as a model of an effective approach to learning. He tells the story of United Airlines

Flight 173 that crashed due to the pilot's failure to notice they were running out of fuel. The pilot was focused on solving another issue, much less serious, with the landing gear.

Within 12 hours of the crash an investigation team had been appointed and was meeting, not to find who was to blame, but to learn from it. As they probed into the evidence they began to notice a pattern that had similarities with a number of previous accidents. In each case the investigators realised the crews were losing their perception of time as they became narrowly focused on solving a single issue. The second similarity they noticed was that the co-pilots or other crew members were not being assertive enough in voicing their concerns to the captain – their deference to the hierarchy was getting in the way of effective dialogue to inform correct decision-making.

Within weeks, the investigation report led to a new module of training for all airlines, focusing on what they called 'crew resource management'. This training led to a new approach of sharing responsibility amongst all crew on the flight deck for monitoring multiple factors during a critical incident. This training focused in particular on the human factors of getting captains to be better at listening, and encouraging other crew members to be more assertive.

Flight 173 was a traumatic incident in which ten people lost their lives, but the learning from it enabled a great leap forward in safety, almost certainly saving thousands more lives. There are a number of features that stand out from this example, which are common to other environments that are exceptional at learning.

1   The amount of energy and time committed to debriefing and reviews, and the speed with which they lead to new ways of working. Team reviews are a key feature of high-performing environments, whether it be elite sports teams like British Cycling, the Royal Marines or high-performing businesses like Pixar. John Lassiter, head of Pixar, surprises people when he reveals how poor the storylines of their movies are in the beginning. In his own words,

> the secret of Pixar's success is not our ability to come up with great stories at the outset – pretty much all of them suck to begin with. It's our process of peer reviews they go through and the continuous improvement this brings about over time.

2   The openness to learning in the culture and, in particular, the openness to learning from failure. Aviation, as an industry, recognises failure as an opportunity to improve. They know their current safety record is built on the rubble of past failures because they have an effective system and open culture that allows them to learn from these failures. Innovation nearly always starts with having a problem in mind that needs to be solved. When we try to ignore failure or do not take time to think about that problem, we allow the source and seed of learning to

die. This raises a critical distinction between accountability and blame. Accountability ensures that people are challenged to review their contribution to a result and learn from it. But the focus is on learning, not blame. It often helps to assume that there are likely to be multiple factors contributing to the result, and not just the actions of one individual. Fear of blame, on the other hand, shuts down learning, as people automatically look for causes outside of themselves. The implication here is that many leaders, in a positive intent to try and create a culture that is 'tough on poor performance', actually hurt the pace of continuous improvement.

3   The quality of feedback that individuals are given in their role, telling them how well they are doing at any point in time. We often make the assumption that experience leads to learning, but this is only true if we have feedback from which we can refine our approach. To illustrate this point, if you were to practise golf every day for 20 years, you would expect a certain level of mastery. But what if you practised in absolute darkness with no feedback on the quality of your shots? Research suggests there is no positive correlation between experience and capability where people have no way of assessing their performance.

One of the more subtle barriers to learning is a linear approach to strategy that is built on a false sense of certainty that we can design the perfect approach from the outset. Contrast this with a more open approach where you start with a number of operating assumptions, and seek to test them and evolve your strategy as you go along. This approach mimics nature's system of evolution, and is at the heart of the learning system in some of the most innovative environments in learning organisations such as Formula 1, 3M and WL Gore.

Use positive feedback and recognition to build confidence and reinforce motivation

Positive recognition for hard work, attitude and progress is one of the two greatest drivers of motivation in high-performing environments (the other driver being a motivating goal, covered earlier). People thrive on genuine and specific constructive feedback.

A final thought

One of my favourite quotes from Jim Collins (author of the bestselling book *Good to Great*) is that 'It takes no more energy to be great than it takes to be mediocre. It is simply a choice'.

Similarly, a colleague from Oxford University, Dr Terry Hill, summed up the underlying message of this chapter beautifully when he was reflecting on a day we had spent with Peter Keen, the first Performance Director of

UK Sport and founder of British Cycling's phenomenal performance programme. 'It strikes me' Terry said 'that these organisations just pay more attention to the environment they create than their competitors. They succeed because they take it more seriously'.

Decide today to make your performance culture a defining strength of your team or organisation. Make some notes in your own words on the insights you take from this chapter and commit to start putting them into action as soon as you can.

Three leadership lessons from the performance environment behind the New Zealand All Blacks – the world's most successful sporting organisation

No team, no brand, has so dominated a sport to the extent of the New Zealand All Blacks in rugby union. In 111 years of test match rugby, they have won 76% of their games. The closest win ratio to this from another rugby team is South Africa (60%) and the nearest national team in any sport is Brazil's football team (63%). The average winning margin in favour of the All Blacks is 25–12, twice as many points as their opposition.

But as well as being one of the finest examples of sustained high performance, this is also a case study of transformation. In the ten years up to and including the 2015 Rugby World Cup, at a time when many external factors have worked against them (fewer young people taking up rugby and many players leaving to play overseas), the All Blacks' win percentage has increased to over 90%. They have just celebrated ten years at the top of the world rankings, and they have not lost a game at their National Stadium in Auckland for 23 years.

Defying the odds

So how is it that a nation considerably smaller than Scotland, and with less than 25% of the registered players of either England or South Africa, can continue to outperform the rest of the world? Yes, their grass-roots structure produces a strong pool of talent from which to select, but this is only part of the story. The real secret of the All Blacks can be found in the performance environment that the coaches and senior players create around a player with potential from the moment they are spotted. The further step change in performance achieved by the current team of coaches and support staff over the last decade is a dramatic illustration of this point. They have been obsessed with a goal to create the best performance environment of any sports team in the world. Understanding the key characteristics of this environment, and what the leaders do to create it, offers powerful lessons for anyone who would like to recreate a little of their magic within their own organisation or team. This case study will take you inside the three pillars on which their performance culture is built:

1   Ambition and high standards.
2   Creating a culture of leadership and responsibility at all levels
3   Speed and effectiveness of learning.

Lesson 1. Ambition and high standards: the All Blacks set the bar higher than anyone else, and are always seeking to raise it further

If you analyse the way the All Blacks play, you may be surprised to notice that they don't do anything particularly different. They simply take the basic disciplines to an extraordinary level of skill and intensity. They pass and catch better than any other team. Their defence in terms of successful tackle percentage is the best, and they are the fittest team in the world.

Take their fitness as an example. It is not uncommon for the All Blacks to be behind with 20 minutes to go – Ireland, Argentina, Scotland and Wales have all been in a winning position in recent years. As the opposition begin to tire, the All Blacks will actually increase their intensity and frequently close out the match with two or three tries. Fitness and physical performance are critical to winning in rugby and theoretically any nation should be able to match them. Strength and conditioning techniques and science are openly understood, yet the All Blacks continue to be the fittest team without exception. Something in the environment drives players to hold themselves to higher standards – what is behind this motivation?

First and foremost, their motivation and drive are grounded in the legacy that was laid down in the team's early years. Losing just one international out of their first 15 test matches, and four of their first 30 between 1903 and 1924, set standards for future generations. Ritchie McCaw, the recently retired captain of the All Blacks who is regarded by many as perhaps the best ever player of the sport, reflects on the fear of letting down the jersey in his recent book by saying that the legacy of previous teams is 'more intimidating than any opposition'.[6]

Critically, it is not enough for the All Blacks to try and live up to the legacy. Each new generation of players is challenged by the culture and environment to add to it. In 2012, having finally regained the World Cup after 24 years of underperformance in the tournament, the coaches and senior players were worried about complacency setting in. Together they created a new ambition to try and become the most dominant team in the history of the game, by pushing their win percentage even higher and becoming the first nation to win back-to-back Rugby World Cups. Over this four-year period, they lost only three games, maintaining a win percentage of 93%; and in November 2015 they did indeed become the first team successfully to retain the World Cup. As we write this case study, a largely new team is holding a series of meetings in the off-season to start setting their goals around the legacy they want to leave.

Applications for business leadership

- Ambition is the lifeblood of every high performing culture. Engage people behind a goal to achieve something special and redefine standards in key areas of performance. Translate this to each individual by challenging them to commit to become the best in their world at what they do.
- Spend time reflecting on the examples of when you have been at your absolute best as a team or organisation, and use these examples as a basis for defining the set of values you want to live up to all the time. It's about learning from and being proud of the great performances that have got you to where you are today, while looking to add to the legacy.

Many organisations try and shape their culture through the creation of a set of values to guide the behaviour of their people. In too many cases this is a largely meaningless process that results in writing up a set of laudable qualities with which any organisation can identify. If, like the All Blacks, it is based on an in-depth examination of the qualities that underpin how people respond and take decisions under the most intense pressure, these stronger and more distinctive values will become a set of aspirational standards against which people can hold themselves accountable on a daily basis.

Lesson 2: Distributed leadership – push responsibility down to empower the organisation and grow capability to think and act as leaders

There are two basic approaches to leadership that an individual can take. The first, a directive approach, is where the leader sees himself/herself as the expert, with the role to give direction to his or her followers. The second, more indirect, approach sees the core role of a leader as being to create an environment that unlocks, makes full use of and develops the talent and potential of the people around them.

From the genesis of their culture on the 1905 tour of the UK, shared leadership responsibility within the team has always been a strong feature of the All Blacks. It is probably grounded in the fact that most of the original players were pioneering farmers who had chosen to leave the UK and make their own way in a new colony. When rugby became professional in the mid 1990s, the opportunities to develop these qualities of self-reliance and leadership outside of the sport were significantly diminished, and the culture started to suffer. Over the last decade, the current generation of coaches and players has sought to make this a defining strength again through a number of innovations that have now become standard practice in other international teams.

The leadership group is made up of seven players (four focused on on-field leadership, three on off-field leadership, and always including at least one younger player), and there is a lot of energy invested in defining the qualities they are looking for in the individuals who make up this group. Beyond the leadership group, every individual is given some leadership responsibility. There are strategy groups looking at attack and defence, other players are given responsibility for a key area of set play (the scrum or kick off for instance) and a different group of players will be asked to analyse video of each opposition team. The point is that every player is given leadership responsibility. From the moment they enter the environment it is made very clear that you are expected to act and behave as a leader. This expectation creates a culture of responsibility and accountability.

One example of this distributed leadership that also reinforces their stated value of a 'yes attitude' in action, was in the lead up to a mid-week game against Munster on a recent tour. The team found that the practise pitch that had been organised was far too small. The assumption was that this was a mistake (it was about half the size of a hockey pitch). Everyone paused to look at it, and you could just see what some of the management were thinking. Then Kevin Mealamu, neither the coach nor the captain, spoke up: 'Don't worry about it guys, we can make this work – just compact it up. Let's make it a great session'. It was a leadership moment, to which the response of many teams would have been to vent their frustration and waste an afternoon. Instead it was one of their best sessions of the week.

Applications for business leadership

- Ask yourself as a leader – 'Am I blocking or unlocking the talent around me?' How effective am I, and our organisation, on a scale of 1–5, at getting the best out of our talent? Here is what to do:
  - Give responsibility – give specific areas of leadership responsibility to a wide network of people from all levels of your team/organisation.
  - Lead with questions – actively seek out people's input and open up an on-going dialogue around the key questions at the heart of your strategy – e.g., how do we get more people engaged in the sport?

Lesson 3: Focus on improving the speed and effectiveness of learning

> Every great All Black has been dropped at some point on their way to becoming great; it's how you bounce back that counts.
>
> Dan Carter[7]

Perhaps the most impressive part of the All Blacks' culture is not that they are invincible – they do lose and they do have poor games. What is so impressive is how quickly they learn from these blips and recover.

The phenomenal performance of the current team is built on the rubble of one of their darkest periods. When Graham Henry became coach in 2004 he was surprised to find that a number of the players no longer enjoyed the All Blacks environment. Following a record loss to South Africa – their second loss in a row following a defeat the week before to Australia – Henry was dismayed that the response of the team was to get ridiculously drunk. On returning to New Zealand, he convened a two-day review with a selection of players he respected and his coaches. The purpose of the meeting was to speak honestly about what was wrong with the culture, and to figure out how they were going to make it a great environment again. From this meeting came a number of important innovations, including the leadership group mentioned above, and a much more rigorous and structured approach to reviews to ensure standards never slipped this far again.

The team now invests an enormous amount of energy in squeezing learning out of reviews and individual feedback. Win or lose, they aim to improve and learn from every game. Here is a flavour of their review process:

- The leadership group meets twice in the off-season to review the previous season.
- They debrief after each game, and after each practice session (albeit briefly).
- Every player is able to search a personalised video of the game by key words like 'missed tackles' or 'passes completed successfully' within two hours of a game finishing.

In the unlikely event that the All Blacks lose two games in a row, it will automatically trigger a review process – this is their key indicator that they need to take a deeper look at what they are doing and what needs to change. This happened again in 2008, but this time (unlike in 2004) they were able to put things right much more quickly.

One of the big areas they have worked on over the last four years is to improve their performance in Rugby World Cup knock-out matches. The key challenge was to review the effectiveness of their game plan during play, and change it as necessary. The need for this area of improvement arose out of their shock defeat to a supposedly weak France in the 2007 Rugby World Cup. Following the review of yet another failure at the tournament, players were trained in a mental model called OODA (Observe, Orientate, Decide and Act). 'Observe' is about analysing the effectiveness of their current strategy in light of what is actually happening, and 'Orientate' is about re-evaluating what they should do. Dan Carter used this mental strategy to help him think through a change in tactics in the semi-final of the 2015 Rugby World Cup against South Africa. Ma Nonu (another senior player) used it to inform a change in strategy at a critical point in the final, just as Australia seemed to be stealing the momentum. He spoke to Dan Carter about the need to be more aggressive, and a Carter kick started a recovery that led to 13 unanswered points.

Applications for business leadership

- How effective are you and your organisation at reviewing performance – corporate and personal?
- How much time do you spend reviewing your own performance? High performers in any field have a habit of reviewing their performance weekly or monthly.
- How open are you and others to learning from mistakes or issues?
- How skilled are you and other managers in your organisation at leading and facilitating collective reviews? A great indicator of our effectiveness in this area is how we respond to bad failures. Do we try and ignore them or explain them away with excuses (which can be very tempting)? Or do we throw ourselves into learning what we need to from them?

A final thought, summing up the most important lessons

- If you were to employ an ex-All Black in your team or as a non-executive director on your board – what would they implore you to do more of?
- Breathe more ambition into your culture – aim higher. Not in a negative 'push everyone harder' way, but in an inspirational way.
- Identify the people, the talent, who you feel have the potential to contribute a lot more than they currently are – and give them leadership responsibility to transform a key aspect of your performance.
- Commit to making learning a defining strength of your culture – both from your best examples and your most difficult failures. Train your managers in coaching and debrief skills for facilitating these review discussions.

John Bull
Genesis Consultant and Associate, 2003 to 2010

Postscript: the All Blacks and the Focus Framework

It is useful to contemplate what the Focus Framework might have looked like to the All Blacks, had they prepared such a document. John Bull and I considered this question and illustrate in Figure 20.1 the vision of success

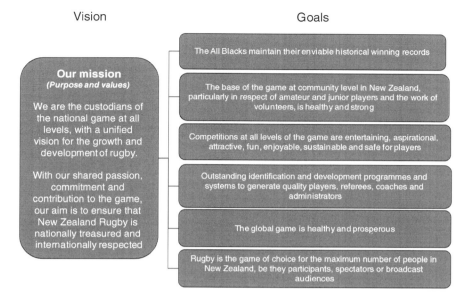

Figure: 20.1 The All Blacks strategy framework. Created by Alistair Gray and John Bull, adapted from annual reports. Source: New Zealand Rugby (2017).

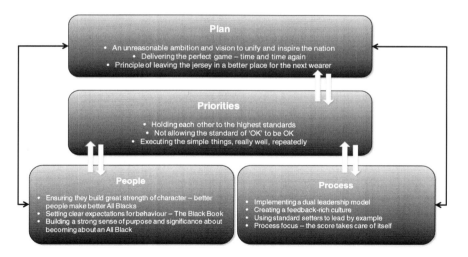

Figure: 20.2 The All Blacks performance framework. © *Powerhouse*, Brian MacNeice and James Bowen (2016).

The Scoreboard

Figure 20.3 The All Blacks scoreboard. Figure created by Alistair Gray from The All Blacks Annual Report (2015).

that would have been the centre of their strategic planning, based on the research and interviews carried out by John in preparation for writing the first section of this chapter.

In their recent book *Powerhouse*,[8] Brian MacNeice and James Bowen suggest the performance framework in Figure 20.2 applied to the All Blacks.

In addition to planning, the All Blacks have a unique approach to deploying a scoreboard to underpin their quest for performance. Their selected key performance indicators represent the basis for their annual report to the sport and other stakeholders. Figure 20.3 is an example from their 2015 Annual Report.

The overall 'score' for the year is 80 out of 100. This not only represents an open and honest assessment of the organisation's performance; it represents the basis for performance-related pay across the organisation. Every employee of the All Blacks has an agreed level of performance-related pay, e.g., 15% of salary. The actual payment in this year would be 80% of 15, i.e., 12%. Such an approach guarantees the interest of all employees, from the receptionist in the Wellington HQ with the trophy cabinet behind her desk to the CEO Steve Tew. Everyone in the New Zealand All Blacks has a stake in the organisation's success.

**New Zealand
All Blacks**

- **Breaking the rules: setting new, higher standards**

  - High standards are an explicit part of the culture and a source of pride for the team. New entrants into the environment are told to expect to be challenged and to be okay with that.
  - As a team, they define what success depends on and then challenge themselves to continually raise their game in each of these areas.
  - Every individual, player or coach, is challenged to try and become the best in the world at what they do.
  - They measure and hold themselves accountable against these high standards – e.g., players get feedback on the percentage of their tackles that are dominant and disrupt the opposition's game.

- **Developing leaders at all levels in the organisation**

  - From the moment an individual enters the environment, it is made clear they are expected to think and act as a leader. Every player is given leadership responsibility for something. They have a leadership team of seven players from within the squad, but other players are given responsibility for looking at a particular area of performance or reviewing videos of an opposition team.
  - A key part of their leadership culture is encouraging candid sharing of views and constructive disagreement. Individuals are encouraged to push through the natural politeness we all bring into group interactions.
  - Everyone is engaged in their quest for performance.

- **Creating a culture of rapid learning**

  - The All Blacks are not invincible – they do lose and they do have poor games. A key secret of their sustained success is their humility in facing up to the fact when they've been poor and the systematic way in which they go about learning from these blips.
  - Win or lose, they put enormous energy into learning from every game, every tour and every season. The goal is to constantly move forward – to 'leave the jersey in a better place than you found it'. The mechanism is focused debriefs and reviews.
  - They mistrust their success. They are constantly on guard against the danger of complacency. Some of their most ruthless reviews are when they have had a big win, because they have learned from the past that a surprise loss often follows such a win.

Notes

1 Thomas John Watson Jr (14 January 1914–31 December 1993) was an American businessman, political figure and philanthropist. He was the second president of IBM (1952–1971), the 11th national president of the Boy Scouts of America (1964–1968), and the 16th United States Ambassador to the Soviet Union (1979–1981). He received many honours during his lifetime, including being awarded the Presidential Medal of Freedom by Lyndon B. Johnson in 1964. Watson was called 'the greatest capitalist in history' and one of '100 most influential people of the 20th century'.

2 *A Business and its Beliefs*, Thomas J. Watson Jr, McGraw Hill, 1964.

3 'Little Town of Champions', Nick Ashdown, *Atlantic Magazine*, March 2014.

4 *Black Box Thinking*, Matthew Syed, John Murray, 2015.

5 *Good to Great*, James Collins, Random House, 2001.

6 *The Real McCaw: The Autobiography*, Richie McCaw, Aurum Press, 2015.

7 Dan Carter – highest points scorer in the history of rugby union and World Player of the Year in 2005, 2012 and 2015. He was repeatedly dropped from the team in 2013 and 2014.

8 For more detail on the research into high-performance organisations please refer to *Powerhouse: An Insider Account in the World's Top Performing Organizations*, James Bowen and Brian MacNeice, Kogan Page, October 2016.

21 All you need is love

Introduction

Over our years in Genesis we have had the opportunity to work closely with sporting organisations in the Republic of Ireland and Northern Ireland. Ireland is a small nation, similar to Scotland in size, and Northern Ireland is the smallest province of the United Kingdom. Unlike Scotland, Ireland has a strong foundation in Gaelic games – hurling, Gaelic football and camogie. These community-based sports have historically produced successful athletes across a number of sports ranging from boxing to rugby union, football and golf. In recent years Padraig Harrington, Rory McIlroy, Graeme McDowall and Darren Clark have all won the British Open and other major golf championships. Paul McGinlay, after a successful professional playing career, performed admirably as captain of the European team that defeated the US team at Hazeltine, Minnesota, in the Ryder Cup in 2016. How can athletes and professionals from a small nation (Ireland) and an even smaller province (Northern Ireland) achieve this level of success in major tournaments competing against the best in the world and from the largest and wealthiest nations in the world?

In preparing for the first part of this chapter I chose to examine the reasons behind the success of Rory McIlroy and Graeme McDowall. I was fortunate to have access to both golfers and their families, as well as to others who had helped them along the way. In times of highly professional sports science, sports medicine and other services, it is refreshing to report that the result of these conversations brought a surprising outcome and set of reasons for their success.

The FIFA World Cup in 2002 in Japan and Korea had yet to start, but the island of Ireland was devastated by the early homecoming of Roy Keane, Ireland's captain, from the training camp in Saipan. Keane had had a major fall-out with Mick McCarthy, the Ireland manager, and had returned home before a ball had been kicked in the tournament. Genesis was asked by the Irish Sports Council to report on the facts of the matter and make recommendations as to how the Football Association of Ireland might better support their international teams and players in the future. Some surprising (and unpublished) findings are contained in the second part of the chapter.

Faith, hope and love – three secrets behind Northern Ireland's major winners

1   **Faith** [feiθ] *noun*, have faith

    Complete trust or confidence in someone or something.

2   **Hope** [heop] *noun*, verb, hoped, hop·ing

    Feeling of expectation and desire for a particular thing to happen or be true.

3   **Love** [lʌv] *noun*, verb, loved, lov·ing

    Feeling of warm personal attachment or deep affection, as for a parent, child or friend.

How can a relatively small region like Northern Ireland (population 1.8m) possibly produce a succession of major winners in golf, at a time when the competitive intensity at the top of the world game is at its greatest in living memory? The towns of Portrush (population 7,000) and Holywood (population 12,000) are two small communities in Northern Ireland, yet both have given birth to, and nurtured, major champions in golf.

Portrush is the home of Fred Daly (1947 Open Champion), Graeme McDowell (2010 US Open Champion, ten European Tour wins, three PGA wins, four Ryder Cups), and is now the home of Darren Clarke (2011 Open Champion, 21 International tournament wins, five Ryder Cups). Just down the road from Belfast in Northern Ireland is Holywood, the home of Rory McIlroy, ranked World Number 1 for 95 weeks, a four-time major winner at age 28 and winner of the order of merit on both sides of the Atlantic in 2012. He has also won 13 times on the US PGA Tour and nine times in other international competitions, representing Europe four times in the Ryder Cup.

Image 21.1 Irish golf major winners: McDowell, McIlroy and Clarke with Harrington and McGinlay. © Getty Images.

How can these relatively isolated communities produce such globally competitive athletes? What special ingredients existed in Northern Ireland that enabled these champions to grow their talent from ages 8–18 to create the platform for their success at the pinnacle of the world class in their sport? Are there lessons that can enhance performance plans and talent development strategies?

In recent years I have been privileged to gain a unique insight into what is behind the success achieved by Rory McIlroy and Graeme McDowell. Through interviews and conversations with the golfers, their families and close associates, it is clear that theirs is a story of faith, hope and love, rather than of science or system, and more about people than process.

In the beginning my aim was to test and validate the questions posed by three core principles in Malcolm Gladwell's book *Outliers*:[1]

1   Was the 10,000-hour standard achieved between 8 and 18 years?
2   Were 'best vs best' opportunities given to the players to sharpen their competitive abilities?
3   Do 'troubles' such as those endured in Northern Ireland have any influence on the development of talent?

I hope this chapter is of interest and a challenge to those designing high performance programmes in sport and business, and at the same time gives credibility to a different emphasis when nurturing talent capable of performing in the world class.

Rory and Graeme – two different players; two different routes to the top

Born ten years apart, Rory McIlroy and Graeme McDowell took different routes to the summit of golf, yet, as I will argue, there are considerable similarities in the environment they experienced that enabled them to build and hone the skills that would eventually lead to success in the majors.

Rory McIlroy's rise to the top of the world in five years from turning professional at 17 was meteoric. Sport, and golf in particular, were clearly ingredients in his DNA. His uncle on his mother's side had played Gaelic football for Armagh, and Gerry, his father, and uncles (on his father's side) were all low handicap golfers. Rory's early interest began in the pram when accompanying his parents to the club. Starting left-handed with plastic clubs and barely out of nappies, the videos of him chipping balls into the washing machine are now the stuff of legend.

McIlroy showed an early interest in Nick Faldo (winner of six Majors, nine US PGA Tour and 30 European Tour wins, 11 Ryder Cups). Rory's talent was clear from an early age and, at age eight, with the brashness of youth, he played with his elders (aged 12–13) at Holywood Golf Club. At the age of ten he entered the Callaway Junior World Championships in 1999, finishing 8th, before winning the event the following year.

At that point Rory's parents, Gerry and Rosie, clearly recognised his talent and potential. Both worked extra hours in their jobs to support the increasing cost of Rory's participation in the game, Gerry taking a bar job at Holywood Golf Club. In their words they used 'all their efforts' to ensure the future success of their only child. Rory responded and the mutual respect between prodigy and parents is obvious, as is the respect shown by Holywood Golf Club to its young talents. The love and respect shown by the club to their younger members is an example for all to follow. There is not an issue of access to the course for young people at Hollywood. The club has 200 junior members of whom 30% are girls. It is open all day, every day, for its youth and the young McIlroy took full advantage of the support and access he was afforded. Winning the Ulster Boys at age 13 and the Irish Boys the next year were further signs of his outrageous talent. In 2005 (aged 16) he won the West of Ireland and Irish Amateur Close Championships.

Naturally gifted at soccer and cricket as well as golf, his talent was recognised and nurtured at Holywood. Gerry asked Michael Bannon to coach Rory at age eight and he has remained at his side ever since as a constant source of advice, turning full-time only in 2012. Not for Bannon the aspiration to become the next swing guru or publish the 'reveal all' blockbuster. The Bangor Golf Club professional is more than happy to play a retiring supportive role in one of Northern Ireland's greatest sporting adventures.

He was professional at Holywood when he first came across Rory. 'Rory owns his own swing. It's not Michael Bannon's' he once said in an interview. He went on:

> I am not just a technical coach. I coach him on having a positive attitude and talk to him about course management. Once I'd watched Rory play, I wouldn't want to watch anyone else hit a ball, his swing is so good.

McIlroy played little junior golf, preferring to test himself against his elders. Winning the Irish Youth Championships (aged 15) – a tournament for Under 21 players with participants from other nations – did little to convince him to spend successive years defending junior titles. Driving back to Holywood with Gerry after winning the event he vowed never to play in the Irish Youth Championships again.

At 16 Rory McIlroy was probably given the best bit of advice he ever received, after his father Gerry had the usual parental interview with the headmaster of Sullivan Upper School. The school motto, which is printed on all the school blazers, is 'Lamh Foisdineach An Uachtar', which is Irish for 'with the gentle hand foremost'. With his gentle hand foremost, the headmaster John Stevenson advised Gerry that 'Rory is never going to be a doctor or a dentist' and proposed that Rory finish school a year early to pursue his passion with golf and get on the road to fulfil his potential. Rory joined Team Faldo, winning an event in Hong Kong. The second piece of good advice came when he was offered a place on the University of East Tennessee State's golf programme. McIlroy duly signed a letter of intent but, on the advice of Sam Torrance (21 European Tour wins, eight Ryder Cups), never crossed the Atlantic. Torrance believed he was too good technically and that he would benefit more from turning professional sooner rather than later. So, at the age of 17, Northern Ireland's outrageous talent played for GB and Ireland in the Walker Cup at the Royal County Down Golf Club in Northern Ireland and then launched himself, as a fledgling professional, on the European Tour to take it and the world of golf by storm.

In his ensuing years as a professional he has enjoyed more elation, and has endured as much gut-wrenching frustration and failure, as many of his peers experience in a lifetime. Above all, his ability to learn from these experiences has propelled him to the top of the golfing world and has armed him for the battle to stay there.

Graeme McDowell's route to the top was longer, more measured, planned and incremental. It was in 2010, at the age of 31, that the dominoes fell for him in a big way, as he became the first European US Open winner since Tony Jacklin in 1970. Golf does not appear to have been in the DNA of the McDowell family. Graeme's father Kenny was predominantly a weekend golfer, and although Graeme and his brother grew up being coached golf by their 'uncle' Uel Loughery, he was not a blood relative.

Graeme was 'OK' at most sports but was not outstanding at any. He grew up playing golf at his local club, Rathmore in Portrush, which had a thriving junior golf scene in which his father and uncle were actively involved. Around 30–40 young players regularly played in tournaments and were notably encouraged by their seniors, with enjoyment of the game paramount. Graeme's father was the junior golf convenor at the club so the game of golf was very much part of the family's lives growing up. Portrush is also home to one of the greatest championship golf courses in the world and a former venue for the Open Championship.[2] Players do the hard yards learning how to play in harsh weather and a tough economic environment.

By the age of 12 McDowell was playing golf at least 20 hours a week and it was clear that he had a deep interest in and enthusiasm for the sport. His first coach was his uncle Uel and he credits his success to the great grounding and stable introduction to the game his uncle gave him. His uncle was not a PGA golf coach or player, but he was a good all round golfer with a great eye for the game and a good swing. He kept things simple for McDowell as a youngster. McDowell acknowledges that his uncle Uel is without doubt his unsung hero.

McDowell was very inquisitive as a youngster, always searching and wanting to learn more. He says himself that if an outsider had looked at him and his brother when they were young they probably would have said his brother was more likely to become a major winner. Just as McIlroy chose Nick Faldo as his role model, McDowell watched video footage of Steve Elkington (one major, ten US PGA Tour wins) to model his swing, However, Graeme's desire to better himself and his own competitive spirit have clearly contributed to his success today. He always had a great attitude to hard work and practice and, in his own words, he has been a grinder.

While growing up, McDowell did not see himself as a winner of majors. He constantly set himself achievable targets and goals and worked towards them. He would pick a particular golfer he admired and work towards bettering himself to that standard. He would continually repeat that process throughout his formative years.

The late Severiano Ballesteros was another very influential role model who inspired McDowell, as he did many others of his generation. McDowell was fixated on statistics, hungry for information on swing and technique and often videoed leading players to emulate their swing technique.

McDowell won six amateur titles during his early career. He spent a year at Queen's University, Belfast, and played for the University golf team, but he realised their goals were more social than competitive so, when he was offered the chance to go to the US on a scholarship at the University of Alabama-Birmingham, he grabbed it with both hands. He credits his university days within the collegiate system in the US as a major factor in the transformation of his golf. Graeme believes the environment of golf in the States is hugely beneficial for the development of the game in youngsters. Golf is very much geared to families and kids and, although some exclusivity still exists, there is generally more accessibility for young people to play than in the UK and Ireland.

The competitive scene in the US is also much more intense than in the UK and Ireland. In Ireland/Ulster there would have been no more than ten tournaments per season, but in the US he would play at least double that number. Coming up against top (best vs best) competition helped to raise his golf to a different level.

McDowell was a leading NCAA player and had a better average stroke/round (69) in his last NCAA season than Tiger Woods (Stanford). High standards were set on and off the course.

There was also no tolerance for slippage in academic studies. He achieved the following at the University of Alabama in Birmingham:

- Awarded Fred Haskins Award for top golfer in the US in 2002.
- 2002 Golfstat award recipient (given to golfer with lowest average).
- Two-time Ping All-American (2002 and 2001).
- Two-time Conference USA Player of the Year (2002 and 2001).
- Nine tournament victories and 24 top-ten finishes.

'I came here as a pretty average amateur golfer and left ready to set out on the pro ranks', McDowell said on a recent return visit to Birmingham, acknowledging his growth on coach Alan Kaufman's team. 'I was very lucky to end up at a college like UAB with a golf programme like this'. When he returned after university in the States, his golf had completely changed. He won five amateur titles that year and it was obvious that his game had been transformed to a new level.

The love of the family and club

There is no doubt that the environment in which both golfers grew up played a huge part in their success. Golf was very much part of a stable family life and was an interest the young players shared and enjoyed with their family at home and with the extended family in the club. This, coupled with their inquisitive nature and desire to better themselves, and the encouragement and support of their parents, coaches and mentors, laid the solid foundations for future golf successes.

It is clear that the environment created in their clubs' junior sections together with the family involvement in the club and the coaching provided by family and friends were key factors contributing to their interest and enjoyment of the game, which ultimately led them to work harder at improving themselves. The focus on early-years coaching was on learning rather than instruction on the technical aspects of golf. They were both given time and space to learn to play at their own pace.

Where McIlroy differs from McDowell is in his early ambition to join the pro ranks and be the best in the world. Common to both is a belief that success comes from sustained hard work and both clearly exemplify a healthy practice ethic; values that are still held dear in Celtic society. As a youth McIlroy preferred the practice ground to the game-boy console, while McDowell preferred the golf course to the attractions of Kellys nightclub complex in Portrush.

Interestingly, Northern Ireland's 'troubles' had little impact on the development of both players. (Gladwell (see above) indicated that challenging environments might be the breeding ground of champions.) McDowell is from a mixed Protestant/Catholic family and McIlroy's parents are both Catholic by denomination. Both are comfortable to be Irish and British and thankfully most of their fans fall in line. Both came from strong communities in Holywood and Portrush where the sense of community was far stronger than any sectarian interest, and neither was exposed directly to significant violence, though McIlroy's great uncle (Joe) lost his life to Ulster Volunteer Force terrorists in 1972. Portrush had few incidents and in many ways was isolated from the atrocities in the likes of Belfast, Strabane and Londonderry.

Irish Golf – national governing body love

Many world-class athletes often comment that they have succeeded despite the performance system put in place by their sport. In Irish Golf we find something completely different. It can be argued that Ireland's provincial system and the approach to allowing young talent to develop played an important part in the development of McIlroy and McDowell. Both players felt that the Irish Golf set-up was generally better and more competitive than that in Ulster. Starting to compete within Ulster, then Ireland, helped both McIlroy and McDowell develop their game to the next stage.

Irish sport is quite different. Most young people are introduced to sport and physical activity through Gaelic games – football and hurling – which are an integral part of the local community. Where the likes of Scotland and England struggle to find identity for their golfers in a structure made up of 15 areas and 50 counties, respectively, the four-province set-up delivers many benefits in terms of focus, scale, pride in performance and teamwork – all key ingredients underpinning high performance. It works in rugby union where three of the four provincial teams regularly compete in the final stages of the Heineken Cup. Young rugby players and other athletes grow up aspiring to play for Ulster, Munster, Leinster or Connaught. There is inter-pro competition from an early age (best vs best) and also teams representing Ireland go abroad to compete against other national age-group squads. This is clearly the case in the island of Ireland at national and provincial level.

Any good performance system in sport must have five main attributes:

1   A growth engine that continuously produces sufficient players and coaches to populate the talent pathway.
2   Structured, simple, systematic yet sensitive performance system that holds features such as '10,000 hours' and 'best vs best' as two essential platforms in the early teenage years.
3   Infrastructure of people (coaches, mentors and administrators) as well as facilities and processes with real capability to nurture and grow talent, keeping young players' emotional tanks full as they journey along the pathway.
4   Supportive, demanding and respectful culture among the key stakeholders that honours the game and participants as individuals as well as celebrating performance.
5   Strong feeling of 'team' even in individual sports that fosters pride and values being part of a team.

In its own way Irish Golf has developed (in my view not necessarily as a result of deliberate strategy or action) a world-class system that enables young golfers with ambition, positive attitude towards hard work and self-belief to achieve their goals.

Northern Ireland – loves to keep you grounded

When both McIlroy and McDowell return to Northern Ireland, people treat them the same way as when they were young, with love and respect. McDowell recollected:

They give me a good slap if I need one. It's great. It puts life in perspective for me. Private jets and frickin' desert islands and playing for millions of dollars. I go back home and see the real world. My buddies tell me what they think. It keeps me grounded. It's what real friends are like.

These are views endorsed by Dame Mary Peters, Northern Ireland's Olympic Pentathlon champion in 1972.

Northern Ireland is well insulated, for a variety of reasons, from the frenzied, headline-grabbing tabloid-driven world of much of the United Kingdom's media. Talented sports men and women can be developed there, ready for the world class, in a caring and supportive environment. Winning is redefined as being the 'best you can be'. Northern Ireland's isolation has cost it economically and socially, yet paradoxically it has enabled it to create an environment where limited numbers of talented athletes, musicians and academics (to name a few) can flourish. Values, established by their forefathers, remain strong.

There is undoubtedly something in the history, culture and attitudes of people in Northern Ireland, and in communities and clubs like those in Portrush and in Holywood, that influenced the development of both golfers and contributed hugely to their ultimate success.

So what?

In trying adequately to draw conclusions from a unique and privileged insight into two great golfers and their development through their early years, I found myself challenging part of the accepted wisdom around the development of performance athletes. In an era where hard science, medicine and analysis is often preferred to soft feelings and emotions, process promoted over people, and facts valued over opinion, I believe there are special ingredients that deserve greater emphasis over the driven and focused attention to data and detail.

McIlroy and McDowell more than adequately repaid the faith and hope their parents, their communities and clubs had in them. Too often, talented youngsters are driven from their sport by overzealous parents and coaches trying to achieve their unfulfilled hopes and ambitions for themselves through their children. The faith, hope and love – tough love at times – as shown to Rory McIlroy and Graeme McDowell during their early formative years undoubtedly made a difference. This shines through in a number of critical areas:

- Support and encouragement to inspire and sustain them during at least 10,000 hours of purposeful practice between the ages of 8–18 – delivered by family, community and clubs.
- Part of a talent development system, relatively unique to Ireland, that provided a calendar of events and opportunities for players to play

Image 21.2 The author with Graeme McDowell at Kingsbarns. ©Alistair Gray.

'best vs best' as well as valuing the importance of the 'team' playing for their province and country.

- The culture that challenged and supported them to succeed while at the same time respecting their need to learn to play, avoiding the hard instructive technical input of skill, technique, science and medicine until demanded by the athlete as part of their development.
- Encouragement to adopt values and mutual respect, at the same time honouring the great game of golf.
- Regular inputs from coaches and mentors to keep their emotional tank full at the low points as well as after the victories in the majors.
- Leaders of performance management systems will draw a number of conclusions and lessons from the development of Rory McIlroy and Graeme McDowell. They would do well to replicate the environment described above that continues to deliver outstanding performers, now driven by real role models and champions. They would be wise to challenge the hard:soft balance of their talent and performance development programmes to make sure there is room for faith, hope and love to flourish.

'And now these three remain: faith, hope and love. But the greatest of these is love.'[3]

Acknowledgements

I would like to acknowledge the support and encouragement given to me during the course of the research. This especially includes the golfers, their fathers Gerry McIlroy and Kenny McDowell, Ian Webb, the former Chair of the General Committee of the R&A, Duncan Weir and Peter Dawson at the R&A for their encouragement, and Joe Macnamara and Pat Finn of the Irish Golfing Union. Their agents also enabled communication to take place. I would also like to acknowledge the contribution from Dr Stephen Martin of the Olympic Council of Ireland and Gary Keegan of the Irish Institute of Sport for the work they are doing to transform high performance sport in Ireland, with faith, hope and love.

In addition Sheila (my wife), Judy and Rick at the Winning Scotland Foundation and Dame Mary Peters helped me get this over the line. They are all great talents in their own right, reared and nurtured in Northern Ireland.

The Genesis Report – The FAI, Roy Keane, the 2002 FIFA World Cup and all that

Without doubt, one of the greatest influences on my consulting career in sport was the review Genesis carried out of the Football Association of Ireland (FAI) in 2002, following Roy Keane's spectacular removal from the squad during their pre-World Cup warm-up in Saipan. Not only did the review provide a game-changing solution for the FAI, it created a template for the modernisation of many other sporting organisations. It also provided a real insight into Roy Keane, the man and consummate professional footballer. Here is the story as never told before.

In the beginning

Before 1988, Ireland's football team had failed to qualify for a single major international tournament. Sometimes they came close but more frequently they did not. The result was always the same – hope followed by disappointment. Success, when it came, was particularly sweet. In 1986 Jack Charlton, one of England's 'heroes of 1966' was appointed by the FAI to manage the Irish team. Charlton's infamous 'granny rule' imported a number of outstanding players and the team broke tradition by qualifying for the 1988 European Championships. They did not make it past the first round but that mattered little. As if qualification itself had not been enough, the boys in green, an unlikely bunch of upstarts who would always 'give it a lash' as the 1990 song went, without really hoping to win a trophy, secured an unlikely 1–0 victory over England in the first match and made national dreams come true.

'Giving it a lash' characterised Irish football during the Charlton era and the fans enjoyed it for what it was. The progress of the national football team prompted a badly needed upsurge in national hope and pride after a particularly grim decade. Ireland's qualification for the 1990 FIFA World Cup was even better still. Thousands of Irish fans travelled to Italy to support the team, which finished eighth, still led by Jack Charlton. A small financial loss was made, but this best-ever finish created immortality around the team management and their particular style. This was reinforced by a good performance in the 1994 World Cup in the USA. The European Championships two years later brought this remarkable and successful streak to an end. Charlton stepped down as manager to be replaced by Mick McCarthy, his former captain. Under McCarthy Ireland did not qualify for the 1998 FIFA World Cup (France) or the 1996 and 2000 European Nations Cup Finals, losing in play-offs for all those competitions.

With his job on the line, it was a relieved manager who watched his team win a World Cup play-off match against Iran to go through to the 2002 finals in Japan and Korea. Expectations were high, not least for captain Roy Keane – the Irish 'player of the tournament' at the 1994 World Cup. Roy Keane first played for Ireland in 1991. Since then he won 55 caps and played in all the major campaigns. He is the third highest capped player in Ireland's history, and was appointed Captain by Mick McCarthy soon after the latter's appointment as Manager. As much as his skill, it was Keane's tactical sense and will to win that characterised his performance – something recognised by his appointment by Sir Alex Ferguson as Manchester United's Captain (from 1997 to 2005). That relentless drive and unsmiling approach was often at odds with the spirit of the Irish team that had relished its status as underdogs and 'good lads'.

Qualification for the 2002 World Cup was McCarthy's first successful campaign since rebuilding the team after 1996. His overall record since makes him, next to Jack Charlton, Ireland's most successful team manager with a win ratio of 43% in 68 matches.

A week before Ireland's first fixture, the team arrived at the Pacific island of Saipan. The idea was to relax after a long season, acclimatise to the region and perhaps engage in a little light training. Unfortunately no one had told the captain. Even gentle exercises turned out to be difficult when it emerged that the training kit and balls were still making their way in skips from Ireland (carrier documents provided evidence they left Dublin three days late). The quality of the training pitch was also unsuitable and potentially dangerous (in Keane's view). Previously critical of the FAI's treatment of players (relative to officials of the FAI), Keane was furious at the 'shocking' facilities in Saipan, which were 'worse than a car park'. He lambasted the lack of ambition, drive and professionalism in the FAI, and crucially in his squad colleagues. The attitude, he said, was one of 'We're the Irish team, it's a laugh and a joke. We shouldn't expect too much'.

Matters came to a head at a team meeting. McCarthy openly criticised Keane over his behaviour and a recently published article in the Irish Sunday press. Keane responded with an expletive-filled tirade, telling McCarthy 'You were a crap player, you are a crap manager'. McCarthy sent him home and, at a stroke, Ireland lost its captain and a world-class player before a ball was kicked in the World Cup.

The issue divided Ireland, and its national and sports media, right down the middle. Even the Taoiseach Bertie Ahern felt compelled to intervene say-ing the nation would 'sleep happier in their beds' if Keane was recalled to the squad. Ronan Fanning wrote in the *Irish Independent* that 'the essence of the differences between Roy Keane and Mick McCarthy is the conflict between ability and authority'. It was a clash of cultures between new and old Ireland.

> We are going home unbeaten . . .
>
> Mick McCarthy in *The Gaffers* by Paul Howard
> (O'Brien Press, 2002)

> We have got to start giving ourselves a bit more credit. We have good players. You get a bit sick and tired of the whole 'Well the Irish will have a good time, no matter the result'.
>
> Roy Keane in *Keane: The Autobiography*
> (Penguin, 2011)

> Soon everyone was singing again – it's what we do best!
>
> Supporters' Association

After the finals (in which a depleted Ireland performed miracles to finish 12th, losing on penalties to Spain in the quarter finals), the Irish Sports Council (supported by the FAI) commissioned Maurice J. O'Connell, a former Governor of the Bank of Ireland, to lead the review and Genesis, with our specialism in reviews of this nature, were asked to undertake the detailed investigation.[4]

Our report concurred with much, if not all, of Keane's critique, though not with the same linguistic panache! McCarthy resigned as Ireland man-ager six months after Saipan. Two subsequent coaches failed to qualify for the finals of any major international tournament.

While Ireland's management and preparation of squads had improved, other countries had moved faster as the business/standard of soccer had grown. Historically, like many nations, the Board of Management of the FAI had frequently been preoccupied with ticketing and accreditation issues, over the factors affecting the performance of their national team on the field. Importantly, no executive or officer of the FAI addressed the clearly deteriorating relationship between Keane and McCarthy during qualifying and preparation for the tournament of their lives.

Our approach

Our approach was to review the performance of the FAI with the key stakeholders in Ireland's international football. In addition, we reviewed and analysed substantial amounts of data including reports on previous tournaments, minutes of Officers and Board of Management meetings and the financial accounts of the FAI and the last three World Cup tournaments. We interviewed/contacted over 100 people in the course of the review including team management, coaches, FAI management, team support staff, voluntary leaders, executives at the Irish Sports Council, Department of Tourism, Culture and Sport, journalists/media correspondents in Ireland, 23 members of the 2002 World Cup squad (and their club managers, many of whom were in England) and, of course, Roy Keane.

In addition, we undertook a comparator analysis of the preparation and planning carried out by three other football nations who we believed to be comparable with Ireland – Sweden, Denmark and Belgium. We also reviewed the preparations carried out by England for the 2002 World Cup and Scotland for the 1998 World Cup. Finally, we examined the approach to managing performance and preparing for major tournaments/fixtures of the following organisations – New Zealand All Blacks, Netherlands Hockey, Rugby Football League, Irish Rugby Football Union.

Winds of change

In 1990, when Ireland played in the World Cup in Italy, the English Premiership did not exist. Twelve years on, it was one of the best and most competitive leagues in the world, with the European Champions League raising this level of competition even higher. The sophistication of demand for services and status for players were at an all-time high level.

The viability of football in Ireland and the FAI as an organisation was closely linked to the success or otherwise of its senior international team, rather than the growth of the game in Ireland. The first half of the 1990s was hugely successful, coinciding with the emergence of the Celtic Tiger economy and a new Irish generation of global citizens. Since then, the competition for Ireland in the second tier of football nations had intensified, with the rapid development of the Asian and African national teams and the emergence of former Soviet bloc nations. Developments such as the migration of international team management, elite coach development and the explosion of satellite television had levelled the playing field in terms of the tactics deployed by international teams.

Many emerging nations were now challenging the likes of Ireland for that second-tier status in international football. The quality and preparation of many so-called smaller nations had improved dramatically over the previous five–ten years. Biggest or oldest had no divine right to be best. Most of the top 20 national associations had professionalised their approaches to the development and management of international squads, developing structured pathways through to the top, often with academy/institute structures supporting the athletes. Football as an international sport was booming after 2000, in terms of growth in participation, broadcast media coverage and sponsorship, and associated commercial opportunities.

Irish players

Irish international players have frequently played their football in England or Scotland, with a few mercenaries seeking their fortunes in foreign leagues, e.g., Liam Brady and Gerry Armstrong. Many became legends in leading clubs, e.g., Johnny Giles (Leeds), Gerry Daly (Manchester United), Niall Quinn (Arsenal, Manchester City, Sunderland), Packie Bonner (Celtic), David O'Leary (Arsenal).

Young players with potential tended to leave Ireland at 15–16 years of age to join a Premiership/First Division club in the UK. (Roy Keane was in many ways an exception, playing under an FAS apprenticeship until he was 18 before joining Nottingham Forest.) They participated in excellent competition in the top English/Scottish Premierships, as well as receiving athlete services of the highest quality in strength and conditioning, technical training, massage, nutrition and other athlete services, as well as the perks of the job.

This experience raised expectations among players (athletes) for a much higher standard of service/support than 10–12 years before. Roy Keane was at the extreme of these expectations:

- Captain and player with Manchester United – in the European Champions League.
- Pupil of Brian Clough and Sir Alex Ferguson.
- Perfectionist, often to the extreme, making him appear more obsessive and intimidating than he was.

Like most national associations, the FAI did not provide additional athlete services directly, other than those associated with the squad's preparation, such as medical and physiotherapy provision, travel and logistics support and security. Liaison with the players' clubs was usually through the team management and was found to be satisfactory in terms of communication, demands on players and condition of players when they returned to their clubs. Most club managers interviewed perceived the FAI as no better or worse than other national associations.

Irish squads performed above expectations in the decade after the FIFA World Cup in Italy. Most people felt this was due to:

- Strong morale and team spirit – almost like a club.
- A feeling of 'we have nothing to lose'.

- A spirit of fun in the squad and 'get on with it' when in adversity.
- A social relationship with one other and with the fans.

Ireland's national economic performance had been exceptional leading up to the millennium. It was unlikely that this position would continue. In line with most other developed economies, public-sector funding for football would be less available than in the past, or to a lesser extent than previous levels of grant. Consequently, the FAI was very dependent on the success of its international teams for financial viability.

Our conclusions

The Irish football team, in achieving a ranking of 13th in the world, consolidated through their performance (12th place) in the FIFA 2002 World Cup, achieved a credible performance, delivered through outstanding performance by a squad in good physical and psychological condition throughout the tournament, coupled with effective planning by the team management for the preparation for the tournament.

The commercial objective of a surplus of €1m was achieved. The ticketing arrangements in particular were considerably better and more professional than in 1994.

The much publicised incidents relating to the late delivery of skips and the quality of the training pitch in Saipan had little technical impact on the performance of the squad in the World Cup. They did result in Ireland's Captain and arguably best player going home and were the final straw in a self-fulfilling prophecy. The seeds of discontent and anger that culminated in the Captain's withdrawal from the squad had been sown many years before and had been well nurtured over an extended period of time. These warning signals had been totally ignored.

Many observers believed the potential of the Irish squad was not fully realised. We concurred with this view. The main factors that may have led to even better performance included more positive action to recover the breakdown in the relationship between Roy Keane, the FAI team management and the FAI, and an improved approach to and management of performance in the FAI.

The overall planning by the FAI was naïve and inadequate for an event the size and scale of the 2002 World Cup. The fact that the eventual outcome was positive (on the field and commercially) was more a matter of luck than effective management practice.

The size, scale and possible impact of participating in the 2002 World Cup were underestimated. Advice given to strengthen the management of external relations was ignored. Any comments on planning excluded that carried out by the team management and a number of very capable individuals, both groups working almost in isolation from the FAI. The inexperienced working group was too informal in its set-up and operation and had little control over the outcome. Elsewhere, outcomes were not planned and no written plans or budgets were prepared (with no formal review processes practised), either before or after the World Cup.

The minutes of the board of management reveal that more consideration was given to issues relating to complimentary tickets or accreditation of officials than to assuring the performance of the team or the commercial outcome for the FAI. No official structure and processes were set up by the FAI to prepare for the 2002 FIFA World Cup. No formal learning was captured from previous major tournaments, or deployed to benefit the planning for this tournament.

The additional workload for the World Cup was allocated to existing staff and contractors – no advanced consideration was given to their existing commitments and the potential impact on staff performance. In general there was not a culture of discipline in the management of the FAI, with most basic management disciplines non-existent. For example:

- No job descriptions existed with performance indicators for day-to-day/normal work, far less for the World Cup.
- The team management, where contracts existed, did not have mutually supporting objectives. None of these focused on achieving an overall performance goal for Ireland or the FAI.
- No plans, minutes or agreed actions were documented. Meetings were held irregularly with few basic disciplines such as agendas or minutes.

There were lots of words written about the FAI, its team and players, before and during the 2002 World Cup. There was, however, little effective communication with stakeholders. There had probably been more written about the incidents in Saipan and Japan than about many major international conflicts between nations.

The management of the crises that emerged before and during the 2002 World Cup left a lot to be desired. This was not new in Irish football, and the whole management of PR/media had not been addressed despite repeated crises over the previous ten years. The experience and expertise of personnel dealing with external relations, especially during the events in Saipan, were inadequate for a major global sporting event. The potential for a media crisis around the FAI was high.

The FAI did not practise performance management (on or off the field), as an organisation, other than that delivered by the senior team and their direct management. The development plan 'One Game; One Association' did not address this in any depth. There was no intention so to do. There were no strategies or plans to develop key areas such as sports science and medicine. Although the senior team manager appeared to have had responsibility for the development of football, there was little evidence to show that this was actually carried out. Given the clear talent emerging from Ireland, this represented an opportunity lost.

In comparison with other nations the following key points emerged:

- Country B – full debriefing carried out with players, management and staff; excellent liaison between senior players and coaching staff.
- Country C – planning by HQ staff and head coach; debriefing planned for later in 2002.
- Country D – had a World Cup Committee, integrating team and technical management; debriefing and reporting to the World Cup Committee.
- The FA (England) began planning in March 2001, with a full-time project manager. No journalists or officials were allowed to travel with the team. All travel was direct, by charter flight.
- The scope and complexity of the activity carried out by the FAI had grown significantly over the preceding decade. Little had changed in the governance and management of the Association over that time.
- Management capacity in the FAI was inadequate given its current, far less projected, workload.
- The structure and practices of the FAI did not enable key staff to perform – any empowerment was effectively by abandonment. The voluntary leadership and professional management structures of the FAI were designed to govern football domestically, and did not address the needs of the international team competing, as it did, at the highest level in the world. They did not provide effective leadership, challenge or support for:
  - High performance sport in football.
  - €10m business (nearer €20m in World Cup years).

They failed even to recognise good organisational practice employed elsewhere in sport, including in Ireland.

At the heart of the matter

Two aspects stood out as fatal flaws in the FAI's organisation. First, its organisation was a total mess, with the General Secretary in the middle attempting to spin plates that regularly went out of control. The General Secretary is illustrated in Figure 21.1 as a 'black hole' – effectively what the position was, potentially reporting to 80 voluntary leaders and responsible for 20 staff, all making demands on a manager endeavouring to carry out 'mission impossible'. The organisation was not capable of being managed effectively even by the most experienced corporate executive. Well-intentioned management had little chance of working in an organisation that was out of control, with few processes or plans to take them forward to an improved level of performance.

Second, the breakdown in the relationship between Mick McCarthy and Roy Keane was an accident waiting to happen, with no one in the

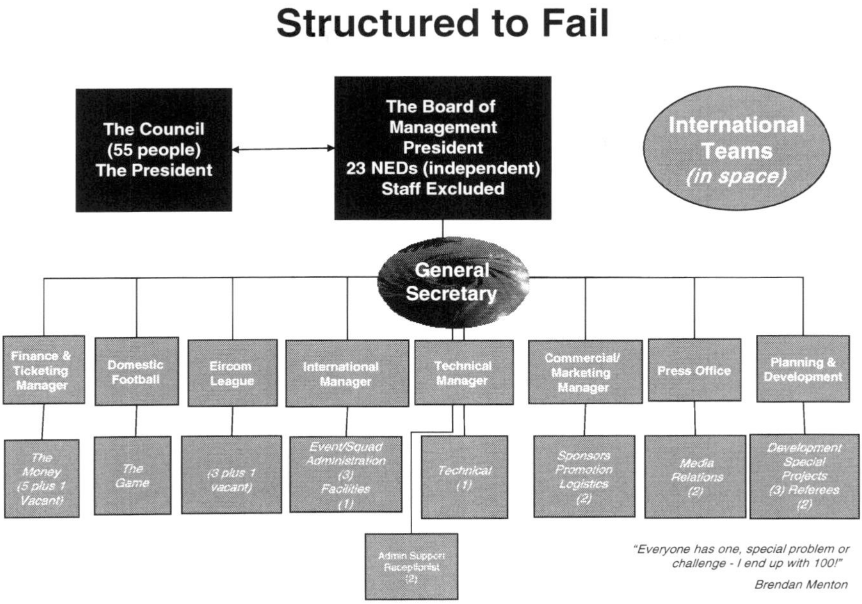

Structured to Fail

Figure 21.1 FAI organisation structure (2002). Diagram created by Alistair Gray.
Source: FAI

organisation bringing both together at any time to resolve their differences. The potential for the relationship breaking down had been there since 1990 in the US and had been exacerbated on a number of occasions since then. No one in the FAI took responsibility to ensure that these issues were addressed.

McCarthy and Keane were two extremely powerful individuals in their own different ways, both with strong personalities. Arguably both had been given too much freedom in the past. Both had perceptions of the FAI that were not positive. Neither really recognised or appeared prepared to recognise the other's needs. They both seemed to operate through agents and authors. Someone from the FAI needed to take responsibility for achieving a good outcome, as it was unlikely the individuals were capable of such a result on their own.

Our recommendations

In presenting our report we challenged the FAI to make one of the biggest choices in their history since their formation in 1921, which was the result of another dispute with the Irish Football Association (now Northern Ireland's Football Association).

The choice was stark and simple. In each case the FAI was required to accept the need for change in the way they did things. They could make a

- The ineffective leadership of the FAI was one of the biggest issues in the breakdown of the relationship between Mick and Roy.
- The sub-plots, which had been festering for some time, had gone unrecognised.

INEFFECTIVE LEADERSHIP

Mick
The Manager

Roy
The Captain

Perceptions of the FAI
Power
Agents and authors
Too much latitude
No recognition of need
Demise of Manchester United in 2001–2002
FAI's management of media

Son of Jack
Captain
Marvellous

Son of Alex
Captain
Fabulous

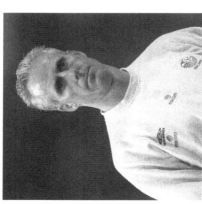

Figure 21.2 Lack of leadership: the big issue. Figure created by Alistair Gray (2002).

Image 21.3 Mick McCarthy. © SportsFile / *The Irish Times* (2002).

Image 21.4 Roy Keane. © SportsFile / *The Irish Times* (2002).

number of modest changes in areas such as travel arrangements, PR/media and the way they treated their players. In addition, they might tighten up management practices, processes and procedures, as well as improving the management and logistics for major tournaments.

But these modest changes would *not* improve their competitive capability or performance in the tough and more competitive world of football, far less resolve the major issues that emerged during the 2002 World Cup. They would also *not* achieve the 'new beginning' or step change desired by almost everyone we consulted during the review.

Alternatively, the FAI could:

- Accept the need for transformation in the way it managed football and the performance of its international teams, as well as recognising the importance of its players as the key and most important stakeholders.
- Recognise that to compete successfully and exploit the growth in football as a sport and business, it needed to modernise and professionalise the leadership and management of the sport.
- Set objectives for success over the following eight years that would result in taking football to a leading position in Irish sport and the FAI to a position as a modern performing organisation, admired throughout the nation and the football world.
- Achieve a period of sustained stability in which to implement the changes proposed and other initiatives already planned. Football needed to be seen as an integrated, inclusive sport.

A new beginning was open to the FAI as a result of the crises in 2002, if it wished to grasp that opportunity. Any revolution needs to be worked out aggressively with the full support of the sport's leaders. We were pleased to receive the FAI's commitment to the latter option.

Our recommendations were grouped in three time phases – the following three months, the next six months, the next year – and can be summarised as follows.

Immediate actions (following three months)

- The FAI must accept openly that there was a need for greater professionalism and that they embraced enthusiastically the need for change.
- They must acknowledge openly the importance of providing for their players and coaches as the first priority and achieve a higher level of attention to detail in planning and managing their arrangements.
- A number of changes were outlined to policies and practices regarding the travel and other arrangements for international fixtures and major tournaments, e.g.:

- o   Charter flights for the team and team management group (business-class-equivalent seating).
- o   Officials and executives travelling with the team should be restricted to members of the international performance group and leading FAI executives – press/media should not travel with the team, or stay in the same hotel.
- o   Crisis/contingency plans should be prepared for major tournaments.
- o   Management and communication with the media should be taken to a higher level of professionalism.
- o   Planning for major events should be undertaken formally by a working group set up for that purpose, with a senior executive leading and an official of the FAI as sponsor of the group.
- o   Greater consideration should be given to the dietary needs of the team prior to the international fixtures and the provision of specialist sports medicine services.

- •   The FAI needed to take action in the following specific areas:

  - o   Finalise and integrate contracts of team management and other key personnel and establish job descriptions with key results areas and performance targets for all key staff.
  - o   Establish a personal performance review process, including career and personal development, backed up by suitable reward and recognition systems.
  - o   Develop and implement a communications strategy and plan, both externally and internally, to establish good practice.
  - o   Develop strategies and plans that build the skills, capabilities and enthusiasm of the FAI's staff.

Developing effective management and functions (next six months)

- •   The FAI needed to make a number of senior appointments to lead and deliver the change to secure sustained performance in international football and to exploit the opportunities that provided. These included the appointment of:

  - o   Chief executive of the FAI, replacing the previous position of general secretary.
  - o   Director of performance – not to oversee the team management but to ensure the integrated challenge and support for Ireland's international teams and the performance pathway.
  - o   Director of football operations – to manage the domestic game in Ireland.

○ Director of marketing and communications – to lead the professionalisation of the Association's relations with the external world and increase its marketing effectiveness.

○ Director of finance and administration – to manage the increased financial resources of the FAI and other corporate service functions in the FAI.

In addition to the appointments we recommended:

- The FAI should prepare an international performance plan for the following four-eight years to include:

  ○ Setting up an international performance group, chaired by a director of the FAI, which:
  ○ Assures the support of the Association behind their international team management and their players;
  ○ Integrates all aspects of support for performance, in Ireland and the UK (the Premiership and Nationwide 1 clubs);
  ○ Manages the planning and logistics for international teams and events;
  ○ Assures the challenge and support to those teams, their managers and players; and
  ○ Plans for football's place in the Irish Institute of Sport.
  ○ Development and implementation of a high performance strategy that supports the development of young footballers with potential in Ireland, building on the recent 'One Game; One Association' strategy.

- The FAI must embrace the need for a culture of discipline and planning within the ethos that was unique and special to Ireland. This should include, for their key functions and teams:

  ○ Setting objectives and making plans.
  ○ Reviewing these plans regularly to secure successful outcomes.
  ○ Developing the skills of their people.

- The FAI should continue their excellent work of developing coaching in Ireland, working with the NCTC (National Coaching and Training Centre in Limerick) to address especially the recruitment and development of future high performance coaches. This should include:

  ○ Use of current senior coaches to coach others.
  ○ The development of a world class coaching module.
  ○ Designing pathways for coaches and targeting international players for induction into coach education.

For the long-term (planned over the following 12 months)

- A new beginning was open to the sport, if it wished to grasp that opportunity. Any revolution needs to be worked out aggressively with the full support of the leaders of the sport. To achieve this there must be:

  o Greater engagement and development of the key stakeholders in the sport.
  o Football in Ireland should undertake a development initiative to simplify and intensify its operations, in time to present a four-year development plan to its members and the Irish Sports Council. All parties in football in Ireland must be brought to the party.
  o The focus for development should be tightened along the lines of the regional developments planned in 'One Game; One Association' with the League of Ireland clubs fully behind these efforts.

- Football in Ireland needed to determine its goals with an accompanying strategy for the sport over the following eight–ten years (say to the 2010 World Cup). These goals should be aspirational and include:

  o International performance.
  o Football as a sport in Ireland – building on 'One Game; One Association'.

- If the FAI was serious about competing in the world class of 21st-century football, it needed to modernise and professionalise to reflect the needs of 21st-century sport. The key areas to address were:

  o Development of effective voluntary leadership, professional management and structures.
  o Reform of the existing board of management and council, providing leadership capable of leading and directing a €10m-plus business in a world-class sport.

The FAI badly needed a period of sustained stability in which to implement these and other changes. It had to be seen as an integrated and inclusive sport. Our recommendations were likely to involve additional financial investment, which we believed could be covered out of their existing and planned revenues.

Support for implementation

Following review of our report and presentation of findings to the board of management of the FAI, the sport discussed and agreed our recommendations. At that point the other key stakeholders in the FAI were engaged in discussion of the summary findings and recommendations, to secure their buy-in to the future implementation of the emerging plan. The Irish Sports Council was especially supportive during the early years of change.

Real progress by 2005

In 2004 John Delaney, the Treasurer of the FAI in 2002, was appointed Chief Executive, a post he holds to this day. Under his leadership, and that of a reformed board of directors, major changes were achieved quickly. In 2005 we were asked by Delaney to review the progress made since the publication of our report at the end of 2002. We were pleased to conclude:

- Substantial modernisation had taken place within the FAI.
- A more professional ethos existed within the organisation.
- There was now a 'culture of discipline' in place that was not evident in 2002.
- A robust and fit-for-purpose organisation structure had been developed to serve the organisation, including the key appointments contained in our recommendations.
- There was real evidence of considerable and positive changes within the operating environment of the FAI.

Image 21.5 John Delaney, CEO FAI, UEFA Council Member. © FAI.

Since then, the FAI has enjoyed a period of relative stability. By 2006 they had implemented many of the recommendations of the Genesis Report. In 2005 they set themselves a number of challenging objectives, most of which were delivered. These included:

* Relocation of their headquarters to Abbotstown – SportsCampus Ireland.
* 2005, technical development strategy and plan objectives secured.
* Planning application submitted for the National Stadium.
* Qualification for the 2006 World Cup secured.
* Eircom merger established with enthusiasm.
* Performance review process linked to corporate objectives for key staff.
* Training plans linked to development needs, performance reviews and corporate objectives.
* International performance group established.
* 2005 operating plan delivered.

The only one missed was qualification for the 2006 FIFA World Cup. They have moved even further forward and were rewarded in 2012 by an accolade from UEFA as a model organisation for a football association. A long-term strategic plan is in place for soccer in Ireland that has underpinned its development as a sport and business. John Delaney was elected to the Executive of UEFA at their Congress in 2017.

The final word goes to Roy Keane

Clearly the success or failure of our review was dependent on the perceived balance and thoroughness of our consultation and associated research. In particular we needed to ensure the contribution of Roy Keane to our consultation. Initial signs were not promising. In the autumn of 2002 Keane was due to undergo surgery on his troublesome groin and also had a court appearance on an assault charge (subsequently dropped) following his infamous and subsequently career-ending tackle on Alf-Inge Håland, in retaliation for a previous challenge four seasons previously. Sir Alex Ferguson did not feel it would be in his player/captain's interest to be dragged through the sorry Saipan incident again.

While sympathising with that view, I decided to pursue other less formal routes and came up trumps having persuaded (with some difficulty) Eamon Dunphy (Keane's agent and long-term critic of the FAI) to undergo an interview. Dunphy was clearly under the impression that

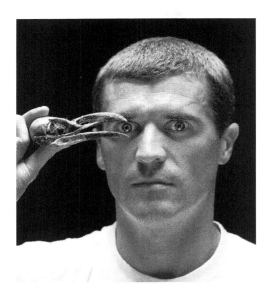

Image 21.6 Roy Keane: a unique personality. © Murdo MacLeod.

we were the FAI's 'hired assassins'. We easily demonstrated that this was not the case and his position and mood improved to the extent that he recommended Roy Keane would make himself available for inter- view. So, with less than ten days to go before we were due to report to Maurice O'Connell, I met Roy Keane at his local hotel in Altringham, near Manchester. Our two-hour conversation covered many topics and he was completely open and, in my view, honest in his thoughts about events in Saipan and also the wider aspects of performance management in football and the FAI.

In general his views reflected those of others, with the added personal insight given freely by a pretty unique personality and a player who grew up under the stewardship of two of the greatest managers in the game – Brian Clough and Sir Alex Ferguson. Keane only understands winning and the commitment and hard work required to get to the top of his profession. His journey to the top had been a hard one and his answers contained few frills and his punches did not miss.

At the end of the interview I was privileged to receive insight from him that he, as far as I am aware, has never published, even in his autobiography. He reflected that 'everyone will have learned lessons from all of this'. The con- versation took the following route, as I dug deep into my reserves of courage.

Me: 'I am sure you are right Roy. What were yours?'
Keane: rocking back in his chair laughing, 'I left myself open for that, didn't I!'
Me: 'Yes and please answer my question'.
Keane: 'I should never have agreed to go (to the World Cup)'.

He then proceeded to explain why. He had had the worst season of his life with Manchester United, winning nothing. He had struggled with injuries for most of the season and kept going with pain-killing injections. On top of this a number of disciplinary matters such as the Håland affair had punctuated his season. He was pressurised by friends and family to go – and not let Ireland down. At the same time he knew in himself that he would last at best two–three games at that intensity before breaking down completely.

He was disappointed with the response of McCarthy to his pleas and requests to improve the preparation of the squad – he had invited him to his home at the start of the qualifying campaign. Subsequent events in matches showed few lessons had been learned. His relations with management and players were strained and often misunderstood, e.g., his no-show at Niall Quinn's testimonial (remember his injury comments). When he turned up at Dublin Airport to be greeted by the Taoiseach, memories of the 1994 World Cup US trip came flooding back. It would take little to send him home.

And so he came home. His homeland split down the middle between those who branded him a traitor who had let down his national team and the Irish nation, and those who branded him a hero and a saint for exposing the failure of the FAI to support its national football team. Inevitably readers will draw their own conclusions. The first section in this, the final chapter, is titled 'All you need is love'. If there was one thing that was missing from the FAI, its officers and players it was love. That is the note on which this story (and case study) should end.

Postscript

The year 2005 saw the publication of *We Declare* by Richard Aldous, who was Head of Archives at University College Dublin, and Niamh Puirséil, a historian of modern Ireland. The book summarises the documents that proved landmarks in the history of Ireland. They range from St Patrick's Confession, the Proclamation of the Irish Republic (1916), the Constitution of Ireland, the Belfast (Good Friday) Agreement – through to the Genesis Report on the FAI (2002).

Taken together these documents tell the story of Ireland from St Patrick – via Purnell, Pearse and de Valera – to Roy Keane.[5]

FAI

- **Broke the rules; challenged existing paradigms**

  - Established a chief executive to replace the general secretary role.
  - Changed the role of the all-embracing Football Development (Technical) Department.
  - Invested in performance management, with a clear strategy and goals, behind an inspiring vision of success. Appointed a performance director.
  - The board and council dramatically changed – board numbers were reduced from 25 to the 'First XI', all with responsibilities to champion key functions of the organisation with executives.

- **They worked it out themselves**

  - Faced reality as it was in 2002 with consistent under-performance as an organisation, lurching from crisis to crisis.
  - Engaged effectively with the clubs and secured support for the recommendations in the Genesis Report.
  - Secured support from key stakeholders, e.g., Irish Sports Council and UEFA.

- **Planned for and achieved a step-change in performance**

  - Prepared four-year strategic plans with goals and outcomes.
  - Key areas like Eircom (now Airtricity) league reviewed along with youth football, amateur football, schools football.
  - New strategies for performance and women's football.
  - Increased focus on diversity.
  - Commended by UEFA for the changes they had made.
  - Committed to being a key partner in building the Aviva stadium.

- **Changed organisational performance**

  - Restructured existing and recruited new staff in line with the Genesis Report and professionalised the organisation of major events, internationals and national finals at all age groups.
  - Executives paired with board members to ensure few conflicts.

- **Leaders at all levels in the organisation championed the new way**

  - John Delaney elected a Vice-President of UEFA in 2017.
  - Strong executive team reporting to John Delaney as CEO. Regular board and executive meetings, well prepared and planned.
  - Used consultants, contractors and advisers, not as strategists or planners but to lead and facilitate the process of change.

Notes

1 *Outliers: The Story of Success*, Malcolm Gladwell, Allen Lane, 2008.
2 Portrush has been named by the R&A as the venue for the 149th Open Championship.
3 Gospel according to St Paul: Letter to the Corinthians; Chapter 13, verse 13.
4 My wife Sheila, herself a World Class Adviser to UK Sport, and John Bull undertook the assignment with me.
5 *We Declare: Landmark Documents in Ireland's History*, Richard Aldous and Niamh Puirséil, Quercus, First Edition, 2008.

Appendices

Appendix 1

Checklist 1: Strategy audit: creating a new beginning
Checklist 2: Process for developing divergent scenarios
Checklist 3: Assessing the state of purpose in a team or organisation
Checklist 4: Assessing the innovativeness of your organisation
Checklist 5: Evaluating a strategy or strategic option
Checklist 6: Cluster-based strategy
Checklist 7: Making mergers work: the identity audit
Checklist 8: National Governing Body of sport: organisation performance
Checklist 9: High performance sport
Checklist 10: Good to great (in sport)
Checklist 11: Building and sustaining a high performance culture
Checklist 12: De-briefing performance

Checklist 1
Strategy audit
Creating a new beginning

Introduction

Creating the future is both more challenging and rewarding than playing catch up. The goal is not to benchmark or wallow in the complacency of the apparent 'best practice' of our own small world, but to develop an independent point of view about tomorrow's opportunities and how best to exploit them.

Frequently in business, well-conceived and designed strategies and plans fail to be implemented successfully, despite the elegance of their theory. Successful implementation is not about the headlong rush of the corporate elite backed up by the resources of corporate planning or a cohort of consultants. It is about people with the necessary skills, capabilities and commitment achieving real (profitable) success through the careful deployment of resources in strategically important areas.

To be effective, any strategy must:

- Be based on sound principles that have stood the test of time.
- Provide a compelling direction.
- Promote relative strengths and exploit any opportunities provided by the external environment.
- Encourage people to strive for excellence by implementing initiatives to lift performance in areas of strategic priority.
- Build in people at all levels superior shared values, commitment and motivation to that of competitors.

With an increase in pressure to deliver immediate performance, it can be easy to lose perspective on the long-term direction of a company. No matter how lean and fit an organisation becomes, to achieve sustained success it still needs a brain.

The key challenge facing corporate leaders today is to develop a competitive and compelling vision of the future, based on well-founded insight into tomorrow's markets.

Future success is about making a difference to customers by exceeding their wildest expectations and reaching into the future to create unimagined products and services. It is also about making a difference in the lives of employees by creating excitement, enjoyment and fun in the pursuit of ambitious aspirations. This is achieved through the provision of hope after re-structuring or re-engineering, and providing opportunities for people to flourish.

Finally, it is about creating a new competitive space; generating new wealth and building an enterprise that will outlast one's own career.

New beginnings

When starting any journey it is important to know where you are now. The following questions will enable you to understand where you are now. They will help you test where your strengths and weaknesses are, both in terms of understanding your markets and competitive positioning but also in terms of your capability to make change happen.

The audit is not meant to be an exact science – it will require judgement based on your own perceptions. The checklist below is at a summary level to simply give you pointers as to where you believe the business is positioned. More detailed questioning can then be developed in each of the 14 sections.

Foundation

Strategic analysis	Vulnerable	Open to question	Industry average	Good	Excellent
Issues of change	Vulnerable	Open to question	Industry average	Good	Excellent
Strategic principles	Vulnerable	Open to question	Industry average	Good	Excellent
Competitive advantage	Vulnerable	Open to question	Industry average	Good	Excellent

Strategy development

Vision	Non-existent or totally internal	Some customer orientation	Addresses customers and values	Clearly stated customer orientation and values	Totally reflects customer orientation and values
Strategic goals	Non-existent	Confused	Poorly expressed	Some strategic goals	Clear strategic goals
Leadership and influence	Little investment in capability	Some understanding of their capability to influence	Developing capability in leading and influencing change	Capability and developing experience	Confident leaders who know how to influence change
Operational objectives	Non-existent	Confused	Poorly expressed	Some objectives	Clear objectives
Plans	Non-existent	Confused	Poorly expressed	Some plans	Well-defined plans

Implementation

Resources/ milestones	No detailed plans in place	Very few plans in place	Some plans in place	Most plans in place	Full detailed plans in place
Organisation and people	No detailed plans in place	Very few plans in place	Some plans in place	Most plans in place	Full detailed plans in place
Performance focus	No challenge to existing performance	Very little challenge	Some challenge but poor process	Performance challenged but variable process	Constant challenge and well-honed process
Innovation	Not innovative	Poor at innovation	Some innovation	Quite a lot of innovation	Very innovative
Learning	No learning	Very little learning	Some learning, no knowledge transfer	Learning focus and some knowledge transfer	Constant learning process with knowledge transfer

Checklist 2
Process for developing divergent scenarios

The key to developing divergent scenarios is to carry out the process with a team of people made up from staff in the organisation, other external representatives of stakeholders or other informed parties. There is always room for a 'wild card' or remarkable person who may add a completely different insight and creativity.

The problem with most forecasting is that any variable or risk metric tends to be in the range of +/− 10–15%. How would that have prevented Cisco losing more than half their revenues in 2001 after corporate America treasurers stopped buying information hardware, or anyone forecasting the impact of 9/11 on industries such as insurance and tourism?

The basic process for developing and engaging in scenario thinking is outlined below:

- Scenario development:
    - Creating the alternative futures.

- Strategic conversations:
    - Engagement.
    - Knowledge input.
    - Understanding.
    - Insight.

- Better decisions about the future:
    - Stronger strategic options.
    - Greater flexibility.
    - Improved ownership.

The key steps along the way, in a suggested two-day process, are as follows.

Preparation

Prepare a position paper on the key future trends. For example, the main trends that have emerged over the last ten years include:

- Polarisation of socio-economic groups:

  o Polarisation of economies.
  o Growing, more mobile, world population and the role of the cities.
  o Rise of global warming and increasing natural disasters.
  o Impact of the internet and technology.
  o Increasing role of the banks – new role post 2008.
  o New roles for the public sector – locally, nationally and internationally.
  o Threat of terrorism (how quickly IS emerged).

Ask participants to contact two–three people they admire who they believe will have a view on the future. Get them to seek an interview with these people and ask them their forecast for the world over the next five–ten years.

Prepare the venue – big wide spaces with walls to write on and lots of self-adhesive flip charts and pens.

Day 1 – to boldly go

1 Right at the beginning – carry out the safety briefing for this flight into the future. It must include guidance to:

  a Leave your baggage at check in – all the limiting assumptions.
  b Unfasten your seat belts – you are not here representing anyone or any organisation – feel free to move around.
  c No headphones please – share your music and great ideas and insight.
  d Mobile phones *off* please – they will interfere with the navigation of this flight.
  e Look, listen, feel.

2 Review the external environment and list out the trends expected in society, technology, the economy, wider competitive environment, politics and legislation – nationally and internationally. The position paper will inform this conversation.

3 Evaluate these trends and decide on the five most important and five most potentially impactful. These will form the basis of your development of axes.

4 Develop your focal question – what would be the one question you would like an oracle to answer? Frame this from consideration of the competitive environment and the issues/opportunities facing your organisation, e.g., 'Where should our business invest to be globally competitive when China overtakes the US as an economy?' 'Should Company X invest $200m in developing sales of Product Y in the Far East markets?'

5 Form a number of sets of axes that are orthogonal (not related) to each other – for example, 'growth of the internet' with 'trends in health care'.

6   Select the pair of axes that best addresses the focal question.
7   Develop the outline scenarios and, in pairs or larger numbers, work on the story lines overnight. Describe what would be going on if this scenario unfolded five–ten years out. A useful trigger might be to write letters to a colleague from that point in the future describing what happened that led to the scenario. The other stimulus to creativity is to think of newspaper headlines that would appear in the scenario.

Day 2 – vision and action

1   Develop each scenario into bullet-point stories:

- What would be going on? Who would be the winners/losers?
- What is the vision of success in the scenario?
- What strategies would lead to the good outcome?
- To what extent would the strategy work in other scenarios?
- Consider alternative strategies?

2   Feedback the scenarios and potential outcomes/strategies to the wider team.
3   Discuss the most likely scenario – not the one you most like or would wish to transpire but the one most likely to appear from your review of the external environment.
4   Consider the strategy that leads to a good outcome in the most likely scenario.
5   Are there strategies from other scenarios that would strengthen the strategy in the most likely scenario without losing focus? They may help to reduce risk.
6   Develop the integrated strategy and associated actions that need to be taken as well as the metrics to monitor the evolution and emergence of the scenarios.

Then go to the pub!

Checklist 3
Assessing the state of purpose in a team or organisation

Question areas to use to survey and assess the state of an organisation's purpose:

1 Think about a time when you were asked to perform a task that you couldn't see any purpose in? How motivated and engaged were you in the task?
2 Imagine if even half of your people had a clear and meaningful purpose. How would your organisation be different? How would it be performing?
3 What is the purpose of your organisation/team in 15 words or less?

  - To what end do we exist?
  - What would happen, or not happen, if we did not exist?
  - If we were setting up from scratch, how would we justify our experience?

4 What is significant and important to me about this purpose? If you don't care, why should the people you lead?
5 What would your people say if you asked them what the purpose of the organisation is? Do they know?
6 What is the purpose of your role relative to the organisation's purpose?
7 What about the purpose of each of the roles in your organisation?
8 How often do you talk about purpose?
9 How much effort are you currently putting in to fuelling both drivers of the performance engine (alignment/achievement and engagement/enjoyment)?
10 How could you create more purposeful leadership for the future?
11 What is your personal leadership purpose? How will you tap into this for energy, resilience and motivation?

Checklist 4
Assessing the innovativeness of your organisation

Below you will find an excellent checklist to assess the innovativeness of your organisation. You can illustrate the scores on a 'spider' diagram to indicate the areas of strength and lack of capability (from 1 = not at all to 7 = all the time). An example diagram is included at the end of the checklist (Figure CL4.1).

Company culture

10A	Culture and change							
10A1	All employees share and contribute towards achievement of vision/mission.	1	2	3	4	5	6	7
10A2	Before we make changes in our product or service we always consider the likely effect on our customers.	1	2	3	4	5	6	7
10A3	The business culture promotes continuous improvement in overall quality.	1	2	3	4	5	6	7
10A4	Our latest products or services are perceived to be almost identical, technically, to those of our nearest competitor.	1	2	3	4	5	6	7

10B	Core business							
10B1	We have a clearly defined core business and manage it effectively.	1	2	3	4	5	6	7
10B2	We are able to sacrifice profit in the short term to achieve growth in market share.	1	2	3	4	5	6	7

10C	New ideas							
10C1	Change is encouraged, accepted and facilitated in this business.	1	2	3	4	5	6	7
10C2	New ideas are approved and progressed quickly.	1	2	3	4	5	6	7

10D	Atmosphere							
10D1	Our management never have sufficient uninterrupted time to think constructively or creatively.	1	2	3	4	5	6	7
10D2	Team spirit is a strong characteristic of this company. We support each other.	1	2	3	4	5	6	7

Employees

11A	Management competence/policies							
11A1	Our average manager fears and resists change.	1	2	3	4	5	6	7
11A2	We see creativity as a major priority in the selection of personnel.	1	2	3	4	5	6	7
11A3	All employees have job descriptions.	1	2	3	4	5	6	7

11B	Training							
11B1	We have a training programme driven by our business needs.	1	2	3	4	5	6	7
11B2	Our training programmes are assessed to ensure their effectiveness.	1	2	3	4	5	6	7
11B3	Where external standards exist, e.g., NVQs, we have linked training targets to them.	1	2	3	4	5	6	7

11C	Performance and rewards							
11C1	My performance targets are set by my boss without consultation with me.	1	2	3	4	5	6	7
11C2	My job is a challenge.	1	2	3	4	5	6	7

Communications and organisation

12A	Communications – style							
12A1	The senior managers regularly spend time on the shop floor and in the offices.	1	2	3	4	5	6	7
12A2	In this company we 'shoot the messenger' who brings bad news.	1	2	3	4	5	6	7

12B	Communications – effectiveness							
12B1	We have no formal or recognisable briefing or listening systems.	1	2	3	4	5	6	7

(continued)

(continued)

12B	Communications – effectiveness							
12B2	Communication is three-way – upwards, downwards and sideways.	1	2	3	4	5	6	7
12B3	The Chief Executive sets aside time for frequent and regular meetings for briefing and feedback.	1	2	3	4	5	6	7
12B4	The marketing and 'R&D' departments work together in the conception of new products and services.	1	2	3	4	5	6	7

12C	Organisation – structure							
12C1	Our organisational structure reflects the objectives and needs of the business.	1	2	3	4	5	6	7
12C2	We use broad-based teams to develop new products, services, processes and procedures.	1	2	3	4	5	6	7
12C3	New products and services are discussed with all concerned at the earliest possible stage.	1	2	3	4	5	6	7

12D	Flexibility							
12D1	When major change is needed, we retrain people to help them in their new roles.	1	2	3	4	5	6	7
12D2	Our organisational structure and attitudes inhibit change.	1	2	3	4	5	6	7

Quality

13A	Quality culture							
13A1	Our business has an explicit quality strategy.	1	2	3	4	5	6	7
13A2	The business culture promotes continuous improvement in overall quality.	1	2	3	4	5	6	7
13A3	Individuals feel personally responsible for their quality of work.	1	2	3	4	5	6	7

13B	Product quality							
13B1	Our product quality is perceived by our customers to be higher than that of our competitors.	1	2	3	4	5	6	7
13B2	We receive systematic feedback from consumers and customers on product quality.	1	2	3	4	5	6	7

| 13B3 | Management make every effort to ensure poor quality products are not passed. | 1 | 2 | 3 | 4 | 5 | 6 | 7 |

13C	*Quality systems and relationships*							
13C1	All aspects of quality are clearly measured.	1	2	3	4	5	6	7
13C2	Our quality processes meet a recognised international standard.	1	2	3	4	5	6	7
13C3	Everyone has knowledge of their internal customers.	1	2	3	4	5	6	7
13C4	Right-first-time behaviour is expected and rewarded.	1	2	3	4	5	6	7

Customers

14A	*Current business*							
14A1	We are more interested in total sales than in sales to individual customers.	1	2	3	4	5	6	7
14A2	We know exactly why our customers buy our and not our competitors' products or services.	1	2	3	4	5	6	7
14A3	Our most demanding customers determine our quality standards.	1	2	3	4	5	6	7
14A4	We do not monitor whether we deliver to customers on time.	1	2	3	4	5	6	7

14B	*Customer relations*							
14B1	We contact our customers frequently.	1	2	3	4	5	6	7
14B2	The Chief Executive visits our customers frequently.	1	2	3	4	5	6	7
14B3	Customer complaints are always communicated to all departments concerned with overall quality.	1	2	3	4	5	6	7
14B4	Our customers accept considerable variation in quality.	1	2	3	4	5	6	7

14C	*Future business*							
14C1	We continually assess the future needs of our customers.	1	2	3	4	5	6	7
14C2	We have no joint venture developments with our customers.	1	2	3	4	5	6	7

Finance

15A	*Financial targets*							
15A1	The financial targets set for new projects in this company are so high that they inhibit innovation.	1	2	3	4	5	6	7
15A2	We can be flexible on the financial targets for new projects.	1	2	3	4	5	6	7

15B	*Investor relations*							
15B1	We hold regular briefing sessions with our main investors, parent organisations and financial advisors.	1	2	3	4	5	6	7
15B2	We aim to balance the need for short-term profits and the need for long-term investment.	1	2	3	4	5	6	7

15C	*Resources*							
15C1	We lack the resources to invest in new equipment to make us more competitive.	1	2	3	4	5	6	7
15C2	Most managers have discretionary funds to back new ideas.	1	2	3	4	5	6	7

Suppliers

16A	*Knowledge*							
16A1	We know which of our suppliers are vital to our business.	1	2	3	4	5	6	7
16A2	We do not know which of our important suppliers also supply our competitors.	1	2	3	4	5	6	7

16B	*Purchasing policy*							
16B1	We buy on the basis of lowest price alone.	1	2	3	4	5	6	7
16B2	We try to minimise the number of our suppliers for each item.	1	2	3	4	5	6	7

16C	Relationship							
16C1	To obtain the best deal we change our suppliers frequently.	1	2	3	4	5	6	7
16C2	We attempt to maintain mutually beneficial relations with our suppliers.	1	2	3	4	5	6	7
16C3	We have joint venture developments with our most important suppliers.	1	2	3	4	5	6	7
16C4	We check every delivery – it is the only way to ensure consistent quality.	1	2	3	4	5	6	7

Competitors

17A	Competitor analysis							
17A1	We know who our main competitors are for each of our products.	1	2	3	4	5	6	7
17A2	We obtain very little useful information on our competitors from our customers and suppliers.	1	2	3	4	5	6	7
17A3	We always analyse our competitors' products or services to see what we can learn from them.	1	2	3	4	5	6	7

17B	Market share							
17B1	We aim to increase our market share until we are in a dominant position.	1	2	3	4	5	6	7
17B2	We aim to increase market share by better delivery and after-sales service rather than product/service differentiation.	1	2	3	4	5	6	7
17B3	We monitor threats from products, processes or services that could fulfil the same need but in a different way.	1	2	3	4	5	6	7

17C	Developing competitive capabilities							
17C1	We aim for unique approaches for improving customer performance.	1	2	3	4	5	6	7

(continued)

(continued)

17C	Developing competitive capabilities							
17C2	Our product development staff do not have regular customer contact.	1	2	3	4	5	6	7
17C3	Our R&D staff have to sell their ideas internally to sales and manufacturing.	1	2	3	4	5	6	7

Technology

18A	Uniqueness							
18A1	Our business depends on technologies and know-how that are unique to us.	1	2	3	4	5	6	7
18A2	We balance our efforts on new technology between cost reduction and launching new products or services.	1	2	3	4	5	6	7

18B	Management							
18B1	We monitor proposed environmental legislation and evaluate the likely impact on the technology we employ.	1	2	3	4	5	6	7
18B2	We monitor competitive technologies and know-how.	1	2	3	4	5	6	7
18B3	We audit our own technologies and know-how at least once a year.	1	2	3	4	5	6	7
18B4	We examine only those products or services which fail in use.	1	2	3	4	5	6	7
18B5	We practice statistical process control.	1	2	3	4	5	6	7

18C	External inputs							
18C1	We have regular contact with universities and research bodies on relevant research.	1	2	3	4	5	6	7
18C2	We invite leading academics and business specialists to visit us and discuss how their work can improve our products, processes and services.	1	2	3	4	5	6	7
18C3	We monitor patents and licence opportunities on a continuous basis in all areas relevant to our products, services and processes.	1	2	3	4	5	6	7

New products and services

19A	Product obsolescence							
19A1	We are committed to making our existing products or services obsolete by the introduction of new versions.	1	2	3	4	5	6	7
19A2	We maintain regularly updated records of the performance and price of our products and services compared with those of our competitors.	1	2	3	4	5	6	7
19A3	Our latest products or services are very similar to those of our competitors.	1	2	3	4	5	6	7

19B	New product/service generation							
19B1	We are happier when our latest products or services are responsible for an increasing share of our sales turnover.	1	2	3	4	5	6	7
19B2	A 'champion' is a vital ingredient of successful new product or services development.	1	2	3	4	5	6	7

19C	Process obsolescence							
19C1	If a process or system is working well we leave it alone.	1	2	3	4	5	6	7
19C2	We maintain regularly updated records on the efficiency of our processes and systems.	1	2	3	4	5	6	7
19C3	I do not consider our processes or systems to be innovative.	1	2	3	4	5	6	7

19D	Operating procedures							
19D1	We review our operating procedures only when problems arise.	1	2	3	4	5	6	7
19D2	We are always looking to see how new technology can assist our operating procedures.	1	2	3	4	5	6	7

Figure CL4.1 Innovation score. Chart created by Alistair Gray (2018).

Checklist 5
Evaluating a strategy or strategic option

In our strategic consulting work with clients we are often asked 'what makes a good alternative strategy or option'? The following checklist has proved useful to clients in their own planning as well as in our assignments together.

Consider each of the question areas and, through providing real evidence, score your strategy. This is also a very good way of testing or evaluating strategic options or alternatives.

Templates for building alternative strategies or options

The strategy

- **Rationale:**
  - What opportunities or issues does this option address?

- **Focus:**
  - What – products, services, technologies?
  - Where – geographic markets, channels?
  - Who – customer segments, partnerships?

- **Position:**
  - How we will be seen by our customers and also our competitors, e.g., low-cost producer, market leader, most innovative?

- **Unique customer proposition:**
  - What solution are we delivering for our customer?

- **Sources of competitive advantage/strategic capabilities:**
  - What makes us unique in this option?
  - Sources of superior performance?
  - Primary capabilities, e.g., assets, skills, technologies, systems?

- **Business model**
  - How we will make money?
  - Direct sales?

- ○   Licences, royalties?
- ○   JVs or alliances?
- ○   Consultancy?

Implementation planning

- **The Business in five years:**

  - ○   Size and shape.
  - ○   Relative to original objective.
  - ○   Financial and real terms.

- **Financial benefit**

  - ○   Describe the total revenue stream.
  - ○   Where is value added?
  - ○   Other corporate benefits, e.g., disposals?

- **How quickly can we move on this option?**

  - ○   Any timing issues?
  - ○   Knowledge gaps to be filled?

- **Potential for interference:**

  - ○   Competitor, customer?
  - ○   New entrant, new technology?
  - ○   Their apparent strategies?
  - ○   Legislation?
  - ○   Ourselves?

- **Fit with scenario:**

  - ○   In which scenario does this option work best?

- **Implications:**

  - ○   Resources – financial, people, capital?
  - ○   Degree of change or transformation required?
  - ○   What does it rule out?
  - ○   Commercial or technical risks?
  - ○   Implementation issues?

Evaluating the options

Consider the evidence and score each option, using each question area, on the basis of:

5:   The strategy/option exemplifies this feature exceptionally well.
4:   The strategy/option exemplifies this feature, but definitely has room for improvement.

3:   The strategy/option is neutral in terms of its impact.
2:   The strategy/option does not particularly reflect this feature; equally it is not totally negative in terms of impact.
1:   Executing the strategy/option would result in a negative impact.

Question area	Evidence	Scoring (5 through 1)
Meets your objective?		
Takes the initiative?		
Builds on real, relative strengths?		
Exploits market opportunities?		
Unity of leadership?		
Flexibility?		
Economic benefit?		

You can then use a table similar to the one below to evaluate the options or alternative strategies you are considering. It is useful to give out copies of this to individuals involved in the evaluation process. This enables the team to make their individual assessment and results in a much more participative and therefore useful evaluation process.

Criteria	Option 1	Option 2	Option 3	Option 4	Option 5	Option 6
Meets the objective						
Takes the initiative						
Builds on strengths						
Exploits opportunities						
Unity of leadership						
Flexibility						
Economic benefit						
SCORE						

Remember that it is not simply the highest scoring option that wins. There may be features of alternative strategies that would add value or strength to the emerging strategy without detracting from its focus.

Checklist 6
Cluster-based strategy

Establishing the potential for cluster development

One of the best ways to establish the potential for deploying cluster development strategies is to use the 'diamond of competitiveness' as outlined in Chapter 9.

It is always useful to start with an overview of the global trends that might apply to any cluster. For example, the following are ten trends that have appeared in almost every scenario-thinking exercise that has been completed over the last decade:

- Polarisation of socio-economic groups.
- Polarisation of economies.
- Growing world population and the role of the cities.
- Rise of global warming and increasing natural disasters.
- Role of the banks – as credit becomes more expensive and debt more strategic.
- Impact of the internet.
- Impact of technology.
- Rise in demand and importance of local/regional government.
- Shape of public services – especially sustainable transport.
- Rise in global terrorism and radical minorities.

In addition, it is important to consider the business trends, especially when many product markets are changing so quickly. Consider:

- Competition is increasing and intensifying through globalisation.
- The best people are the scarcest resource.
- Industries are consolidating.
- Profit margins – where there are few barriers to entry.
- The increasing profile of company brands over product brand.

The diamond of competitiveness

Consider each element and evaluate those trends/factors that are positive or negative towards genuine competitive advantage of any sector.

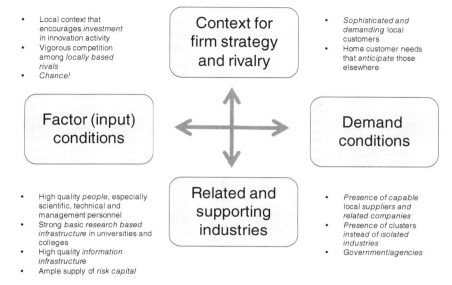

- Local context that encourages *investment* in innovation activity
- Vigorous competition among *locally based rivals*
- *Chance!*

Context for firm strategy and rivalry

- *Sophisticated and demanding* local customers
- Home customer needs that *anticipate* those elsewhere

Factor (input) conditions

Demand conditions

- High quality *people*, especially scientific, technical and management personnel
- Strong *basic research based infrastructure* in universities and colleges
- High quality *information infrastructure*
- Ample supply of *risk capital*

Related and supporting industries

- *Presence of capable* local *suppliers and related companies*
- *Presence of* clusters *instead of isolated industries*
- *Government/agencies*

Figure CL6.1 The diamond of competitiveness. Created by Alistair Gray.

Testing the potential

The cluster potential test is used for evaluation in cluster preparation. However, it can also be used at every stage of cluster development in support of internal and external evaluation. The tool provides an overview of a complex system of interactions between various success factors. It shows gaps and deficits and makes possible rapid assessment of the cluster development potential.

Brief description

The test distinguishes three dimensions, each with five factors. The three dimensions are *cluster strength, implementation strength* and *functional strength.*

- **Cluster strength** evaluates the joint competitiveness of the potential cluster partners and the cluster's performance strength (critical mass).
- The **implementation strength** evaluates the cluster's self-organisation ability.
- The **functional strength** reviews how far the conditions for performing key cluster functions are satisfied.

The three dimensions are inter-dependent. Successful cluster development cannot take place in the absence of any one of them. A cluster needs competitive strength, it needs the potential for implementation using its own resources, and it needs functionality.

Benefits

The cluster potential test provides a quick overview of the strengths and weaknesses of potential clusters, and it shows the opportunities of and threats to cluster formation.

The test is also suitable for comparisons between clusters (benchmarking). However, it cannot replace a thorough analysis. Instead it simply provides an orientation for determining where more detailed analysis needed and where further development should be initiated.

Cluster potential test

Cluster strength

A: Cluster market strength

1   Does the cluster offer a forward-looking and complex product group with very good market prospects, a lot of development possibilities as well as high quality and innovation advantages?
2   Standard and completeness of technological, product-related and organisational strategic capabilities along the value chain?
3   Is there clearly identifiable and complementary potential among the businesses involved?

B: Lead businesses

1   Does a sufficient number and quality (market, technology, knowledge, qualification, capital and profitability) of key businesses in various industries exist, that can assume important lead functions for the cluster?
2   Do the lead businesses contributing to the cluster project have domestic and international market experience, experience with strategic alliances, clear ideas about the goals and topics for cooperation, as well as a willingness to collaborate and are of high priority to the cluster project?

C: Supplementary businesses and related areas of economic activity

1   Number and quality (market, technology, knowledge, qualification, capital and profitability) of businesses in the upstream and downstream segments of the value chain and in related areas of economic activity.
2   Balance between lead businesses and supplementary businesses.
3   Significant share of turnover within the cluster.
4   Sufficient similarity in the goals and expectations.
5   Geographical proximity.
6   Efficiency of networks and links with businesses.
7   Innovation potential from proximity to other clusters or cluster-like economic structures.

D: Supplementary service institutions and infrastructures

1   Are there sufficient supplementary high-quality institutions that are also close to the businesses and related to the cluster, particularly in the fields of research, development, consulting, qualification, quality control, information transfer, strategic alliance brokering and internationalisation?

2   Do these institutions have a strong service and quality orientation and are they up to international standards?

3   Is the environment in the region supportive of innovation and business-friendly?

E: Regional consolidation

1   Geographical proximity of cluster businesses and institutions relevant to the cluster.

2   Existence of geographical cores or sub-clusters that promote each other.

Implementation strength

A: Clear benefits

1   Are businesses, services and infrastructure providers clearly recognising the benefits of participating in cluster development?

2   Can the benefit of cluster participation be communicated to all the relevant businesses and institutions in a comprehensible and credible manner?

3   Are the central cost–benefit relationships known and accepted?

B: Co-ordination and management potential

1   Are there public or private institutions with organisational capacity and know-how for cluster development?

2   Can private-sector promotion be integrated, and is it equipped for the specific tasks of cluster promotion?

3   Do the structure and services of the cluster development organisation ensure that the focus is on the interests and needs of the businesses?

C: Readiness and ability to cooperate

1   Would the potential cluster actors contribute experience with cooperation along the value chain and in the development of the products and services?

2   Are there functional commercially successful cooperation projects already in existence in the cluster that can serve as examples, are scalable and can initiate further strategic alliances?

3   Are there distribution networks already in place, and can they be expanded?

D: Human resources

1   Do cluster actors have enough highly qualified personnel?
2   Are there adequate human resources available within cluster businesses for the cluster project?
3   Does the cluster project engage outstanding national and international experts for the businesses and cluster projects?

E: Political support

1   Are the country's key politicians as well as business and social partners backing the cluster project?
2   Are politicians, administration, businesses and supporting institutions appropriately functionally integrated into the project?
3   Is the project solidly embedded in the regions?

Functional strength

A: Internal networking

1   Is there intensive cooperation and networking between the key actors in the cluster and in its support system (R&D, training and advanced training, controlling, consulting)?
2   Is there a solid basis of trust between competitors while maintaining functional competition?
3   Is there a transfer of knowledge between the various sub-systems in the cluster?
4   Are existing groups (local networks, strategic alliances, distribution networks, etc.) attracting new partners and prompting emulation effects?
5   Are there institutionalised technical discussions on a regular basis concerning the further development of the cluster as a whole?

B: External networking

1   Are key actors well networked (know-how, capital) with businesses outside the cluster and with comparable or similar clusters?
2   Does a strong export orientation exist and is the strategic development in the cluster focused on ongoing improvement of international competitiveness?
3   Is there accessible monitoring and benchmarking of international competitors?
4   Are international research alliances in place?

C: Quality orientation

1   Is there a consistent focus on competition through quality and customer satisfaction, as well as on quality standards that are continuously evaluated and adapted for growing demand and market requirements?
2   Are adequate professional quality control and consulting services available?

3 Is there an integrated quality management in place that applies vertical networking of standards and controlling?

D: Innovation orientation

1 Does a networking of competences exist between research and business?
2 Is the market knowledge and experience of cluster actors visible and accessible for call-up and ongoing updating (innovation)?
3 Is innovation being managed in the cluster, both between and within cluster sub-systems?
4 Are common IT packages being used and do networks or incentives exist to upgrade the internet performance of the individual cluster actors?

E: Location marketing

1 Is the region (also) marketed as a location promoting an appropriate image (brand name, trademark, logo) domestically and internationally?
2 Are the cluster actors aligning their products and services with the common location's philosophy and investing in regular quality improvement of the location?
3 Is a professional marketing team available for these tasks?

The results of the cluster potential test can be presented graphically, as Figure CL6.2 shows.

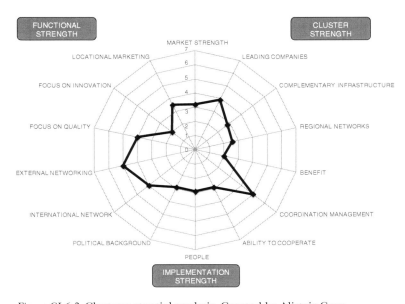

Figure CL6.2 Cluster potential analysis. Created by Alistair Gray.

Checklist 7
Making mergers work
The identity audit

An identity audit reveals what makes an organisation unique in the eyes of its employees and stakeholders. It also reveals the degree of alignment among different constituencies regarding what the organisation stands for. For example, a business may be commonly viewed as a high-technology company, while a good deal of its identity may be anchored in its nationality or ownership structure.

An identity audit consists of three steps:

1   Careful study of available data – current, historical and internal (such as company documents and white papers) and external (everything from annual reports to news coverage). This step captures how managers, employees, shareholders, customers, competitors and the media portray the organisation. The result of this step is a list of possible identity anchors to be validated and refined in the next two steps of the process.

2   The second step consists of a series of in-depth interviews of representative members of key stakeholder groups. The interviewees are invited to reveal their understanding of the organisation's identity anchors through a discussion of a list of past actions, strategic decisions and, when applicable, controversial episodes.

3   The final step in the audit consists of large-scale validation of the identity anchors that surfaced in the first two steps. Auditors create a questionnaire, to be completed by a large sample of key internal and external stakeholders, that asks respondents to express their degree of agreement with a series of statements, each corresponding to an identity anchor.

Analysis of data from the survey yields a reduced list of identity anchors that make the organisation unique in the eyes of its key stakeholders, and an assessment of the degree of alignment between various perceptions of the organisation's identity.

When the audit is conducted in conjunction with a merger or acquisition, either of two extreme outcomes should raise a red flag – strong consensus among the target's stakeholders around an identity that could hinder the realisation of synergies, or a high level of divergence among stakeholders about the target's identity.

Here is an example of an initial questionnaire to use at the beginning of post-merger integration work. It helps in getting an appreciation of the cultural challenges the new organisation will face.

Making it happen, together

Ensure the input will be kept strictly confidential. However, for analysis sake, respondents should indicate the company (pre-merger/acquisition) and the operational area in which they are currently working.

Top people questionnaire. Making it happen, together

	Question area	Strongly agree	Agree	Disagree	Strongly disagree	No opinion	Comments
1	The new set-up will open up a brighter future for the success and the expansion of the organisation.						
2	I now feel more motivated in contributing to added value in the new enterprise.						
3	I believe that the strategic directions of the firm are sound and clear.						
4	I believe that the reorganisation of the group will improve my personal career prospects.						
5	I believe we have the marketing capabilities to take advantage of the market opportunities available.						
6	I have confidence in my colleagues in the new organisation.						
7	The new organisation will require a significant improvement in leadership skills.						

(continued)

(continued)

Top people questionnaire. Making it happen, together

	Question area	*Strongly agree*	*Agree*	*Disagree*	*Strongly disagree*	*No opinion*	*Comments*
8	I am willing to modify my cultural approach if this is needed to foster business growth through cooperation.						
9	I would generally be open to any change that would improve the way things are done here.						
10	This new organisation seems very open to suggestions about how we can improve the business.						
11	Which is the ONE immediate action you believe the executive teams should consider to make for the success of the new organisation?						

Ensure that respondents are clear as to the confidentiality of the returned input data and that individual questionnaire returns, no matter how simple, will be destroyed. It is also advisable to utilise an external party, e.g., your change consultants or advisers, to carry out the analysis on a confidential basis.

Checklist 8
National Governing Body of sport
Organisation performance

Those involved in leading or managing sport may find the questions below helpful when developing or refreshing a strategic plan. The questions were those used with the FA and were also part of an on-line survey to which thousands of individuals contributed. The results represented a powerful 'vox pop' as an input to the strategic planning process.

Key questions

Please consider the following questions, answering with your thoughts as succinctly as possible:

1   Looking back at the sport and the National Governing Body (NGB) over the last four years:

   - What have been the real highlights or major successes (max of 3)?
   - What have been the real lowlights or big failures (max of 3)?

2   What are the key objectives the NGB should be targeting over the next four years – as a sport and as an organisation (max of 3)?

3   Which organisations should we compare/learn/benchmark ourselves with? Why?

   - Within sport in our nation or elsewhere? (max of 3).
   - Any other organisations (profit and non-profit) (max of 3).

4   How are our relationships with external stakeholders? Comments:

   - The general public/fans.
   - The leagues.
   - International and national federations.
   - Government and key departments.
   - Sports councils.
   - National Olympic Committee.
   - Broadcasters and media (journalists).
   - Local authorities.

- Sponsors.
- County/regional associations.
- Unions or player representatives.
- Other parties (please list):

b   If applicable, how could the relationship with various stakeholders be improved?

5   Given unconstrained resources, what would be the three big initiatives you would take as CEO of the NGB?

6   What would be the 'one big success' that would be a really good outcome from the strategy process:

- For the NGB?
- For the sport?

7   Are there any other points that you would like to make or issues to raise that need to be addressed?

Planning to win

The two forms that follow (Figures CL8.1 and CL8.2) provide a useful outline of the action planning that is required to take forward the leading strategic projects. Keeping the discipline of these two pages drives the focus for implementation and also provides a format that can summarise progress and highlight areas for action through use of a simple 'traffic light' process. This can be summarised as:

- Green: on plan; on budget; no action required.
- Amber: not on plan; action proposed to return to plan.
- Red: Not on plan; no recommended action – needs discussion of options to return to plan.

Logo	Txt box	Txt box/Vision

Text box

Text box/Framework

Text box

Strategic goals

Operating objectives for improving key processes

Strategic architecture	Goals	Vision summaries	Targets

Text box

Figure CL8.1 Strategic initiative – action plan (page 1)

| Completion of agreed actions | Achievement of operating objectives | Achievement of overall objective and our ambition |

Actions

Strategic initiatives	Status	Planned outcomes/100 day plans	Responsibility
	RED		
	AMBER		
	GREEN		

Text box

Figure CL8.2 Strategic initiative – action plan (page 2)

Checklist 9
High performance sport

Table CL9.1 High performance assessment (based on Mission 2012)

Sporting organisation: performance assessment					
Name of organisation	Criteria	Score out of 10			
		Athletes	System	Climate	AVERAGE
1. Vision and strategy					
	1 Strategic planning (S)				
	2 Performance pathway (S)				
	3 Strategy into action (C)				
2. Results and progress					
	4 Results – performance (A)				
	5 Results – Development (A)				
	6 Results – Athlete progression (A)				
3. Mood in the camp					
	7 Leadership (C)				
	8 Behaviours (C)				
	9 Team environment (C)				
	10 Innovation and creativity (C)				
	11 Monitoring and perceptions (S)				
4. Structure and systems					
	12 Management – internal (S)				
	13 Management – external (S)				

(continued)

Sporting organisation: performance assessment					
Name of organisation	*Criteria*	*Score out of 10*			
		Athletes	*System*	*Climate*	*AVERAGE*
	14 Integrated planning and organisation (S)				
	15 Coaching workforce (S)				
	16 Competition/training camps (S)				
	17 Sports medicine support (S)				
	18 Sports science support (S)				
	19 Team recruitment and confirmation (S)				
	20 Communication and information (S)				
	21 Competition opportunities (S)				
5. Athlete support					
	22 Individualised athlete support (S)				
	23 The coaching experience (A)				
	24 Athlete welfare and lifestyle support (A)				
	25 Injury and health management (S)				
	26 Athlete commitment (C)				
	27 Anti-doping culture (A)				
6. Resources and partnerships					
	28 Facilities (S)				
	29 Equipment (S)				
	30 People development (C)				
	31 Financial management (S)				
	32 Key partnerships (C)				
	AVERAGE				

Checklist 10
Good to great (in sport)

In this checklist the 5-Blob model, introduced in Chapters 17 and 18, is expanded into a number of areas, seeking real evidence against which to assess current performance.

A: We exemplify this trait exceptionally well – there is little room for improvement.
B: We often exemplify this trait, but definitely have room for improvement.
C: We show some evidence of this trait, but our record is patchy.
D: There is little evidence that we exemplify this trait, and we have obvious contradictions.
E: We operate almost entirely contrary to this trait.

Feature	Source of evidence	Score (A, B, C, D, E)
Number of players and coaches regularly competing close to international level.		
A systematic approach to performance management of an integrated pathway to professional sport.		
Quality infrastructure supporting the pathway in terms of facilities, coaching and other resources.		
Culture of performance and learning in all areas of the sport.		
Each international team performing as a club with strong purpose and values.		

Checklist 11
Building and sustaining a high performance culture

In both business and sport the creation and maintenance of a culture of high performance is by far the most important aspect of leadership and management.

Assessing the performance culture

Score using a scale of 1–5 from Excellent (5) to Very poor (1) for 'The climate I experience' in the left-hand column and 'The climate I create' in the right-hand column.

The climate I experience   The climate I create

1   *Clarity of focus and engagement – around both what we are trying to achieve and how*

- Clarity of purpose – the extent to which our work is focused on a clear long-term purpose and set of goals, giving everyone a crystal clear focus for *what* we are trying to achieve.
- Engagement – how well our people buy-in to what we are trying to achieve and their energy for it.
- Clarity of focus on *how* – how clear are people about where to focus our energies in order to maximise our performance?
- Individual clarity of role – how effective are we at translating our overall goals into what this means for each individual role, both in terms of what we need from them and how they can maximise their value?

2   *High standards*

- Level of challenge in the standards we set – 'Excellent' would mean the standards we set ourselves in each key area of performance are based on what would make us among the best in the world.
- Ownership of the drive for improvement – how motivated are people at all levels of the organisation to raise our game in key areas of performance?

- Challenge at an individual level – to what extent is each individual challenged to maximise their contribution?
- Our effectiveness in challenging both poor and mediocre performance.

3 *Focus on unlocking and using talent*

- Involvement – how effective are we at actively encouraging people to think about and contribute their ideas on how we can improve performance in key areas and then listening to these ideas?
- Autonomy – how effective are we at giving and trusting people with clear areas of responsibility into which they can pour their creativity and initiative in pursuit of our goals?
- Support – how effectively are people supported in meeting the challenges of their role and in fulfilling their potential with high quality coaching and mentoring?

4 *Recognition*

- How effective is the environment at making people feel valued, important, and that their work matters?
- To what extent is excellent work and exceptional effort recognised and rewarded?
- How effective are we at celebrating our achievements and making progress?

5 *Feedback and learning*

- Bigger picture feedback – 'Excellent' would mean everyone knows exactly how we are performing as an organisation against our goals and key measures at any point in time.
- Individual feedback – to what extent do individuals get frequent high-quality feedback, enabling them to accurately judge how well they are performing and to learn from the effectiveness of their actions?
- Using reviews, pilots, etc. to drive rapid improvement – how effective are we at driving rapid improvement in focused areas of performance?

6 *Teamwork and collaboration*

- Collective identity – to what extent is there a feeling of all being a part of a united team with a shared set of goals and priorities? To what extent does this translate into good collaborative and supportive behaviours between people?
- How clear are people on where we should focus our collaborative efforts to have the greatest impact on performance?
- How effectively do we work with other teams and departments to maximise our overall value to the organisation?

Leadership capability – the key skills of performance leadership

Understanding the above framework gives leaders a tangible way to evaluate their effectiveness and focus on where to improve. Applying it requires a desire to be exceptional, not just good, and a level of skill and self-awareness most managers fall short on.

The table below summarises the key skills we have found most critical to performance leadership – again, rate yourself and your managers to highlight the most important development needs.

Score (1–5).

High standards, ambition and drive – high level of personal energy for driving performance

- Ability to engage people behind the goals – to ignite a commitment for the goals in others.

Performance insight – able to distil and focus people's energies on what matters most

- Skill based on unlocking and developing people's potential:
  - See potential in people, and give them the opportunity to develop it by letting go and giving them responsibility.
  - A very high standard of coaching skills for drawing out and developing people's potential.
  - Feedback skills: giving frequent effective feedback on performance to individuals, both positive recognition and on areas for improvement.
  - Supportive and accessible: good at 'picking people up' and supporting them when they need it.

Facilitating reviews – skilled and disciplined approach to facilitating reviews to drive momentum and learning

- Skilled in and willingness to deal with poor performance – have the courageous conversations.

Team development skills – able to pull people together around common goals and create an environment where collaboration is a defining strength

- A never-ending commitment to keep developing your own leadership skills.

Source: Checklist created by John Bull, Tall Tree Performance Leadership, permission granted.

Checklist 12
Debriefing performance

This is perhaps my favourite checklist. It is only made up of three questions, and it has led to many major changes in client performance in business and sport.

In my experience the best performers and their organisations are expert in debriefing, for example:

- National Olympic committees, institutes of sport, governing bodies and their performance directors after major games or championships.
- Coaches and players, together, at the end of a season or cup campaign.
- Boards of companies, local authorities or not-for-profit organisations at the end of a fiscal year.
- Project teams at key milestones.

Many have elaborate questionnaire-driven approaches. Our own approach to debriefing is made up of three simple questions:

- What went well – what were the successes or highlights?
- What might have been done differently to secure a more successful outcome?
- What were the lessons learned for the future?

Debriefing is undertaken too often after failure or under-performance and in a climate of negativity that too frequently sucks the energy out of a team or board through a debilitating process. By starting with what went well the emphasis is on positive improvement and a commitment to achieving better performance in the future. The process, more often than not, surprises participants with the extent of positive performance achieved even in defeat. The best organisations debrief after success as well as disappointment.

Appendix 2
Bibliography
50 books that have influenced me

Here are 50 books and publications that have influenced me over my business and consulting career.

Strategic management

Brown, Shona L. and Eisenhardt, Kathleen M. *Competing on the Edge*, Boston: Harvard Business School Press, 1998.

Davidson, Mike *The Grand Strategist*, London: Macmillan, 1995.

Day, George S. and Reibstein, David J. *Wharton on Dynamic Competitive Strategy*, Hoboken: John S. Wiley and Sons Inc., 1997.

Hamel, Gary and Prahalad C.K. *Competing for the Future*, Boston: Harvard Business School Press, 2003.

Kim, W. Chan and Mauborgne, Renée *Blue Ocean Strategy*, Boston: Harvard Business School Press, 2005.

Markides, Constantinos C. and Geroski, Paul A. *Fast Second*, Hoboken: John S. Wiley and Sons Inc., 2005.

McGrath, Rita Gunther and MacMillan, Ian *The Entrepreneurial Mindset*, Boston: Harvard Business School Press, 2000.

Mintzberg, Henry *Mintzberg on Management*, London: Macmillan, 1989.

Musashi, Miyanoto *The Book of Five Rings*, Woodstock: The Overlook Press, 1982.

Ohmae, Kenichi *The Borderless World*, London: Collins, 1990.

Porter, Michael E. *Competitive Advantage*, New York: The Free Press, 1985.

Porter, Michael E. *Competitive Strategy*, New York: The Free Press, 1980.

Sminia, Harry *The Strategic Manager*, Abingdon: Routledge, 2014.

Young, Arthur *The Managers Handbook*, London: Sphere Books, 1986.

High-performing organisations

Ahrens, Thomas *Driving the Tiger*, London: Business Books Ltd, 1991.

Bossidy, Larry and Charan, Ram *Execution – the Discipline of Getting Things Done*, New York: Random House/Crown Business, 2002.

Collins, James C. and Porras, Jerry I. *Built to Last*, London: Century Business, 1995.

Gibson, Clive, Pratt, Mike, Roberts, Kevin, Weymes, Ed *Peak Performance*, London: HarperCollinsBusiness, 2000.

Hickman, Craig R. and Silva, Michael A. *Creating Excellence*, London: Unwin Hyman, 1985.

MacNeice, Brian and Bowen, James *Powerhouse*, New York: Kogan Page, 2017.

Moore, Geoffrey A. *Inside the Tornado*, New York: Capstone Publishing, 1995.

Peters, Tom *Thriving on Chaos*, London: Macmillan, 1988.

Peters, Thomas J. and Waterman Jr, Richard H. *In Search of Excellence*, New York: Harper and Row, 1982.

Tichy, Noel M. and Sherman, Stratford *Control Your Destiny or Someone Else Will*, New York: HarperBusiness, 1994.

Inspirational individuals

Basquali, Catherine *Intimate Portrait of a Champion*, Sydney: Macmillan, 2000.

Campbell, R.S. and Skinner, Andrew S. *Adam Smith*, Beckenham: Croome Helm, 1982.

Carnegie, Andrew *The Empire of Business*, New York: Books for Business, 2001.

Gates, Bill *Business @ The Speed of Thought*, New York: Penguin Books, 1999.

Herman, Arthur *How the Scots Invented the Modern World*, New York: Three Rivers Press, 2001.

Isaacson, Walter *Steve Jobs*, New York: Simon and Schuster, 2011.

Jones, Peter and Skinner, Andrew S. *Adam Smith – Reviewed*, Edinburgh: Edinburgh University Press, 1992.

Roddick, Anita *Body and Soul*, London: Vermilion, 1992.

Leadership and people

Davis, Stanley M. *Managing Corporate Culture*, Cambridge MA: Ballinger Publishing, 1984.

Davis, Stanley M. *Future Perfect*, Boston: Addison-Wesley, 1987.

De Geus, Arie *The Living Company*, London: Nicholas Brealey, 1997.

Drummond, Norman *The Spirit of Success*, London: Hodder and Stoughton, 2004.

Gardiner, John W. *On Leadership*, New York: The Free Press, 1990.

Gratton, Lynda *Living Strategy*, London: Financial Times/Prentice Hall, 2000.

World-class manufacturing

Goldratt, Eliyahu M. *The Goal*, Great Barrington: North River Press, 1984.

Gunn, Thomas G. *21st Century Manufacturing*, New York: Oliver Wight/HarperCollins, 1992.

Weill, Peter and Vitale, Michael R. *Place to Space*, Boston: Harvard Business School Press, 2001.

Organisations and change management

Handy, Charles *The Empty Raincoat*, London: Random House Ltd, 1994.

Handy, Charles *The Age of Unreason*, London: Century Hutchison, 1989.

Handy, Charles *Understanding Organisations*, London: Penguin Books, 1976.

Kanter, Rosabeth Moss *The Change Masters*, London: George Allen and Unwin, 1984.

Kanter, Rosabeth Moss *World Class*, New York: Simon and Schuster, 1995.

Kanter, Rosabeth Moss *When Giants Learn to Dance*, London: Simon and Schuster, 1989.

The future and scenario thinking

Fahey, Liam and Randall, Robert M. *Learning from the Future*, Hoboken: John Wiley and Sons Inc., 1998.

Georgantzas, Nicholas C. and Acar, William *Scenario-Driven Planning*, Westport: Quorum Books, 1995.

McCorduck Pamela and Ramsay, Nancy *The Futures of Women – Scenarios for the 21st Century*, New York: Warner Books, 1996.

Schwartz, Peter *The Art of the Long View*, New York: Doubleday, 1991.

Appendix 3
NCR Dundee
A source of future entrepreneurs

Many NCR engineers went on to become entrepreneurs in their own right. Of those, Chris van der Kuhl and Ana Stewart stand out. Both grasped the opportunity of vacation employment while at college to enjoy a 'once-in-a-lifetime' experience and made contributions to NCR's success story that is the stuff of dreams. Both were exposed to leading US customers in their tender years and created platforms that were the basis of NCR's future ATMs, as well as giving them a launchpad for their future careers.

Chris van der Kuhl

Chris van der Kuhl, the entrepreneur specialising in online markets and interactive digital entertainment, was fortunate to work as an intern just after the implementation of SuperPlant commenced. Now the Chair of 4J studios, he created Minecraft for XBOX 360 with Mojang and Microsoft, and is currently working on all PlayStation and XboxOne versions.

He was initially engaged by NCR in 1988, aged 19, as an intern in John Fry's product engineering department while at the University of Dundee. They were working on 'hugely pioneering' projects and he was allocated to the team developing customer solutions for networks of fixed machines. This was central to NCR's development and at the heart of the change demanded by 'SuperPlant', integrating product engineering, production engineering and manufacturing departments. The company had a specific enquiry from a customer in Michigan to develop a relationship database. Having worked on ORACLE and IBM DB2 as part of his studies, Chris readily volunteered for the project and prepared a project plan to address the enquiry. The project involved not only meetings with the customer but also establishing links with potential suppliers in Silicon Valley as well as at NCR's Dayton headquarters. The £15,000 cost was above Jim Morrison's (Deputy Director of Engineering) ex-budget approval and required authorisation by Jim Adamson himself.

Energised by his passion for the project and the prospect of his first visit to the US, Chris entered the CEO suite at lunchtime (did he know in advance the secretary would not be there?) and knocked on Jim's door.

Always open to youth and their ideas, Adamson listened attentively to Chris's project plan before asking the killer question – 'What will this do for NCR's advantage?' Satisfied with the answer, Jim approved the proposal and Chris was duly empowered to execute the project. With new NCR business cards in his pocket, the intern set off on his journey and delivered a successful prototype and project. So successful, in fact, that he was retained and returned on a number of occasions during his final year.

Chris was most impressed with the entrepreneurial spirit and levels of empowerment promoted by Jim Adamson, a spirit that drove and fast-tracked future development. NCR was effectively the source of Chris's business, and that of another colleague at NCR, Ana Stewart – the queen of the cash machine.

Ana Stewart

Ana Stewart can claim to be the first person to have spotted the potential versatility of the humble cash machine. She also took the opportunity of a summer job at NCR (out of a chance baby-sitting experience for an NCR executive), and there began a story that would see her play a key role in the transformation of the cash machine into an all-singing, all-dancing sales and marketing tool.

She began designing digital media around a 16-colour palette on a 386 PC as an art student in Dundee. Ana started out designing digital files that helped make ATMs look more attractive and easier to use – moving them away from the green and black typefaces of early models. In recurring stints at NCR she was given far more responsibility than an undergraduate might expect, and did so well that NCR even lent her a cash machine on which to show her wares at her degree show in London. The work experience made a more lasting impression than the average summer job would on Ana, who realised her design skills could be in demand in the emerging world of hi-tech manufacturing. Such was the early-stage development of the 'new NCR' that this undergraduate effectively became, within two–three months, NCR's design hub and a leading player in the design department. Imagine her excitement at being whisked off to the US to spend two weeks with FedEx in the US, followed by a series of presentations to a number of the world's leading banks and other customer partners.

She was a pioneer in aspects of the whole graphical interface and quickly realised there was a real market for her skills and creativity. She was given responsibility way beyond someone of her years. The company gave her a PC during her final year at college to enable her to continue working for them on key projects in her spare time.

Similarly inspired by what was going on at NCR as Chris van der Kuhl, she left university to found iDesign, which led to the business developing ATM-ad, a revolutionary software application for ATMs. Ana and Chris worked together on projects, e.g., interactive touchscreen and app development, and both founded their initial business ventures on the same day. After two years, NCR became a major customer of her business. She floated the business on AIM in 2007 and it was acquired by Cardtronics in 2013. Still based in Dundee she is on the board of Cardtronics.

Reflecting on her time at NCR, Ana was fulsome in her praise of the people she worked with there:

> They showed such belief in me. This gave me huge confidence and self-belief as well as a platform from which to develop my skills and ultimately my business. The people I worked with at NCR had a real 'can-do' attitude – telling me just to get on with it . . . give it a go.

Such empowerment, coupled with her own sense of responsibility, made for a successful 'win–win' relationship.

The examples of Ana Stewart and Chris van der Kuhl bear testimony to the culture that Jim Adamson nurtured and grew at NCR. Gone were the 'no-can-go' attitudes of the cash-register days that focused on labour productivity, controls and work-study engineers. In a few small weeks these entrepreneurs were conceived and born; both went on to global success and, to this day, both champion the inspiration they experienced during a few short weeks – locally and globally – at a pivotal point in their careers.

Appendix 4
Postscript

My personal renaissance – 'You've got to find what you love'

Steve Jobs (February 24, 1955–October 5, 2011), Founder and CEO of Apple

In 2008 the world encountered the tsunami of recessions, the deepest and longest recession in my working life (since 1970). The resultant fallout had a devastating effect on strategy consulting firms. We had to effectively close our operations in Ireland, downsize in Scotland and merge with another firm in England. In 2010 I reflected on what we had achieved and the potential future options. In my own case, through the vehicle of Renaissance & Company, and other key members of Genesis through their own endeavours, we have continued to deliver value to our clients. My own chosen path to the future was highly influenced by reading the Stanford commencement address by Steve Jobs, CEO of Apple Computers and Pixar Animation Studios, delivered on 12 June 2005 at Stanford University (Source: The Stanford News*). Here are a number of extracts.*

I am honoured to be with you today at your commencement (graduation) from one of the finest universities in the world. I never graduated from college. Truth be told, this is the closest I've ever gotten to a college graduation.

Sometimes life hits you in the head with a brick. Don't lose faith. I'm convinced that the only thing that kept me going was that I loved what I did. You've got to find what you love. And that is as true for your work as it is for your lovers. Your work is going to fill a large part of your life, and the only way to be truly satisfied is to do what you believe is great work. And the only way to do great work is to love what you do. If you haven't found it yet, keep looking. Don't settle. As with all matters of the heart, you'll know when you find it. And, like any great relationship, it just gets better and better as the years roll on. So keep looking until you find it. Don't settle.

Your time is limited, so don't waste it living someone else's life. Don't be trapped by dogma — which is living with the results of other people's thinking. Don't let the noise of others' opinions drown out your own inner voice. And most important, have the courage to follow your heart and intuition. They somehow already know what you truly want to become. Everything else is secondary.

When I was young, there was an amazing publication called *The Whole Earth Catalogue*, which was one of the bibles of my generation. It was created by a fellow named Stewart Brand not far from here in Menlo Park, and he brought it to life with his poetic touch. This was in the late 1960s, before personal computers and desktop publishing, so it was all made with typewriters, scissors, and Polaroid cameras. It was sort of like Google in paperback form, 35 years before Google came along: it was idealistic, and overflowing with neat tools and great notions.

Stewart and his team put out several issues of *The Whole Earth Catalogue*, and then when it had run its course, they put out a final issue. It was the mid-1970s, and I was your age. On the back cover of their final issue was a photograph of an early morning country road, the kind you might find yourself hitchhiking on if you were so adventurous.

Beneath it were the words: "Stay Hungry. Stay Foolish." It was their farewell message as they signed off. Stay Hungry. Stay Foolish. And I have always wished that for myself. And now, as you graduate to begin anew, I wish that for you.

Index

Page numbers in *italics* refer to figures.